BUSINESS AND CORPORATE AVIATION MANAGEMENT

On-Demand Air Transportation

John J. Sheehan

MCGRAW-HILL
New York Chicago San Francisco Lisbon London Madrid
Mexico City Milan New Delhi San Juan Seoul
Singapore Sydney Toronto

The *McGraw·Hill* Companies

Library of Congress Cataloging-in-Publication Data

Sheehan, John J.
    Business and corporate aviation management: on demand air transportation / John J. Sheehan
        p.   cm.
    Includes index.
    ISBN 0-07-141227-1
    1. Local service airlines—Management.   2. Airlines—Management.
3. Airports—Management.   4. Aeronautics—Flights—Management.   5.
Aeronautics, Commercial—Management.   6. Aeronautics, Commercial—
Charters.   7. Airplanes, Company.   8. Private flying.   9. Business travel.
I. Title.
HE9785.S54   2003
387.7'428'068—dc21   2003051245

1 2 3 4 5 6 7 8 9 0   DOC/DOC   0 9 8 7 6 5 4 3

ISBN 0-07-141227-1

The sponsoring editor for this book was Scott Grillo, the editing supervisor was Daina Penikas, and the production supervisor was Sherri Souffrance. It was set in the HB1 design in Times Roman by Wayne A. Palmer of McGraw-Hill Professional's Hightstown, New Jersey composition unit.

Printed and bound by RR Donnelley.

This book was printed on recycled, acid-free paper containing a minimum of 50% recycled, de-inked fiber.

DEDICATION

To Peggy, my True Course.

CONTENTS

Chapter 5. Flight Department Management $\qquad$ *5.1*

Chapter 6. Operations

Chapter 7. Maintenance 7.1

FOREWORD

Transportation is a necessary component of economic growth and improved quality of life. In Biblical times, King Solomon's power was tied to his system of roads that enabled the peoples of his domain to be effective traders. Nations with the most capable sailing fleets dominated European trade in the centuries before trains and planes. The first U.S. president, George Washington, urged his newly formed Congress to build roads and canals, for to do so would reap rewards. President Lincoln pledged if elected in 1860 to complete the transcontinental railroad to bind the nation and advance commerce. In the mid-twentieth century, President Eisenhower championed legislation that resulted in the interstate highway system, which proved to facilitate significant advances in the nation's economy and the well being of its citizens.

Today, aviation is the principal form of transportation for business. No other means of communication supports the fast pace of commerce. Fax machines, cell phones, videoconferencing, and all the marvels of the communications revolution have not negated the need to travel. Rather, they have simply quickened the pace of business and necessitated the need to be face-to-face with a company's customers and enterprise partners before someone from the competition gets there first.

Think about your own business life. Has your cell phone caused you to slow down or travel less? Has your fax machine taken the place of a visit to a customer or potential customer? Are you comfortable building a bond of trust using the Internet? Do you want to launch your development plans using the telephone or e-mail?

Nothing takes the place of face-to-face in keeping clients and growing your business.

While there is universal acceptance that transportation is a necessity for economic development, many business leaders think only of scheduled airlines as a means of satisfying their travel needs. They have yet to understand and use a particularly advantageous form of travel known as *business aviation*.

Scheduled airlines provide safe, secure, and frequent connections between major cities throughout the world, albeit lacking the flexibility to serve many less populated cities and ill structured to provide time-efficient travel itineraries involving multiple stops. Limited by the strictures of their self-imposed hub and spoke system, scheduled airlines provide frequent and timely service to about 10 percent of the 429 commercial airports that have scheduled operations by air carriers. In fact, nearly three-quarters of all airline passenger enplanements occur at fewer than 50 locations.

Business aviation, the use of general aviation aircraft for business transportation, provides safe and secure access to about 5000 locations within the United States and many more internationally. With the ability to transport employees in a timely fashion, unencumbered by limited airline service and inefficient schedules, companies are able to enhance the productivity of a firm's two most important assets—people and time.

Increasingly, business leaders and planners are looking to business aviation as an effective tool for enhanced productivity and growth. No longer misunderstood or maligned by the specter of an uninformed press, business aviation has emerged as an important travel resource that should be part of a company's travel equation. Over 10,000 U.S. companies own business aircraft, and about 90 percent of the public companies that return the highest dividends and capital gains to shareholders employ some form of business aviation. Worldwide, nearly 14,000 companies own company aircraft. Knowledgeable travel specialists, however, suggest that the number of companies that could employ some form of business aviation advantageously exceeds 100,000.

Business aviation complements rather than competes with scheduled airlines. Members of the National Business Aviation Association (NBAA) are the most active users of business aviation in the world, yet they purchase over $10 billion in airline tickets annually. Companies need to travel, and the most enlightened firms use the airlines when it is most efficient to do so and employ business aviation when that form of transportation is most productive. Thus, understanding business aviation and determining how it can be applied profitably to serve a company's travel needs is a challenging yet beneficial management task.

Also, business aviation comes in several forms, ranging from chartering an aircraft for occasional use, through owning a fractional share of an aircraft managed by a fractional ownership provider, to full ownership by a company and the establishment of a corporate flight department. The enlightened user has access to all aspects of business aviation, selecting the form that best satisfies the company's varying needs. Thus the company with an established in-house flight department also should know when and how to select supplemental lift using charter, for example. The availability of business aviation options reflects the sophistication of this form of business transportation.

Business and Corporate Aviation Management by John Sheehan is a most appropriate and authoritative reference for the company or individual seeking a full understanding of business aviation and its capabilities. Authored by an aviator, educator, and lecturer with 40 years of relevant experience, this handbook encompasses John Sheehan's considerable knowledge of the business aviation community gleaned from years of consulting with the world's safest and most successful flight departments. In his role as a safety auditor over the past 20 years, John has earned the respect of business aviation's leading practitioners. He has prepared and presented seminars on flight department management for the NBAA for more than a dozen years and is scheduled for continuing activity for NBAA members in the areas of business aviation operations.

Good management concepts and techniques are essential to capitalizing on the benefits of business transportation. I recommend *Business and Corporate Aviation Management* by John Sheehan for seasoned flight department managers as well as for company travel department personnel who are exploring how business aviation can benefit their company. This handbook also should be required reading for students seeking to grasp the breadth of transportation capabilities inherent in business aviation. Furthermore, John Sheehan covers the elements of business aviation as a transportation resource in a comprehensive and insightful manner that adds to the handbook's value.

John W. Olcott
President
National Business Aviation Association
November 2002

ACKNOWLEDGMENTS

The following people made material contributions to this book through their ideas, experience, and encouragement: Roger Phaneuf, of PAI; Jack Olcott, David Almy, Bob Blouin, and Greg Jackson, of NBAA; Jim Cannon, Rich Messina, Steve Nielsen, Jim West, Len Beauchemin, Pat Cunningham, and Steve Hawkes, flight department managers *par excellence*; Walter Kraujalis, Bloomer DeVere, and Mark Twombly, of WestWord; Frank Hofmann, of IAOPA; Dennis Wright, of FlightTime; Steve Quilty, of BGSU; and Shelley Carr, of McGraw-Hill.

In a larger sense, all my clients and workshop participants through the years actually wrote this book; I just recorded their experiences and observations.

A special thanks to my wife, Peggy, without whose ideas, encouragement, editing, and moral support, this book would never have seen the light of day.

INTRODUCTION

WHY THIS BOOK WAS WRITTEN

This book was written as a consequence of 13 years spent helping individuals and companies to choose the types of aircraft they needed to fulfill their on-demand air transportation needs and to evaluate their flight departments. Certain central themes and patterns of success in business aviation operations have emerged over the years, ideas that I felt should be shared with those desiring to engage in on-demand air transportation.

Finding the Right Aircraft and Method of Delivery

The advantages of having one's own aircraft are evident—creating your own travel scheduled, time saved, security, and the ability to go many places that the airlines cannot are all compelling reasons to use on-demand air transportation. Yet few people are sufficiently familiar with the breadth and detail of this form of aviation to choose efficiently among the options available.

Deciding to use on-demand air transportation consists of two tasks: selecting an aircraft and the method of delivering the service. Choosing the aircraft is not as simple as buying an automobile; there are many different types of aircraft, each incorporating a variety of features not apparent or well appreciated by the novice buyer. Seating capacity, runway performance, range versus payload tradeoffs, and interior appointments and amenities all make a difference in how the service is delivered. The days of the boss asking the board of directors for $30 million to buy a Gulfstream aircraft without justification are a fond memory in most companies; the board and the boss want to know what they are getting for their money and what the downstream consequences of their purchase are. Likewise, an individual selecting an aircraft and delivery method is faced with a wide variety of choices and combinations much too complex to absorb at a single inquiry.

The common issue left out of the aircraft acquisition equation is, "What are my/our on-demand air transportation needs?" Many acquisitions are made on the recommendation of a trusted acquaintance, senior corporate officer, or aircraft broker, none of whom have a good idea of your total transportation needs or those of the company or what value the aircraft will bring to the equation. An air transportation analysis must be done to determine the types and number of aircraft needed and how the service should be delivered.

While thousands of individuals and companies own and operate aircraft worldwide, other options exist: charter, aircraft management companies, fractional ownership, joint ownership, and combinations of these. Service levels and both capital and operating costs vary widely depending on the type of transportation delivery method chosen. Unfortunately, many of these essential points are lost in the rush to acquire an aircraft or sign up for a fractional share.

The first three chapters of this book address these important issues, attempting to provide insights that will be useful in creating a substantial understanding of how people and companies use their aircraft and decide how the service is to be delivered.

Operating the Flight Department

Running a flight department effectively and efficiently seems to be easy for some but difficult for others. My evaluations originally consisted of examining flight departments for compliance with Federal Aviation Administration (FAA) regulations and the operator's policies to ensure that they were safe. While this was a major responsibility (and the principal factor in causing the evaluation to take place), my work increasingly looked at the business side of the operation. Management, business skills, handling people, administration, reports, planning—all the elements necessary for the effective operation of a flight department became increasingly important in my evaluations. Not that the safety and compliance aspects were any less important, but it soon become evident that there were some clear distinctions between the good and the not-so-good departments I visited. The single element that made the difference between the two types of departments boiled down to *management.* The desire to take the department's operations beyond tomorrow's flight schedule and the ability to systemize processes, to create control mechanisms, and to handle people well—all these elements of management became evident either by their presence or absence shortly after my arrival at the departments.

At first, it seemed so simple—to detect the differences, catalog them, prescribe remedies, and rapidly leave town. However, it slowly came to me that many of the people with whom I left my remedies did not *understand the management process.* They had never been trained, never been expected to create order out of a complex operation, did not appreciate the value of control and feedback, and never worked in a corporate environment. Many of the flight department managers, chief pilots, and directors of maintenance were *winging it!* These people were fish out water, out of their natural environment. These good people were used to thinking in terms of flight plans, weather forecasts, air traffic control clearances, maintenance inspection schedules, life-limited parts, and recordkeeping—not budgets, reports, human resources, and long-range plans.

With very few exceptions, these people were bright, well-motivated, sincere people; I knew they could be helped. How best to help them? Some had had elementary management training at a point in their past, some had business degrees, and some had no training at all. There was little common ground from which to start. Thus I fell on the idea of writing a book that would link the theoretical tenets of management with the practical needs of day-to-day flight department operations.

Over the past 11 years, I helped to develop and present workshops for the National Business Aviation Association (NBAA) on developing flight department maintenance and operations manuals and managing small flight departments. These workshops provided me with a wealth of information as a consequence of facilitating thousands of participant interactions about how flight departments should and should not be operated.

The result of my observations and interactions, which you hold, represents my learning experiences from working closely with people in hundreds of aviation organizations over the past 13 years. This is a composite of large and small aviation organizations, low and high usage operations, companies with large jet transports and those with a single piston-powered twin, and one-person departments and those with more than 100 people. I have attempted to draw on the best practices from each segment of the aviation community, but in doing so, I must issue a note of caution: *There is no single right way to make any orga-*

nization work effectively and efficiently. Rather, there are as many ways as the human imagination and creativity can conjure; there are literally thousands of *right* ways.

Flight department management must constantly evaluate the organizational culture, economic environment, personnel assigned, mission, and resources to adapt their operations to meet user needs. It is this ability to adapt, to reorient, and to intelligently change the organization and its procedures that makes the difference between the good and not-so-good departments. However, adherence to core value systems and cultural norms is necessary to provide substance and integrity to any organization. Therefore, it is the balance between maintaining values and adjusting to the demands of the environment that can mean the difference between success or failure.

THE AUDIENCE

This book was written with two basic types of people in mind:

- Individuals seeking information about how to get into the on-demand air transportation business, whether for business or personal reasons
- Flight department managers, their bosses, and those who would become flight department managers

While all these types of people are closely related, they are not necessarily close in outlook, immediate and long-term needs, or background. Yet they all need varying amounts of practical, real-world information to do their job; this is the factor that links them in their common quest for providing safe, reliable, and efficient on-demand air transportation.

Individuals

Whether visiting grandchildren, traveling to a vacation home, or talking with an advisor, individuals have found that going via aircraft and their own scheduled makes life simpler and enjoyable. The aircraft may work out to be a modest single-engine piston-powered four-seater or a medium-sized turbojet, yet selecting and operating the aircraft sometimes can be a confusing and lengthy task. Where does one begin to understand both the aircraft options and the methods of delivery? And once the decision is made, how is the service to be managed? Similarly, those who work with and advise individuals must understand these features if they are to properly assist their clients and friends.

Business Executives

The harried entrepreneur, chief executive officer (CEO), and senior manager are all victims of the same deficiency: *not enough time.* This is usually coupled with the need to visit with customers, deal makers, and company personnel who will make a difference for their future. They slowly come to realize that they must *make more time for themselves.* Doing so can be difficult, but if they travel frequently, cutting down on their travel time will enable them to get out and back more quickly, spend fewer days (and nights) on the road, and be more productive enroute. All these features are the reasons why businesspeople choose on-demand air transportation.

The chairman, CEO, and senior staff are prime candidates for this book, but others within the company will benefit as well. Foremost is the staffer charged with either seeking the right answers to the air transportation questions or attempting to justify the decision made regarding an aircraft type or delivery method made somewhere above his or her level. Such a staffer probably has not thought of all the potential uses of the service nor of the different means of providing it. In doing so, he or she will feel much better about his or her choice and confident about implementing it.

Human resources, finance and accounting, risk management, planning, and legal personnel also need to understand why the company either has an aircraft or will soon get one. Theirs is a need to justify or comprehend the process but, more important, to assist the flight operation in succeeding in its mission. By understanding the operation and needs of the flight department, they can become partners in its success.

Finally, for middle managers or salespeople who are desperately attempting to satisfy their pressing travel needs, this book will provide ideas about how to get management's attention and justify their own on-demand air transportation needs. Business aircraft are not just for the few executives at the top of the company, they are business tools that should be used where they make the most sense.

Flight Department Managers

Flight department managers, including the department manager, chief pilot, head scheduler, director of maintenance, and chief inspector, are the front-line, buck-stops-here people who must produce reliable, safe, and on-time on-demand air transportation. Yet their one- or two-aircraft airline does not have the depth of personnel or virtually any other resource an airline has. They must keep a number of balls in the air constantly; they are master jugglers, with few assistants to relieve them of their many tasks. Before we become overwhelmed with pity for these poor souls, it is well to realize that they also have some of the most rewarding jobs in aviation.

They are highly autonomous, operating in a location remote from the corridors of power and often with a financial independence that is the envy of their peers within the company. In the great majority of cases, they are "aviation junkies," having risen through the ranks of pilot, scheduler, or aviation maintenance technician; they love airplanes and get paid to work with them. What could be better?

This question takes on a new relevance when the CEO is waiting for a mechanical problem to be fixed on the only available aircraft, or the budget proposal is 20 percent over what the boss wants, or word just arrived that the Gulfstream's left engine melted down and it is in Melbourne (Australia, not Florida)! As the old adage goes, this is why they pay the manager the big bucks.

With privilege comes responsibility. With responsibility comes the need to organize, plan, foresee events, and grasp the big picture of where the organization should be in 1, 3, or 5 years. The pilot or technician fresh from the ranks, testing the heady mantle of boss, manager, or leader, may not have had the opportunity to practice the types of skills necessary to assume the responsibilities that accompany the title. He or she rapidly learns that the skills needed to run the show are considerably different from those required of one of the performers.

The Boss

This is person to whom the flight department manager reports either in a company or in private operation. This is the person to whom the CEO or principal casually assigned management and oversight of the aviation department, not appreciating that this person's total aviation experience comes from enjoying the perquisites of the first class section of an airliner. In a significant number of cases, the addition of the aviation department to this manager's already impressive list of tasks was not something for which he or she would have volunteered.

These people are typically an executive vice president, senior vice president of administration, vice president of finance, or director of facilities. As far as they are concerned, taking on the aviation department is like assuming the job of elephant master at the circus; airplanes, pilots, and mechanics are strange and sometimes messy animals. However, the fact that they have been put in charge brings pressure to bear—how can they manage it if they do not understand it? Certainly, they must accept the word of their subordinates within the flight department, but this sort of trust only goes so far when the safety of lives and a $2 million annual budget are involved. What are they to do?

The advice of getting smart fast about corporate aviation may be good but largely unattainable for most. The new reporting senior can talk to peers in other companies, talk to his or her friends on the golf course, read everything he or she can lay hands on, or hire a consultant. If only there were a single source of information about everything that goes on out at the airport. This book obviously does not have all the answers, but it will provide a sturdy foundation.

Would-be Managers

An axiom in the airline business states that if you take the most senior line captain and make him or her the chief pilot, you lose the best pilot and gain a lousy manager. This presumes that the captain never had any management training or experience—a reasonable assumption, given the normal career progression of a professional pilot. The same situation is probably not true for an aviation maintenance technician, since there is a logical progression of positions within the maintenance world that requires supervisory and management skills. All this spawns close parallels within the corporate flight department business.

The existing flight department manager may receive a better offer, finally decides to retire, or cannot pass the aviation medical exam—this sets the stage for the senior pilot or technician to succeed to the throne. The call comes from the company reporting senior for a meeting, the offer is made and accepted, and yesterday's happy-go-lucky pilot or technician has just landed in the fire. It is likely, too, that this new-found manager has not been privy to the inner workings and hidden mechanisms that make the flight department run. In essence, this person's new boss has unceremoniously thrown him or her into the deep end and told him or her to start swimming.

The old adage that the best time to know an emergency procedure and the worst time to learn it is in an emergency applies here. If the fresh-caught manager has been preparing for this eventuality for more than a few months, he or she has a head start. With no preparation, the new kid on the block is at a real disadvantage. This book was not specifically designed as a cookbook to be used in the heat of the kitchen, but it will enable the new manager to keep the departmental potatoes from burning while the peas and chicken are tended to.

Finally, the student who is taking a course in aviation management will gain valuable insights regarding the real world of business aviation by reading the book. Note that I said *reading*, not *studying*; this material may enhance and bring reality to a more basic text. Therefore, this book should be considered supplementary reading and not a primary text, since I do not cover all the basic elements associated with planning, finance, personnel management, and the like. With luck, I may convince someone starting in an aviation career to gravitate toward business aviation instead of an alternative.

Satisfying the Needs

Each of these people has a significant need to know how a flight department should be run and the tools required to make that happen. Much of what they use to accomplish this task comes from prior experience in aviation or outside it. In most cases, this experience is neither appropriate nor fitting to the job at hand. Thus this book attempts to describe a range of flight department operations and present alternative management methods that will enable the preceding classes of individuals to cope and perhaps thrive.

However, this book alone will not solve all the needs or problems of those interested in business aviation and how it operates; this is just a beginning, a guide, a starting point for those would manage. It takes curiosity, tenacity, sensitivity, resoluteness, and vision—a wide range of characteristics and traits that mark both leader and manager. These are the skills that draw primarily from life experience, character, and values. The principal characteristic that makes it all work is the individual's *will* to manage or *motivation* to do the job; without these, this book is of little value.

THE BOOK

This book was written to be a practical guide for those who would undertake to manage an on-demand aviation operation, large or small. While the book contains some theory, the majority of its contents are very practical, based on a variety of observations and insights gained from my work with on-demand flight operations. Experiences gained from working with airlines, repair stations, and air taxi operations are used liberally throughout as well.

I realize that there are many different ways to operate a flight department, some of which may be better or more appropriate to a specific situation than a suggestion made within this book. However, it is my intent to provide the uninitiated and those seeking solutions to problems with a starting point for many of the common situations faced by companies and individual operators. Some of the more significant situations described herein contain several alternatives in an attempt to provide flexibility and options, but many offer just a starting point.

While the book may be read cover to cover as a conventional text, the real value should come from its use as a reference. Regardless of how the book is used, however, Chapters 4, "Running the Business," and 5, "Flight Department Management," should be read by all. These chapters serve as starting points for the neophyte and as a refresher for the old hand.

Some sections of this book are more detailed than others, recognizing the fact that some aspects of the manager's job have proved to be either more important or more interesting to managers. Sections as diverse as small flight departments, budgets, safety, working with people in the parent company, and marketing the flight department have been chosen for special, extended treatment. Choosing these aspects of running the flight department over others was difficult, but it is these subjects that have given flight department managers the most trouble or provided the greatest advantages.

The Index should lead readers to the desired topic, if not the general subject area. Readers are encouraged to seek answers to questions in several different topic areas rather than just a single one. The Glossary is designed primarily for those not experienced in aviation issues, attempting to give them a head start in the arcane and voluminous jargon endemic to the world of aviation.

For those wishing to cut to the chase, to get to the real answers of how to run a flight department successfully, see Chapter 9, "Putting It All Together." There I try to sum up the superior performance and wisdom I have witnessed over the years to portray the best methods of serving your company and ensuing flight department survival.

The Chapters

Chapter 1, "Setting the Scene," provides a background to on-demand air transportation, relating reasons for its existence, its definitions and characteristics, and a means for justifying it. An attempt is made to predict the future of the genre, done with more enthusiasm than precision. Each method of delivering this service—employee/owner-flown, in-house flight department, charter, fractional ownership, etc—is further defined and explored to provide a brief idea of how each one works and might be used to satisfy a company's air transportation needs.

The big issue of determining the shape and size of the air transportation need is discussed in Chapter 2. The air transportation analysis process, evaluating the options for service delivery and evaluating the costs of the venture, is examined. Most important, advice on how to select from among the alternatives is presented in a straightforward manner.

"Getting Started" is the title of Chapter 3, showing in brief form how to begin one of the several types of aviation operations. Emphasis and detail are given to owner-flown and in-house methods, since these are the most common types of operations. Practical advice on finding the right people, setting up a schedule method, and arranging for maintenance is provided.

Chapter 4, "Running the Business," examines the planning, administrative, human resources, and financial details of operating a flight department. A special section is devoted to the small flight department, those operating two or fewer aircraft. This is the most common form of flight department and the type with the greatest burden because of their many tasks and few people available to complete them.

"Management 101" may be a better title for Chapter 5, "Flight Department Management." This covers the background and elements of the practice of management, attempting to show how they can best be used in the context of running a flight department. The chapter examines the flight department manager as a business executive, putting this person into the larger corporate frame of reference.

How the flight operations details of the department work is the subject of Chapter 6, "Operations." It is in this chapter that the details of the flight department are explored: scheduling, standard operating procedures, security, training, and safety. Particular emphasis is placed on the subject of standards and limits to be used in a flight department.

"Maintenance," Chapter 7, is a short but meaty chapter. While much of the glamour associated with flying goes to the operations end of the hangar, maintenance is what really makes it go. The somewhat obscure but essential issues regarding maintenance are covered to provide perspective for technician, pilot, and nonaviation manager alike.

Safety is given special treatment in a chapter of its own, Chapter 8. The enviable safety record of business aviation does not happen by accident; dedicated staff and a conscious adherence to safe operating procedures make it happen. The chapter provides a number of insights and sampled safety programs to use.

Chapter 9, "Putting It All Together," attempts to take all the information imparted in the previous chapters and put it into perspective, attempting to achieve the maximum utility from the more detailed sections of the book. Skim this chapter first, since it contains many of the valuable insights my clients have taught me.

Finally, a Glossary and Appendix provide useful reference sections. And then, for research, the Index permits fast access to the variety of information provided in the body of this book.

No one book can possibly contain sufficient material to cover a subject it in its entirety. This book is no exception, primarily because of the great diversity of operations represented within on-demand aviation. However, this book also contains references that will lead readers to a variety of other, more comprehensive material on the subject. Again, no one work can be truly comprehensive; this is just a beginning.

Being of a mindset that I should continue to improve my work until I get it right, I would sincerely appreciate reader comments about this book. I would especially be grateful for comments concerning the mix of information and appropriateness of material included for all types of flight departments. You can reach me through the publisher—the second edition will be better because of your comments.

John J. Sheehan
Wilmington, North Carolina
November 2002

CHAPTER 1
SETTING THE SCENE

Four years ago we had four plants and today we have eleven and the only way we have been able to expand our company and to get these locations has been in our own aircraft.

—CORPORATE CEO

ON-DEMAND AIR TRANSPORTATION

Within all forms of transportation there are two basic divisions, scheduled and nonscheduled. *Scheduled* is self-explanatory and well understood. Airlines, railroads, buses, and ferry boats operate according to set schedules. *Nonscheduled* requires further explanation; the term expresses a sense of randomness or irregularity, concepts not useful when attempting to define the process. However, *on-demand transportation* is a more descriptive term, signifying that the transportation should be available when requested or needed. Therefore, the purpose of this book is to describe the various types of on-demand air transportation and to tell readers how they can best choose and use the methods comprising it.

Many different people use on-demand air transportation: Individuals, corporate executives, technical troubleshooters, sports teams, entrepreneurs, and families all benefit from the advantages brought by this form of flying. The object for all is to travel to some distant point as safely and comfortably as possible. Some wish to do so in high style, others more economically; some rapidly, others at a more leisurely pace; some doing the flying themselves, others leaving those tasks to professional flight crews. However, all do so because they want to create and maintain their own schedule and control their lives more fully.

This book will examine this form of aviation from two basic perspectives: personal and business aviation. This distinction is made because of the fundamentally different motivation for each, one to serve a personal lifestyle and one to create efficiency in the workplace.

On-Demand Air Transportation Defined

The International Civil Aviation Organization (ICAO) states that all civil aviation operations are divided into three categories: commercial air transportation, general aviation, and aerial work. They are defined as follows:

- *Commercial air transport.*   An aircraft operation involving the transport of passengers, cargo, or mail for remuneration or hire.

- *Aerial work.*   An aircraft operation in which an aircraft is used for specialized services such as agriculture, construction, photography, surveying, observation and patrol, search and rescue, or aerial advertisement.

- *General aviation.*   An aircraft operation other than a commercial air transport operation or an aerial work operation.

For the purposes of this book, we will consider only the first and last types, since they both provide on-demand air transportation, with the fundamental difference being whether the operation is conducted for compensation or for hire (Fig. 1.1).

On-Demand Air Transportation—The transportation of passengers and cargo by aircraft from one point to another in a manner and at a time designated by the person exercising operational control.

Personal aviation may be provided by the owner-operator's own aircraft or by a commercial venture supplying air transportation on demand. Therefore, personal aviation may be a subset of either commercial or general aviation.

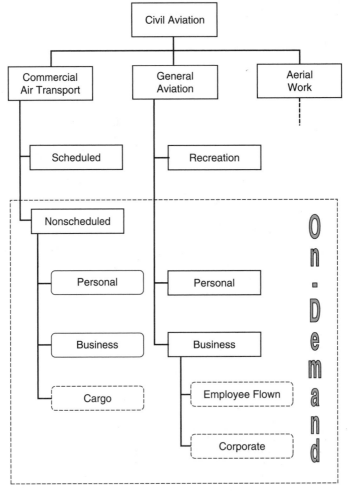

FIGURE 1.1   Civil aviation elements.

Business aviation covers all types of aircraft operations flown in pursuit of business matters. Within this broad classification are employee-flown and corporate operations. Employee-flown operations are predominately owner-flown aircraft, yet these flights may be piloted by any employee, carrying other employees or customers. The key factors involved in employee-flown operations are that the aircraft is operated by a company using a pilot or pilots not specifically employed or compensated to fly the company aircraft. Corporate aircraft operations are distinct from employee-flown operations in that they are operated by a company for its business purposes, using professional pilots (normally two) compensated specifically for their piloting duties. The National Business Aviation Association (NBAA) defines *corporate aviation* as "aircraft owned or leased and operated by a corporation or business firm for the transportation of personnel or cargo in furtherance of the corporation's or firm's business and which are flown by professional pilots receiving a direct salary or compensation for piloting." Note that in either employee-flown or corporate methods, the aircraft does not necessarily have to be owned or leased by the company; it can be rented or even borrowed (some restrictions apply to these operations, however).

Aircraft charter and fractional ownership also may be used to satisfy business requirements for on-demand air transportation.

Personal Aviation

The best means of explaining this segment of air transportation may be via an analogy. Both buses and automobiles are available to people wishing to travel, yet the automobile dominates our ground transportation for obvious reasons: comfort, convenience, and schedule. The automobile provides ground-based on-demand transportation to individuals and groups willing to pay for the service. This is preferred to public transportation for the reasons listed. Perhaps the most important reason for our preference for the automobile is that we wish to create our own schedule and change it at will. Buses (and airliners) seldom permit us this luxury.

There are approximately 350,000 general aviation and aerial work aircraft worldwide, of which an estimated 150,000 are used at least in part for personal transportation. Perhaps one-third of these are used for true on-demand purposes, possessing the ability to fly in weather and to carry two or more passengers. Therefore, personal air transportation constitutes a significant worldwide activity, complementing other forms of transportation that support the needs of individuals. Whether it be a family seeking the fastest and most hassle-free transportation to the ski slopes, an individual flying to a mountain retreat, or a person seeking the best shopping venue in a major city, personal aviation has come of age. These are just a few of the reasons individuals, families, and friends use aircraft.

Some people use an aircraft for recreational, sightseeing, or sport purposes, but these do not constitute on-demand air transportation because transportation, i.e., flying people or things from point A to point B.

Personal air transportation uses a wide range of aircraft, from small, four-seat, single-engine, piston-powered aircraft to large, multiengine turbojets carrying scores of people over intercontinental distances. However, in this book I will concentrate on three broad classes of personal air transportation: owner-flown operations, those provided by a company as a service, and in-house flight departments using professional flight crews.

Personal and business aviation are separated by a single factor: *purpose*. The organization, regulations, and mechanics of the two operations are essentially the same; only the motivation for the on-demand air transportation services is different. At the lower end of aircraft types used, single-engine aircraft capable of carrying more than two passengers during instrument meteorological conditions (IMC), personal aviation generates an estimated 80 percent of usage worldwide; at the upper end of the spectrum, turbine-powered aircraft are used an estimated 90 percent of the time for business purposes.

Yet both types are organized, regulated, and operated in a similar fashion—the principles are the same. Therefore, within this book, business aviation will be used as the predominant example because it often requires the highest level of organization and standards, therefore making it the form more inclusive of the factors to be considered in many aspects of on-demand air transportation. Where differences exist, they will be discussed.

Our aircraft has enabled my family to be together more frequently and to more fully enjoy those times.

—AIRCRAFT OWNER

Business Aviation

In an average year, hundreds of millions of people travel for business purposes worldwide. This is done in an effort to establish firm connections between businesses, to communicate ideas, to act on opportunities, and to establish a face-to-face connection. While many inter-business communications can be made by telephone, e-mail, fax, and mail, the deals are made, the problems solved, and new frontiers forged by people meeting in person.

Twenty years ago, technology mavens were forecasting a dramatic decrease in business travel due to the advent of cell phones, the Internet, and teleconferencing. Their theory stated that face-to-face meetings were no longer necessary due to the superlative new communications devices; teleconferencing was the next best thing to being there. While these new communications devices did relieve the more routine travel needs, a strange thing happened: Both teleconferencing and business travel increased. Productivity gains provided by communications technology generated the opportunity for more business, which, in turn, generated more business travel. The two connectivity methods worked together to help the productivity of such countries as the United States, Germany, and Japan become the highest in the world.

The need to be face-to-face in the business world never seems to decrease, only increase. New and important deals are made in person, seldom over the phone or Internet. Customers are cultivated, pampered, listened to, and helped in-person, and new product and services are introduced in-person; business travel is a long-term growth industry. However, there are other means of getting business travelers to their destinations via air.

Most business travel, perhaps two-thirds, is accomplished via the airlines. Every year the world's airlines carry an average of 1 billion passengers domestically and 550 million passengers internationally, with roughly one-third of these people traveling for business purposes. The airlines serve thousands of airports, providing frequent, safe, and fairly reliable service to the world's business travelers, yet there are alternatives.

With frequent airline service available to the far corners of the earth, why do we need other aircraft to transport a few people to many of the same destinations? Isn't this much more expensive that the airlines? And how safe is it? These are just a few of the questions asked by both the curious and the critical when considering business aviation.

As this book is being written in 2002, more than 13,000 operators fly in excess of 21,000 turbine (turbojet and turboprop) aircraft worldwide in support of business (Table 1.1 and Figs. 1.2 and 1.3). Three-quarters of the operators and aircraft are located in North America. In the United States, each of the approximately 14,000 turbine aircraft flew an average of 450 hours, transporting an estimated 18 million business travelers in 2001.[1] Interestingly, four-fifths of U.S. business flight operations have just one aircraft (Fig. 1.4).

TABLE 1.1   Business Aircraft
by Country, 2001

United States	14,079
Brazil	667
Canada	656
Mexico	540
France	431
Germany	378
Venezuela	288
United Kingdom	283
South Africa	247
Argentina	216
Australia	213

Source: International Business
Aviation Council (IBAC).

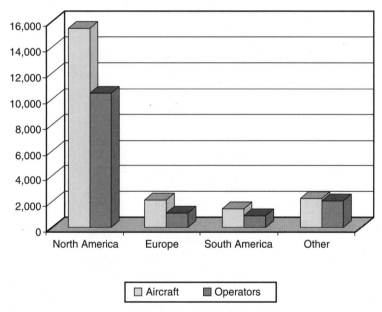

FIGURE 1.2   Turbine-powered business aircraft distribution. (NBAA.)

Of the Fortune 500 companies, only 29 percent choose not to operate at least one corporate aircraft. The productivity, net income, and sales of companies operating corporate aircraft dramatically exceed those of comparable nonaircraft operators. These companies use their aircraft as productivity tools, as a means of controlling their busy travel schedules, and as a convenience for their executives who need to pack every ounce of productive work into each day. In essence, the aircraft becomes a time machine, a modern magic carpet to safely and rapidly transport executives to the next business opportunity.

On-demand air transportation has become a part of corporate culture and promises to be a fixture in the business world for the foreseeable future. It did not take long for companies to discover that having an aircraft of one's own created advantages that the competition did

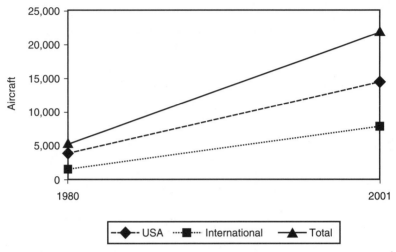

FIGURE 1.3 Business aviation turbine-powered aircraft. (NBAA.)

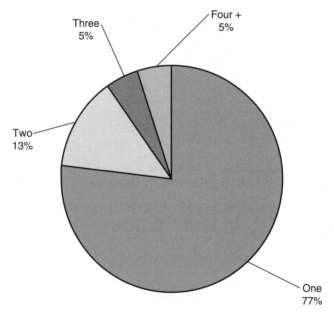

FIGURE 1.4 Average aircraft per company. (NBAA.)

not have. The time savings, flexibility, efficiency, privacy, and security that corporate aviation offered were convincing enough to justify aircraft devoted to a company's exclusive use. However, softer, more intangible benefits accrued to its use too. Increased time at home, the ability to reach even the most remote locations directly, comfort, and fewer airport hassles became sufficient reasons for most to gravitate toward this type of transportation.

The real clincher, the reason that keeps the board of directors and stockholders happy, is the ability of corporate on-demand air transportation to increase productivity for its executives. The corporate aircraft becomes a time multiplier, offering convenient access to as many as 5000 airports in the United States (compared with just 500 that airlines serve) with turbojet speed and an ease not possible on the airlines. It makes little sense to consume 2 days in getting star corporate performers to and from a remote location when the corporate aircraft can get them there, provide a half-day on site for business, and have them home for dinner, *all in the same day*. It is this measurable productivity multiplier effect that keeps selling corporate aviation every day.

Even the accounting department realizes that business flying makes sense. Studies show that companies using their own aircraft have better sales growth, earnings per share, long-term return to investors, and productivity (sales per employee) than companies that do not use business aircraft. The evidence is compelling: Business aircraft are good for the bottom line. The airlines continue to drive executives to corporate aviation in increasing numbers. As scheduled air transportation is forced to restrict and segment its schedules and routes to be more competitive, as airlines overbook and bump passengers in increasing numbers, and as airline terminals become more unmanageable, corporate aviation can only increase in importance; the airlines may be the best reason for using corporate aircraft.

As the global village increasingly becomes a nation's marketplace, the use of corporate aircraft will facilitate this transition. Intercontinental corporate aviation has been a reality for some years and increasingly will serve our interests abroad. Corporate turbojets having nonstop New York to Tokyo and Los Angeles to Paris range are a reality and the hottest-selling aircraft in the business fleet.

Yet corporate aviation is not immune to the business cycle. The health and well-being of the company flight department may be directly tied to the state of the economy, with boom times signaling increased aviation activity and recessions creating not only less activity but also fewer aircraft, hours, and people as well.

> The Honeywell Corporation, a leading supplier of turbojet engines and avionics to corporate aviation, predicts that 7600 new business aircraft, valued at $121 billion, will be delivered between 2003 and 2013.

There will continue to be good times and bad as the economy pursues its mood swings. Despite the bad times, corporate aviation will persist and become stronger as the concept of on-demand air transportation becomes more deeply entrenched in many corporate cultures.

The Beginnings

Personal aviation began with the Wright brothers in 1903. Their objective was to provide a new form of transportation that would enable people to get from point A to point B as rapidly as possible. Their initial 129-ft trip signaled the beginning of personal air transportation. Before the end of the first decade of the twentieth century, individuals were using the airplane as a legitimate, although limited, form of transportation. It was the initial desire for individuals to travel by air rather than groups in larger public aircraft that drove early aviation forward. While interrupted by World War I, personal aviation continued to grow and grow steadily until Lindbergh's transatlantic crossing in 1927, a watershed event for all aviation.

Business aviation began shortly after World War I. Plentiful war-surplus open-cockpit, two-seat biplanes were used to promote various companies' wares via barnstorming trips and advertising courtesy of product logos painted on the fuselage. Hearty entrepreneurs flew or rode in these aircraft to sales opportunities around the country. Yet the rigors of open-cockpit flying and less-than-reliable engines kept these risky trips to a minimum through the 1920s. The world's oil companies, Standard Oil, Texaco, Continental, and Royal Dutch Shell, became the pioneers of true business and corporate flying in the 1920s, using the first multiengine, usually trimotor transports to service their far-flung drill sites.

Standard Oil's chairman, Robert W. Steward, concluded that the advantages of airplane versus train travel "...more than compensate for the expense and make the airplane an economical method of travel...as safe and comfortable as transcontinental train."[2] Despite this glowing endorsement, relatively few companies took advantage of business aviation until the late 1920s. It was the simultaneous availability of closed-cabin monoplanes (with more reliable engines) and Charles Lindbergh's solo transatlantic flight in 1927 that served as the basis for corporate aviation as we know it today.

The Lindbergh flight, combined with national authorities regulating civil aviation, gave travelers new confidence in this fledgling form of transportation. Airlines suddenly sprouted, proving to the world that air travel was safe, efficient, and mostly reliable. Business executives and entrepreneurs, ever seeking a competitive advantage, immediately saw company operated aircraft as a means to facilitate their business activities. The 1930s saw the availability of aircraft specifically designed for business applications, including small single-engine and medium-sized multiengine aircraft. Oil companies again took the lead, using fleets of aircraft, including airliners, to service their international business activities. The growth of business aviation during the 1930s is remarkable in that the great depression curtailed much other business expansion.

Similarly, personal aviation benefited greatly from Lindbergh's transatlantic flight, turning all eyes to the skies. During the 1930s, scores of new aircraft were introduced with the thought of providing personal transportation for the masses. Despite the constraints of the poor economic conditions, light aviation flourished and grew. Business aviation and the airlines provided the new developments and the infrastructure that benefited personal flight.

World War II called a temporary halt to civil aviation development, but in a very real sense, it prepared the world for the aviation boom that followed the cessation of hostilities. Hundreds of thousands of people learned about and became acclimated to the concept of air transportation during their wartime service, leading them to transfer their skills and knowledge of aviation to the business environment. Postwar boom times and the availability of surplus military transports fueled a rapid growth in both personal and business aviation. Significantly, the rapid advances of wartime aviation technology made civil flying much safer, more reliable, and even practical. Improved communications and navigation equipment, more reliable engines and aircraft systems, and the beginnings of a real air traffic control system facilitated the move toward business and personal aviation.

While business and personal (general) aviation grew substantially during the 1950s, it was introduction of the business jet at the end of the decade that made the industry take off. In 1957, the Lockheed Jetstar made its first flight and ushered in a new era of speed and convenience for corporate travelers. Fast, comfortable, and practical, "airborne board rooms" became a reality with the jet age. Followed shortly by the Sabreliner and Hawker/deHaviland 125, the jets provided a quantum increase in business travel effectiveness and efficiency. Then, in 1964, the first Learjet brought jet travel within economical reach of most corporations. The Learjet cost $550,000 and provided speeds of up to 485 mph over distances as great as 1800 mi, accommodating up to seven passengers. Business aviation had arrived.

Commercial helicopters were available as early as 1946, but it was the advent of the Sue-Est Alouette turbine-powered helicopter in 1958 that brought a practical rotary-wing aircraft to business applications. While thousands of business helicopters are used worldwide for business aviation, their numbers remain small relative to the number of fixed-wing aircraft working for business. Yet their importance for specialized applications make them valuable and permanent assets in the corporate transportation inventory.

Personal aviation benefited from these developments, taking aerodynamics, radio, and infrastructure improvements for its own. During the 1960s and 1970s, personal aviation grew rapidly, attempting to reach the dream of practical and safe flying for all. The late 1970s and early 1980s saw a peak in the number of pilots and aircraft produced, essentially realizing the dream within the bounds of economic practicality. Finally, small general aviation aircraft could be used as a practical form of personal transportation through most weather conditions and at speeds and distances that made sense to the consumer.

Through the mid-1970s, business aviation aircraft growth was modest, with fewer than 100 turbine-powered aircraft being produced for the business community in 1972. Good economic times in the late 1970s and early 1980s produced a miniature boom in business turbine aircraft, with more than 400 such aircraft produced at the peak in 1982. During the same year, more than 2000 piston-powered light general aviation aircraft were produced, a significant number destined for business uses. In 2001, more than 1200 turbine-powered business aircraft were shipped worldwide, approaching the 1800 piston-powered airplanes produced in the same year; the emphasis is clearly turning to turbine-powered business aircraft.[3]

In 1986, some 14,000 turbojets and turboprops flew for business around the world; that number had grown to more than 21,000 by the end of 2002 (11,000 of these are turbojets), 50 percent growth in just 15 years. Importantly, 13,000 operators worldwide sponsored all these aircraft. The rate of increase is growing, perhaps as rapidly as 4 percent per year. Business aviation has earned itself a permanent place in the world's corporations.[4]

Personal aviation has taken its place as a practical transportation alternative throughout the world with an estimated 150,000 aircraft used for safe, reliable, transportation.

Travel Is Important for Business

Corporations of all sizes increasingly focus on their travel expenditures, which often represent the third largest expenditure within many companies. As such, corporate stakeholders traditionally have viewed business travel from the narrow perspective of costs as opposed to its relationship to corporate productivity. Understanding the need to better define the corporate perception of travel and the role of travel management, the Institute of Business Travel Management (IBTM) commissioned an environmental scan to assess the value senior corporate executives place on business travel and travel management in meeting corporate goals and objectives.

With participants ranging from chief executive officers (CEOs), senior vice presidents, vice presidents, and chief financial officers (CFOs) of Fortune 500 companies including Boeing, EDS Corporation, Johnson & Johnson, Microsoft, and The Limited, Deloitte & Touche conducted the first research project of the IBTM.[5]

Key findings included the following:

- *Travel is important to meeting company goals and objectives, and travel management programs contribute significantly to companies.* As a result of the combination of an increasingly global economy and increasing company growth fueled by the economic boom of the last few years, companies have strategically channeled more funds into the cost of conducting business. Like other business units, travel is expected to increase the corporation's return on investment and increase process efficiencies. The findings of this study clearly indicate that senior executives value the role of travel and effective travel management. Further, the study found that senior executives believe that travel management programs make significant contributions to the corporation and support the achievement of corporate missions and goals.

- *Few companies use sophisticated models to calculate the contribution of travel management to company bottom lines and shareholder value.* While senior executives value the contributions of the travel management programs, the study found that few companies use sophisticated means to calculate the true value of their travel programs. Although executives implicitly understand that travel affects other areas of the company such as sales, marketing, and operations, most travel management programs do not employ measurements that effectively calculate travel's bottom-line impact on the corporation. As a result, travel's impact on the company is strongly recognized, but a mechanism to quantify its impact has not been fully developed.

- *Senior management's highest travel priority is to optimize time while being very sensitive to the balance between time and cost.* While minimizing costs for any company is critical, the study found that those interviewed also understand that "time is money." Thus, in crafting travel policy, entering supplier relationships, and developing performance measurements, travel managers should develop methods that integrate the time and cost elements of travel.

The Reasons[6]

Deciding how to travel—via the airlines, via company or charter aircraft, or even by driving or taking a train—involves many considerations. While several of the benefits of business aircraft are tangible and measurable, some are challenging to quantify precisely. Progressive managers routinely consider all the costs and realistically evaluate all the benefits of every travel option before deciding how to go. According to the NBAA these benefits include the following:

Saving Employee Time. Efficient employee scheduling and employee time saved are key advantages of business aircraft use. Because business aircraft have the ability to fly nonstop between any of the 3500 small, close-in airports—ten times the number of locations served by scheduled airlines in the United States—highly efficient employee time management becomes a very real benefit. Additionally, the value of employee time often exceeds its cost to the company by substantial margins, further increasing the importance of employee time savings. Simply stated, business aviation helps a company obtain maximum productivity from its two most important assets—people and time.

Increasing Productivity Enroute. High levels of employee productivity enroute to a business destination—in a secure office environment that is free from interruptions, distractions, or eavesdropping—can have substantial value to an employer. A Louis Harris & Associates survey showed that executives felt that they were 20 percent more productive in the company jet than they were in the office. Conversely, they felt that they were 40 percent less productive in an airliner due to distractions and lack of privacy.

Group productivity, maximized due to the common availability of club seating and tables, often is unique to business aircraft. Strategizing before meetings and debriefing afterwards are common practices facilitated and encouraged by business aircraft cabin configurations (Figs. 1.5 and 1.6).

Minimizing Nonbusiness Hours away from Home. Family time before and after traditional business hours is critical to most employees. Because a stable, supportive family can have an acute effect on employee morale and productivity, scheduling that minimizes time away from home can be a key benefit.

Ensuring Industrial Security. For many companies, the protection of personnel from uncontrolled public exposure alone is justification for business aircraft use. Avoiding

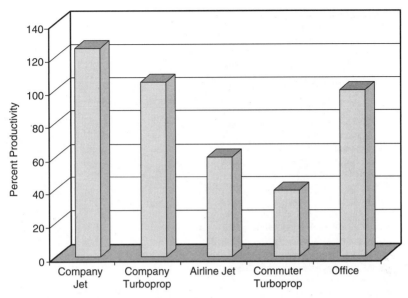

FIGURE 1.5   Productivity compared. (*NBAA.*)

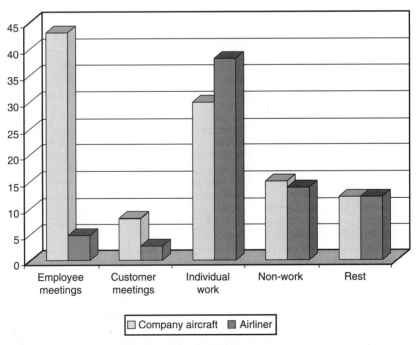

FIGURE 1.6   Passenger activity aboard aircraft. (*NBAA.*)

eavesdropping, reducing travel visibility, and eliminating unwanted and unnecessary conversations and interruptions all support the use of business aircraft to safeguard company employees and the sensitive information they carry.

Maximizing Personal Safety and Peace of Mind. Turbine-powered aircraft flown by two-person professional crews have a safety record comparable with or better than that of scheduled airlines. The peace of mind that results from complete company control over the aircraft flown, passenger and baggage manifests, pilot quality and training, aircraft maintenance, and operational safety standards is substantial. This benefit also can include the rescheduling of flights if weather, mechanical, or other considerations suggest that this is the appropriate course.

Exercising Management Control over Efficient, Reliable Scheduling. The near-total scheduling flexibility inherent in business aircraft—even changing itineraries enroute—can be a powerful asset. Since aircraft can arrive and depart on the passenger's schedule, typically waiting for them in the ordinary course of business, meetings can be moved up, back, or extended without penalty, risk, or unnecessary scheduling pressures. Overnight trips also can be avoided. If managed proactively, this benefit can improve business results.

Projecting a Positive Corporate Image. For customers in particular and often for vendors, the arrival and departure of company employees via business aircraft are the sign of a well-run company, signaling the progressive nature of an organization with a keen interest in efficient time management and high levels of productivity. If used for charitable purposes, significant public service contributions, as well as possible public relations benefits, also can be realized.

Attracting and Retaining Key People (Customers Included). The right person in the right place at the right time can change everything. Finding and keeping such people can hinge on many factors, including the ability to maintain reasonable travel schedules, maximizing personal productivity and ensuring family time. Holding on to valuable employees also can prevent companies from spending time and resources on training replacement employees.

Reducing Posttrip Fatigue and Increasing Posttrip Productivity. Schedules that require late-night travel or longer-than-necessary trips often result in posttrip fatigue, damaging productivity in the day(s) after the trip. Because they can facilitate more efficient scheduling, business aircraft can minimize this loss.

Optimizing Payroll. Under "rightsizing" initiatives, many organizations have rediscovered the need to maximize the productivity of the same or fewer employees to accomplish equal or greater amounts of work and ensure their competitive position and long-term success. As business aircraft improve employee time management and efficiency, they can help eliminate the need for additional personnel, reducing payroll costs, and help to maximize a company's competitive market advantage.

Truncating Cycle Times. The compound effect of increased productivity and saved travel time is that more can be accomplished in less time. Consequently, many companies attribute reductions in *cycle times*—when facilities are brought online sooner and projects finished faster—to business aircraft use. Although it is challenging to quantify or attribute entirely to business aircraft use, this benefit often can be substantial.

Charging the Entrepreneurial Spirit. By minimizing or eliminating many of the barriers to travel, business aircraft allow business opportunities to be considered and acted on more readily. Business cultures and their strategies change as markets, facilities, and customers in rural areas of the country—once practically unreachable and unconsidered—are newly accessible.

How Companies Use Aircraft[7]

There are a nearly infinite variety of ways to use business aircraft. From the obvious, getting the executives out and back rapidly, to transporting teams of specialists, to going out and getting customers to witness your excellent manufacturing or service organization, companies have learned that these and other applications make sense.

The NBAA has studied how companies use their aircraft. Here are just a few ways that organizations have discovered to use their aircraft (Table 1.2):

Key Employee Travel. This is by far the most frequent use of business aircraft. Getting to essential meetings, conducting site visits, and keeping customers happy are all reasons for the right people to get to the right place in a *timely manner*. The timeliness of these trips means choosing the right time for the trip and then getting out and back as quickly as possible. We all know intuitively that the business adage "time is money" is true, so we try to maximize our time where it counts most. Spending time waiting at airports in security lines does not meet this criterion.

Key employees can be anyone of any rank who is indispensable to a task, not just the CEO. Financial experts, attorneys, technicians, and quality control specialists are all candidates for using the company aircraft when hours count. Not surprisingly, an NBAA study revealed that top-level executives were not the most frequent flyers in company aircraft; middle managers were.

TABLE 1.2   Business Aircraft Utilization Strategies (NBAA)

Key employee travel.   Getting the right person in the right place at the right time.
Customer visits.   Visit customers on their turf.
Customer trips.   Bring customers to you.
Scheduled customer service.   Routine trips to service customer accounts.
Emergency customer service.   Rapid response trips to fix what's broken and "put out fires."
Humanitarian and charitable flights.   Being a good corporate citizen; helping employees.
Sales and marketing blitzes.   Multiday/multicity sales trips covering a region or sales area.
Charter revenue flights.   Offering your aircraft for use by a charter operator.
International flying.   Regularly outside the United States.
Helicopters.   Used to go directly to specific destinations; not just between airports.
Management teams.   Transporting management teams to organization sites.
Engineering teams.   Transporting production or engineering teams to critical work sites.
Corporate shuttles.   Regularly scheduled flights between organization facilities or customer sites.
Make airline connections.   Making airline connections, particularly international flights.
Carry priority cargo, parts, or mail.
Special projects.   Such as advertising shoots.
For goodwill/lobbying.   Transporting elected officials or candidates; going to lawmakers.
Utilitarian purposes.   Mapping, aerial surveys or inspections, etc.
Market expansion.   Evaluating new markets/sites.
The airborne office.   Working/conferring enroute.
Personal travel.   Employees and their families.
Attract and retain key people.   A tool to facilitate work or get people home more nights.
Maximize employee safety and industrial security.   Better than the airlines.

Saving Time and More

A control-valve manufacturer in Milwaukee was in the final stages of signing a major contract with a potential customer located in Asheville, North Carolina. A major sticking point arose over a number of issues, including final design, production rate, and costs. The situation was deemed "critical" by the company executive vice president. Clearly, a meeting of the minds was in order. A visit to the Asheville customer was planned.

As is often the case, finding a 3-day window for the meeting for all concerned (at both locations) was difficult. Why 3 days for a meeting that should require at most 6 hours? Airline service from Milwaukee to Asheville was such that the five travelers had to depart the day before and return the day after the meeting. Therefore, the executive vice president chose the only day available to all and scheduled the company aircraft for the trip.

The team rose early on the day of the trip, went to a conveniently located general aviation airport in suburban Milwaukee, boarded the aircraft on arrival (no waiting or processing necessary), and 1.5 hours later arrived in Asheville. Exactly 7 hours later (a little longer than they expected), they reboarded their aircraft and arrived back in Milwaukee in time for a stylishly late dinner.

Not only did team members save an aggregate 60 productive hours, they also saved more than 120 hours of their personal time in the process. Moreover, the 3-hour roundtrip was used profitably in strategy and implementation meetings in the company aircraft. The best part: The cost of the company aircraft was 20 percent less than the combined fares would have been on an airline.

Business aircraft are used commonly by key employees to

- Extend management control and bring operational areas to a manageable size
- Facilitate company, supplier, and/or customer meetings in multiple cities per day
- Take practical and routine daily on-site supervision of facilities in different cities
- Reduce, sometimes dramatically, travel times to multiple locations versus public transportation
- Facilitate emergency meetings, including those involving the board, partners, and customers
- Efficiently reach remote locations
- Strengthen relationships with customers through shared private time enroute to a destination
- Facilitate rapid action on mergers and acquisitions, particularly for companies in remote locations

Customer Visits.   Most businesses place customer contact at the top of their priority list. An integral part of such contacts involves face-to-face visits—visits to introduce new products, discuss existing product lines, explore new customer needs, and in general, be nice to the people who ultimately pay the bills. However, getting to customer locations, which frequently are poorly served by the airlines, can be a several-day chore. Since business aircraft have access to many more airports than do the airlines, a number of customer visits can be made in one day with the company "magic carpet."

Visits via business aircraft can be used to

- Attend customer-sponsored events, such as a grand opening.
- Service more than one destination in a day.
- Efficiently increase face-to-face contact with the customer, relationship building, interaction between people. "They think more highly of us when they see more of us."
- Facilitate a lean senior staff. "We have a lean management, so it has to cover a wide area quickly." Consequently, business aircraft can facilitate senior management participation in selling.
- Enable a team approach rather than a one-person attempt. "If there is a new business opportunity that requires a team visit, we dispatch them out on that call."
- Demonstrate capability; establish or reinforce an image
- Support a customer in trouble. "Being there sometimes helps."

Market Expansion. The attractiveness and potential of new geographic markets may be limited by a lack of physical access to those markets. Business aircraft can open potential new markets, including international ones, and provide dramatically improved access especially to rural areas. Market expansion is facilitated as much by attitude as by access. Business aircraft, because they can facilitate access, can lessen or remove perceived barriers to the management of new markets.

Prospecting within new markets is the first step, often for potential local business partners. Business aircraft sometimes are used to facilitate meetings that take place at a halfway point into these new markets. A new class of business aircraft with nonstop ranges in excess of 7000 miles is making access to global markets practical and common. Almost every flight on business aircraft has an element of market expansion to it.

Management Team Travel. Management team travel is the most common use of business aircraft. These teams provide a critical mass of expertise, talent, and experience that can be applied to problems and challenges not found at the home base. Getting these individuals out to the problem area and back expeditiously makes good business sense.

Management teams have a substantial aggregate hourly value to their employers. The combined costs of air services, employee travel time (door to door), and other trip expenses (such as hotel, meals, rental cars, etc.) often compare favorably to airline travel between second-tier cities or rural locations. When the value of employee time is considered along with the value of productive time enroute and nonbusiness hours away from home (family time), the comparison of business aircraft travel versus public transportation often becomes problematic.

Some progressive companies have or are installing conference facilities in corporate hangars to facilitate off-site meetings. Corporate hangars also are being equipped with transient manager offices that can be used for private conversations, study, or sending and receiving e-mail.

Transporting Customers. A corollary to customer trips is the practice of bringing customers to your facilities to witness your excellence and to impress them with your knowledge and insight. Moreover, fetching customers in the company airplane makes a substantial impression on them; this means that they are very important people to you.

The practice of transporting customers can

- Be used to pick them up, bring them to company facilities, meetings, cultural, entertainment, or sporting events, and then return them home as quickly as is practical, often on the same day

Letting Them See Your Excellence

A major office furniture manufacturer provides its products to a worldwide audience; however, most of its sales occur in the United States. Early in its life it saw the need for bringing customers to its Midwest headquarters, first by car and train and then by company aircraft. The investment in customer transportation has paid off, making the company a member of the Fortune 500 and a world-class provider of office furniture.

"We can show them what we make in catalogs and showrooms," says a member of the company's marketing team, "but getting them on our turf and showing them how all the pieces fit together and how dedicated we are to quality is a powerful marketing tool. We couldn't do this without the company airplanes."

- Provide an opportunity to build relationships and ease communications
- Help those in need to restore service by moving their personnel and equipment
- Improve customer access in both directions
- Be used as a courtesy to correct for company-induced delays
- Engender goodwill
- Facilitate approvals for the delivery of products or services
- Facilitate customer contract signing

International Trips. The allure of emerging markets—both as potential suppliers and as customers—in China, India, and Russia is of increasing interest. Hundreds of business aircraft fly every day between North America and Europe, Asia, Africa, or South America. A surprising number of the aircraft used for this purpose are small to midsized jets.

Many companies transport management teams internationally for multicity visits, some covering dozens of cities over multiple weeks. Given the limited airline service in some regions, this can be a highly efficient practice. Importantly, as the teams travel, they have an increased opportunity to confer and plan during lengthy enroute legs because of the uniquely private and communicative environment provided by the business aircraft cabin.

Canada, Mexico, Central America, and the Caribbean are the most frequent destinations for U.S. companies; many of these markets become closer via business aircraft than cross-country U.S. markets. As major markets and producers move offshore, the need to get to those sources becomes increasingly important; business aviation provides ready access to these areas at greatly reduced cycle times.

Specialty Teams. Teams of engineering, troubleshooting, survey, and financial employees are commonly dispatched to rural or remote areas to

- Rapidly restore service at "down" facilities or sites
- Monitor, inspect, and review construction progress
- Install, modify, or dismantle equipment
- Deliver and install emergency parts
- Evaluate potential construction sites
- Attend or facilitate critical meetings
- Visit suppliers

Not only do the teams get there faster, using a business aircraft sends a message to the passengers and customers alike: This is an important job that deserves attention.

Team Efficiency

A major U.S. catalog clothing retailer regularly ensures the quality of its products by sending quality control teams to its contractors' manufacturing plants to inspect the operation. When the manufacturing took place within the United States, normally in the southeastern part of the country, these visits were relatively simple and quick, involving a week on the road, via airline, at most to cover four to six plants using a team of five to seven inspectors. However, when most of the manufacturing activity went offshore, primarily to Central America and the Caribbean, the inspection teams began to spend more than 3 weeks to accomplish their task.

A chance meeting between the company flight department manager and head of quality control spawned a scheme to make the company more efficient and to get the inspection team home more rapidly. By using the company Learjet, up to seven team members could be taken to the offshore plants, sometimes two per day, in about half the time required by international airline travel. This scenario is now played out several times a year, allowing the company to visit its suppliers more frequently while reducing wear and tear on its inspectors. Importantly, using the company jet saves tens of thousands of dollars on travel and trip expenses.

Sales/Marketing Campaigns. Sales and marketing blitzes can be of nearly any scope and duration, depending on the stamina of the participants and their families. Such blitzes can be highly efficient and concentrated direct selling opportunities. Because they are time-efficient, participants are able to spend more time in the office and less time in airports.

In some companies, business aviation is the prevailing method used to get senior officers into a specific marketing territory to visit customers and vendors. Because time is so limited, multiday trips facilitate maximum exposure in a limited time.

Sales and marketing blitzes can intensify seasonally, during new product introduction cycles, for initial public offerings (IPOs) or investment/investor swings, during downturns in the economy, or following a restructuring. Potential customers and distributors also can be the target of multiday trips.

Attract and Retain Key People.

Attraction:

- Companies commonly use business aircraft as recruiting tools to facilitate the interview and negotiation process for key prospective employees or business partners and their families.
- The greater the distance and the more rural the recruiting base, the greater is the apparent benefit of a company aircraft.
- Anything that helps motivate key employee recruitment is critical.
- The value of the first impression left on a prospective employee is very important.
- The use of business aircraft rapidly establishes credibility.
- Companies make regular flights to universities to recruit graduating students.

Retention:

- Companies can keep personnel longer by making their days shorter.
- The use of business aircraft for commuting or other personal travel can be negotiated as part of a personal services contract.

- Extra "no cost" passengers can fill empty seats as a reward to high-performance employees and their families on certain trips scheduled for business reasons, although this type of travel may be taxable as personal income to those passengers.

- A company philosophy that stresses family-friendly scheduling—reducing nonbusiness hours away from home through the use of business aircraft for efficient day trips—can be very attractive.

- A surprising number of goodwill flights seem to be flown, typically very quietly, to facilitate employee medical treatments.

Corporate Shuttles. Some companies with multiple operating bases have found it advantageous to institute a scheduled flight operation between those bases to save both time and money relative to airline service. Airline schedules frequently do not fit the daily commute nature of many work requirements, driving companies to establish what amounts to their own private airline. Time savings in airport processing delays with the airlines greatly reduces an employee's availability to accomplish work productively; a private shuttle may reduce this wasted time by as much as 80 percent. Moreover, with just a modest number of travelers, significant cost savings may be realized with a shuttle.

Shuttles are most appropriate for larger companies with decentralized operations and facilities or for companies with repetitive tasks, such as safety checks, management reviews, ongoing employee training, or a need to make airline connections from rural locations. Shuttles are not always permanent, often operating for short periods for specific projects or startups. High-priority personnel can be transported regularly via helicopter to several company locations in a major metropolitan area, saving many hours of tedious ground travel.

Priority Cargo, Parts, or Mail. This subject has immense potential. Many companies use aircraft to carry high-value cargo, replacement or spare parts, or interoffice mail. This practice is common and often unquantified but of substantial commercial value in displaced overnight delivery charges. Any material that cannot be moved practically by conventional shippers due to size, weight, susceptibility to damage, or other physical limitations, and particularly those which need to be delivered within hours, often are best transported via business aircraft.

Projects. Usually business aircraft are used for infrequent or "one shot" projects, such as multilocation advertising photography "shoots" involving a multidisciplined team of experts. The combination of both personnel and an unusually large amount of project-specific equipment can trigger business aircraft use as the most efficient and cost-effective travel alternative, specifically for transporting delicate equipment of extreme value to the project.

It's just essential for us to get out in the field....Aviation is the most time-efficient way for us to do that.

—Marketing Manager

Utilitarian. Business aircraft are used commonly as a convertible platform for mapping; aerial surveys, inspections, and photography; cattle ranching and herding; flying laboratories for airborne experiments or other research and development; educational laboratories; surveillance; and power-line and pipeline patrols, in addition to other uses.

Public, Press, and Investor Relations. Progressive companies often manage opportunities to project a positive corporate image using business aircraft either as a symbol of efficiency or as simple transportation to facilities or events to further this purpose. Publicity generated by the use of aircraft for noble purposes, such as the rapid delivery of relief supplies after a natural disaster, can be of substantial public relations benefit.

Personal Travel.   Just because the aircraft is operated by a company does not preclude its use for personal transportation. However, the company must define personal-use policies and provide methods for employees to pay for these services.

Emergency Evacuation/Response.   Business aircraft also are used to remove company employees from harm's way, usually as a result of a medical emergency, natural disaster, civil strife, or other security threat, particularly in areas of limited or uncertain scheduled airline service. Similarly, the ability to place key personnel at the scene of an oil spill, manufacturing plant fire, or tornado-damaged office site rapidly makes good business sense. Getting to the scene early with the right people may save additional damage and costly downtime.

Goodwill.   Business aircraft also are used for personal customer or employee needs, such as travel associated with family emergencies, or as a favor. There is not always an immediate, tangible business benefit from the use of business aircraft for customers or employees with special needs or for public officials. A longer view, however, may suggest that the company's strategic interests can be best served by this practice depending on individual circumstances.

Lobbying.   Business aircraft can be used to transport elected or appointed officials. The use of business aircraft for the carriage of public officials is common at all levels of government. Specific Internal Revenue Service (IRS) regulations govern this practice. Legal restrictions also can limit the availability of sponsored travel for certain government employees. All travel of this type is routinely and publicly reported. In rare instances, business aircraft also are used to carry government officials to company-sponsored events. These can be unusual and invaluable opportunities for information exchange.

Other.   Any need to travel can be accomplished safely, reliably, and efficiently with the company aircraft. After beginning to use their aircraft, companies rapidly discover many collateral uses. The only limit on these uses lies in the minds of the users.

Justifying Business Aviation

Most businesspeople identify quite well with the advantages of on-demand air transportation, yet the inevitable question becomes, "Isn't all of this rather expensive?" The answer is a qualified "Yes."

Much of what a company does requires large quantities of investment capital and operating funds to achieve desired goals and objectives. Yet there is a vision behind every capital and operating expense that permits the company to move ahead and compete effectively in the marketplace. Granted, the company always must be cognizant of bottom-line and rate-of-return concerns, but it is the vision of an individual or small group of individuals that carries a winning project forward to its destiny; such is the case in most companies when the concept of safe, reliable, and efficient transportation is being considered.

In evaluating transportation alternatives, tangible and intangible benefits must be defined to begin to realize the value of on-demand air transportation.

Tangible and Intangible Benefits.   Business aviation creates a number of benefits for individuals and the company. Some can be measured, and others elude quantification. Nonetheless, all these factors are very real and should be considered when evaluating on-demand air transportation options.

The most obvious and quantifiable advantage of on-demand air transportation is the amount of time saved for the passengers. Access to 10 times the number of airline airports, fewer check-in formalities, direct routing, landing near the business destination, and no waiting for luggage save major portions of days for single trips and full days for multiple-leg trips. The time saved means more time on task for employees, greater productivity enroute, the ability to confer with fellow travelers enroute, and fewer distractions during the entire travel process that detract from focus on the issues at hand.

Operational flexibility, or the ability to react intelligently to changing business situations, often serves companies well. Being locked into an inflexible airline schedule and lack of alternative flights at the last minute serve as sources of frustration for business travelers. Schedule changes, even in-flight, can be arranged easily for on-demand transportation.

While often perceived to be more important to the traveler than to the company, the number of days and nights spent on the road are important to both. The company needs its key personnel to be operating at maximum productivity as much as possible; nights in motels and days in airline terminals seldom make it possible to achieve this goal.

The preceding items are quite important features of business life and are measurable. Yet some of the most important aspects of business aviation are immeasurable.

- Security concerns have become very important for all travelers. The very personal, private, and well-controlled nature of business aviation makes this a very secure form of transportation, one that allays the concerns of most travelers.

- Fatigue is a major negative component of travel, especially when public transportation modes are used. Business aviation provides a secure, hassle-free environment that promotes a relaxed travel experience. Further, it is a lot easier to rest in the peace and quiet of an intimate personal space offered by business aircraft.

- "Road warriors," those who spend a major portion of their time traveling, may become discouraged or even depressed at the thought of suffering the indignities associated with airline travel, innumerable nights on the road, and the stress associated with the entire process. On-demand air transportation provides a morale boost for weary travelers, permitting them to regain a better lifestyle and become more productive.

- While the concepts of prestige and image are not normally considered in the employee business equation, the ability to use on-demand air transportation creates a very positive reaction in business travelers. Companies promote additional image and prestige items in many aspects of an executive's life. Why not in the way they travel? This feature will permit the company to attract and retain the best and brightest performers.

- Companies rely on privacy and confidentiality in their daily operations to gain advantage over the competition. These features are also important in ensuring the safety and security of business travelers. It is difficult to work on confidential information in airport terminals and airliners because of prying eyes and ears. On-demand air transportation offers complete privacy, with just a few trusted operational personnel aware of destinations, schedules, and manifests.

- Finally, comfort and convenience may be overlooked or discounted as significant factors in business travelers. One has but to ask busy executives why they value the company aircraft, and these features usually will be among the most frequently mentioned.

The airplane is an extension of our office; we probably have our most productive meetings there.

—Corporate CEO

Value of Time.   *Value* in this case refers not to the intrinsic monetary benefit of on-demand air transportation but to the worth in terms of usefulness, utility, and merit. The following set of statements will illustrate this: (1) "A coach airline fare to Ft. Wayne will cost X, whereas the company airplane (or charter) will cost $X+$" and (2) "Getting the vice president of marketing to Ft. Wayne tomorrow morning will save the Acme contract."

There are several issues at work here:

* How important is the Acme contract?
* What *value* does the contract hold for the company?
  * Projected revenues
  * Future business
  * Criticality to other products/services
* Can anyone get to Ft. Wayne via the airlines by tomorrow morning?
* Will such a flight require an overnight stay?
* What else could the vice president of marketing be doing with his or her time?

Before we look at any of these variables, it is important to examine the *value* of an employee's time. Many companies mistakenly equate the value of an employee's time with his or her compensation level. For instance, if the vice president of marketing receives $250,000 in total compensation, some would say that this person is worth $125 per hour ($250,000 divided by 2000 hours of work time per year). Yet this would be short-sighted and would sell the *value* of the employee short, as well.

Human resources accounting recognizes employee skills, training, and experience as a capital asset. This field is based on the fact that employees are vitally important to the success of a company. Studies indicate that profits are due in large part to the actions and expertise of management personnel. Human resources accounting places a value on people rather than a cost. These values have been recognized and quantified by the insurance industry through key-person insurance policies for business. The theory behind this insurance is the potential loss to a company as a consequence of the injury or death of a key person; life insurance is issued in the name of the key employee, with the company listed as the beneficiary.

Easier to understand is an inherent belief that each employee must have the power to bring in sufficient revenues beyond his or her compensation to achieve profitability. If this were not true, the company would only pass through revenues to the employees as compensation and have nothing left over for profit. The assumption of an employee's ability to make a profit for the company is understandably higher for upper-level executives, but the expectation is nonetheless levied on each employee within the company. In recognition of this expectation, key-person insurance is written as multiples of an employee's compensation, generally in the range of 2.5 to 15 times salaries and other forms of compensation.

If this concept is to be believed, then the inherent *value* of an employee becomes some multiple of his or her compensation. By extension, this value should extend to all aspects of the employee's work life, including examination of low-level administrative tasks, supervisory duties, and the use of travel time. Therefore, if, in our example, the marketing vice president can be expected to bring revenues of 4 to 6 times compensation, then every aspect of his or her time carries the same value, including travel time. At the higher multiple, this executive is worth $750 per hour, making the value of travel time a pricey commodity. If this executive has to leave the office 3 hours before a scheduled airline departure, spend an overnight at the destination due to inadequate airline schedules, drive a rental car 1 hour from the destination airport to the real destination, and invest another day returning to base, the waste of time, talent, and ultimately, dollars adds up rapidly.

All the travel variables involved in computing the time-value equation have proved too complex in the past to permit rapid or real-time calculation. However, the NBAA has devised a sophisticated software tool to compute just such values. *Travel$ense* is a tool designed to help management better analyze and understand business travel. With surprising accuracy and flexibility, this tool automatically calculates the actual business hours, productivity, trip expenses, and family time saved by traveling via business aircraft versus airline alternatives. For each trip, the tool accounts for and calculates

- *Trip purpose and outcome.* The benefit in cost-benefit terms.
- *Cost of air service.* On two business aircraft *and* comparable airline flights using real-time data.
- *Cost of employee travel time.* Door to door for each passenger, leg, and trip on three aircraft.
- *Other travel expenses.* Including overnight costs.
- *Value of employee travel time.*
- *Value of productive time enroute.*
- *Nonbusiness hours away from home.*
- *Productive hours saved and other trip statistics.*

Executives and flight department personnel have found *Travel$ense* to be a powerful tool to illustrate the extraordinary business advantages of business aircraft.

I gain an additional productive month each year with the time I save by using the company airplane. Love those 13-month years!

—CEO OF A MAJOR SERVICES COMPANY

Creating Shareholder Value. Once the value of time is appreciated, it is relatively easy to calculate the per-trip cost alternatives versus value to the company. Ultimately, some person or persons within the company must fully appreciate the potential benefit of on-demand air transportation to the company and act as a catalyst and spearhead to make this happen. However, others have studied the process from a macro viewpoint and reached some interesting conclusions.

Anderson Consulting assessed the potential financial benefits of operating business aircraft to companies and their shareholders by examining peer groups of companies distinguished by their use or nonuse of business aircraft.[8] The study looked at the companies comprising the Standard and Poor's (S&P) 500 list, which represents the largest U.S. publicly held companies according to their market capitalization. The S&P 500 were classified into 24 industry groups, evaluating each of them as to the number of aircraft operators and nonoperators. Financial performance and share price information were examined for the period 1992 through 1999.

The results showed that aircraft operators earned 146 percent more in cumulative returns than nonoperators from 1992 through 1999 (609 versus 463 percent). Increased shareholder returns primarily were due to improved business performance. Executive interviews revealed that business aircraft were essential "to conduct due diligence for a number of potential targets" and to "get our financial teams into and out of hard-to-reach locations." Aircraft operators achieved sales and earnings growth nearly double that of nonoperators. Key drivers of sales growth include the ability to identify and execute strategic transactions and alliances.

The aircraft helps us increase and protect revenues.

—CORPORATE CFO

Other key areas of business performance yielded margins for aircraft operators of up to 100 percent above their nonaircraft peers.

- Average cumulative earnings before interest, taxes, depreciation, and amortization (EBITDA) growth
- Increased productivity
- Asset efficiency ratio (sales to total assets) decline

Quality improvements emerged as a theme that supported several drivers of shareholder value. As one chief financial officer (CFO) stated, the chairman's methodical oversight of the company's network made possible by using business aircraft "sets the tone" across the United States and around the world, helping to ensure a single level of quality. Another executive said that her company used the fleet to "sell time to our executives by executing trips in hours instead of days." As another CFO of a financial services company explained, the key profitability benefits of business aircraft derived from increased productivity and efficiency for top executives—benefits that are "obviously there, but hard to quantify."

Corporate performance relative to the use of company aircraft was revealed in four factors:

- *Strategic transaction orientation.* Being able to facilitate critical transactions was associated most regularly with direct shareholder value creation. Rapid transaction value is essential in several industry sectors, especially those in consolidation.

- *Customer service orientation.* Time-sensitive requirements, such as emergency customer services, supported sales retention and sales growth and could be met most efficiently by some companies using business aircraft (no ready substitute).

- *Process and quality improvement orientation.* Being better able to manage and execute far-flung operations was found to be the most extensively cited trait. Business aircraft enabled executives to visit multiple locations, sometimes more than once a year, by customizing schedules not possible on commercial airlines. Executives were able to review operations, efficiency, quality, and customer service.

- *Meritocracy orientation.* When a company uses aircraft to treat all employees as an important asset, it achieves uncommon results. Because the workday could be lengthened without sacrificing employee family time, shuttling employees between company facilities offered significant productivity gains. Enhanced employee safety and security and the security of intellectual property were characteristics of this orientation.

Our executives often use the aircraft to reach meetings they couldn't otherwise attend, closing transactions that would fund the flight department for years to come.

—CFO

The study concluded that there was a strong correlation between business aircraft benefits and shareholder value creation. Its central finding was that business aircraft can make a substantial difference in how a company performs its mission, in many cases generating significant gains in the drivers of shareholder value. Increased mobility was at the core of these gains—satisfying management's need for greater organizational agility, knowledge integration, and transaction speed.

Significantly, in the study's interviews with CFOs, more than 75 percent confirmed that disposing of their business aircraft could, for the same reasons, potentially harm their company's value. In many cases it was found that there often were no ready substitutes for business aircraft without diminishing company performance or losing new business opportunities.

Hands-On Helps

A manufacturer of emergency-response municipal telephone systems introduced a new line of equipment and attempted to market it via conventional means using sales personnel to call on clients in the field. Unfortunately, the innovative features of the equipment were difficult to describe to potential customers. Simulator boxes, call-in demonstrations, and videotapes were employed in an attempt to demonstrate the features of the equipment, with little result.

The vice president of marketing convinced the CEO to use the company's Citation aircraft to bring representatives from two municipalities to company headquarters to attend a hands-on demonstration of the equipment. The first visit achieved a sale to one community and a promise to send municipal officials back for further evaluation. Based on this and subsequent successes, the company aircraft now brings potential customers to headquarters for demonstration once a week. The passengers are impressed with the fact that they travel in a corporate jet and are back home the same day. Best of all, they are able to fully assess the benefits of the product by observing it in operation.

Fortune 500[9]

The Fortune 500 list of the largest U.S. industrial and service companies has long been regarded as the elite roster of American businesses. Among the Fortune 500, 356 companies operate business aircraft, and approximately 80 percent of those operating companies are NBAA members. Among the Fortune 100 companies, 89 have business aircraft.

Aircraft-operating companies in the Fortune 500 have enjoyed superior financial performance. Also, users of general aviation aircraft for business transportation dominate *Fortune*'s list of the top 50 corporations in terms of dividends and capital gains returned to shareholders.

A detailed analysis of the financial performance of aircraft-operating Fortune 500 companies in 2000 revealed the specific financial advantages that these operators of business aircraft enjoyed over nonoperators. The study, performed by Aviation Data Service of Wichita, Kansas, showed that

- There were more than twice as many aircraft-operating companies as nonoperators among the Fortune 500.

- Sales of all Fortune 500 aircraft operators were $6.1 trillion, whereas sales of nonoperators totaled approximately $1.0 trillion.

- The net income of all operators was more than $394 billion in 2000; nonoperators' total income in that year was $60 billion.

- Operators collectively had over $15 trillion in assets; nonoperators' assets totaled $2.7 trillion.

- Net income per employee for operating companies was more than $19,000, whereas net income per employee was only $16,000 for nonoperating companies.

- Stockholders' equity in operating companies was over $2.5 trillion; equity in nonoperators was approximately $360 billion.

The bottom line is that business aircraft are good for the bottom line. Business aircraft operators consistently outperform nonoperators in key economic performance measures, such as annual sales volume, number of employees, value of assets, stockholder's equity, and annual income.

Safety

Companies engaged in business aviation activities choose to operate or contract for their own aircraft as an alternative to the airlines and charter operators. In doing so, they expect that their operations will be as safe as or safer than the public transportation option. Therefore, company aviation operations work under safety programs that provide the desired level of safety.

Corporate aviation operators are justifiably proud of their excellent safety record, equaling or exceeding the airline accident record for their turbine-powered aircraft operations. For instance, the airlines experienced 2.4 accidents per million flight hours during 2001; on the same basis, corporate operations experienced only 1.1 accidents.[10] Even though this in an enviable record, business aviation operators strive for a perfect record of no accidents; while this goal has not been achieved, it remains a credible goal for the industry.

Most corporate aviation flight departments voluntarily exceed the minimum operating standards imposed by their national regulatory agencies (such as the Federal Aviation Administration) for their type of operation. In fact, corporate operators' standards and limits closely resemble those used by the airlines and charter operators. Two experienced pilots, certified to airline standards, fly company aircraft and undergo recurrent training in airline quality simulators; maintenance technicians use state-of-the-art techniques and materials to keep the aircraft in first-class condition; and all personnel are trained in ground and flight emergency procedures.

Owner- or employee-flown business aircraft enjoy a considerably better safety record than the whole of general aviation but lag slightly behind that of their corporate aviation brethren. This is understandable because these pilots are probably less experienced and fly aircraft that may be less capable than a corporate turbojet. Yet, while comparisons are difficult, traveling in an employee-flown business aircraft is safer than traveling an equivalent distance in an automobile.

Companies and their pilots, technicians, and support personnel demonstrate their pride in safety through the NBAA Flying Safety Awards. Each year at the NBAA convention, hundreds of individuals and companies receive recognition for their many years of safe operations. A number of companies have achieved the 50 Year Safe Flying Achievement Award, indicating that they have had a corporate flight operation for that long without having had an aircraft accident. Similarly, at a recent convention, more than 900 pilots received recognition that they had flown at least 1500 accident-free hours. These awards are cumulative, often honoring pilots who have achieved tens of thousands accident-free hours and technicians amassing scores of accident-free years of service.

Business aviation operators take safety seriously, since their jobs and reputation depend on each and every flight. All operations are planned carefully and executed in accordance with mature standards and procedures stemming from industry best practices.

The Future

Business flying in the United States is expected to grow faster than any other segment of general aviation, with the number of jet aircraft increasing an average of 3.5 percent annually, and flying hours are forecast to be up 4.1 percent through 2010.[11] Honeywell Corporation's forecast, revised downward to reflect the impact of September 11, 2001, on the world economy, calls for deliveries of 7600 business aircraft in the next 10 years, valued at some $121 billion. Moreover, the U.S. fractional ownership market is forecast to grow to over 1600 aircraft and 13,500 share owners by the end of 2006,[12] making it the fastest growing segment of the industry.

Whether these forecasts will come true is problematic. What is clear is that on-demand business air transportation for business purposes has earned itself a solid place in corporate life worldwide. And as airline travel becomes more complicated and often inconvenient, the demand for business aviation will increase. While there may be some natural constraints on the system in the form of airport and airspace availability, air traffic control congestion, and environmental concerns, business aviation is a sufficiently major part of the business economy to weather most of the storms to come.

Most interesting, from the standpoint of the owner-flown aircraft is a project in progress known as the Small Aircraft Transportation System (SATS). SATS is a partnership among various organizations including the National Aeronautics and Space Administration (NASA), the FAA, the U.S. aviation industry, state and local aviation officials, and universities. The system partners intend to relieve the nation's current problems of highway gridlock and airport delays. At equivalent highway system costs, SATS will reduce transportation times to more communities by half in 10 years and by two-thirds in 25 years. With over 5000 small airports already in place across the country in almost every locality, a small aircraft transportation system that is both a safe and affordable alternative to current transportation systems could provide an effective solution. SATS will accommodate higher volumes of air traffic at small airports, provide for lower weather operating minimums at these airports, create safer aircraft systems, and devise procedures to integrate these aircraft into the air traffic control systems. Initial results of the project are scheduled in 2005, and operational capability is anticipated by 2010.

Additionally, a private turbojet taxi service has been proposed that operates much like earth-bound taxi or car services. The service will use up to 1000 small turbojet aircraft spread across North America to provide essentially on-call service for as little as $600 per hour. The thought is that this will make the service competitive with full coach airline fares. The service proposes to avoid the current constraints facing commercial aviation infrastructure by taking advantage of the large network of general aviation facilities surrounding the nation's metropolitan areas. Commercial airlines traditionally have been excluded from such facilities as a result of their dependence on hub-and-spoke architectures, large airframes, and extensive ground facilities. The service largely will depend on an innovative new turbojet aircraft design that will greatly reduce both purchase price and operating costs of the aircraft.

Faster helicopters, tilt-rotor aircraft, and supersonic corporate business jets all promise a bright future for the upper end of business aviation. And while we are waiting for these wonders, business aviation continues to grow and serve the world's businesses with safe, reliable, and economical on-demand air transportation.

Business aviation is strong and healthy in North America. In Central and South America, four countries are in the largest 10 business aircraft fleets of the world, so it would appear to be solid in the south.

However, in Europe and Asia, business aviation is not used to its potential. Although Europe has a major position in the world's economic and corporate infrastructure, business aircraft in Europe only represent 10 percent of the global fleet. In Asia, the political and economic realities have restrained growth. Fees and charges have tended to be very high. However, there appears to be a resurgence of interest.

New business aviation associations in Japan and the Asian region are active and helping to foster improved access with more realistic charges and fees. Certainly, Asia is seen as an area for potentially significant increases in business aviation in the near future.

—INTERNATIONAL BUSINESS AVIATION COUNCIL
(IBAC) BUSINESS AVIATION FORECAST 2002.

AIRCRAFT

Aircraft come in two broad categories: airplanes and helicopters. Airplanes are what we normally see at the airport—an engine-driven heavier than air device supported by the dynamic action of the air on wing surfaces. Helicopters are marvelous devices that move through the air supported by a rotor revolving above the fuselage; really, the helicopter moves its "wing" before the fuselage moves, as is the case with a conventional airplane.

Each of these devices, in turn, is classified by the type of powerplant used, either piston- or turbine-powered. The piston engine is usually installed in smaller single- and twin-engine versions used in employee-flown aircraft. Similarly, employee-flown helicopters may be powered by a piston engine more often than the more sophisticated turbine engine used for corporate applications.

Turbine engines come in two varieties: turbojets and turboprops. While their propulsive force relies on a gas turbine in both cases, the turbojet relies entirely on its ability to accelerate air through its interior to move it forward. The turboprop uses its gas generator to drive a propeller through reduction gears, which pulls it through the air.

Any aircraft (including both airplanes and helicopters) may use one or more engines to propel it through the air. Smaller aircraft tend to have one engine. The larger the aircraft, the more likely it is to have more than one engine.

Aircraft Characteristics

A four- to six-seat, single-engine, piston-powered airplane is considered ideal for some owner- and employee-flown operations. Its simplicity and relatively low operating cost make it ideal for an entry-level aircraft. This aircraft is ideal for trips of less than 500 miles carrying not more than three passengers; yet it will carry five passengers up to 600 miles when necessary. Importantly, in ideal conditions, it can operate safely on runways just 2500 ft long, whereas airliners normally require at least 6000-ft runways[13] (Table 1.3 and Figs. 1.7 through 1.15).

The next step up is a four- to eight-seat, twin-engine, piston-powered airplane, also normally used in owner- or employee-flown operations. The additional engine provides increased load carrying and speed capability along with increased safety. Incremental increases in both speed and range are realized over the single-engine aircraft.

A single-engine turboprop is the next level in the upward progression of both capability and costs. The powerplants used in single-engine turboprops are smooth-running and quite reliable. These aircraft also normally are employee-flown, although many companies use either a full-time professional pilot as the principal pilot or as a part-time copilot for the owner/pilot. Additional experience is required for operators of turbine aircraft to obtain reasonably priced hull and liability insurance.

The twin-turboprop is the entry-level professionally flown aircraft, yet owners may pilot this type as well. This versatile aircraft is ideal for trips of less than 700 miles while carrying up to four passengers, although most can fly up to 900 miles nonstop with up to six passengers. In general, this type of aircraft can operate out of smaller airports than can pure turbojets; a 3500-ft runway is considered adequate under ideal conditions.

While a number of single-engine turbojets are under development, entry-level turbojets currently all have two engines. This class of airplane generally will accommodate four to six passengers with a flight crew of two pilots. They will carry two to four passengers 1500 miles nonstop at speeds approaching 400 mph.

The next step up is a midsized-cabin twin-turbojet featuring up to eight passenger seats and capable of flying nonstop coast to coast, west to east (nonstop westbound transcontinental flights are seldom possible in many of these aircraft due to headwinds, especially

TABLE 1.3   Business Aircraft Characteristics

			Typical Business Aircraft Types			
Type of aircraft	Example	Passenger seats	Normal cruise speed (mph)	Range with half seats full (mi)	Acquisition cost new ($)	Direct operating cost ($/hr)
			Airplanes			
Single-engine piston	New Piper Saratoga*	5	180	750	450,000	120
Single-engine turboprop	TBM 700*	5	320	1500	2,300,000	300
Multiengine turboprop	Raytheon Beechcraft King Air B200	7	275	1400	4,500,000	700
Small twin-engine turbojet	Cessna Citation Bravo	7	400	1750	5,450,000	900
Medium twin-engine turbojet	Bombardier Continental	8	520	3000	16,000,000	1,400
Large twin-engine turbojet	Gulfstream G-V	14	520	7400	43,000,000	1,800
			Helicopters			
Single-engine piston	Robinson R44	3	120	325	350,000	150
Single-engine turbine	Bell Jet Ranger 206B	4	130	400	850,000	250
Twin-engine turbine	Eurocopter Dauphin EC 155	5	70	500	6,000,000	600

*Primarily employee- or owner-flown.

during the winter). The range of airports that will support this type becomes smaller because they require at least 5000-ft runways to operate safely under normal conditions.

The large-cabin aircraft accommodate up to 14 passengers and have substantial range capability. Although not possible with all seats full, some of these aircraft can easily make it nonstop from New York to Paris.

Finally, the true intercontinental turbojet can carry 15 to 30 passengers in comfort for distances of up to 7400 miles. These aircraft require airline-sized runways and more extensive support facilities.

On the helicopter side, the entry-level single-piston-engine aircraft will carry three passengers 325 miles at 120 mph. The more capable single-turbine helicopter will carry four passengers 400 miles at 130 mph. The high-end twin-turbine helicopter accommodates up to seven passengers on journeys of 350 miles at 140 mph.

FIGURE 1.7   New Piper Saratoga. (*Courtesy New Piper.*)

FIGURE 1.8   SOCATA TBM 700. (*Courtesy SOCATA Aircraft.*)

FIGURE 1.9   Raytheon Beechcraft King Air 200. (*Courtesy Raytheon.*)

FIGURE 1.10   Cessna Citation Bravo. (*Courtesy Cessna Aircraft.*)

FIGURE 1.11   Bombardier Continental. (*Courtesy Bombardier.*)

FIGURE 1.12   Gulfstream V. (*Courtesy Gulfstream.*)

FIGURE 1.13   Robinson R44. (*Courtesy Robinson.*)

FIGURE 1.14   Bell 206B. (*Courtesy Bell Helicopter.*)

FIGURE 1.15 Eurocopter EC 155. (*Courtesy Eurocopter.*)

ON-DEMAND AVIATION METHODS

One of the great advantages of on-demand air transportation is the number of methods of delivering this service. Companies or individuals do not have to own or even lease their own aircraft, although this is the most common form of operation. Importantly, more than one type of delivery method is often employed to meet emerging user requirements. For example, a company owning an airplane may contract for charter services on occasion to meet unusual requirements or heavy demand. Similarly, an individual may purchase a share of an aircraft from either a company or private owner to form a joint ownership agreement or from a fractional provider to augment existing aircraft.

In each of the methods listed below, the relative advantages and disadvantages will be discussed for each form of delivery. A full appreciation and understanding of these features is not available until the unique requirements of an individual company are known. Therefore, those contemplating on-demand air transportation should seek a wide variety of information sources to be fully informed prior to making a decision.

On-demand aviation includes the following methods:

- Owner/employee-flown
- In-house flight department
- Management company
- Joint ownership
- Interchange
- Time share

- Charter
- Fractional ownership

Owner/Employee-Flown

This is the entry level of on-demand air transportation; in many cases, a businessperson or individual discovers the advantages of on-demand air transportation through others and either learns to fly or uses an already qualified employee to fly an aircraft and manage its operation. The aircraft is purchased and used primarily for either business or personal purposes, depending on the situation.

An aircraft may be purchased, leased, or rented, depending on personal or company preferences. However, most aircraft are wholly owned. In most countries, all administrative and operational costs may be fully charged as business expenses when the aircraft is being flown for a business purpose.

The majority of these operations fall into the single- or twin-engine piston or turboprop airplane category, although an increasing number of these applications use helicopters and small turbojets. While it is difficult to determine the actual number of aircraft used for this type of flying, literally tens of thousands of these applications exist worldwide. In the United States, FAA statistics showed that during the year 2000, 25,000 aircraft were used primarily for employee-flown business operations.[14]

National aviation authorities governing this type of flying impose only the most basic standards governing civil aviation. Holders of a private pilot license may carry passengers anywhere, even internationally. However, insurance requirements and good operating practices dictate that more than minimum standards be employed for this type of flying.

In-House Flight Department Using Owned/Leased Aircraft

Most companies engaged in corporate aviation or receiving personal transportation services in larger aircraft use this form of operation. It is self-descriptive, indicating that an owner/operator uses in-house assets to administer, fund, and operate his or her own aircraft. This form of operation may be most popular because it affords the user the maximum amount of control over the aircraft; i.e., all choices regarding ownership, scheduling, crewing, and training the crew, and maintaining and operating the aircraft remain with the user; outside individuals or companies have no role in operation of the aircraft.

Control over these functions is important to corporate travelers and individuals because they want their aircraft to be available when they want them and crewed and maintained by people they know and trust and they want to have full control over the financial aspects of operation. Seeing familiar faces in the cockpit and around the hangar give passengers a sense of control and comfort often deemed essential.

These flight departments report to either the principal user or a subordinate regarding aircraft operations. All personnel required to schedule, fly, maintain, and administer the aircraft report to the flight department manager or chief pilot. All functions regarding budgeting, scheduling, and operation of the aircraft are the responsibility of this manager. Ultimate control of the aircraft and its personnel rests with this individual.

The decision of whether to own or lease an aircraft is a matter of company fiscal policy or personal preference, with no common denominator driving this decision. Carrying a major capital asset like an aircraft on the company books and enjoying the benefits of depreciation appeal to some companies, whereas others prefer to expense all costs associated with aircraft operation through a lease, thereby avoiding the carrying costs of a major asset. Synthetic leases provide the combined features of both owned and leased aircraft, creating a third option.

Management Company

In this option, a company or individual owns or leases an aircraft but contracts with a management company to provide all functions required to operate it. This includes scheduling, crewing, maintaining, bill paying, and management oversight of the entire operation. This option is often used by those new to corporate aviation or not wishing to be bothered with the details of aircraft operation. Typically, a fixed management fee is paid to the management company, and all operational, administrative, and employee compensation costs are passed through without additional fee to the owner/operator.

Management companies have the advantage of providing their services to a number of companies and benefiting from the resulting economies of scale. For instance, the flight crew assigned to Company X's aircraft also can be used on Company Y's aircraft when the former aircraft is not active. Management companies typically operate an air taxi operation to complement their management operations, offering to use managed aircraft for their charter operation to provide their owners with income that can be used to offset their operating costs. However, in doing so, users relinquish significant amounts of control over their own schedule and how the aircraft is to be used.

Joint Ownership

In this arrangement, two or more companies or individuals jointly own an aircraft. One of the owners employs and furnishes flight crew and arranges for scheduling, maintenance, and administrative services. The other owners pay their share of all operating, employment, and administrative costs.

Joint ownership lowers operating costs for owners who do not fully use an aircraft; however, the method of determining who can use the aircraft at a particular time can prove difficult if clear scheduling guidelines are not established up-front. Yet a significant number of companies and individuals operate well under this method, especially if the nature of their use patterns complements one another. For instance, if a company typically only uses the aircraft during the week and a private individual normally uses it on weekends, the two requirements tend to be mutually exclusive and noninterfering.

Managed companies also provide their services to joint owners, providing them with fully outsourced operations.

Interchange

This option involves an entity leasing an aircraft to another person in exchange for equal time, when needed, on that person's aircraft. No charge, assessment, or fee is made except that a charge may be made equal to the difference in the operating costs of the two aircraft.

Those entering into interchange agreements do so primarily to provide themselves with a locally positioned backup aircraft for use when their aircraft is either scheduled or in maintenance. The ability to occasionally use, at relatively low cost, an aircraft with appreciably different capacity or operating characteristics is another reason to enter into this type of arrangement.

Time Share

This approach is really a method of lending one's aircraft for discrete periods to a second party and recouping a portion of the operating costs. In this arrangement, a company essentially leases an aircraft, with flight crew, to another person for the cost of operating the aircraft for that flight. The real advantage of this method is that it is not considered to be a commercial venture in the United States and other countries and therefore is not subject to air charter regulations.

A formal time-sharing agreement must be established between the parties involved. While this is an excellent method of providing transportation to company employees who desire to use the aircraft regularly for personal purposes and to favored individuals, some tax and liability consequences are incurred by the party sharing the aircraft.

Charter

Aircraft charter is the normal on-demand air transportation entry point for most users. Charter companies offer a wide range of aircraft types with a corresponding range of prices designed to suit a variety of tastes and uses.

Legitimate charter companies must possess an air taxi operating certificate issued by their national regulatory authority to legally offer their services to the public. With the same philosophy that requires the airlines to provide a higher level of safety to the traveling public than afforded by general aviation, charter operators must operate to a higher set of regulatory standards too.

Typically, a person desiring air charter services will find a provider meeting his or her requirements and call them to determine availability and the costs involved. Normally, few other formalities are required except for telling the charter operator when and where the service is needed. Arranging for this service is normally a simple transaction; however, determining the right charter provider to use can be difficult if high-quality, reliable, and cost-effective services are to be found.

A small number of in-house and managed flight operations, perhaps 10 to 15 percent, offer their aircraft for charter use as well. Either they obtain their own authorization (operating certificate) from the regulatory agency to provide charter service, or they enter into an agreement with another company possessing an operating certificate to make their aircraft available. Offering one's aircraft for charter is done primarily to recoup some of the aircraft operating costs from the charter revenue, especially if the aircraft is not being fully used. However, most people who operate their own aircraft do not offer them for charter because of additional regulatory requirements, interference with their schedules, and added wear and tear on their aircraft.

Fractional Ownership

This form of transportation delivery is essentially a large-scale joint-ownership operation. Instead of buying into just one aircraft, the owner buys into a fleet of similar aircraft. While the owner buys a share (as little as one-sixteenth) of one aircraft, the fractional provider also makes a fleet of identical aircraft available to fractional owners through an interchange agreement. This provision allows owners to lease their aircraft to another person participating in the fractional program in exchange for use of the other's aircraft. In this manner, the chances of a like aircraft being available when the owner wants to use it are very good, as opposed for waiting in line for a single aircraft in the case of a single jointly owned aircraft. In fact, availability is guaranteed, utilizing contract charter aircraft when necessary.

Owners purchase a fraction of an aircraft and are entitled to all tax and depreciation benefits of their share of ownership. Additionally, they pay a monthly management fee and an hourly operating charge in exchange for guaranteed response times (4 to 12 hours) and utilization levels (a one-eighth share receives 100 occupied hours annually) in either their aircraft or an identical one. The minimum term of the contract is normally 5 years, at which time owners can renew or sell their share for a predetermined value. All of this occurs as an all-inclusive service with all required support functions provided, virtually invisible to the owner.

This form of transportation is the fastest-growing form of on-demand air transportation, with more than 5000 fractional owners of approximately 700 aircraft as of mid-2002. It is attractive because of its joint-ownership features, guaranteed availability and response times, uniform service levels, and hassle-free operation.

Fractional ownership is considered private (personal) transportation in the United States but a commercial operation in most of the rest of the world.

Choosing the Best Method

Each of the preceding methods of supplying on-demand air transportation has advantages and disadvantages for prospective users. However, the number of variables involved in determining the ideal form of transportation are many and interact to make the choice difficult.

To evaluate their needs properly, prospective users must conduct an analysis of their transportation requirements to gain insight into their needs. This analysis does not have to be extensive or detailed, but the more detailed it is, the better is the set of requirements that results. Chapter 2 explores this subject in detail.

As a rule of thumb, if a company intends to use an aircraft less than 100 to 150 hours annually, charter is probably the best option from a cost standpoint. For between 100 and 300 hours of use, joint or fractional ownership makes good economic sense. For above 250 hours, efficiencies of scale begin to make full ownership or leasing more attractive.

Again, if seeing familiar faces in the cockpit and around the hangar is important to on-demand users, a wholly owned or leased aircraft is the way to go. While fractional ownership gets a participant closer to the service provider, personnel flying the aircraft may be different for every trip.

Yet the most important factor is the degree of control exercised over the aircraft operation—scheduling responsiveness, flight crew quality, level of training, amount and type of maintenance, administrative and financial controls, and level of customer service (see Chap. 2). Most individuals and companies are very particular about levels of service; in-house operation usually provides the best opportunity to receive the highest levels. Conversely, some travelers care little about the details of their on-demand air transportation services, regarding it in the same way they do their limousine service—a means to an end. Therefore, it is important to place the personal imprint of the principal passengers onto the services rendered.

The airport runway is the most important main street in any town.

—NORM CRABTREE, OHIO AVIATION DIRECTOR

REFERENCES

1. National Business Aviation Association. *NBAA Business Aviation Fact Book 2002*. Washington: National Business Aviation Association, 2002.

2. Winant, John H. *Keep Business Flying*. Washington: National Business Aircraft Association, 1989.

3. General Aviation Manufacturer's Association. *General Aviation Statistical Databook, 2001*. Washington: General Aviation Manufacturer's Association, 2001.

4. International Business Aviation Council. *IBAC Business Aviation Outlook 2002*. Montreal: International Business Aviation Council, 2002.

5. Deloitte and Touche. *A View from the Top: Perceptions of Travel Management and Business Travel*. Washington: Deloitte and Touche, 1999.

6. National Business Aviation Association. *The Real World of Business Aviation*. Washington: National Business Aviation Association, 1997.

7. National Business Aviation Association. *Business Aviation Utilization Strategies*. Washington: National Business Aviation Association, 2000.

8. Anderson Consulting. *Business Aviation in Today's Economy: A Shareholder Value Perspective*. Washington: Anderson, 2001.

9. NBAA *National Business Aviation Association Fact Book, 2002*. Washington: National Business Aviation Association, 2002.

10. National Transportation Safety Board Preliminary Aviation Accident Statistics, 2002.

11. Federal Aviation Administration. *FAA Aerospace Forecasts, 2002*. Washington: Federal Aviation Administration, 2002.

12. Aviation Research Group press release, April 2002.

13. Business and Commercial Aviation "Operations Planning Guide, 2002," in Business and Commercial Aviation and Conklin and deDecker (eds.), *Aircraft Cost Evaluator*. Quincy, MA: Conklin and deDecker, 2002.

14. Federal Aviation Administration. *General Aviation and Air Taxi Activity Survey CY2000*. Washington: Federal Aviation Administration, 2002.

CHAPTER 2
DETERMINING THE NEED

The airplane has made us faster and better. We're cutting our time in airplanes and airports down by probably a third.

—Corporate CEO

AIR TRANSPORTATION NEEDS

Individuals seeking on-demand air transportation often select a method as a consequence of either a recommendation from an acquaintance or minimal research. The resulting service may serve many of the individual's needs, yet another type of aircraft or method may be better suited to their needs. Therefore, a comprehensive analysis of one's travel needs and alternative methods of meeting those needs will provide a more satisfying and efficient transportation process.

Similarly, companies spend a large amount of resources on employee travel. As travel costs increase, companies become increasingly aware of the tremendous number of resources expended on getting their employees from point A to point B. At some point, reliance on one's secretary or administrative assistant to make reasonable, economical travel arrangements becomes too much for an individual or group of individuals not well versed in the subject of travel. This is the time that companies set up their own travel department or outsource the function to travel professionals.

While this event marks a milestone in a company's existence, turning over the travel arrangements to professionals does not solve the unique travel requirements of certain employees. Senior executives and teams of marketing, sales, or quality control personnel or troubleshooters requiring rapid, short-notice travel are often overlooked by travel departments. If these individuals are to accomplish their unique missions and goals, they must fend for themselves, often stretching, or even breaking, existing travel policies. In short, these employees' travel needs are not well taken care of.

Normally, these special classes of employees begin to realize that scheduled air transportation does not serve their needs. They may start exploring features of the most readily available and affordable alternative, aircraft charter. Yet, having never before contracted for these services, such employees are at a disadvantage in determining which charter operator will provide the most cost-effective, safe, reliable, and high-quality service. The selection then becomes a hit-or-miss proposition, exposing such employees to a range of service levels that may prove to be a turn-off or excellent, based more on the laws of chance than on intelligent choice.

Alternatively, contact with an aircraft salesperson or broker or the opportunity to take a trip on another company's aircraft may provide sufficient impetus to investigate the possibility of a company aircraft further. Whatever the introduction to business aviation, the desire to investigate further is usually strong. Unfortunately, prospective users of on-demand air transportation seldom perform a thorough analysis of their needs and options. Perhaps this is because the concept is new and the initial impetus is compelling. Whatever the reason, a rush to embrace one method of on-demand air transportation without investigating the full range of options inevitably will leave the user unsatisfied. There are better ways of doing this.

Why Individuals and Companies Use On-Demand Air Transportation

A number of the following issues were covered in the last chapter, but viewing them in a slightly different way will prove useful in opening this chapter.

Create One's Own Schedule. The airlines have created a transportation network that connects the world's major cities and, through regional airlines, many of the smaller cities. Yet few would say that using the airlines is an easy task. Inconvenient schedules, multiple connections, and departure processing delays waste much of a busy executive's time. When you want to go or arrive, there is seldom the right flight schedule or combination of schedules; even when the schedules accommodate your needs, seats may not be available; you can only get to within a 2-hour drive of your ultimate destination due to lack of airline service— sometimes it seems that you can't get there from here!

While we have all endured some or all the phenomena just listed, the on-demand transportation option is always available, 24/7, to as many as 10 times the number of airports served by the airlines. Creating one's own schedule and destination is truly a liberating experience. Further, it often makes good business sense; having the tools to determine what makes sense will easily lead to the liberating experience.

The Value of Time. We all have just three resources available in pursuit of our goals: time, people, and money. While the latter two are certainly important, the asset over which we usually exercise the least amount of control is time—time to research, time to plan, time to react, time to produce. Therefore, the conservation and allocation of time are important to everyone, even more so to those who make the decisions and initiate actions.

Conforming to an airline schedule, waiting in airline terminals, and being subject to the whimsy of airline delays do not conform to a philosophy that will permit the efficient use of available time.

The Need to Be Face-to-Face. The communications revolution of the past few decades has made personal and business contacts easier and faster. Cell phones, fax machines, the Internet, e-mail, teleconferencing, and electronic whiteboards have all enabled individuals to be more productive and aware of their environment. Yet the big decrease in travel predicted as a result of using these modern marvels has not materialized. In fact, these electronic tools actually have increased our need to travel simply because they have increased our productivity and improved our view of the marketplace. Moreover, these electronic marvels have increased the speed with which we receive information about markets to the point where rapid and decisive action is required to take advantage of the information received.

While many issues can be handled remotely, people still subscribe to the following truisms:

- Deals are made in person.
- Individuals like to be courted in person.
- People learn more when they can see, touch, and hear in person.

Increased Productivity. Everyone strives to do more with less and to be at the right place at the right time—in short, to efficiently take advantage of what the environment and markets have to offer. Increased productivity has become the holy grail of the modern world.

This requires individuals and companies to use their scarce resources effectively and efficiently. In doing so, information databases, communications tools, and intelligent delegating are provided as tools to empower and enable people. Yet these same valuable individuals and employees spend countless hours waiting in airports, languishing in hotel rooms, and driving hours to far destinations, all because the airlines cannot get them rapidly to where they want to go, when they wish, and back again in the shortest possible time. The millions spent on productivity gains are often squandered on lost productivity during the airline travel process.

Safety, Security, and Confidentiality. We all wish to protect our loved ones, especially when they are away from us. Similarly, key employees are highly valued by their companies because of their ability to make a competitive difference in the environment. Extraordinary methods are taken to protect them from hazards, to put them in the finest hotels, to hire bonded limousine services to carry them around in distant cities, and to contract with security services to protect them from harm. Yet, with all these protection methods, our valued acquaintances and executives are exposed to the vagaries of airline travel.

The ability to take advantage of superior information about the markets presupposes that only your company knows about this valuable information and that the competition will not find out about it until you have taken advantage of it. However, travel schedules of key personnel attempting to take advantage of unique opportunities may be readily found out by a determined competitor. Moreover, the same competitor can overhear sensitive conversations between your employees and observe their work papers and laptop screens during the travel process; airline travel is neither secure nor confidential.

Intangibles. While the following issues seldom create a compelling reason for the use for on-demand air transportation, experienced travelers can instantly associate with and appreciate their negative impact on both their productivity as employees and the quality of their private lives:

- Airline travel hassles
- Travel-related stress
- Nights on the road
- Fatigue

All these quality-of-life issues have an impact on lifestyle issues and the ability of companies to keep employees relatively happy and productive. Burnout as a result of repeated and excessive doses of the items listed above is a very real concern; anything that can be done to alleviate these issues creates greater peace of mind and relaxed individuals and employees. None of us wishes to subject our loved ones to these unattractive consequences of airline travel.

Defining the Requirement

Individuals and families who travel frequently normally can forecast their transportation requirements at least 6 months and often 1 year in advance. Vacations, trips to residences, meetings with friends, and a certain number of pop-up trips are usually well known sometime in advance of the travel date. Some time spent with a simple monthly planning calendar should yield a reasonably accurate view of their on-demand travel requirements. Going through this exercise is useful in determining the correct type of on-demand method to be used.

Individuals who use on-demand air transportation for their personal needs often have business reasons to travel as well. Board meetings, property inspections, and consulting with advisors all provide business purposes to their travel calendar. Estimating these events can be made easier by using elements of the air transportation analysis that follows.

A company may concentrate on the travel needs of just its top three to five executives, or it may spread its net wider, including a variety of employees, some of whom may be classified as middle managers or below. It is important for a company to define its needs accurately before commencing an air transportation analysis. If this is not done, important requirements may be overlooked that may yield the wrong type of aircraft, or too many aircraft may be purchased; these features tend to create a negative impression on all concerned.

While the most common use of business aviation involves the travel needs of a top few executives within a company, these needs seldom fully utilize the aircraft. Most business jets operate on average about 450 hours per year but have the capability to operate as much as 700 to 800 hours annually. Well-defined repetitive schedules, such as corporate shuttle operations, can provide 1200 to 1300 hours from a single aircraft. Therefore, making the aircraft available to just a few people in the company will unnecessarily restrict its utility and reduce its efficiency.

Corporate Culture.   The personality of a company determines how it conducts its business. Its level of aggressiveness in its markets, its risk behavior, its relations with its employees, its communications style, and its degree of formality all determine its culture. All these factors are important determinants of how a company approaches opportunities and problems, reacts to stimuli, and in general, makes its mark on the landscape.

Corporate culture is in large part a result of the personality and style of the chairperson or chief executive officer (CEO). This person's personality is often strong enough to be transmitted into the entire organization through subordinates, including level of participation desired in decision making and degree of aggressiveness in approaching the market. All these features spread throughout the organization via goals and objectives, policies and procedures, and informal communications. These elements combine to define the *nature of the company*; a lasting culture soon follows.

Aggressive companies seize opportunities rapidly and extend themselves throughout a wide range of market possibilities; analytical companies usually examine potential markets carefully and with in-depth analyses; entrepreneurial companies are more extensions of the nature of the founder/president than they are true corporate entities. Each of these company types reacts differently to opportunities and challenges. Knowing the corporate culture is essential in determining the type of aviation operation, aircraft, and aviation personnel best suited for a company.

It is important to note that this culture changes over time. The entrepreneurial, aggressive company of yesterday may have evolved into a more cautious, measured entity in a 5- or 10-year period. Realizing the new culture and its changing needs is necessary to ensure the proper fit between company and flight department. Also, new senior management inevitably brings changes in the culture, although these changes may take years to make. (See "Corporate Stages of Development" in Chap. 5.)

Situational Needs.   Certainly, priorities must be established that recognize the relative importance of higher-level executives. In doing so, arguments regarding who should use the company aircraft are rarely encountered. The primary point of this discussion is to recognize that not just a few select individuals should be permitted to use a company aircraft. Situational demands placed on a variety of individuals may easily make on-demand aircraft the preferred method of travel.

All processes of a company must be examined to determine eligibility to use on-demand air transportation:

- Marketing and sales often send a number of representatives to one or more locations to work with prospective or existing customers. If the destinations are remote and airline schedules are incompatible with the teams' workload, on-demand transportation may make sense.
- A remote manufacturing facility, either the company's or a customer's, experiences a technical problem. Sending engineering and technical teams in the company aircraft will get the problem solved faster and get the team back to their regular duties more rapidly.

- Customers can be brought to see your display area and manufacturing facilities in a minimum amount of time while transmitting the message to them that they are VIPs.
- A team of company attorneys must take multiple depositions in a remote location. The company airplane may cut 2 days off their travel time.

A list of possible aircraft users and uses should be compiled before starting the air transportation analysis process. Without this list, determining aircraft usage will prove difficult. Chapter 1 discusses a number of potential uses.

Transportation Solutions.   Obviously, an owned or leased aircraft may not be the means of on-demand air transportation chosen for primary use within a company or for private users. Charter, fractional ownership, or joint-use operations may prove the best method for either long- or short-term use. Becoming wedded to the concept that a single aircraft is the only on-demand method that should be considered for travel, regardless of how many users/uses are justified, unnecessarily restricts the range of travel options available. In doing so, decision makers miss the big picture of what they are attempting to accomplish by using on-demand air transportation.

Companies traditionally list profitability as their principal goal. How they achieve profitability within their chosen niche requires a variety of methods and plans. The same is true for transportation.

Just because the principal airplane is booked or that the preferred charter operator does not have an aircraft available when someone wants it should not mean that the individual is doomed to use the airlines for his or her trip. Rather, creative scheduling may permit the use of either aircraft for a multimission role on the day in question, another charter company may be used, or a prearranged interchange agreement with another operator on the field can be used to supply the desired trip.

On-demand air transportation is a method designed to support some business or personal requirement; it is not an end unto itself. All methods of on-demand air transportation must be viewed as means to an end—as *transportation solutions.*

AIR TRANSPORTATION ANALYSIS

Companies must conduct a survey to determine existing and anticipated travel patterns, thereby correctly determining their actual requirements. Determining these needs based on anecdotes and gut instinct often will overlook essential company travel needs.

An air transportation analysis examines three aspects of a company's travel:

- A historical view of airline and on-demand travel
- Planned and expected travel needs for the near future
- Solutions for these needs

The historical view is designed to provide the company with a look backwards at its past 12 months of travel, permitting a view of recent travel. While this will not necessarily predict future usage, understanding existing travel patterns is useful when setting the stage for the future.

Planned and/or expected travel is determined through interviews with key company personnel, reviewing strategic plans, and a knowledge of future products and services to be offered.

Suggested solutions use information from the first two sections of the analysis and develop a range of possible solutions to provide recommendations to decision makers (Fig. 2.1).

The object of this analysis is to create a picture of anticipated travel of key players and to describe the benefits of on-demand air transportation in terms of convenience, time savings,

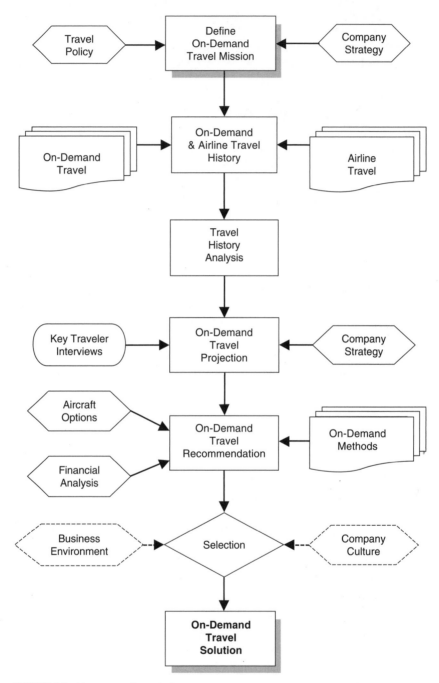

FIGURE 2.1   Air transportation analysis process.

and access to markets. The National Business Aviation Association (NBAA) has some excellent materials available to facilitate the travel analysis and aircraft selection process. While aircraft manufacturers and brokers also will perform this analysis or assist with the process, realize that they are selling a product or service and that this may bias the outcome of the analysis. Independent consultants will perform this analysis for a price; their work may be less biased. Alternatively, company or private analysts should be able to perform the basic analysis with little difficulty.

Travel History

The travel history analysis phase should look at all company travel, not just executive travel. This is done to determine the total travel requirements for the company so that the on-demand solution can be used to fit as many possible transportation needs as efficiently and economically possible. A major selling point for a business aircraft is that it will serve the needs of the entire company, not just the senior executives.

Start the analysis by examining airline travel records from the past year (more that 1 year's worth may be counterproductive because of the changing nature of corporate travel patterns). These records usually are available in a database either from the company travel department or from the company travel agent; such an analysis is usually known as a *city-pair analysis.* (Table 2.1). Similarly, Table 2.2 provides aircraft charter destination information. Use available analytical features associated with the database to determine the following:

- Most popular destinations
- Trip frequencies
- Level of personnel traveling to those destinations
- Cost per trip (ideally, cost per seat-mile)

From this information, a graphic representation for destinations and frequency of travel versus distances (Fig. 2.2), a map of these destinations, and some qualitative description of relative convenience may be developed. This should be done for both key executives and other selected company employees. Obviously, executives will be the principal beneficiaries of the aircraft, but it also may be desirable for others within the company to use the aircraft. Employees from the CEO down through middle managers should be considered in this research. While all these employees may not be granted regular use of on-demand air transportation, knowing how a range of managerial and technical employees travel will produce a more complete picture for use in the analysis.

This analysis also should be done for on-demand transportation used by company employees during the same period considered for the airline city-pair research. Records of aircraft charter, fractional ownership, and company aircraft travel, if any, will complete the travel picture for employees.

An essential part of the analysis is a section, usually toward the end, that compares on-demand air transportation with the alternative modes of transportation and includes tradeoff features arising from not using on-demand methods, including

- Extra nights on the road
- Lengthy travel days
- Poor airline connections causing circuitous routings or delayed travel
- Lost productivity due to additional hours and days on the road
- Poorly located airline airports requiring lengthy rental car trips
- Intangibles—frustration, employee satisfaction, security, airport hassles

TABLE 2.1 Sample City-Pair Analysis

MSP-LGA   921 mi   Between Minneapolis and NY LaGuardia

Airline	First Fare	First Flight	Business Fare	Business Flights	Economy Fare	Economy Flight	Other Fare	Other Flights	Totals Fare	Totals Flight	Avg	CPM	%
NW	$3000	2			$14,300	22	$4500	9	$21,800	33	$660	$0.72	97
UA	$3000	2			$3,500	5			$3,500	5	$700	$0.76	13
					$17,800	27	$4500	9	$25,300	38	$666	$0.72	100

MSP-LGW   4,295 mi   Between Minneapolis and London Gatwick

Airline	First Fare	First Flight	Business Fare	Business Flights	Economy Fare	Economy Flight	Other Fare	Other Flights	Totals Fare	Totals Flight	Avg	CPM	%
CO	$7000	1			$14,400	12			$21,400	13	$1646	$0.38	80
AA	$7000	1			$3,500	3			$3,500	3	$1166	$0.27	20
					$17,900	15			$24,900	16	$1556	$0.36	100

TABLE 2.2   Sample Charter Destinations

Irvine	Trips	Greenville	Trips
Houston	16	Owensboro	4
Greenville	8	Houston	3
Washington	6	Baltimore	3
Calgary	5	Hilton Head	3
Chicago	5	Washington	2
San Francisco	4	Peoria	2
Bartlesville	3	Gary	2
Atlanta	2	Savannah	2
Dallas	2	Columbia	2
Teterboro	2	Philadelphia	2

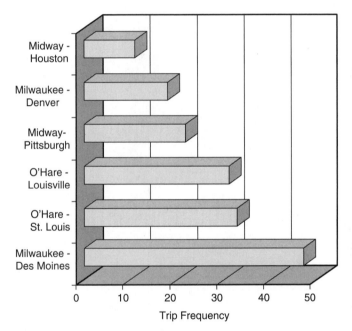

FIGURE 2.2   Sample airline city-pair graph.

These stories are best told anecdotally, bringing the human element to bear—everyone has a airline tale of caution and woe to relate. While the numbers developed in the trans-portation history section are useful in depicting how employees have traveled in the recent past, how people actually use and react to the travel experience become invaluable when contemplating the future.

The Future

Emphasis must be placed on *anticipated* travel needs for the analysis to be of value to the company. Reliance on past travel needs or merely extrapolating those needs incrementally—

Strategic Plans

These are the broad-brush plans for coming events within a company. While lacking in detail, they provide a sense of direction for the company. Items of use for the air transportation analysis include

- New products and services
- New or closing plant/office locations
- New geographic or business-line markets
- Competitive forces
- Strengths and weaknesses
- Resource availability
- Timeliness
- Contingencies

Importantly, these items will serve as entry points for the interviews to be conducted.

Transportation Analysis Interview Questions

- Interviewee's position and duties
- Recent company travel history
- Views concerning travel convenience (ask for specific examples)
- Concept of the company's and interviewee's department future growth (1- and 3-year projections, if available)
- New products and services planned (and travel implications)
- Personal and departmental (especially direct reports) travel plans for the next 18 months
- How can on-demand air transportation help achieve department goals?

"We probably will be on the road in the Northwest 15 percent more next year"— likely will provide an inaccurate or biased requirements picture. Determining the future travel needs of a company is often difficult because future plans may not be well defined.

Each company (and flight department) should have a long- and short-range view of its future, articulated through a series of strategic and operational plans. The goals and objectives flowing from these plans become action items that drive the company toward its view of the future. These plans often will contain the information necessary to gain insight into upcoming travel needs. Unfortunately, these plans often are not well developed or articulated, instead relying on chance and personality to drive the organization forward. And even if they are well formed and documented, they may not tell the full story.

The rate of change of the business environment has given rise to a more ad hoc planning style, with many companies preferring to remain flexible enough to react to a rapidly changing marketplace. Yet, within each chairperson, CEO, chief operating officer (COO), or other top executive resides a central focus, a vision of where the company will be in 1 year, 3 years, and if they are brave, 5 or more years. It is this vision that will provide the impetus for the corporate engine to receive its power and direction. Therefore, it is this direction that must be discovered to determine the air transportation needs of the company.

The company vision likely will include new products and services, new or different locations to produce or provide those commodities, and certain people to bring shape and form to the dream. It is the people who will provide the details of the vision.

An important part of the air transportation analysis involves interviewing those who make corporate decisions and those who will actually do the traveling. In addition to putting flesh on the bones of often hastily written plans, interviews serve as a mechanism to focus attention of the on-demand air transportation issue throughout the company. The act of asking about travel needs often will serve to stimulate interest in the subject and drive it forward to some conclusion. Without the opinions of the decision makers and travelers, the data analysis portion of the study may prove a meaningless exercise.

Certainly the CEO, COO, corporate officers, and senior managers should be asked about their views of the future to provide an overview. However, the real focus should be on what may be considered the company's "movers and shakers," those who will bring the corporate vision to reality. These are typically senior managers or officers charged with applying substance to the ideas of top-level executives. It will be their hard work that will bring projects to fruition, and it will be these individuals and their direct reports who may be most in need of on-demand air transportation.

The interviews should be distilled into a report providing principal and anticipated destinations, frequency of visiting them, and broad justifications for the trips (Table 2.3). An essential part of the report must speak to the efficiency and convenience gained by using on-demand air transportation. Information gained during the interviews may be used as the principal source of future travel needs within the company. The picture gained from the interviews may not be precise, yet it constitutes the best possible view of the company's future travel plans provided by the people who know more about the subject than anybody else.

Solutions

Once all research and interview information has been assembled and analyzed, a total picture of air transportation requirements must be constructed. Much of this travel will not warrant the use of on-demand air transportations; rather, a majority may be better suited to airline travel.

At some point the criticality of the mission, time value of the trip, value of employees, number of employees traveling together, and need for rapid action will tip the scale in favor of use of something more rapid, reliable, and confidential than the airlines. Finding this point will vary widely with the type of company, stage of corporate development, market forces, future plans, and so on. However, such a point must be identified and well defined if the decision to use on-demand air transportation is to be made. Accurately defining this point may be the most important aspect of the analysis because it is this point around which the whole issue of mass versus private transportation revolves. Therefore, significant effort should go into defining this point. (See the discussion of NBAA Travel$ense software in Chap. 1.)

TABLE 2.3 Sample Interview Results

Company Air Transportation Requirements—5/03–11/05				
Department	Destination	Frequency	Mission	Remarks
Manufacturing	Ft. Wayne	6	Plant construction	With two direct reports
Manufacturing	Springfield	2	Product conversion	with QC, facilities
Manufacturing	Jefferson City	3	Plant addition	with engineering
Manufacturing	Rockford	2	Merger discussions	with finance, marketing, legal
Manufacturing	NYC	2	Financing presentations	with CEO, finance, legal
Manufacturing	Ft. Smith	2	Plant shutdown	with facilities
Manufacturing	(Midwest)	2	Location search	with CEO, facilities
Legal	Rockford	4	Merger discussions	
Manufacturing	Chicago	4	XYZ lawsuit	
Marketing	(Round-robin)	4	New product intro	Six Midwest cities
Manufacturing	Rockford	1	Product fam	Team of six

TABLE 2.4 Sample Consolidated On-Demand Requirements

Projected On-Demand Air Transportation Requirements for 2004				
Destinations	Distance (mi)	Frequency	Passengers	Remarks
Chicago, Des Moines, Rockford	Up to 300	22	2–6	Plant related, personal
Winnipeg, Kansas City, Grand Rapids	300–400	36	2–4	Merger, acquisition, expansion
Ft. Wayne, Springfield	400–600	28	2–8	Construction, new products
Buffalo, Memphis	600–800	6	2–4	Acquisition
Houston, New York	800–1200	12	2–6	Financial
Phoenix, Seattle	>1200	5	2–4	Partners
(Undefined, round-robin)	—	22	2–6	Marketing, site search

Once this point is defined, a table can be developed that provides the composite requirements for on-demand air transportation for the company (Table 2.4). The table should portray sample destinations, distances to those destinations, anticipated number of passengers for the trips, and any relevant remarks that will assist in understanding and justifying the projected trips. Since interview information serves as the source for this table, justification for projected trips should prove relatively easy.

This table normally assumes that just one aircraft will supply all the on-demand air transportation needs of the company. However, what if high-priority missions destined for widely separated destinations are required on the same day? Or what if the aircraft is unavailable due to an extended maintenance inspection? How are high-priority trips accommodated? Can a single aircraft provide more than 700 to 800 hours per year of service? How many multiple-day trips will be required? The point is that one or two aircraft may not be sufficient to meet all legitimate travel needs. Therefore, either more than one aircraft will be required to meet those needs or a number of transportation delivery methods will be needed. (Alternative delivery methods, including charter, fractional ownership, and interchange, will be discussed later in this chapter.) These facts must be included in the decision analysis to provide a complete picture regarding transportation needs; to do less sends an incomplete and incorrect message to decision makers.

Presentation of these trips may be made more understandable and graphically pleasing if a map covering the destinations can be created that displays the proposed trip frequencies with arrows denoting trip frequency by varying the width of the shaft. This presentation will figure prominently in the decision on the type of aircraft to be used in providing the service (Fig. 2.3).

Utilization Factors

Typically, aircraft are only available for service 90 to 95 percent of the time due to scheduled maintenance requirements. This and other factors make it difficult to claim that a single aircraft is available 24/7/365. Factors that reduce aircraft availability include

- Multiple trips to different destinations (schedule conflict)
- Multiday trips
- Need to reposition the aircraft from a previous one-way trip
- Scheduled maintenance
- Flight crew duty time limits
- 700 to 800 hours per year are the effective maximum for most applications

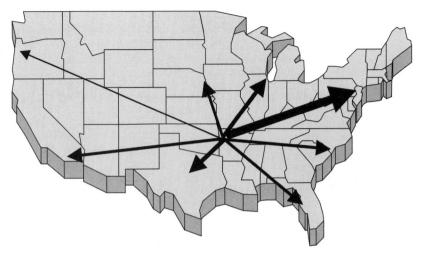

FIGURE 2.3 Depicting frequently flown routes.

For a more complete list of items involved in the air transportation analysis, see the "NBAA Air Transportation Needs Analysis Checklist" in the Appendix.

Evaluation of Aircraft Types. The majority of trips shown in Table 2.4 are less than 800 miles, a range easily attainable by most turboprop and turbojet aircraft carrying six passengers, the passenger load factor called for in a majority of the trips. Aircraft range and payload are not independent of one another; rather, they are closely linked. Most airplanes are designed so that if their fuel tanks are full, they cannot also fill all passenger seats due to weight limitations. Therefore, with all seats full, the maximum range of the aircraft is reduced. When flights exceed 800 miles, a number of factors, such as departure airport temperature and altitude, winds aloft, and destination weather, may make an enroute fuel stop necessary. Some passengers prize the ability of an aircraft full of passengers to make a transcontinental flight nonstop, whereas others either do not care or relish the thought of a stop every 3 to 4 hours. The extra range required to make a nonstop trip may double or even triple the purchase price of an aircraft. This capability seldom may be required; therefore, desired aircraft performance characteristics should be defined carefully prior to selection (see the "Aircraft Characteristics" sidebar on the next page).

Much is made of an aircraft's speed, although this performance characteristic must be placed into perspective. While an aircraft may be capable of speeds in excess of 500 knots, it must climb high, normally above 35,000 ft, to achieve this speed. If many of the expected trips are 300 miles or less, the aircraft will either spend much of its time climbing and descending or be unable to reach its maximum speed. Therefore, its effective speed between departure and destination, *block speed,* is often considerably less than its maximum. Air traffic control congestion and delays also will reduce the effective speed of an aircraft, especially on the heavily traveled East and West Coast routes. And the difference between a 500-knot and a 400-knot aircraft over a flight of 350 miles is just 11 minutes; the difference in purchase price between the two types is $13 million.

Cabin size figures prominently into aircraft choices too. The smallest turbojets have a cross-sectional diameter of barely 5 ft and are 11 ft long; a large-cabin aircraft cross section is more than 6 ft and 50 ft in length. The difference can accommodate many additional amenities, including a full-size lavatory, seats that recline into beds, and a full galley,

Aircraft Characteristics

Selecting an aircraft depends on choosing among a number of factors, some of which are interdependent:

- Seating capacity
- Cabin dimensions
- Cabin amenities—lavatory, galley
- Baggage capacity
- Weight—empty, maximum, useful load, payload
- Speed—maximum, normal, long range
- Range—maximum, seats full
- Ceiling—certified, service, engine out
- Runway performance—landing, takeoff
- Costs—purchase, operating

including crystal and silver. The difference in cost of the two aircraft types is $20 million. Moreover, the larger aircraft cannot operate into smaller airports, an important feature to some companies. Conversely, the larger aircraft will carry double the passenger load for several times the range of the smaller aircraft.

Airport Factors. Not all airport runways are created equal: Some are shorter, narrower, and have less weight-bearing capacity than others. Many on-demand aircraft users take advantage of the many nonairline airports available to them, since many airline airports are not close to their desired destinations. For instance, there are more than 15,000 airports available to private aircraft in the United States but just 500 available to the airlines. More realistically, even small turbine-powered aircraft are limited to not many more than the 4500 public-use airports in the United States, still a major increase over the number available to the airlines.

Larger, faster aircraft normally require longer, wider runways due to their performance characteristics. The required takeoff field length is defined by runway performance tables contained in the airplane flight manual, taking air temperature, airport elevation, and weight of the aircraft into account. These are mandatory minimum values under a country's operating regulations. For instance, a small-cabin turbojet may require just 3000 ft of runway for takeoff; a large-cabin jet may require twice this amount. However, these runway performance requirements may be reduced if the aircraft is not operating at its maximum permissible weight, but they may be increased if there are high temperatures and/or a high-elevation airport is used.

The "Annual Purchase Planning Handbook" (normally the May issue) of *Business and Commercial Aviation* and Conklin and deDecker's *Aircraft Cost Evaluator* are excellent sources of detailed aircraft operational and cost data.

Some of these decision points are performance-related, some are financial, and still others may be considered lifestyle choices. Certainly, a small seven-seat turbojet with a range of 1000 statute miles will meet the needs of many companies' and individual's on-demand air transportation needs, but additional seating, performance characteristics, and interior appointments have created a large market for more than 20 smaller aircraft and 30 turbojet aircraft designed for business purposes. The tradeoffs must be considered carefully to ensure that the company or individual user is provided with the right mix of features that will serve his or her needs.

An important feature in making this choice is talking with others who currently use on-demand air transportation for business or private purposes. Although each will value aircraft characteristics differently, their experience will prove invaluable to assisting you and/or your decision makers to find the right aircraft and delivery methods to provide suitable transportation solutions. Finding representatives of these companies can be accomplished easily by asking local fixed-base operators (aircraft service companies), aircraft brokers, and business acquaintances for their opinions and experiences regarding their company aircraft and/or service providers. Affiliates of the International Business Aviation Council (see Appendix) can supply contact points.

Making the Decision. Deciding which aircraft type or combination of types will adequately serve the needs of the individual or company may be a simple process of presenting a number of recommended solutions to the proper decision makers. Or it can prove complex and labored, depending on whether the proper decision makers have been chosen, internal politics, and the financial state of the company or individual. Ensuring that all these factors have been covered carefully prior to the ultimate presentation will make the decision process smoother and relatively painless.

Gaining a consensus of middle- and upper-level employees and executives often will provide sufficient weight of opinion to sway top-level decision makers regarding aircraft type and delivery method. Yet many chairpersons and CEOs may have strong opinions about air transportation methods because they will be the principal passengers, foreseeing many hours riding in the aircraft. Knowing how the boss perceives air transportation will ease the decision process

There is no substitute for allowing company representatives to try a number of aircraft types before the final choice is made. If a clear choice is not made after presentation of the air transportation analysis, the finalists in the competition may be tested via several methods. The primary method of doing so is by chartering a specific aircraft for an actual trip. This will enable a number of decision makers to experience the actual environment they may choose to travel in for some time to come. If the type chosen does not meet decision-maker preferences, another type can be tried. And charter may prove to be the best method of providing air transportation for the company's on-demand needs. Unfortunately, a full range of aircraft types may not be readily available from local charter companies, and therefore, this method may not be accomplished easily. It is possible to find virtually any aircraft type available for charter, but the distance it must travel to provide the demonstration may be considerable, effectively increasing the cost of the charter, due to the costs of transit time with the aircraft empty.

Another method of experiencing different aircraft types is to arrange for a demonstration flight in a new or used aircraft through the manufacturer's sales force or an aircraft broker.

Healthy Flyers

A health care provider operated eight different hospitals from Minneapolis to Oklahoma City. The company was based in St. Louis, and its executives and managers became TWA frequent flyers, attempting to keep up with the growing organization. Marketing, finance, and the executive officers were the most traveled within the company, so much so that three key managers left the company because of the amount of travel involved. The company began using occasional charter aircraft to ease the travel burden and soon discovered the advantages of on-demand air transportation.

A brief air transportation analysis showed that the company could easily justify an aircraft based on the fact that more hospital acquisitions were anticipated and increasing numbers of people needed to travel. Soon thereafter the company leased a used Beechjet and was soon putting more than 500 hours per year on it. The good news is that two of the managers who had left the company were lured back into the fold because of the better travel arrangements.

While these flights are often not very long, they will allow passengers to get the feel for the aircraft. Alternatively, demonstration flights often can be arranged to accommodate actual business trips, with the company receiving the transportation paying only the direct operating costs for the aircraft. This type of demonstration is preferable because it shows the aircraft in its operational mode and allows the passengers to actually work and confer on the flight, experiencing its positive and negative attributes.

CHOOSING THE METHOD

As previously discussed, on-demand aviation services may be supplied by one of the following methods:

- Employee/owner-flown aircraft
- In-house flight department
- Management company
- Joint ownership
- Interchange
- Time share
- Charter
- Fractional ownership

Each of these will be discussed in this section, but it is useful first to examine what customers really want from flight service organizations.

What Users Want in On-Demand Air Transportation

At first glance, the answer seems simple: providing high-quality on-demand air transportation service to the passengers. This is easy to say, but what are the components of this service? Even better, what do the principal user, CEO, senior executives, and just plain passengers really want from a flight services provider? If they are asked directly, they may not provide either an honest or a meaningful answer. "On-time service" or "Just keep on doing what you're doing" will not help to define the essential components and level of service to be delivered.

After having spoken with many individuals and company executives regarding their expectations for their flight operations, impressions are formed that probably represent a majority opinion. Importantly, many of these passengers did not precisely articulate desires for high levels of safety and value, yet the specific examples they give point directly to those issues.

Safety. While the principal passenger will almost never grab the flight department manager or other provider by the lapels and say, "You'd better be safe!" this is an inherent expectation. On-demand aircraft are used as an alternative to the airlines; passengers expect their alternative to be at least as safe. While many may say that such an expectation "goes without saying," it may be useful to remind all concerned of the primacy of safety on a regular basis. The key feature to look for is that every decision made within a flight operation begins and ends with a realistic assessment of the risk factors involved. If so, the outcome probably will prove safe.

Reliability. If a provider says that he or she will pick up passengers at 9 A.M. on Friday, this forms a contract. Not being there and ready to go as promised jeopardizes the reputation of the provider and perhaps future contracts. Granted, every provider experiences mechanical or weather delays, but these should be precious few. Once dispatch reliability gets below 98 or 99 percent, passengers may adopt a more surly attitude toward the service provider. Good contingency plans and backups help prevent these embarrassing moments.

Good News About the Provider.   If other customers say nice things about an on-demand aircraft provider, this tends to build confidence about that provider. Fortunately or unfortunately, bad news seems to travel twice as fast as good news, so getting the word on one provider or another is not difficult. Yet the news may not come automatically; ask for references on a regular basis. Providers who deliver knock-your-socks-off service will cause all concerned to sing their praises. The occasional delay will pass easily if the service provider receives mostly favorable comments.

Good Service.   Passengers paying up to $7500 per hour for upper-end aircraft services deserve and usually demand the highest levels of service. On-time departures, immaculately clean and well-maintained aircraft, courteous schedulers and flight crew, excellent meals or snacks, continuous information about the progress of the flight, and on-time arrivals—as permitted by air traffic control and weather—are all standard expectations in the on-demand aircraft business. Moreover, superb service in all aspects of the operation are a *given,* especially if the service provider desires a long-term relationship with the contracting company. Moreover, the provider should be supplying added value for the user, not just charging for indifferent service.

Value is a combination of level of service and cost. That is, the lowest-cost operation does not necessarily provide the best level of service. Instead, a desired level of service is provided at a reasonable cost. There are no blank checks here; the cost of operation is not the primary consideration in providing the service.

In essence, users look for three elements in an on-demand air transportation service provider:

- Safety
- Service
- Value

The ability to provide excellent on-demand air transportation service while also providing good value can best be accomplished if the user has total *control* over the operation. The best means of ensuring the highest levels of control are to maintain a completely in-house flight department—scheduling, operations, maintenance, and personnel are an integral part of the company. Let's take a look at each type of service provider to examine pros and cons.

It's All About Control.   In the final analysis, companies seek the highest level of control over their on-demand flight operations. Whether it be schedules, personnel qualifications, service quality, or level of maintenance, these and other factors drive companies to choose one form of transportation over another. Table 2.5 lists the various factors of on-demand air transportation and grades them by the level of control each method provides. It is important to note that the grading system does not imply that one form of transportation is better than another, merely that the level of control over the factors listed is either higher or lower.

For instance, just because the in-house operation shows four asterisks in the service consistency category does not necessarily mean that any in-house operation is necessarily better or worse than a charter operation showing two asterisks. Rather, this means that the user has the opportunity and means to control this issue better than he or she would have when contracting with a charter company.

Control over the aircraft schedule is perhaps the most important issue in on-demand air transportation. An in-house operation clearly has the edge on this factor because the aircraft

TABLE 2.5　Flight Operations Control Factors

Factors	In-House Flight Dept.	Managed Aircraft	Joint Ownership	Fractional Ownership	Charter
Aircraft					
Availability	****	***	***	****	**
Response	****	***	***	****	**
Maintenance	****	***	***	***	**
Security	****	***	***	***	**
Service	****	***	***	***	**
Personnel					
Qualifications	****	***	***	***	**
Training	****	***	***	***	**
Costs					
Capital	****	***	***	***	n/a
Operational	****	***	***	**	*
Liability	****	***	***	**	*

Note: The number of asterisks indicates the ability to control the factor mentioned, not the absolute value of the factor itself.

operator/owner has the ultimate level of control over this feature. Although a scheduling conflict or unscheduled maintenance on the aircraft may reduce the availability of the aircraft, scheduling remains firmly in control of the company operating the aircraft. Note, however, that fractional ownership provides similar or perhaps greater availability and response capability due to the additional pool of aircraft. Yet the intelligent shuffling of trip priorities by the user still may provide a higher level control over this feature.

Service quality and consistency are prized by many on-demand users as the most important features offered by this form of transportation. The in-house flight department clearly has the edge on this method of transportation because the company dictates its standards and performance desires to the flight department directly with no middlemen interfering with the communication. Other passengers (probably a minority) prize on-time operations more than service quality. In reality, most users demand and receive both. Again, corporate culture or the preferences of the principal passengers set the tone for on-demand air transportation activity.

The ability to dictate and control overall aircraft use policies and procedures is very important. Delegating such factors to a management company or fractional provider or sharing them with another in joint-ownership arrangement is often not favored by users. Similarly, knowing who is maintaining and flying the aircraft provides reassurance to many travelers. Yet some users consider the availability of an on-demand aircraft just another support service, such as a limousine or information technology service; ultimately, all services can be outsourced to one degree or another.

Each of these features comes with a cost and gives rise to tradeoffs with other features mentioned. Yet cost alone is rarely the principal determinant of satisfaction among on-demand air transportation users. Deciding which features are important and their relative importance before you embark on choosing a transportation method will ensure happier travelers over time.

Methods

Each of the following methods provides a slightly different type and level of service. Some of these differences carry a fee; others do not. No one method is ideal for any class or type of company; individual preferences and unique needs dictate the proper methods. *Note: Each of these methods involves a number of financial, regulatory, and legal issues that cannot be covered in this section because of the complexities involved. Prior to entering into any of these agreements, experienced legal and financial counsel should be sought. Additionally, some of these methods, such as interchange and time share, may not be available in all countries.*

Private-Use/Employee-Flown Aircraft.   This is the most basic form of air transportation used by companies and individuals. It is normally initiated by the company owner or individual, either bringing a love of aviation (and an aircraft) to the job or acquiring a desire to learn to fly for private purposes. In either case, the desires and preferences of one of the users determine an air travel policy, with this person flying his or her own or a company aircraft. The key factor in defining this type of flying is that the individual flies the aircraft as an adjunct to his or her normal duties; he or she is not compensated for transporting either himself or herself or other employees/friends.

The best reason for using individually flown light aircraft is the flexibility they provide. The ability to create one's own travel schedule and then to modify it as conditions and opportunities dictate makes good personal and business sense. Rapid reaction to changing events is accomplished easily with this type of operation. The efficiency generated by this travel mode can be great.

While many aircraft used for this purpose are small single- or twin-engine piston-powered aircraft, a growing number of turboprops and turbojets are being employed. Comfort, convenience, and speed must be balanced against the utility desired and the costs involved.

In many business applications, the CEO or other senior employee uses the company airplane for their near-exclusive benefit, making company employees seek other forms of on-demand transportation. This is not necessarily a bad concept because in small and entrepreneurial companies it is the principal who makes most of the deals and whose time is most critical. It is common that companies begin with an owner-flown aircraft and then progress rapidly to the point where a corporate turbojet flown by professional pilots can be justified.

There is some concern regarding the safety of this type of aircraft. However, business flying is statistically much safer than the more inclusive group, general aviation. This is so because the equipment used is usually superior to most general aviation aircraft and the pilots are better trained and are more mature and cautious. Companies that insure sophisticated aircraft generally require higher pilot qualifications and training standards than they do for general-purpose flying.

Costs vary widely depending on the type of aircraft used. A single-engine piston-powered aircraft capable of carrying four passengers over ranges of up to 800 miles will cost $450,000 to purchase new and roughly $120 per hour to operate. A twin turboprop capable of carrying five passengers up to 1200 miles would cost $4.5 million new and $700 per hour to operate. Purchasing either of these aircraft on the used market easily could reduce the acquisition cost by half.

Liability exposure is usually no higher than that encountered with any other venture. Insurance policies should name the company or any associated enterprise as an additional insured if the aircraft is privately owned; sufficient liability limits should be purchased to ensure company viability in the event of a serious accident. Again, pilot qualifications and training and aircraft maintenance practices should be better than required under national aviation regulations to ensure safe operations and create the image of concern for corporate liability.

Employee-flown aircraft occasionally may reduce the productivity of the employee if a proper balance is not struck between work and travel. This situation should be monitored carefully, and a full-time professional pilot should be hired when flying interferes with the work of the employee pilot.

These types of operations usually begin as a consequence of a personal motivation to fly. The love of flying is seen as a means to support travel activities. If done with the business or personal travel needs as the principal motivator, these operations make good sense. For companies, they also may lead eventually to upgraded business aviation operations using larger aircraft and professional flight crews.

In-House Flight Department. This is the most common form of on-demand air transportation in the world. In this method, an owned or leased aircraft is flown by full-time professional pilots to support the user's on-demand air transportation needs. The aircraft are based at a conveniently located airport and housed in a rented, leased, or wholly owned hangar that contains office space for flight department personnel and, often, maintenance shops for aviation maintenance technicians. However, operators sometimes opt to have all maintenance services outsourced to a local contract maintenance facility or number of facilities.

Passenger scheduling is done by either a part-time company employee or a personal assistant of the principal user; occasionally, a full-time scheduler/administrator, normally located with the other flight department personnel, may be employed. Company human resources, information technology, accounting, security, and legal personnel support flight department operations; individual users must rely on contractors for these services

This method affords users the highest level of control possible of any method of providing on-demand air transportation and, potentially, the highest-quality transportation. Direct policy and procedural control over scheduling, response time, aircraft utilization, flight operations, maintenance, and expenses should ensure that the operator receives exactly what is desired from this form of transportation. No other provider interposes his or her standards and procedures that may tend to reduce service quality. However, depending on one's own limited number and type of aircraft and personnel, this form may reduce options that may be available via a fractional ownership or charter operation. These other types may be used to supplement one's own aviation resources, when needed. Additionally, interchange and time-share agreements can provide additional aviation assets at little additional cost.

Capital and operational costs associated with an in-house operation are borne by the operator. The aircraft may be either wholly owned or leased, depending on a company's willingness to assume debt and/or carry major assets on its balance sheet or the preference of the individual user.

While users appreciate the total control of their aviation assets afforded by this method, administration and management of the aircraft are borne fully by the user. These details are tracked and accomplished by an aviation department manager who is normally also a pilot or aviation maintenance technician. This person usually reports to the principal, CEO, or other senior manager. Ideally, the flight department becomes an integral support function of the user's overall operation, contributing to its success by providing safe, effective, and efficient on-demand air transportation to its passengers.

Management Company. Under this method of operation, a company or individual contracts with an aircraft management company to provide all necessary elements to operate the aircraft. For a monthly fee (typically $3000 to $7000 per aircraft, depending on size and complexity), the management company provides personnel, training for the personnel, a base of operations, passenger scheduling, and aircraft maintenance, services. Salaries, benefits, fuel, hangar rent, aircraft maintenance, and other operational costs are all collected by the manager and passed through to the owner. This is essentially a turnkey operation, which relieves the aircraft owner of the great majority of the responsibilities of aircraft operation.

The management company often manages aircraft for others and may be able to provide some operational efficiencies through the use of pilots and technicians employed for the other aircraft. This procedure provides a ready pool of trained and qualified individuals, but the same flight crew members may not be available to operate the owner's aircraft on a daily basis, a feature prized by some.

Additionally, management companies often provide air charter services using their client's aircraft. In essence, the client's aircraft is leased to the management/charter company for the purpose of providing charter services; in return, the client whose aircraft is used receives a portion of the charter revenue that can be used to offset some of the fixed operating expenses associated with their aircraft's operation.

The use of a managed aircraft for charter services reduces the owner's scheduling flexibility because charter trips scheduled in advance make the aircraft unavailable to the owner for last-minute trips. In addition, additional aircraft utilization created by the charter trips accelerates the aging process of the aircraft and exposes it to users who may not treat it as kindly as the owner does. Attempting to regain major portions of the fixed expenses associated with aircraft operation may prove difficult unless the charter revenue is substantial. In attempting to increase charter revenues, the aircraft becomes less available to the owner. If this method is chosen, a balance must be struck between availability to the owner and desired revenue levels.

Management companies can provide excellent services to owners not wishing to become involved in the details of operating a flight department. In so doing, however, control over policy, procedure, costs, and desired quality levels is shared with the management company; absolute control over the asset is no longer possible. While many of the technicalities and complexities associated with operating a sophisticated aircraft become the responsibility of the management company, full understanding and appreciation of available options may not be possible. However, the use of management companies has increased in popularity within the past few years, principally as a method for aircraft owners to rapidly enter the ranks of business aircraft owners with little or no knowledge of the subject required.

Joint Ownership. Under this arrangement, two or more entities (individuals or companies) become registered joint owners of an aircraft. One of the owners employs and furnishes the flight crew, and each of the owners pays a share of the charge specified in an agreement. Administrative, financial, and operating details usually are assumed by the owner employing the aviation personnel. Otherwise, this type of operation is quite similar to the more traditional in-house flight department. The principal advantage is having others share the fixed costs of the aircraft, which, depending on a number of factors, may comprise one-third of the total aircraft expenses.

This method works well when the owners, normally two, use the aircraft infrequently and at times that complement one another. For instance, a company may use the aircraft mainly during the week for business trips, and the coowner, who uses the aircraft for personal trips, may use the aircraft primarily on the weekends. Scheduling conflicts may be the main problem area for these arrangements, although many partners use this method with little conflict.

A detailed joint-operating agreement is an essential part of a successful joint-ownership operation. Scheduling priorities and conflict-resolution methods should be worked out and tested before the final agreement is signed. Successful joint-ownership operations liken their arrangement to the give and take found in a good marriage—an appreciation of the other's needs is the key.

The advantages and disadvantages of taxes, depreciation, and liability are shared by the partners. Control over all aspects is shared by the owners, somewhat diluting the ability of any partner to dictate all elements of the operation. Yet the shared-ownership aspect usually provides motivation to create and maintain a high-quality flight operation.

Interchange. This in an arrangement, available principally in the United States, whereby an owned aircraft is leased to another entity in exchange for equal time in that entity's aircraft when needed. No charge or fee is made for this service, except that a charge may be made not to exceed the difference between the cost of owning, operating, and maintaining the two aircraft. This method requires that each party own their aircraft and exchange their aircraft on an hour-for-hour basis.

This arrangement is often used to advantage by two companies based at the same airport and using similar aircraft. An interchange agreement will allow one company to use the other's aircraft as a backup when its aircraft is unavailable due to an existing trip or maintenance. The two operators "borrow" one another's aircraft when needed, and if there are cost differences between the aircraft, the companies settle up on a periodic basis. Interchange provides the option of infrequently using another's aircraft without the need for a more formal and binding joint-ownership agreement.

Individuals and companies also use this method to provide a different type of aircraft when needed. For instance, an individual operating a twin-engine turboprop strikes an agreement with a company at the same airport that operates a medium-sized turbojet aircraft. The parties then have the option to use the turboprop for short trips and the turbojet for longer ones interchangeably. At the end of the quarter or year, the individual operating the turboprop compensates the company (if required) for the differential costs associated with operating the more expensive turbojet.

Again, a detailed interchange agreement must be signed by the parties to protect them and to ensure that they have a full understanding of one another's obligations and privileges. Tax and liability issues must be addressed specifically. Perhaps most important is an understanding that specifically provides scheduling, cancellation, and conflict-resolution procedures.

Time Sharing.   A U.S. time-sharing agreement means an arrangement whereby a person or company leases its airplane with flight crew to another person, to whom direct operating expenses of the aircraft may be charged. These expenses include

- Fuel, oil, lubricants, and other additives
- Travel expenses of the crew, including food, lodging, and ground transportation
- Hangar and tie-down costs away from the aircraft's base of operation
- Insurance obtained for the specific flight
- Landing fees, airport taxes, and similar assessments
- Customs, foreign permit, and similar fees directly related to the flight
- In-flight food and beverages
- Passenger ground transportation
- Flight planning and weather contract services
- An additional charge equal to 100 percent of the fuel and oil used

Since this arrangement does not compensate the owner for a major portion of the aircraft operating costs, specifically its fixed expenses, such an arrangement is used in only limited cases. Among such cases are agreements to provide company executives with personal use of the company aircraft or the occasional use by friends of the owner of an individually owned aircraft. These uses traditionally constitute a minor portion of the total operation of the aircraft because the owner wishes to use the aircraft for normal travel purposes. Tax and liability considerations must be addressed when entering into a time-share agreement.

Time share, interchange, and joint ownership all tread a fine line with regard to other Federal Aviation Administration (FAA) and Internal Revenue Service (IRS) regulations in the United States regarding private and common carriage; similar restrictions exist in other countries where these options are available. *Common carriage* means that an operator holds itself out to provide transportation of persons or property from place to place for compensation—airlines and charter operators provide common carriage. *Private carriage* differs from common carriage in that the private operator does not *hold itself out* (advertise, market, etc.) as a provider of air transportation to the general public.

Aircraft Charter.   Chartering an aircraft is just about as easy as calling for a limousine— find a charter company in the Yellow Pages, tell them where you want to go and when, complete a few formalities such as a credit check, show up at the appointed time, and you are on your way. This may be the easiest and least expensive means of obtaining on-demand air transportation, especially in the short term. Moreover, using a number of charter providers and a variety of aircraft will provide you with a good sampling of what the market has to offer in terms of aircraft types. This is the easy, low-risk way to enter the air transportation business. Yet the critical nature of providing on-demand air transportation services for compensation should make one more discriminating about the operator selected.

In virtually every country, national regulatory authorities certify and oversee air charter or air taxi operators in an effort to protect the traveling public. The United States will be used as an example to relate what is required of these operators.

Air taxi operators offer on-demand air transportation services to the public and by law must be certified by the FAA by meeting stringent operational, maintenance, and safety rules. In addition, pilots must be specifically qualified in both the type of aircraft to be flown and the type of operation.

The regulations for air taxis provide for a high level of safety and control. They address flight operations, maintenance requirements, and crew member training and testing. They also address crew rest and physical examinations and mandate a drug testing program. The FAA closely monitors air taxi operators to make sure that they conform to the established standards of performance. Your safety depends on flying with a legally certified air taxi operator.

Yet, even with federal oversight of air taxi operators, there are wide variations in the levels of service provided. With more than 3500 air taxi operators available in North America alone, it may be seen that checking their background and reputation makes good sense to find the best available. Also, realize that the FAA regulations covering air taxi operators specify certain minimum operational standards that do not relate to the level of service provided.

Charter Aircraft Rates (per Hour)

Single-engine piston, 3 to 4 passengers	$300
Twin-engine piston, 5 passengers	500
Twin-engine turboprop, 7 passengers	1000
Twin-engine turbojet, 7 passengers	1800
Twin-engine turbojet, 10 passengers	4000
Intercontinental turbojet, 14 passengers	7000
Single-engine turbine helicopter, 4 passengers	700
Twin-engine turbine helicopter, 7 passengers	2500

(North America, late 2002.)

Asking a few basic questions of the air taxi operator is all that is needed to be certain that you are dealing with an FAA-certificated air carrier (this is the official name for an air taxi operator) and that the operator is authorized to provide the type and kind of service you require (see Chap. 3 for methods).

Available charter aircraft range from small single-engine piston-powered models up through large intercontinental airline-type airplanes. Each charter aircraft has unique speed, range, payload, and comfort features that should be evaluated carefully prior to selecting an aircraft type and charter operator. Each of the features mentioned has an associated cost, some modest and some not so modest; the careful consumer will consider all desired aspects of the prospective air transportation prior to choosing. In addition, it pays to shop around for these services. Considerable savings can be realized by a bit of extra inquiry and planning.

Note that all hourly charter fees are determined by block time, which includes taxi time (taxi time averages 12 minutes per leg flown). If the aircraft must be sent to your location from another airport, you pay for the amount of flight time required to position it both before and after your flight.

Most charters are subject to a 2-hour daily minimum charge; time spent waiting for passengers may be subject to charges of up to $100 per hour. If you wish the aircraft and crew to remain overnight, a fee of approximately $700 will be charged. Federal excise taxes of 7.5 percent and domestic segment fees of $3 per leg are applicable to most flights. Extraordinary catering, airport use fees (landing/parking), and international customs fees normally are billed at the operator's cost.

Is charter a good choice to provide you with on-demand air transportation services? If your travel needs do not exceed 100 to 150 hours per year of block time and you have found a good, reliable provider, then air charter may be right for you. However, getting the same aircraft or flight crew from trip to trip may be difficult, unless you have a good relationship with the provider. And consistently high-quality service may suffer due to the inability to get the same aircraft and flight crew for every trip. Yet most charter operators strive to provide these service features as a matter of good business practice.

Fractional Ownership.   Fractional ownership is a relatively new concept in the world of on-demand air transportation. It was first introduced in 1986 by Executive Jets Aviation and named *NetJets*. The founder recognized that there was a portion of the population whose aviation needs were not being met through chartering or full aircraft ownership. Charter users wanted their own aircraft that they could count on when they wanted it, yet some could not justify the full purchase price of an aircraft; the compromise was fractional ownership.

Fractional ownership offers the option, instead of buying an entire business aircraft, to purchase shares of one. As little as one-sixteenth of an aircraft can be purchased, which will provide around 50 flight hours of usage per year, or as much as one-half of an aircraft can be purchased, depending on how many hours are needed. The most common amounts purchased usually are one-eighth and one-fourth.

Fractional owners pay a fractional percentage of the purchase price for an aircraft commensurate with the amount of hours they want available per year; e.g., one-eighth share receives 100 occupied hours, one-fourth share receives 200 hours, etc. Most fractional providers offer a variety of aircraft to choose from, ranging from small turboprops to large intercontinental turbojets. Hourly and monthly fees are charged over the period of the contract, normally 5 years.

Fractional owners are guaranteed that their aircraft or another aircraft of the same model will be constantly available to them with as little as 4 hours' advance notice. The fractional provider assumes responsibility for scheduling, staffing, flight planning, weather, communications, maintenance, catering, and insurance. At the end of the initial contract, the owner's fractional share will be purchased by the provider at "fair market value," or the contract may be renewed or upgraded.

Fractional Ownership

The pros:

- Lower purchase price for the aircraft
- Depreciation and tax benefits of ownership (limited to the fraction purchased)
- All costs stated up-front
- No waiting or positioning fees
- Guaranteed rapid response time—normally 4 to 8 hours
- Consistent service standards
- Ability to trade up or down for other aircraft types

The cons:

- High hourly costs when compared with charter
- Rapidly escalating hourly fees after fractional share hours are used
- Built-in positioning fees—normally two-tenths of an hour for each flight hour
- Schedule "blackout dates"
- Rarely ride in the same aircraft or use the same flight crew
- Aircraft maintenance preformed by a variety of contractors
- Penalties apply for early termination of contract
- Accelerated reduction in aircraft value due to heavy use

The last point in the sidebar requires some explanation: A wholly owned corporate aircraft normally is used at a rate of 450 hours per year. A fractional aircraft accumulates 1200 to 1500 hours per year, thereby reducing the book value of the aircraft at an accelerated rate.

The subject of liability remains a vexing problem for fractional owners. Although an aircraft may be insured for a single-limit liability of $200 million, a one-sixteenth owner may only be insured for $12.5 million. Depending on the development of case law associated with fractional ownership, all owners of a particular aircraft may be held liable for an accident, even though those owners were not on board at the time of the accident.

Each fractional share sold requires signing up to five separate contracts, which contain the purchase and management contracts, interchange and resale agreements, and an acknowledgment of operational control obligations of the owner. This last issue is important because under the law the fractional owners incur certain responsibilities and obligations regarding the operation of an aircraft over which they have control. These include an obligation to comply with applicable aviation regulations and the exposure to significant liability concerns.

Is fractional ownership right for your company? Do you plan to fly between 100 and 300 occupied hours per year? Is the guaranteed availability attractive? Is part ownership a desirable feature in your corporate financial plan? If you can answer to these questions, take a close look at a program that has captured the interest of more than 5000 companies and individuals worldwide (Table 2.6).

TABLE 2.6 Typical Fractional Ownership Costs (Quarter Share, 200 hours per year)

Aircraft	Purchase	Annual Fee	Hourly fee
Twin turboprop	$1.1 mil	$180,000	$ 900
Small turbojet	1.8 mil	250,000	1500
Medium turbojet	3.5 mil	320,000	2000
Large turbojet	8 mil	550,000	3300

Multiple Methods. Just as one type of aircraft or method of providing on-demand air transportation service does not fit the needs of all users, one method or type of aircraft may not fit the total needs either. Having a single small turbojet may satisfy the majority of the needs but may not be suited for long-range flights, ones transporting more than seven passengers, or those operating into short runways. These specialized trips may be handled by charter, interchange, or fractional ownership methods.

Provisions should be built into an on-demand air transportation plan to provide for the full range of known needs. Too often users attempt to solve all their on-demand air transportation needs with a single aircraft or aircraft type, which is normally not possible, given the wide range of transportation needs. The flight department and those setting transportation policy must be trained to seek solutions for their transportation requirements from a range of providers, not just their own flight department.

Charter may be used as a backup for multiple trips in a single day, unscheduled maintenance on the owner's aircraft, or supplemental lift for trips in which the number of passengers exceeds available seats. A small fractional ownership share may solve the occasional long-range trip requirement or be used for multiple trips in a single day. An interchange agreement with another flight department based at your airport may solve all the extra requirements already mentioned.

International Operations

A growing publishing company gradually began acquiring European periodicals and book publishing houses. To support these operations, company executives and managers used readily available international flights between New York and London, where the majority of the business was located. However, as the European interests grew, companies in Frankfurt, Madrid, and Warsaw were purchased, making additional intra-European flights necessary. These routes often were not served by readily available flights that met the schedules of the headquarters teams. An aircraft capable of flying to Europe and onward to other locations on the continent appeared to be an attractive alternative.

Since the company already used two Citations for domestic operations, management was aware of the advantages accruing to the use of business aircraft. While the purchase of an aircraft capable of regular transoceanic flights was deemed to be too expensive, further investigation revealed that a quarter-share of a Gulfstream IV would provide the limited access the company wanted to European markets at a more reasonable price. The ocean-spanning aircraft permits enroute conferences and shaves approximately a day off the traditional European trip.

RUNNING THE NUMBERS

Each aircraft type and transportation delivery method comes with a cost. Each user has a philosophy regarding the desirability of carrying capital assets on the balance sheet, asset control, debt-equity ratios, and operating cost controls. Making a match between these sets of features often yields more than one option; choosing an option may be considered an artform rather than a cold financial decision. Achieving closure on an option requires knowledge of the market and an ability to evaluate the financial consequences of the options. Yet evaluating on-demand air transportation methods based on financial considerations alone is insufficient to make an informed decision.

Even though the air transportation analysis may have determined that a medium-sized turboprop or small turbojet will be the ideal candidate, the principal's desire for a midsized turbojet obviously deserves consideration. After all, it is he or she who will be riding in the aircraft most of the time, plus realizing that the aircraft has many uses and applications. Sometimes the principal's instincts are good and contain a vision of what will come instead of what is happening at the moment. This section will look at the costs associated with the several types of air transportation discussed earlier.

Cost Components

As with any enterprise, the associated costs include both capital and operational expenditures. Capital costs are associated with both the initial purchase of an asset and subsequent upgrades or any improvements that will extend its useful life or increase its value.

Purchase versus Lease. Capital expenditures are only incurred if an aircraft is actually purchased for an in-house flight department, managed operation, or fractional ownership. However, the aircraft need not be purchased outright; leasing is also a possibility for aircraft acquisition. The decision to lease or purchase traditionally is based on a core financial philosophy and willingness to carry significant amounts of debt.

Users not familiar with high-end aircraft often are surprised to learn of the high residual values associated with these assets (Table 2.7). Because of these high residual values, the net cost of either ownership or leasing is actually less than the cost normally associated with large capital assets. The resulting differential between tax and book depreciation can prove useful in budgeting as well. In good economic times, some popular aircraft actually appreciate in value over the first 10 years of ownership.

Leasing the aircraft protects cash reserves and keeps the asset off the balance sheet. Aircraft leases take advantage of a user's ready cash flow without adversely affecting its debt-equity ratio. Lease amounts are based on the difference between the asking price and residual value;

TABLE 2.7 Residual Values of Typical New Aircraft (%)

	Length of Ownership (Years)		
	5	10	20
Turbojet	85	70	50
Turboprop	70	60	40
Piston	65	55	45
Helicopter	70	50	35

high residual values for popular aircraft tend to reduce the overall cost of a lease. Leases may be attractive for companies unable to take advantage of accelerated tax depreciation advantages. The decision to lease or buy is extended by the concept of the *synthetic lease*. This method of financing permits a user to receive many of the benefits of ownership while keeping any associated financing costs off the balance sheet, thus reducing apparent debt. The synthetic lease allows an operator to treat lease payments as an operating expense and to take the tax advantages associated with depreciation.

As with any major capital expense, the decision to purchase an aircraft must take into account the value of money used in the purchase. If the aircraft is purchased for cash, the net present value involved must be computed; if the aircraft is financed under a loan, the interest charged also must be accounted for. In either case, the cost of ownership must account for these money costs, effectively increasing ownership costs over time.

The purchase of a fractional share of an aircraft is usually arranged through the fractional provider and financing arranged, if necessary. Aircraft brokers and manufacturer's sales personnel will present a number of purchase options designed to fit an operator's financial condition and philosophy.

Operating Costs.   Operational costs are pure expenses and are divided into fixed or indirect and variable or direct expenses. Fixed costs accrue to the aircraft whether it flies or not; variable costs are incurred only when it flies. The expenses shown in Table 2.8 are typical for

TABLE 2.8   Sample Annual Aircraft Operating Costs

			Flight Hours per Year		
		Cost Item	250	450	600
Variable/direct costs					
Fuel (price × gph)	($2.037 × 270)	$550	137,500	247,500	330,000
Maintenance					
Labor (hrs/flt hr × rate)	(1.6 × $70)	$112	28,000	50,400	67,200
Parts		$99	24,750	44,550	59,400
Engine reserves					
Resortation allowance		$210	52,500	94,500	126,000
APU/reverser overhaul		$27	6,750	12,150	16,200
Landing/handling fees		$14	3,500	6,300	8,400
Crew expenses		$135	33,750	60,750	81,000
Catering/supplies		$40	10,000	18,000	24,000
Total variable costs		$1,187	$296,750	$534,150	$712,200
Fixed/Indirect Costs					
Crew salaries/benefits (2)		$175,000	175,000	175,000	175,000
Hangar		$5,500	5500	5500	5500
Aircraft Insurance		$43,000	43000	43000	43000
Training		$33,000	33000	33000	33000
Flight planning/weather		$3,500	3500	3500	3500
Flight publications/data		$4,500	4500	4500	4500
Other fixed					
Total fixed costs		$264,500	264,500	264,500	264,500
Total costs			$561,250	$798,650	$976,700
Total cost per hour			$2,245	$1,775	$1,628
(Per hour cost savings)				−21%	−27%

a single small turbojet aircraft operation. Note the effect of increased flight hours on cost per hour; this is due to the effect of spreading the fixed costs over a greater operating period.

Aircraft maintenance consists of both scheduled and unscheduled types. Scheduled maintenance is required by regulatory authorities to ensure that the aircraft remains airworthy; it occurs at regular intervals, based on hours flown, engine start cycles, and elapsed time. Unscheduled maintenance occurs when a discrepancy with the aircraft, its engines, or its accessories is discovered during normal operations or an inspection. Both types comprise the total maintenance and parts costs shown in the table. New aircraft typically come with a 5-year warranty for parts and some labor costs; this substantially reduces these costs for a new aircraft.

Engine reserves refer to the advisability to accrue funds, normally on an hourly basis, to perform required engine, auxiliary power unit (APU), and thrust-reverser overhauls. Alternatively, engine operating insurance and overhaul services will provide most required and unscheduled engine maintenance for a set hourly fee.

Landing and handling fees are charged by airports and service facilities to accommodate the aircraft as it operates at those facilities. Crew expenses are primarily for living expenses while on a trip and for overnight stays.

Under fixed expenses, the largest item is that associated with crew compensation; note that benefits are included in the item. This compensation will vary considerably depending on the size of aircraft, cost of living for the operating base, experience of the pilots, and longevity with the company.

Hangar costs are for either maintenance on an owned structure or rent for a leased facility. Utilities and associated costs usually are included in this amount.

Insurance covers personal and property liability associated with the operation of the aircraft and the value of the aircraft itself (hull value). Rates vary depending on use of the aircraft, nature of the operation, and hours flown. Financed and leased aircraft normally incur provisions for minimum coverage amounts.

Training expenses are for just flight crewmembers in this case, who normally undergo recurrent simulator training twice annually. If aviation maintenance technicians and other support personnel are included in the flight department, their training costs will be shown here.

Flight planning, weather services, and required navigational reference publications/data-bases are both customary and necessary expenses for such an operation.

More detailed charts of accounts are employed by some companies to better understand the expenses of a flight department. A more complete chart of accounts may be found in the *NBAA Management Guide.*

Management Fees. Aircraft management and fractional ownership companies charge a monthly management fee to cover their costs. This fee should be negotiated with management companies to obtain the best possible price. However, the ability of the management company to provide fuel, maintenance, and other discounts should figure prominently into the overall costs of a managed operation. The management fee charged by fractional providers is not normally negotiable.

Defining the duties of the management company should be a detailed part of the management contract. Virtually every aspect of the aircraft operation and the expenses associated with those functions should be included in the management fee. Oversight and management of the entire operation, scheduling, operations, maintenance, administration, and finances should all be performed for the owner and accounted for in detail (see Chap. 3 for more detail).

Evaluating the Options

Many people make the mistake of looking at just a combination of the purchase price of an aircraft and its first-year operating costs. Unfortunately, this may provide a skewed view of the total cost of owning/leasing an aircraft. Table 2.9 shows the costs of aircraft ownership over a 5-year period. The cost of capital and depreciation expenses figure prominently into the overall cost of ownership, modifying the total-cost picture significantly. The purchase of a new versus a used aircraft will alter the cost picture as well. New aircraft come with a comprehensive warranty, normally covering most parts and labor costs for the first 5 years of ownership. However, this is offset by the high depreciation cost incurred during the first few years of asset ownership. Conversely, purchasing a used aircraft will increase maintenance costs while avoiding high depreciation rates. *A word of caution:* While corporate aircraft hold their value well and, if well maintained, will remain serviceable for 30 to 35 years, aircraft more than 20 years old may incur higher maintenance costs while sometimes yielding lower reliability rates. A good broker/salesperson should be able to lay out the tradeoffs associated with the purchase of a new versus a used aircraft. However, once the tradeoffs are understood, a life-cycle cost analysis always should be performed to the anticipated holding period of the aircraft.

TABLE 2.9 Sample Costs of Aircraft Ownership

	In-House Flight Dept.	Managed Aircraft	Joint Ownership	Fractional Ownership*	Charter[†]
Single-Year Cost of Ownership, No Depreciation					
Hours flown	400	400	400	400	400
Direct costs/hour	$1,000	$1,000	$1,000	$1,500	None
Fixed costs/each	$300,000	$300,000	$150,000	None	None
Management Fee/month	None	$4,500	None	$40,000	None
Charter Rate/per hour	None	None	None	None	$2,000
Cost/year[‡]	$700,000	$754,000	$550,000	$1,125,000	$860,000
Cost/hour	$1,750	$1,885	$1,375	$2,813	$2,150
Cost per nautical mile	$4.28	$4.61	$3.36	$6.88	$5.26
Five-Year Cost of Ownership, with Depreciation					
Purchase price	$7,500,000	$7,500,000	$3,750,000	$3,750,000	
Operating expenses	($3,500,000)	($3,770,000)	($2,750,000)	($5,625,000)	($4,300,000)
Depreciation[§]	($7,068,000)	($7,068,000)	($3,534,000)	($3,534,000)	
Operating (loss)	($10,568,000)	($10,838,000)	($6,284,000)	($9,159,000)	($4,300,000)
Loan interest rate	8%	8%	8%	8%	
Interest expense	($1,624,377)	($1,624,377)	($812,189)	($812,189)	
Residual resale %	90%	90%	85%	80%	
Sale proceeds	$6,750,000	$6,750,000	$3,187,500	$3,000,000	
Brokering fee	1%	1%	1%	7%	
Brokering cost	($67,500)	($67,500)	($31,875)	($210,000)	
Taxable gain	$6,250,500	$6,250,500	$2,939,625	$2,574,000	
Before tax (loss)	($5,941,877)	($6,211,877)	($4,156,564)	($7,397,189)	($4,300,000)
Income tax bracket	40%	40%	40%	40%	40%
Income tax benefit	$2,376,751	$2,484,751	$1,662,625	$2,958,875	$1,720,000
Net expense	($3,565,126)	($3,727,126)	($2,493,938)	($4,438,313)	($2,580,000)

*One-half share.
[†]No positioning fees included.
[‡]Includes 7.5 percent FET for fractional/charter.
[§]Five year MACRS.

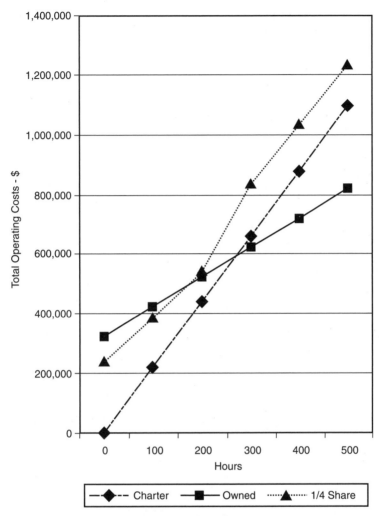

FIGURE 2.4   Sample operational costs versus hours flown.

Note in Fig. 2.4 that as aircraft use increases, the relative advantages of one type of on-demand air transportation give way to another. For instance, in this example, aircraft charter provides the least expensive form of transportation up to about 250 hours of use based on fixed and variable costs. Fractional ownership provides lower total operating costs compared with full ownership for the first 150 hours. Joint ownership and managed operations will shift this equation one way or another based on the lower or higher fixed costs involved. Again, the operating costs form just one dimension of a more complex calculus involved in evaluating the proper type of services to obtain; control over those services and life-cycle costs also figure prominently into the decision process. A supplementary value of this figure is that it shows that the more an aircraft is used, the lower will be the unit operating costs.

TABLE 2.10   On-Demand Air Transportation Comparisons

	In-house Flight Department	Aircraft Management Company
Service quality	• Highest level of control/service possible • Immediate availability likely • If aircraft not available, may use charter, airlines, time share, or interchange • Best possible confidentiality/privacy	• Potentially excellent; may be customized • Immediate availability likely • If aircraft not available, may use charter, airlines, time share, or interchange
Aircraft administration	• Owner maintains total control over and manages aircraft operations • Personnel are owner's employees	• Owner maintains control over but delegates management of aircraft operations • Personnel are management company employees
Crew quality	• Consistent; owner-controlled • Owner controls training of crew and maintenance personnel	• Consistent, owner input, crews may be assignable to other activities • Owner delegates control of pilot and mechanic training
Security	• Dictated and controlled by company policy	• Subject to management company interpretation of company policy
Operating costs	• Variable; utilization-dependent lowest cost of operation at reasonable utilization levels • Subject to positioning expense	• Variable; utilization-dependent • Annual costs maybe higher than an in-house flight department (due to management fee) • Subject to positioning expense
Cost offsets	• Charter option may offset some costs	• Charter option may offset some costs • Possible fuel & crew training discounts
Liability	• Completely liable	• Liability shared with management company
Capital commitment	• Full negotiated purchase price	• Full purchase negotiated price
Tax consequences	• No commercial federal excise tax applicable • Noncommercial fuel tax applies • Maximum depreciation benefit	• No commercial federal excise tax • Noncommercial fuel tax applies • Maximum depreciation benefit
Aircraft acquisition and disposition	• Lease, purchase or sale of any aircraft at negotiated price • Full authority of aircraft make/model, interior and exterior selection	• Lease, purchase or sale of any aircraft at negotiated price • Full authority of aircraft make/model, interior and exterior selection

Note: Concept Courtesy of NBAA.

Joint Ownership	Fractional Ownership	Charter
• Same as in-house department • Availability requires coordination and planning • If aircraft not available, may use charter, timeshare, or interchange	• Service levels may vary • Aircraft availability guaranteed • Advanced notice required (4–8 hours, blackout dates imposed) • Charter aircraft may be substituted	• Service levels may vary • Possible inconsistent service vendor to vendor • Availability depends on market demand; no guarantee
• Owners maintain control and manage operations • Personnel on owner's payroll	• Owners maintain control, but delegate aircraft operations management • Provider supplies people	• None, not applicable • Provider supplies personnel
• Consistent, owner-controlled • Owners control training of crew and maintenance personnel	• Crew changes likely, specific, crew possible • Owners delegate control of pilot and mechanic training	• Crew changes likely, rotating from pool • No control of pilot or mechanic training
• Dictated and controlled by company policy	• Security program in place, standardized	• Federally required security program in place
• Variable; utilization-dependent • Subject to positioning expense	• Fixed fee plus hourly charges • Higher hourly charges when exceeding yearly allotment	• Uniform hourly charges • Misc. charges; catering, landing, etc. • Aircraft positioning expenses charged
• Charter option may offset some costs	• None	• None
• Liability shared with co-owner	• Provider/co-owners share liability	• Charter provider completely liable
• Owners share of purchase price	• Fractional share of purchase price	• None
• Shared tax liabilities/benefits • No federal excise tax • Fuel tax applies • Owners share depreciation benefit	• Shared tax liabilities/benefits • Federal excise tax on direct operating costs • Owners share depreciation	• Federal excise taxes imposed on charter rate • No depreciation tax benefit available as no aircraft are owned
• Shared lease, purchase or sale of any aircraft at negotiated price • Can jointly select aircraft make/model, interior and exterior	• Shared purchase/sale • No aircraft customization • Remarketing fee charged for aircraft disposition • Early withdrawal penalties	• None, no ownership

Decision Factors

Since a variety of factors, both quantifiable and unquantifiable, are used in making the decision regarding the acquisition of an aircraft, it makes sense to set out some decision-making criteria. The following is a list of factors:

- Air transportation needs

  - Normal trip load factor
  - Average/maximum trip/leg length
  - Trip frequency
  - Multiple trips in a single day
  - Payload versus range tradeoff
  - Minimum airport size anticipated in normal operations
  - Cabin size and amenities

- Debt structure and sensitivity to debt

- Level of control desired over operations

- Anticipated aircraft retention period

- Top-level management preferences/commitment

The acquisition of an aircraft should not be taken lightly because entering most types of on-demand air transportation agreements requires long-term financial and management commitment. Often companies (especially entrepreneurial companies) jump at aircraft ownership more on whim than sound judgment. The elation associated with a few good contracts and two good financial quarters leads many to believe that this performance will continue forever. The urge to commit to the purchase or lease of a whole or fractional aircraft is often irresistible, given the obvious advantages of this form of transportation. The rush of the two good quarters can rapidly give way to two bad quarters, cooling one's enthusiasm for the significant expense and commitment associated with the corporate aircraft.

One should first carefully evaluate transportation needs and base the correct solution on a long-term commitment. Many use charters for an extensive period to more fully understand the operational features of on-demand air transportation while exploring ownership options with a variety of sources. These sources must include a representative sample of similar operators who have used their form of transportation for a number of years. It is these testimonials that provide the real insights into the pluses and minuses associated with a particular form of ownership, management, and aircraft type; research with peer users is essential. Table 2.10 summarizes the features of the principal forms of on-demand air transportation.

I was the one who, for many years, said, "No, we're not going to get a jet," but it's really paid off—it's doubled our productivity.

—CORPORATE CFO

Flying has torn apart the relationship of space and time; it uses our old clock, but with new yardsticks.

—CHARLES LINDBERGH

CHAPTER 3
GETTING STARTED

FIRST THINGS

Once a decision has been made to take advantage of on-demand air transportation methods, it is essential to understand one's motives for this in some detail. Doing so will complete the analysis for the chosen method and communicate guidelines for its use to the entire organization.

Failure to set the scene will give rise to confusion among passengers, managers, support personnel, and the flight services provider. However, a surprising number of companies and individuals put their multimillion-dollar asset in place and literally just begin flying trips for all comers or a select, yet undefined portion of the comers. Doing so creates anxiety, ill will, and discontent among all who have to deal with the aircraft. Even if the intent is to use the aircraft for the transportation needs of just principals or top management, defining who those individuals are should be the first step.

The easiest method of setting the scene is to develop an aircraft use policy for the company. (Note that this chapter discusses just the basic elements of getting a flight department up and running; administrative and operational details and more comprehensive issues of flight department operations are covered in subsequent chapters.)

Aircraft Use Policy

The use policy should be a simple, relatively short document that provides the central repository for

- How the aircraft is to be used
- Who can use it
- How the aircraft is scheduled
- Special cases
- Operating restrictions

The document serves as an essential tool to communicate the basic operating rules for the entire company, whether the reader is the owner, chairperson, or the accounts receivable clerk.

> *We operate our aircraft and use charter air transportation as a management tool in improving efficiency and effectiveness in the marketplace. The rationale for use of on-demand air transportation must be consistent with the overall management policies and practices of the corporation.*
>
> —CORPORATE CEO

The Purpose. Without stating the basic purpose for the company's chosen method of on-demand air transportation, this essential business tool may be easily mistaken for a high-level perquisite or executive toy. While it also may be a perquisite for some company employees, its basic mission is hopefully more utilitarian. Therefore, a succinct and credible purpose must be listed at the beginning of the policy document.

A use statement may not seem important for an individual user, but creating one will serve to continuously remind you of why you purchased the aircraft in the first place. Not doing so may give rise to indiscriminate use or underuse of this valuable asset.

The preceding quote is a good example of such a statement. However, both more lengthy and more terse examples are available. Perhaps one of the most pithy is the following one from a chief executive officer (CEO) who was obviously a true believer: "The company airplane helps us beat the competition—use it wisely."

Ace Widget operates a Cessna Citation aircraft to provide air transportation services for its employees and customers. This aircraft is capable of carrying up to seven passengers for distances of up to 1200 statute miles. Certain other restrictions such as minimum runway length and maximum weight apply to the aircraft. Additional on-demand air transportation is available via aircraft charter.

Some basic operating characteristics or operational limitations of the aircraft should be listed to create the proper expectations among passengers. The preceding example may be a bit elementary. For instance, a typical Citation cannot always carry seven passengers and their baggage for a full 1200 miles if the runway used for takeoff is short, significant headwinds prevail, or the weather at the destination is such that a alternate airport with better weather is necessary. Yet it is impossible to detail all operational limitations in such a brief policy document. Some operators provide examples of typical missions that demonstrate some of the more significant limitations encountered.

Note in the preceding quotation that aircraft charter is listed as an option. Doing so will create the expectation that use of this method of transportation is an option when the company aircraft is not available or incapable of accomplishing the assigned mission. However, it also should be stated that the user must pay the bill for the charter services and that such arrangements must be made through a central point within the company, normally the flight department itself. This latter point is necessary to ensure that only high-quality, safe, and economical charter services are used.

Individuals occupying the following positions within Ace Widget may authorize the use of on-demand air transportation:

Chairman	*Strategic planning*
Chief executive officer	*Corporate counsel*
Chief financial officer	*Administration*
Group presidents	*Treasurer*
Government affairs	*Marketing*

These individuals may authorize on-demand air transportation for use of their direct reports and other activities directly related to essential business purposes, when required.

Eligible Users. While it may be that only the top three or four people in the company or family group are eligible to use the company aircraft, a wider range of personnel traditionally is authorized for use. In the preceding quotation, specific individuals are not named as being eligible; rather, named positions are shown as being authorized to schedule the aircraft. This leaves the decision of who may use the aircraft up to them, based on circumstances, providing greater flexibility and utility.

Some companies choose to list specific employees and/or divisions within the company as being eligible to use the aircraft. This method leaves little doubt as to who may schedule the aircraft; unfortunately, it does not allow for contingencies or unusual situations that may occur. Many different methods of designating who may use an aircraft are employed by companies; the important issue is that all concerned know what the rules are.

Although not specifically mentioned in the preceding example, many companies use their aircraft for transporting customers and potential customers. This can be a powerful marketing and sales tool to bring customers to your location to view new products and processes or just to discuss proposed or ongoing business. Sending the company airplane to pick up customers sends a strong message—that they and their business are important enough to warrant the use of the company's "magic carpet."

Those authorized to use on-demand air transportation will supply the following information via e-mail/fax to the Aircraft Coordinator as far as possible in advance of the requested use date:

- *Dates desired*
- *Business purpose(s)*
- *Type of aircraft desired*
- *Detailed itinerary, including specific times and locations*
- *Passenger manifest, including applicable cost centers*
- *Special requirements*
- *Ground transportation required*
- *Catering requests*

Travelers will make their own lodging arrangements.

Scheduling. Specific details regarding a proposed flight must be obtained from the passenger in order to ensure that the flight is planned correctly. The list shown above is a good start; however, some additional specificity is needed. For instance, although the term specific location is used, passengers or their assistants may not realize that several airports in a locale and locations on those airports may be available. The more information available about the exact business destination desired, available ground transportation, and time of day, the more the trip will be satisfactory for the passenger.

Type and location of ground transportation designated to meet an arriving flight constitute another example of details critical to the success of a trip. While the principal portion of the trip involves only the aircraft, the passenger sees the process as a seamless event beginning at his or her office or home and ending at the desired destination, either a hotel or business address. Therefore, scheduling ground transportation in conjunction with the flight is quite important to the success of the entire trip.

The preceding examples demonstrate the need for an experienced individual to act as the aircraft scheduler/coordinator. The more information this individual has about the flight operation, aircraft operating characteristics, passenger preferences, and desired destinations, the greater are the chances for a successful travel experience. Many single-aircraft in-house flight departments use a senior executive's secretary or administrative assistant to fulfill this task, often to good advantage. Yet this individual must be able to devote sufficient time to the process to ensure the success of a trip. Since trips seldom are flown as initially scheduled, the ability of the scheduler to follow-up on and track scheduled trips is essential. A dedicated scheduler/flight coordinator working for the company flight department is probably the best form of scheduling control available for users, regardless of the size of the flight operation.

Charges for the Citation will be computed at the direct operating cost for the aircraft, currently $900 per flight hour. Charter charges will be actual costs billed by the charter company.

Chargebacks

For the uninitiated, a corporate aircraft *chargeback* is an internal charge levied on the user of the corporate aircraft. In essence, it is an attempt to recover all or a part of the cost of air transportation services from a corporate user. Chargeback income usually is deposited into an overhead account designed to partially fund the aircraft's operation. Beyond this simple definition, there are literally hundreds of ways to apply this charge.

On the surface, the concept appears to be just another internal accounting exercise, shifting money from one pot to another. Yet the manner and rate with which the chargeback is applied may have a direct effect on the health and well-being of the flight department. More important, chargeback rates communicate a sense of *perceived value* of on-demand air transportation to the beneficiaries of the service.

Charge or Not?   If there is no internal charge for use of the aircraft and the aircraft is readily available, there is a risk that users may not appreciate the value of the service they receive— "If it's free, it can't be worth much." Further, allocation of the aircraft must be established by an organizational policy or some other prioritization scheme because "market" price is not used—a process fraught with the possibility of abuse and misallocation. Happily, the risk involved in not charging internally for an aircraft appears slight because fully one-half of National Business Aviation Association (NBAA) members impose no chargeback fee.[1]

Company employees are accustomed to being charged for transportation, computer services, and in the case of centrally allocated companies, every support service used: human resources, cleaning, mechanical repairs, and maintenance of office plants. Why not the aircraft they use?

Those companies choosing not to levy chargebacks have made the conscious decision that the value of offering on-demand air transportation services to selected employees and customers justifies absorbing the cost of the service in a corporate overhead account. This is particularly true for small companies in which close control is exercised over the aircraft. As the size and diversity of the company grow, the aircraft allocation problem usually becomes more difficult. As a result, a chargeback policy may be imposed both to recover at least a portion of operating costs and to better allocate the asset. Only 30 percent of companies with sales of less than $100 million employ chargebacks; fully two-thirds of companies with sales in excess of $10 billion charge back some portion of aircraft expenses.

How to Charge?   Two-thirds of the companies charging for their aircraft services do so by the hour. The next most popular method, by aircraft distance flown, is employed by just 20 percent of those reporting. Available passenger seat mile and standard industry fare level (SIFL) methods are negligible compared with the two most popular schemes. While it may be easiest for the accounting department to charge one cost center for use of the aircraft, many companies prefer to charge individual passengers or cost center subaccounts. In this manner, a precise account can be kept of who used the aircraft and, possibly, for what purpose.

How Much? The most popular basis for chargebacks (44 percent) is full direct operating cost expressed either as an hourly or per-mile charge. Direct operating cost plus a percentage of fixed cost is the next most popular method, used by 24 percent of companies. Some fraction of direct cost and fully loaded cost follow in order of choice by companies. Significantly, only 33 percent of companies with sales exceeding $10 billion chose the direct operating cost method, whereas 43 percent of companies with sales of less than $100 million used it.

Clearly, the rationale for using a particular chargeback method goes to corporate culture and, perhaps, the value placed on aircraft use by senior management. That is, if the use of a corporate aircraft is an integral part of corporate life at a company, the company will make it easier for key employees to use it. While this does not necessarily mean that the company will employ the percentage of direct operating cost chargeback method, it will allow sufficient travel funds to be placed in budgets to ensure access to the aircraft.

In a number of companies, chargebacks are used to control aircraft use. In other words, the chargeback rate, which normally is based on a percentage of direct operating cost, is adjusted periodically to ensure a target utilization rate for an individual aircraft. For example, if the target utilization for a Citation Ultra is 500 hours per year and utilization in the past 6 months indicates that the annual rate will reach only 400 hours, the chargeback rate is lowered from $1100 to $950 per hour in an attempt to stimulate use. A company also may supplement chargebacks with written use policies to discourage frivolous use.

At the other end of the spectrum, the fully allocated chargeback method may be so onerous as to stifle aircraft use for the majority of employees. This has the effect of reserving aircraft use for those with the largest travel budgets. If fixed costs and book depreciation are added to the Citation Bravo's direct operating cost, the hourly tab easily can exceed $2500, more than three times direct cost. While this may make the bean counters happy with tidy sums, the company's transportation needs may not be well served.

Significantly, about 75 percent of all companies using aircraft absorb all or part of their operating costs in some sort of corporate general and administrative account.

The "Right" Method. Sorry, no "silver bullet" chargeback method is available that will suit all companies. Corporate culture and senior management policy control the method used. Unfortunately, these characteristics are subject to internal politics that may tend to defeat the purpose of having corporate aircraft in the first place.

When a company decides to acquire an aircraft, it hopefully does so with the expectation that the asset will add value to the company and provide a useful service. The decision to acquire an aircraft represents a significant commitment of capital or operating funds or both. Whether an aircraft is purchased or leased, a significant amount of money will be tied up in the transaction, money that could be used for other business purposes. Capital and/or fixed costs become sunk costs and therefore unavailable for other uses. Given the expense, the aircraft should be used to some optimal level to realize a maximum return on the investment.

Optimizing Aircraft Use. Rather than imposing some arbitrary fee on the use of a valuable business tool, why not establish chargeback rates designed to make the best use of the aircraft? This is the conclusion that a majority of companies seemed to have reached, either by default or by design. Determining optimal use for an aircraft is based on examining the intended purpose or mission of the asset. If the aircraft is to be used as a business tool to increase the company's ability to compete in the marketplace, then the essential elements comprising the competitive factors must be studied. Strategic use, customer service, marketing, operational control, and emergency use are just a few reasons to use the aircraft—how does your company value these factors? Enlightened management will facilitate use of the aircraft to optimize these factors by making the aircraft available to the *right* people and purposes. Chargebacks are a means of achieving this end. Alternatively, the realization that on-demand air transportation is an essential corporate tool may be sufficient motivation to eliminate the use of chargebacks.

The knowledge and expertise of senior corporate executives is such that the loss of more than one of them may jeopardize the continuity and smooth operation of the company. Therefore, in an effort to manage the risk associated with such losses, the following travel restrictions apply:

1. *No two persons in the Office of the Chairman may travel together.*
2. *Not more than five corporate officers may travel together.*
3. *Not more than one direct report may travel with a Group President.*

Restrictions.   Some companies restrict the travel of key executives on the same aircraft in an attempt to protect their business from interruption or loss of revenue as a consequence of an accident in which one or more essential employees are disabled or killed. This policy is usually applied to all forms of transportation, regardless of relative risk.

The rationale for such policies stems from the concept that a business may be harmed or actually fail if certain key employees are not able to continue their work. Key employee insurance is a prime manifestation of this concept, with companies insuring employees, usually essential officers, against loss of life and/or productive time. However, this concept normally applies to individual employees and not groups. Therefore, companies may restrict simultaneous travel of more than one of their essential employees.

Companies not having travel restrictions fall into two categories: those feeling that they do not need one and those feeling that they do. The former feel that the depth of their executive talent is such that barring a near-total loss of the company hierarchy, they could continue to function quite well after the loss of any group of executives. The other category of companies believes that they have raised the issue of concurrent key employee travel restrictions with senior management and have been told either that it was not important or that it would be "taken up at a higher level."

There have been only a few corporate aircraft and charter aircraft accidents within the past 15 years in which the number of key personnel killed or severely injured materially affected a company's performance. However, anecdotal evidence indicates that airline and automobile accidents may have created similar problems for a greater number of companies. Therefore, having a policy restricting group travel for all forms of transportation may be prudent.

The simpler the policy, the better chance it has of application and survival. More important, a group at the highest level within a company or perhaps the board of directors must decide what types and combinations of key employees warrant travel restrictions. Key factors in this discussion should be

- Which individuals are responsible for the highest levels of strategy formulation and execution?
- Which employees have key technical or process information that, if removed, might cause long-term damage to the company?
- What combinations of employees, if removed from the workplace, would cause significant temporary or permanent damage to future company business and/or revenues?
- How practical is the imposition of proposed restrictions on concurrent travel for these groups?
- Finally, will the imposition of these restrictions create additional hazards for the employees; that is, if one employee has to drive a long distance in lieu of aircraft travel, will this expose the employee to a higher risk of injury?

Whatever the policy desired, making it applicable to all forms of transportation and enforcing the policy are important features to be included.

In general, carriage of candidates for elected office or their agents must be paid for by the candidate prior to the flight. Carriage of office holders is generally prohibited except in cases where fact-finding trips or activities in which substantial participation by the official are involved. Obtain clearance from Corporate Counsel prior to carrying any candidate or office holder.

Special Uses. There are several special uses of company aircraft that require special treatment and are subject to special aviation and tax rules and regulations. While the rules associated with these uses may seem complicated at first, once a system has been established to accommodate them, they are relatively simple. Importantly, these special uses may extend the utility of the aircraft appreciably and prove to be important features for the company.

Carriage of Candidates and Elected Officials. As an example, in the United States, the Federal Election Campaign Act of 1971 (FECA) prohibits a corporation from making any contribution to a federal candidate, including in-kind contributions such as transportation services. Therefore, a corporation may not permit a federal candidate or his or her campaign to use its corporate aircraft free of charge or at a discount. Rather, the federal candidate must reimburse the corporation in advance for such use in the amount of (1) first-class airfare if the flight is to a city served by regularly scheduled commercial service or (2) the usual charter rate if the flight is to a city not served by regularly scheduled commercial service.

The U.S. Senate and House of Representatives have relatively similar rules with regard to providing services on behalf of a member of Congress (gift rules). For example, a private entity may not pay for a member's expenses for which the House or the Senate usually provides official allowance (i.e., expenses related to official trips that are "required" by the member's office, such as trips to hold hearings). If a trip is personal or related to the official duties of the congressperson or senator but is not required by his or her office, then the gift rules become applicable.

The gift laws of the various states govern providing air transportation to state officials. Each state has its own distinct gift laws ranging from freely permitting such service to absolutely prohibiting it.

Anyone considering carrying an elected official or candidate on his or her own or his or her company's aircraft should exercise caution. Even though elected officials and candidates should be knowledgeable about the rules and regulations appropriate to their office and circumstances, any failure on their part to adhere to these various rules and regulations could jeopardize the business aircraft operator. In addition, because the different government entities involved do not always coordinate or clarify their rulings, the business aircraft operator might find other facets of his or her operation jeopardized, even if the elected official or candidate does adhere to the rules.

Many countries have similar rules and regulations governing carriage of officials. Therefore, all business aircraft operators are urged to closely examine all the ramifications of carriage of elected officials, including taxes, insurance, and the possibility of compromising the integrity of an elected official or candidate when considering carriage of these individuals, their families, and their staff.[2]

Personal Use. Similarly, many countries provide rules for the circumstances in which an employee is provided a flight on an employer-provided aircraft, and sometimes the flight is potentially taxable to the employee. This also may be true when a nonemployee guest or family member (spouse or dependent children) of an employee is aboard. The value of employee, guest, or family member's transportation may be considered additional income to the employee, not the guest or family member.

For example, in the United States, the valuation rule applies to personal flights on employer-provided aircraft. These flights can be either primarily for business or primarily for personal reasons. If an employee combines personal and business flights and the employee's trip is primarily for the employer's business, the employee must include in income the excess of the value of all the flights that would have been taken had there been no personal flights. However, if an employee combines personal and business flights and the employee's trip is primarily personal, the amount imputed to the employee's income is the value of the personal flights that would have been taken had there been no business flights.

Under the valuation rule, the value of a flight is determined using the aircraft valuation formula (also known as the SIFL formula). This is done by multiplying the SIFL rates by the mileage attributable to the flight, multiplying that product by the appropriate aircraft multiple, and then adding in the terminal charge. The terminal charge is not a landing fee or user charge levied by an airport operator but a base amount to cover certain fixed expenses incurred when providing a seat to a passenger, which is added to the other values. The SIFL rates, expressed as the cost per passenger seat mile, are calculated by the Department of Transportation and are revised semiannually.

If 50 percent or more of the regular passenger seating capacity of an aircraft is occupied by individuals whose flights are primarily for the business of the employer, the value of the flight on that aircraft by any employee (spouse and/or dependent child) who is flying for personal use is deemed to be zero.

Personal use of company-controlled aircraft is a complex issue, with the Federal Aviation Administration (FAA) and the Internal Revenue Service (IRS) often disagreeing on essential points. A full understanding of the issue is essential to protect the interests of both the company and the employee/guest. Yet personal use of a company aircraft is a regular feature of flight department operations and should be covered in the policy document, whether permitted or not.[3]

Although both corporate and charter aircraft activity is regulated by the FAA, those regulations provide only minimum operating standards. It is the desire and policy of this company to provide the safest possible air transportation offering the highest service standards to its employees and customers.

Therefore corporate aircraft operations will be conducted in accordance with the Flight Department Flight Operations Manual. All aircraft charter operations provided will incorporate the provisions of the Standards for Qualifying Outside Charter Companies, attached to this directive.

In all cases the Pilot In Command of the aircraft has full authority over the conduct of that flight and shall not be interfered with.

Aircraft Operating Standards. There is a lot to know about what creates a safe operating environment and, conversely, what reduces safety. Much of what is done in the company flight department, charter operator, or fractional provider is designed to increase the margin of safety. Standards, procedures, training, and equipment are designed to reduce risk in the environment in which we operate.

It is important to appreciate that business aviation providers live not only by the national aviation authorities' rules but also by a series of standards, limitations, and procedures that they adhere to voluntarily. The national regulations form the foundation for safe operation, but they constitute only *minimum standards.* Following only the basic regulations would be like taking a small boat beyond sight of land with no training, no survival equipment, and no navigation aids—legal, but unwise. Rather, to ensure that flight operations are as safe as possible, additional restrictions are imposed on those operations and placed in a document known as the *Flight Operations Manual*. The national regulations and the manual provide the basis for the total operation.

It is these standards, limitations, and procedures, adopted through years of experience and research, that provide for an in-depth safety shield to protect all operations. Significantly, everyone in on-demand aviation, from scheduler through pilots and technicians, follows these rules day after day. An attempt is made to do things the same way every time. It is this discipline that provides the predictable consequence of safe operations.

Initial and recurrent training prepares aviation personnel for the worst that can happen. Simulator training and ground school received at least annually keep pilots and technicians sharp. The nuclear power industry trains the same way, using simulators to create worst-case scenarios that enable employees to face just about every possible combination of plant and environmental failure know to humanity. Additionally, specialty training in weather radar, international operations, aircraft troubleshooting, and medical emergencies further hone skills so that department personnel may benefit from the best of what the aircraft has to offer. Conferences and conventions focused on on-demand air transportation keep participants abreast of the latest equipment and techniques in the field of high-speed, high-altitude aviation.

On-demand aviation operations, especially those belonging to individuals and companies, meet and exceed the maintenance and inspection requirements imposed by both aircraft manufacturers and the national regulatory authority. These operations rarely scrimp on parts, never leave a worn part to chance, and fix discrepancies before the aircraft can fly again. Technicians receive recurrent training to keep them up-to-date on the latest changes in the aircraft and on repair techniques.

Pulling It All Together. All the issues just mentioned are set forth in the flight department Flight Operations Manual. Everything the aviation operation does—every policy, standard, and procedure are contained in this manual. Deviation from these items is rare.

It is important for everyone in the company to realize this, for many of the standards and limitations contained in the manual materially affect how operations are conducted. For instance, aircraft normally cannot take off from an airport when the visibility is less than one-quarter mile. This is so because with less than this value, there is insufficient forward visibility to discontinue a takeoff in the event of a mechanical malfunction or to see potential obstacles on the runway. Similarly, most aircraft cannot land at an airport when the ceiling and visibility are less than minimum values prescribed for that approach. And loading the aircraft beyond specified limits is not permitted under national laws.

Finally, the person in charge of the flight, the pilot in command, must be accorded full and absolute authority regarding the safety of a flight. Moreover, he or she is charged with this responsibility under the International Civil Aviation Organization (ICAO) rules and those of the country in which the aircraft is registered.

Because these items contained in the manual are so important, it is recommended that the principal or CEO sign an appropriately worded preface page to lend sufficient weight to its contents and to communicate to the company that all employees must abide by its provisions. For a complete sample aircraft use policy, see the Appendix.

Oversight

When initiating on-demand air transportation services for an individual or company, those services must be overseen and managed by some person. This entity will be responsible for the following functions:

- Devising and maintaining the aircraft use policy
- Managing the interface with the transportation provider

- Either scheduling the aircraft services for passengers or coordinating/overseeing those services
- Tracking air transportation utilization
- Oversight of the financial issues associated with the air services

These oversight functions are quite important to the overall success of the aviation services effort for the company. If strong, well-developed policies and procedures and positive management and leadership are not imposed on the operation, important service details may be overlooked and financial details not tracked, leaving both passengers and the owner displeased with the overall level of service.

Managed in-house and charter operations often promise seamless turnkey air transportation experiences for clients, but without a company central office or person in charge of the operation, important details will be missed. For instance, when two people in the company wish to use an aircraft simultaneously, to whom will the contractor provide the aircraft? The type and amount of charges imposed for a particular trip or type of trip may not be well advertised or understood by the controlling passenger, leading to misunderstanding and conflict regarding the bill. And complaints regarding the service may not be channeled or articulated properly, given an uncertain relationship with the contractor.

With an in-house flight department, aviation personnel generally are located at the base airport, creating an artificial barrier to good communications and regular interaction not only with passengers but also with company or the principal's support personnel. It is this remoteness and autonomy that may create misunderstanding and conflict with the flight department. The same issues that may arise with a managed or charter operation also apply to the in-house flight department unless a strong connection is established between the company and the flight department. Table 3.1 presents a flight department startup checklist.

Getting Organized. While the CEO's or principal's secretary may be able to handle the day-to-day scheduling and billing activities associated with on-demand aviation services, they may not be the right person when it comes to authorizing flights, resolving scheduling conflicts, and settling billing disputes and other inevitable consequences of an outsourced operation. Rather, some midlevel or higher manager should be assigned the responsibility for on-demand air transportation oversight. This person will be able to interact easily with the management company or charter provider director of operations or chief financial officer (CFO). Daily routine operations may be assigned to a lower-level employee, but at least a "dotted-line connection" should exist between this person and the manager given oversight responsibility to ensure continuity. Typically, a financial or facilities manager is assigned the task of coordinating the contract flight operation.

Typical flight department reporting seniors within a company:

- Executive vice president
- VP facilities
- VP administration
- Director of human resources
- Chief financial officer
- Director of real estate

When an in-house flight department exists, a stronger, more formal tie should exist between the flight department and the company. It is important to have the aviation department manager or chief pilot report to the proper person and level within the parent organization. If the single aircraft is used mainly by the principal or CEO, the department probably should report directly to that individual. In reality, the day-to-day communication and coordination probably will take place between the chief pilot and CEO's administrative assistant or executive secretary.

TABLE 3.1   Flight Department Startup Checklist

Assumptions
  • Aircraft selected (see Choosing the Aircraft Checklist on page 3.15)
  • Ownership method decided (sole/joint ownership, leasing, etc.)
  • Chief pilot selected/hired (see Table 3.3)
  • Pilots/technicians trained
  • Safety program/procedures discussed with senior management

Management
  • Reporting senior lines of communications established
  • Policy and control procedures established—operations manual drafted

Administration
  • Insurance purchased (see Table 3.2)
  • Operating base/hangar selected
  • Other personnel selected/hired (with corporate human resources)
  • Aircraft use policy drafted
  • Passenger scheduling system devised

Maintenance
  • Line maintenance services selected
  • Maintenance record tracking system chosen
  • Inspection/maintenance provider selected
  • Maintenance logbook records custody decided
  • Regulatory compliance issues checked

Operations
  • Trip sheet format established for passengers and flight crews
  • Flight log sheets devised
  • Recordkeeping requirements decided
  • Regulatory compliance issues tracked/checked

Accounting
  • Develop detailed chart of accounts with accounting
  • Draft budget—variance reports system setup
  • Billing/invoice handling system established
  • Aircraft business/personal use codes and procedures devised

---

When a single aircraft is used by more than a few top executives or the department has more than one aircraft, the person to whom the top aviator reports becomes more problematic. If the owner or CEO is not the principal user of the aircraft, the department probably should report to some other high-level executive or assistant for both administrative and operational control. Whatever the job function, the executive should have sufficient power within the company to defend and support the flight department. Most important, the individual should be motivated to accept this responsibility; without this, the department may become an orphan, subject to the whims of other top executives.

The following are desirable features to be embodied in the relationship between the flight department manager and the reporting senior:

• Quick decisions

• Direct communications

• Appreciation for the role of the flight department

• Resolves conflicts and aids scheduling

• Budget and expenses resolution

• Keeps politics away from the department

While all these traits may not exist between the flight department and the company reporting senior, a more useful and stable relationship will exist if they are present.

An Integral Part of the Company.   On-demand air transportation probably is quite different from any other function within the company. Because of this, and because of its remote location, the flight department often suffers from the out-of-sight, out-of-mind syndrome. If the aircraft shows up on time and the passengers are treated reasonably well, the flight department is permitted to continue in its autonomous ways. This is a mistake.

The charter operator, aircraft management company, or flight department provides a valuable service to the company, and it must be managed as such. On-demand aviation should be considered to be a vital support service for the company in the same manner as information technology, human resources, finance, and legal functions. If this is true, then it should be held to the same standards and performance measures required of other support functions within the company.

Unfortunately, because of the remoteness of the aviation function and its high level of complexity, it may be left to shift for itself. Few individuals within the company wish to take on something seemingly as complex and different as aviation, and besides, isn't that why we hired the management company/charter operator/flight department manager? Yes, those companies/people are being paid to perform the aviation service function, but they also should be held accountable for their actions and required to provide reports of their performance.

There must be a strong link between the aviation services function and the company if service levels are to meet company expectations and if the flight department is to know and understand the air transportation needs of the company. The aviation services function should provide *transportation solutions* to the company, not just supply an airborne limousine on call. The aviation manager should be an integral part of the company management team and provide ideas and suggestions as to how the company can be made more competitive and productive. In order to do this, the link between the company and the aviation manager must be strong, permanent, and part of the corporate culture.

Staying Informed

Business aviation is a rapidly changing field. New aircraft, regulations, restrictions, products, and opportunities are constantly arising; missing some of these new features can prove costly and inopportune. The principal method of staying informed is through member associations that both represent the interests of members within the industry and with the regulators that keep the membership informed about not only what the association is doing but also what else is happening in the field that is important or of interest.

Joining and participating in a business aviation organization is essential to ensure that the environment in which the aircraft operates remains favorable to business aviation and to stay abreast of events currently affecting this field. The International Business Aviation Council (IBAC) represents a number of affiliated nationally based organizations (12 at the time this book was published) that look after business aviation interests. In the United States, the National Business Aviation Association (NBAA) has represented its members' interests for more than 50 years, carving out a credible and proud place for itself in the aviation industry, U.S. Congress, and FAA. The membership fee is relatively small compared with the level of representation and information received as a consequence of membership. Similarly, other IBAC affiliates perform the same services in the countries they serve.

The IBAC family of organizations represents companies that operate business aircraft, not pilots. The Aircraft Owners and Pilots Associations (AOPA) has been representing the interests of pilots and aircraft owners in more than 55 countries for as long as 60 years. Its reputation is excellent in securing the best possible regulations and operating environment for its members.

Other specialized organizations represent charter operators, fixed-base operators, aircraft brokers and manufacturers, aeronautical repair stations, and aviation maintenance technicians. All have something to offer their niche members. See the Appendix for a listing of these organizations.

Finally, a number of periodicals are published to meet the information needs of business aviation users. Subscribing to one or more of these publications will keep you current in the ever-changing aviation environment. Most of these are distributed free of charge to qualified operators. See the Appendix for a listing.

OWNER/EMPLOYEE-FLOWN OPERATIONS

This is the entry level of on-demand air transportation, actually do-it-yourself air transportation. The essential prerequisite for this form of business aviation is a pilot capable of both flying an aircraft and performing some other company function. It is this combination of skills that makes this form work. Significantly, it may be difficult for this multitalented employee to find a balance between flying and his or her principal company function. Such an individual may lose sight of the fact that his or her principal value company lies in his or her nonflying job, not the other way around. (*Note:* Since owner/employee-flown business aircraft is a relatively unique operation, the subject will be covered in its entirety in this section.)

Purpose of the Business Aircraft

The on-demand aircraft is a valuable asset. The most valuable benefits provided are time savings and operating flexibility for the owner/operator. Moreover, multiple-stop trips are particularly well suited to small aircraft use. While the owner or senior company officials are the customary users of this type of aircraft, virtually any company employee or acquaintance who has travel needs can make good use of this means of transportation. Expanded access to the aircraft increases its utility and cost-effectiveness.

However, for businesses, the aircraft must be used like any other business tool, with profitability and competitive advantage in mind. Trips that can be completed more efficiently or economically on the airlines should be made using that mode. However, the intangible benefits of business aircraft also must be factored into the transportation decision. The opportunity to set one's own schedule, return home rather than waiting for tomorrow's airline flight, the cachet of flying oneself to visit a customer, and the option of changing schedules at will to take advantage of emerging opportunities are compelling reasons to use an aircraft.

Learning to Fly

Not every person who becomes an employee-pilot comes to the job with a pilot's license or sufficient experience to carry out piloting duties successfully. Sometimes a need is identified and combined with the desire on the part of an employee to learn how to fly; the outcome is often beneficial to both the individual and the company.

Human beings have been intrigued with flight since the beginnings of time. The ability to evade the normal ties to earth and to enter a new realm of transportation has fascinated millions of people to the point of learning to fly—more than a million people worldwide are qualified to fly aircraft. Combining the ability to fly with business and personal pursuits has fascinated people since the early part of the twentieth century, enabling many to combine the joy of flight with practical pursuits.

A Dream Come True

The CEO had always been fascinated with flying, but the press of business and family activities had kept him from learning to fly. A hunting trip in a friend's aircraft convinced him that the time had come to realize his dream of flight.

A local flight training school agreed to fit its schedule to the CEO's, providing an aircraft and instructor, often on short notice, to accommodate his busy schedule. After solo, flight training was continued, frequently combining instruction with business trips. Within months, the CEO became a licensed private pilot and the proud owner of a new six-place Beechcraft Bonanza.

He now flies the aircraft more than 200 hours per year for business and 100 hours for pleasure, the latter mostly on family vacations.

Learning to fly is not necessarily difficult, but it does require discipline and attention to detail to ensure the safety of flight. However, most people motivated enough to learn to fly have little problem with these details. Every pilot of a conventional aircraft must be licensed by a national aviation authority to operate a specific category (airplane, helicopter, etc.) and class (single-engine, multiengine, etc.) of aircraft. Additionally, each pilot must possess a current medical certificate issued by a physician designated by the national authority. The medical certificate is not difficult to qualify for in the case of a private pilot; most adults who can qualify for a driving license also can qualify for a pilot medical certificate.

After approximately 50 to 70 hours of flight instruction and some academic study, a student pilot takes written, oral, and flight proficiency examinations in order to qualify for a pilot certificate. Once certified, the pilot is able to carry passengers in a small single-engine aircraft during good weather. Flight in clouds requires additional training leading to an instrument rating. Increasing levels of proficiency and confidence for the new pilot are gained through experience, an essential feature when contemplating the use of an aircraft as a reliable transportation tool.

Role of the Owner/Employee-Pilot

The owner/employee-pilot is also the flight department manager. Responsibilities of this position include

- Aircraft acquisition
- Aircraft financial and accounting requirements
- Setting standards for aircraft use and operation
- Scheduling
- Maintenance management
- Regulatory compliance
- Record keeping

While all of these items may sound rather daunting in prospect, most will take care of themselves once a *tracking system* has been devised. The concept of a systematic approach to aircraft management cannot be overemphasized; the personal/business pilot has more than enough nonaviation items to occupy his or her time without considering the recurring details of aircraft operation. The core of such a comprehensive system is flight and financial records (described below). If these are maintained on an ongoing basis and in sufficient detail, the system will work well.

A set of policies and procedures should be developed to accommodate the routine requirements of aircraft operation. Once developed, these procedures should be delegated as much as practicable to the operator's assistants and clerical personnel. However, even though these bookkeeping tasks are delegated, the overall responsibility for management of the aircraft should be retained by the principal operator. Through a series of normal and exception reports, the operator will be able to ensure that all essential required items associated with aircraft operation are accomplished, costs are controlled, and safety is maintained.

Many pilots are not in a position to delegate required functions of aircraft management. For this group, a systematic approach to record keeping and operational oversight is essential. Managing a business/personal aircraft requires adherence to standard procedures and accurate documentation, especially when dealing with the tax consequences of aircraft use for business.

Acquiring the Aircraft

A central theme or idea often drives a company or individual toward the acquisition of an aircraft. Exposure of the owner or senior management to another company's or friend's aircraft can serve as the catalyst to begin the investigation process. More typically, an aviation-oriented person realizes the potential value of an aircraft and begins using his or her own or a rented aircraft to meet personal and/or business travel needs. However initiated, the combination of time savings, flexibility, and efficiency involved is a compelling reason for using an aircraft.

Once the decision to acquire is made, a number of additional questions arise:

- What type of aircraft is suitable/desirable?
- What does it cost to acquire and operate?
- How should the aircraft be used/scheduled?
- When should the airlines (or charter) be used?
- Should the aircraft be leased or purchased?

These challenging questions require informed evaluation based on facts. A transportation needs analysis derived from past and anticipated travel patterns is the usual method of determining executive air transportation requirements (see Chap. 2).

Considerations When Acquiring an Aircraft

- Age of the aircraft
- Aircraft limitations [*read* the limitations sections of the Airplane Flight Manual (AFM)/Pilot's Operating Handbook (POH)]
- Paint and interior condition
- Inspection methods used and current status
- Damage history
- Status of airworthiness directives and service bulletins
- Aging aircraft/corrosion requirements
- Noise classification and potential airport restrictions
- Engine status—overhauls, interim inspections, life-limited items
- Anticipated operating costs—fuel, oil, routine maintenance
- Anticipated extraordinary costs— inspections, airworthiness directives, aging aircraft, life-limited items
- Availability of parts and knowledgeable repair facilities (orphan aircraft)
- Desired upgrades

The travel analysis will provide significant information for aircraft selection. Such factors as passenger capacity, speed, range, and runway requirements will become obvious. Choosing among available aircraft types and models, however, is difficult because no aircraft can do all things equally well, and cost is usually a major consideration. Even the best selection will be a compromise. Be willing to seek advice from knowledgeable sources.

New versus used, turbine- versus piston-powered, cabin size, interior amenities, ability to operate from small airports, and potential resale value are but a few of the variables that must be addressed during the selection process. A variety of opinions from operators of the candidate aircraft will prove very useful in the process.

Reference materials to assist with the aircraft selection process are available from *Business and Commercial Aviation* (Annual Buying Guide), Conklin and deDecker Associates (aircraft performance comparison and cost evaluations), and individual aircraft manufacturers.

The capabilities and experience of the pilots who will fly the aircraft also should be considered in the selection process. A low-time pilot with little multiengine experience may not be a good candidate for a pressurized twin. A natural check on the capabilities of a pilot rests with the broker or underwriter who insures the aircraft, however. Such companies will not insure an inexperienced pilot to fly a sophisticated aircraft or will add a hefty surcharge to the normal premium if the candidate is marginally qualified.

Once the analysis has been completed and provisional selection made, some judgment must be exercised in selecting an aircraft. There is no "right" aircraft for an individual company. Several types will be adequate for a company's needs; final selection is not too different from selecting an automobile or a house. The big difference between these more common consumer items and an aircraft is complexity and price. Thus expert assistance is needed. More than one voice should be heard in the process.

Acquisition Assistance

Once a decision has been made regarding an aircraft type, a broker may be useful in the search for the desired aircraft. Remember, brokers and dealers bring some bias to the acquisition process; therefore, it may be desirable to approach several sellers/brokers and solicit advice or actual bids. Lists of aircraft manufacturers and used aircraft vendors are available from the General Aviation Manufacturers Association (GAMA), the National Air Transportation Association (NATA), the National Aircraft Resale Association (NARA), and NBAA. The recommended method of selecting an aircraft purchase advisor is a word-of-mouth recommendation from an associate you trust or a company operating the type of aircraft you want.

Unless you have considerable experience with the type of aircraft to be purchased, a prepurchase inspection should be done. There are too many hidden limitations, restrictions, costs, quirks, skeletons, and anomalies associated with a business-type aircraft for the uninitiated to consider. Just because an aircraft is presented with a "fresh" set of inspections does not necessarily mean that it is in good condition;

Aircraft Acquisition Advisors

Questions to ask the broker/advisor/dealer:

- How long have you been in business under this company name?
- Are you a member of NATA or NARA and follow their standards?
- Provide five references of people to whom you have sold/leased aircraft.
- How familiar are you with the class of aircraft being considered?
- How many aircraft have you sold/leased within the past year?
- How will you support my operations after the sale/lease?
- How is your fee calculated?

experienced eyes must make that determination. A prepurchase inspection should be performed by an *expert* specializing in the *particular type* of aircraft to be acquired. The inspection report should address most of the preceding considerations and come with a guarantee or warranty against unknown or unanticipated surprises about the aircraft. To qualify the potential inspector, ask essentially the same types of questions you asked the dealer/broker. Finally, the prepurchase inspector should have no conflict of interest with regard to owners, operators, manufacturers, brokers, dealers, or the like.

A number of preowned aircraft are usually on the market. Popular aircraft are scarce and command a premium price; unpopular aircraft are plentiful and may be susceptible to heavy price negotiation. The point is that the aircraft market is constantly changing, driven by financial, regulatory, technological, and preference factors. Therefore, market timing is important for both new and used aircraft. Markets that are awash in good, low-time aircraft will cause all prices to soften and be subject to negotiation. Conversely, if the aircraft to be purchased is in short supply, an acceptable one may not be available, regardless of price.

Advisors selected for the purchase process will be reacting to these market features; their advice must be evaluated carefully to get the best possible deal. If the market for the type of aircraft desired is bad at the time the decision to acquire is made, a short-term lease of the desired aircraft type may be desirable. Charter, rental, or a lease also may be used to wait for better market conditions.

Insurance

Insurance should be obtained before commencing any business aircraft operation. Before any aircraft lease or purchase agreement is signed, an insurance binder must be in hand to ensure that coverage is in place. This includes insurance for both aircraft operations and the facility at which it will be based. If the aircraft is leased, or if a lien is attached to it, the lessor or financial institution will stipulate certain insurance limits to be carried. The base facility (hangar) probably will not be included in this requirement.

As with so many other professional issues, several quotes should be obtained for insurance. This process also will provide you with an education about the components and provisions of aircraft insurance. Before the search for insurance begins, however, a risk advisor, facilities director, or legal counsel should be consulted regarding a risk philosophy and insurance. The Apendix of the *NBAA Management Guide* contains an excellent primer on the subject of aircraft insurance (see also Table 3.2).

Employees using their own, rented, or borrowed aircraft must ensure that the company is adequately protected against liability exposure. This normally means that the company must be a named insured on the aircraft insurance policy and that the coverage is adequate. Additionally, employees require special coverage under worker's compensation insurance; pilots' premiums are usually higher than those of most employees.

Flight Records

A permanent record of each flight should exist, detailing

- Flight times/cycles/landings
- Costs incurred
- Destinations
- Passengers carried
- Business purpose, if any

TABLE 3.2   Aircraft Insurance Checklist

Coverage
- Hull—all risk, motion and nonmotion
- Liability—bodily injury, passengers and property damage
- Medical payments
- Lienholders interest endorsement
- Guest voluntary settlement
- War risk
- Foreign operations
- Broad form expansion
- Hangar keepers/airport liability

Points to know about
- Deductibles for each coverage category
- Actual liability coverage and limits
- Substitute/loaner engines/accessories coverage
- Acceptable pilots/required training
- Depreciation effects on hull damage coverage
- Loss of use/substitute aircraft provisions
- Additional insured possibilities/provisions
- Salvage rights
- Provisions for lienholders interest endorsement (breach of warranty)
- Effect/compatibility of corporate umbrella policy cover
- Coverage outside country of registry
- Interaction between hangar keepers and aircraft coverage
- Legal defense coverage
- Exclusions due to regulatory violations
- Owner/operator obligations
- Areas not covered by the policy

General
- Read and understand the policy *thoroughly*— details are very important.
- Have legal counsel review the policy.
- Ensure that all members of the flight department know essential provisions of the policy.
- Review policy annually with corporate risk manager and broker.
- Report minor incidents promptly to your insurance company.

Maintaining such a record will satisfy the FAA and IRS, your accountant, and your own need for information. A separate record should exist for each day on which the aircraft is flown. The form should be completed whether the aircraft is used for business or not; the continuity of information is important, regardless of the use of the aircraft. Once completed, these records of individual flights should be placed in a file away from the aircraft and kept for a minimum of 3 years after your income tax return is filed. If a record of past flights is needed in the aircraft, carbonless duplicating forms may be devised to provide this function. A typical flight record form is shown in Fig. 3.1.

While some people may wish to include maintenance discrepancy and other airworthiness information on the flight record form, the flight itinerary and passengers carried may be considered confidential and not appropriate for release to maintenance personnel or a contractor, therefore dictating the use of a separate form for these purposes (see Fig. 3.2).

For complete record control, the daily flight records may be entered into a computer database for future reference. This process will allow the data to be manipulated so that information concerning your operation may be obtained readily, and this is especially useful when questions arise regarding the use and utility of the aircraft. While some proprietary software is available for this purpose, a simple spreadsheet program can accomplish almost as much as the commercially available programs. Clerical personnel can be trained easily to do this job (see Fig. 3.3).

Care should be taken to accurately reflect the purpose of each flight. This IRS requirement, which attempts to connect a specific flight with a business purpose, does not impose an unreasonable burden on the individual. Extensive explanations are not required, but a clear purpose should be recorded for each leg of a trip if it is different from the previous leg. If the purpose of the flight is personal or pleasure, it should be so noted on the flight record.

Carriage of passengers also should be connected with the flight purpose. If the passenger is being carried for a different reason than the primary flight purpose, it should be noted on the flight record. Passengers being carried for personal reasons may be subject to additional tax treatment; the *NBAA Management Guide* and other NBAA tax publications contain additional information on this subject.

Date_____   Aircraft _____

Pilot _____

	Leg 1	Leg 2	Leg 3	Leg 4
From				
To				
Hobbs In *				
Hobbs Out				
Hobbs Time				
Takeoff Time				
Landing Time				
Miles				
Passengers				
Flight Purpose				
Expenses				
Remarks				

* Assumes Hobbs meter records engine time vs. time off/on.

FIGURE 3.1   Sample employee-flown business aircraft flight record.

Aircraft _____

Discrepancy		Corrective Action	
Pilot	**Date**	**Technician**	**Date**

Discrepancy		Corrective Action	
Pilot	**Date**	**Technician**	**Date**

FIGURE 3.2   Sample employee-flown aircraft discrepancy record.

Standards

An operations manual that provides operational and administrative standards for the operation of an aircraft whether it is used for business or not is essential. The manual will define procedures that enable the operation to comply with federal aviation regulations and establish standards and limits that exceed federal standards when deemed necessary. The operations manual is designed to create a sense of professionalism that will enhance safety, efficiency, and effectiveness.

The process of developing the operations manual is probably more important than the manual itself. This is so because the introspection and research required to create the manual will lead to a realization of the essential factors that make up a well-run, safe flight operation. Once this realization has taken place, setting those factors into policies and procedures will promote a more structured and efficient operation. A suggested table of contents for this manual is shown in Table 3.3.

The resulting manual may be referred to on an ongoing basis to accommodate both normal and unusual situations. If the manual is to be truly useful, it must be reviewed and updated to reflect the changing needs of the individual and the company using it. A brief review at least annually should prove to be sufficient for most operations.

	May 2003	May 2004	12 month average
Trips	6	6	5
Legs	17	16	13
Miles	4140	3885	2880
Hours	23	21	16
Passengers	9	7	5
Average			
Hours/trip	3.8	3.5	3.2
Miles/trip	690	647	576
Passengers/leg	0.5	0.4	0.4
Costs -$			
Direct	4225	3570	2640
Indirect	3220	2990	2515
Total	7445	6560	5155
Direct cost - $:			
Hour	185	170	165
Mile	1.02	.92	.92

FIGURE 3.3 Sample owner/employee-flown aircraft report.

The Business of Safety

Every pilot makes a commitment to safe flight operations at one time or another. Experience has shown, however, that the "one time or another" is not sufficient. Safety demands a full-time, conscious commitment to continuous, safe operations. Conforming to good operating practices and exercising good judgment must be accomplished every time you fly, not just on bad-weather days or on more challenging flights. By analogy, a person uses accepted standards and good decision-making techniques daily to survive in the social or competitive business world. If these techniques are good for these applications, they should be good for flying as well.

Unfortunately, the person who typically uses an aircraft in the pursuit of business or targeted personal reasons may tend to put most of his or her effort and concentration into those matters to the exclusion of other activities. Family and personal relationships may suffer as a result of overconcentration on business matters, as well as the individual's physical and mental health. So it may be with flying.

If the pilot views flying in the same manner as he or she does running a core business or family affairs, in terms of risk and profit and loss, a healthy frame of reference will develop. Flying home in instrument meteorological conditions (IMC) late at night after a full day on the job should be considered risky business in the same manner as expanding into a new market without market research, capitalization, and personnel resources. Achieving safety in flying is really a business or core personal decision.

Training

A structured initial and recurring ground and flight training program will sharpen your compliance to standards and prepare you for the unexpected. The thought process that drives

TABLE 3.3   Owner/Employee Operations Manual

Administration
• Purpose of the business aircraft
• Safety
• Operational control
  • Scheduling
  • Flight following procedures
• Use of the aircraft
• Recordkeeping procedures

Flight operations
• Health and fitness
• Duty time
• Standard operating procedures
• Operating limitations
  • Pilot
  • Aircraft
• Training

Maintenance
• Maintenance program
• Discrepancy control
  • Recording discrepancies
  • Deferred maintenance
• Maintenance provider selection
• Maintenance away from home base

Note: This is an abbreviated outline. For a more complete outline, see the Appendix.

one to train regularly serves to reinforce other safe attitudes. And training itself will create a mind set that fosters adherence to standards and professionalism. There is no regulatory requirement that pilots in general aviation operations undergo any recurrent training for non-type-rated aircraft. Once pilots receive their initial training for a pilot certificate or rating and perhaps some small amount of transition training for a specific aircraft, little or no training is accomplished by the average business or pleasure pilot. However, airline and charter pilots are required to undergo at least annual flight and ground training, and it a rare corporate flight department that does not send its pilots to recurrent training at least as frequently. Since the mission of the owner/employee pilot is often as challenging as that of the corporate pilot, it makes sense to receive some form of initial and regular recurrent flight and ground training.

The best safety device in any aircraft is a well-trained pilot.

—FLIGHT SAFETY INCORPORATED

Initial Training.   Before flying any sophisticated aircraft that will be used for business purposes, some form of transition training should be undertaken. Vendors offer type-specific transition courses that provide both ground and flight training. These courses often include a day or more of ground training to introduce aircraft systems and limitations and a number of flights in an aircraft or simulator to practice normal and emergency procedures. Such instruction is often given by instructors who have thousands of hours of experience in the type of aircraft and can impart more than just procedures and limitations specified in the pilot's operating handbook.

Prior to authorizing an individual to act as pilot in command (PIC) in an unfamiliar aircraft type, the aircraft insurer may specify a certain amount of training or flight time supervised by a qualified instructor. The insurer's requirements should be considered a minimum requirement and not a final qualifying authorization, however.

Recurrent Training.   Although a pilot may fly a specific aircraft hundreds of hours each year, experience in airline, military, and corporate flying has shown the need for periodic retraining. Recurrent training allows pilots to practice unusual and emergency procedures not encountered in the normal course of productive flying. Moreover, it detects undesirable habit patterns that may have crept into an individual's piloting technique over time. Finally, it provides a review of aircraft systems and limitations that often are forgotten during normal operations.

Because business and personal pilot operations are at least as challenging as those for corporate pilots, it makes sense to undergo recurrent training at least annually. The most desirable form of training is formal classroom and simulator training provided by a recognized training vendor. Since this type of training may not be available for all types of aircraft or at convenient locations, use of local training facilities and experienced individuals may be necessary and certainly is a very helpful experience. At a minimum, the training should be accomplished in accordance with a formal syllabus and should include ground training as well.

Other Training.   Many pilots stop their training activities after recurrent training in the aircraft they normally fly. However, there are other related issues and skills that should be either learned or reviewed on a regular basis. Some of theses subjects include

- Avionics/systems
- First aid and CPR
- Survival
- High altitude (altitude chamber)
- Crew resource management/pilot judgment (see below)
- Advanced weather analysis, including weather radar
- International operations
- Air traffic control/instrument procedures

Constant Learning.   The safe pilot is naturally curious about the environment and should always be probing the edges of his or her existing store of knowledge. One's ability to gain a sufficient variety and amount of aeronautical experience before it may be needed is quite limited; knowledge fills the experience gaps. Use your fellow pilots and especially experienced flight instructors to assist in this process. Staying up-to-date with selected aviation periodicals is another means of constant learning.

Compared with discrete training sessions, the learning process should be continuous and never-ending. Detailed aeronautical knowledge may provide the best insurance policy, and the premiums are surprisingly low.

Duty Time

The term *duty time* comes from national regulations that specify how much time a professional pilot can be in a condition of readiness to fly, regardless of whether or not he or she actually flies. This concept recognizes the fact that being on duty eventually will create an unacceptable level of fatigue.

Airline pilots have strict and complicated duty time limits that are guaranteed by regulations and their union contracts. While the idea is under consideration, most national regulations currently do not limit duty time for corporate flight crews. Most flight departments, however, include duty time limitations within the corporate flight operations manuals. Since corporate flying is closer to business flying, the norms used in such operations will be used for examples and comparison.

Fatigue creates a degradation of mental and physical skills that can prove harmful or even dangerous if taken to extremes. If allowed to progress too far, fatigue may conspire to create a hazardous situation. Knowing the warning signs will help avoid the onset of fatigue, but the ideal way to avoid fatigue is to set and abide by personal flight and duty time guidelines.

Because business and personal transportation embraces a combination of flying and other activities, it is difficult to provide strict guidelines for duty time. Each situation and pilot characteristics are quite variable, necessitating an assessment of each set of circumstances.

Symptoms of Fatigue

- Accepting lower standards of performance
- Decreased reaction time
- Reduced attention span
- Sloppy or rough flying
- Distorted or impaired judgment
- Irritability

Perhaps the most significant variable regarding fatigue is the type and amount of business and personal activities conducted either before or after a flight. Intense, contentious dealings tend to drain most people and bring on fatigue earlier than business involving more routine events or participation in a large meeting. Only the individual can evaluate the effects of a full day of activities on the prospect of flying. Therefore, individuals must be honest in making their preflight stress and fatigue assessments.

Guidelines for a maximum-length business/flight duty day:

Duty Time Factors

- Length and complexity of the business day
- Time zone changes
- Flight time
- Number of legs
- Type of flying, e.g., good/bad weather, day/night, etc.
- Cumulative working/flying days

- *Total day:* 16 hours (waking hours)
- *Business and flying:* 12 hours (productive business + flight-related activities)
- *Maximum flying-only day:* 7 hours (all flight-related activities)
- *Reductions due to type of flying* (reduce flying or business and flying day by 1 hour for each):
  - Two legs over an initial two
  - Each leg flown during the hours of darkness
  - Each IMC leg more than one

Duty and flight time are only half the total picture. Adequate periods of rest must be interspersed between duty periods. Rest, too, is a subjective measure that is difficult to quantify. Time spent sleeping is considered good-quality rest time. However, if "rest" is spent divided between doing business "homework" and fitful sleep in a high-noise and light environment, it may not adequately fulfill the intent of rest time.

Guidelines for minimum rest time:

- 10 hours between duty periods

- If a period of only 8 hours of rest is available, reduce the following duty day by 2 hours
- One period of at least 24 consecutive nonduty hours (including 10 hours of rest) for each 7 consecutive day period

Note that these guidelines are just that—guidelines. All guidelines are subject to modification based on situation and circumstance. These have been formulated from a mix of corporate flight department duty times and the National Aeronautics and Space Administration (NASA) fatigue study guidelines. The most important aspect of these limitations is not the absolute numbers stated but the fact that the individual has taken the time to think through the fatigue problem and arrive at personal restrictions.

Limitations

Just as each aircraft has limitations imposed on it, flight departments and individual pilots often have restrictions imposed on them. Airlines have limitations imposed on them not required of private operators in recognition of the higher level of safety afforded those who pay for their transportation. And the majority of corporate flight departments operate under self-imposed restrictions oriented toward individuals and aircraft alike.

Therefore, it makes sense that business and personal operators, who may be flying less capable aircraft with less experienced pilots, also should impose limitations on their operation. These restrictions do not have to be extensive or draconian, but they should take into account the capabilities of the individuals involved in company aviation operations. Limitations should be imposed before the fact and not based solely on inputs derived on the spur of the moment. See the Appendix for suggested employee-pilot limitations

Maintenance

Responsibility for the airworthiness of an aircraft is shared jointly by the owner/operator and the PIC for each individual flight. Responsibility for required maintenance and inspections, however, belongs solely to the aircraft's owner/operator. In most business flying operations, the PIC and owner/operator are usually the same individual, making this person totally responsibility for the continuing airworthiness of the company aircraft.

Many pilots attempt to transfer responsibility for ensuring that the aircraft is maintained in an airworthy condition to their maintenance contractor or vendor. However, it is *not the responsibility* of the maintenance provider to ensure the airworthiness of the aircraft, only to comply with the national maintenance, repair, and recordkeeping requirements. It is the *owner/operator* who must ensure that the maintenance and inspection are accomplished.

Selecting a Maintenance Vendor. Maintenance and inspection may be performed on an aircraft by either of two entities: a licensed aircraft maintenance engineer or an approved maintenance/repair organization. [In the United States, these are known as an FAA airframe and powerplant (A&P) mechanic or an FAA-certificated repair station.] Either is capable of performing normal maintenance and inspection tasks on most aircraft and approving it for return to service. While repair stations are held to the same performance standards as the A&P mechanic, or aircraft maintenance technician as they are now being called, they are required to have inspection systems in place and supervision and training for personnel that exceed what the A&P mechanic is required to have. Further, repair stations are specifically rated to accomplish certain tasks and to work on specific equipment, whereas the individual A&P mechanic does not have such requirements.

Whatever method chosen, the principles of good business-consumer relationships apply. A recommended method for determining whether a vendor is suitable is to ask someone who has used the vendor's service in the past. When doing so, it is important to ensure that the person providing the reference has used the vendor recently for a similar service. Obviously, the person providing a reference may not be as discriminating as you regarding quality of work, time to complete work, and cost. Therefore, try to ensure that the person used has similar standards when making his or her evaluation.

Ask national aviation regulatory authority personnel (the local FAA Flight Standards District Office in the United States) if they have any negative information regarding the prospective vendor.

Vendors should have some experience with your type of aircraft. A Beech Baron probably would receive more expert care from a Beechcraft service center than from one specializing in Cessnas. However, the vendor's affiliation with a manufacturer does not necessarily mean that it is an excellent shop.

While cost is a major consideration in the selection process, quality and reliability of the work performed should rank at least as high, if not higher, in the selection process. Ask the following questions of the prospective vendor:

- How long have you been in business?
- How much experience do you have with my type of aircraft?
- What type and amount of initial and recurrent training do your technicians receive relative to my class and type of aircraft?
- Describe the process you use to obtain spare parts for aircraft? (Quality and price are important.)
- Do you use written work orders and provide a detailed breakdown of work completed on your invoice?
- Describe the warranty you provide for both labor and parts.
- Provide the names of three recent customers flying my type of aircraft.

Maintenance Control. The owner/operator is solely responsible for anticipating airworthiness requirements and dealing with discrepancies that render an aircraft unairworthy. In reality, however, the owner/operator relies heavily on the maintenance vendor to assist with these tasks. A well-functioning relationship between pilot and maintenance provider ensures that required maintenance and inspections are accomplished in a timely manner.

A schedule of maintenance actions should be used to trigger inspections and time-controlled maintenance, whereas aircraft discrepancy reports are used to initiate repairs. Work orders are commonly used both to initiate actions and to determine their progress toward completion. Only after the work has been inspected and signed off on should the aircraft be released to other work or for service. Ideally, when required maintenance has been completed, a maintenance release will be signed by the vendor, certifying that the aircraft is airworthy and can return to service.

Airworthiness compliance should be viewed as a partnership between owner/operator and vendor. Both should consult prior to any maintenance performed on the aircraft, whether scheduled or nonscheduled. It is important to specify in writing exactly the work to be accomplished. This serves as a formal authorization for the vendor to commence work and also should outline the extent of the work to be accomplished. Orders for major work such as upgrades, refurbishment, overhauls, and modifications should be quite detailed and specify completion times and standards. It is this chain of paperwork that provides a firm method of communication between owner and vendor and serves as a series of contractual arrangements between the two parties. This system will create a written record of expectations and promises that will prove valuable many times to both parties.

AIRCRAFT CHARTER

Charter services are a useful means of providing on-demand air transportation for companies and individuals who need just 100 to 150 hours service per year—this equates to approximately 30 to 50 domestic round trips per year, one every week or so. However, charter also should be considered to supplement other forms of business air transportation, such as an in-house operation or fractional ownership.

There are a significant number of charter providers to choose from in most locations around the world. While each of these operators should be officially sanctioned by operating under an air taxi or charter operating certificate issued by their national regulatory authority, levels of service among charter operators may vary widely. Therefore, it is wise to perform a market survey of charter operators in an attempt to obtain the safest and best possible service. Choosing the first charter operator listed in the Yellow Pages may provide disappointing results—take time to investigate the options.

Using a number of charter operators and different aircraft is a good means of exploring what on-demand aviation services have to offer. Service levels, aircraft types and configurations, and associated aviation systems should rapidly become evident to the traveler, providing a useful background for subsequent choices in the field of on-demand air transportation.

As with any other service, reputation and word-of-mouth recommendations may provide the best indicators of service levels. Asking your peers or peer companies should give you a general idea of what is available in the local area and which may suit your needs.

Yet one charter user's needs and standards may not match your requirements. For instance, a charter user may be quite pleased with a small, older turboprop aircraft obtained from a local provider. If your needs tend toward a larger cabin, faster turbojet aircraft, no matter how good the turboprop provider's service is, it will not satisfy your requirements. Therefore, when asking for recommendations, ask for the following service discriminators:

• What type of aircraft do they have/did you use?

• How long was the trip?

• How many passengers were carried on the trip?

• Did they depart and arrive on time?

• Was the aircraft clean and apparently in good condition?

• How were the passengers treated?

• Was the billing as quoted?

• Do you feel that you received good value from the experience?

• Would you use this company again?

Once you have obtained a good idea of what is available through others' recommendations regarding local services, look in the Yellow Pages for other companies that may provide national charter service and make their services available through a toll-free telephone number. The Internet is also a good source of national and international charter service providers. Additionally, *The Air Charter Guide* is a subscription-based periodical (also available online) that provides detailed information about worldwide charter services. Finally, charter brokers are available who, through their knowledge and expertise, will attempt to obtain the best possible charter deal for you, for a price.

Checking the Record

Armed with the recommendations of those who have used the charter service and other information that you may have gained in your research, you need to know some basic facts about the company. The amount of money involved and criticality of the services provided warrant checking into the operator's record with the national regulatory authority.

Since each air charter company has been issued an operating certificate by their national regulatory authority, that agency maintains records on them, gained from surveillance of their operations. First, call the provider to determine its regulatory status and then, using contacts the supplier has provided, contact the regulatory authority to find out how the supplier has performed under the regulations. Here are a few basic items you should know about an air taxi company:

- Air taxi (charter) operating certificate number
- Name of the company as it appears on the certificate
- Location and telephone number of the local aviation regulatory authority having jurisdiction over the company [In the United States, this is the FAA Flight Standards District Office (FSDO).]
- Name of the person assigned oversight responsibility for their operation [This is the FAA Principal Operations Inspector (POI) in the United States.]
- Is the company or has it ever been under investigation by the regulatory authority (FAA) for a violation of applicable national regulations (Federal Aviation Regulations)?
- Has the company ever experienced an incident or accident reportable under national regulations (National Transportation Safety Board)?
- What is the experience level of the flight crew that will fly the aircraft? (The PIC of a charter aircraft must have a minimum total flight time of 1200 hours in many countries; however, most reputable companies provide PICs with 3000 hours or more of flight experience. Helicopter pilots operating under visual conditions may have as few as 500 pilot hours, although 1500 hours is customary.)
- Liability insurance limits carried on your aircraft
- Names and telephone numbers of people who have used the charter services within the past month (to be used as references)

Then contact the named regulatory authority and ask about the supplier's violation history or any other safety-related issues. If the air taxi operator is unwilling or reluctant to provide the answers to the preceding questions or does not want you to contact the regulatory agency for verification, you would be wise to consider another operator to fill your travel requirements.

Charter evaluation services are available worldwide to perform all of these tasks for a fee. Most provide their information as a subscription service, sending an initial comprehensive evaluation followed by periodic updates. These services can be quite useful because they are performed by experts and cover virtually every aspect of the charter provider's operations. Moreover, evaluation services are available for major charter operators worldwide. They may be found by contacting the national regulatory authority, the charter operator itself, or a national organization representing business aviation and/or charter operators (in the United States, see *nbaa.org/prodsvcs*).

Charges

Many charter companies are not based at a local airport; rather, the charter provider may be located hundreds of miles away and will ferry (position or deadhead) the aircraft to the client's location. The charter client is charged for this positioning, normally at the same rate as for occupied service. These charges may add substantial amounts to the total trip charges, leading the wise consumer to consider carefully the use of a local charter operator who may not have exactly the aircraft desired or the best service terms available.

Additionally, landing fees, catering charges, flight crew expenses, wait fees, and overnight charges also may be added to the final bill. Transportation or use taxes often are added to the fee by local or national authorities, further driving up the total charge. Therefore, a detailed quotation stating all anticipated charges should be obtained prior to finalizing arrangements for the service. Figure 3.4 shows a sample quotation.

Evaluation

While you may be an infrequent user of charter services, having a single person in charge of these services is highly desirable. Tracking the various providers and their service levels and charges will provide service continuity and overall satisfaction for both travelers and the company. This person will be able to observe overall utilization and perhaps even perform a central scheduling function as well.

Determining whether each charter flight met the expectations of the passengers will prove useful in evaluating the various providers' services. The charter coordinator/scheduler should keep a record of each flight, noting both statistical details and quality-of-service comments, both observed and asked of the passengers. Exhaustive questionnaires or in-depth interviews are not necessary for this function; casual comments received from the passengers normally are sufficient for this function. Some service quality issues that can be recorded include

- Did the flight depart and arrive on time?
- Was the aircraft clean and apparently in good condition?
- How were the passengers treated?
- Do you feel that you received good value from the experience?
- Would you use this company again?

There are many charter providers available to clients in most areas of the world, and the charter operators are aware of this essential fact of business competition. While you should

September 30, 2003

Quotation for: Ace Widget Company

Date	ETD	Depart	Arrive	ETE	ETA	Pass
10/15/03	8 AM	Wilmington-ILM	Birmingham-BHM	1:30	8:30 AM	6
10/15/03	5 PM	Birmingham-BHM	Wilmington-ILM	1:30	7:30 PM	6

Cessna Citation Bravo Aircraft @ $1,900 per hour x 3 hrs *	$5700
Federal excise tax @ 7.5%	428
Segment fee @ $30	60
Crew wait fee @ $100 per hour x 5.5 hrs	550
Landing/ramp fees	350
Catering – breakfast and evening snack x 6	250
Total	$7338

Total time may vary according to weather and air traffic conditions. Crew and fuel expenses included.

FIGURE 3.4   Sample aircraft charter quotation.

remain aware of this basic tenet, the most successful services are derived from a mature and open relationship developed over time between the provider and the recipient of the charter service.

FRACTIONAL OWNERSHIP

Fractional ownership offers travelers the ability to purchase shares of a business aircraft. As little as one-sixteenth of an aircraft can be purchased, which offers 50 flight hours of use per year, or as much as one-half of an aircraft can be purchased, depending on how many hours are needed. The most common amounts purchased usually range from one-eighth to one-quarter shares.

Fractional owners pay a percentage of the purchase price for an aircraft, commensurate with the amount of hours they want available per year; e.g., one-eighth share receives 100 flight hours, one-quarter share receives 200 flight hours, etc. Most fractional providers offer a variety of aircraft to choose from, ranging from small turboprops to large intercontinental turbojets. Hourly and monthly fees are charged over the period of the contract, normally 5 years.

Fractional owners are guaranteed that their aircraft or another aircraft of the same model will be constantly available to them with as little as 4 to 8 hours of advance notice. The fractional provider assumes responsibility for scheduling, staffing, flight planning, weather, communications, maintenance, catering, and insurance. At the end of the initial contract, the owner's fractional share will be purchased by the provider at "fair market value," or the contract may be renewed or upgraded.

Fractional owners use the service because they appreciate the following aspects:

Fractional Comparisons

Ask the fractional provider to compare its services with those of other on-demand air transportation methods.

- Fixed costs
- Variable costs
- Scheduled response time
- Aircraft range versus payload trade-off
- Resale value/options
- Customer service
- Level of control over operational features
  - Scheduling response
  - Service levels
  - Pilot qualifications and training
  - Maintenance
- Contract options/flexibility

- Guaranteed availability
- Consistent scheduling practices
- Predictable service levels
- Usage ranging from 100 to 200 hours per year
- Relatively small investment that fits the corporate financial plan

Investigating the Service

Many potential fractional owners are veterans of aircraft charter services who are seeking a more predictable or higher level of on-demand air transportation service. While charter services can be quite good, especially if one establishes a relationship with a single provider, the desirability of owning at least a portion of one's own aircraft can be a powerful draw for customers. The "always available" nature of the service is also a positive aspect. And the turnkey, no-hassle nature of the service has convinced thousands of travelers worldwide that fractional ownership is the way to go. However, there are details of the service that must be known prior to committing to the program.

Researching the potential providers of fractional ownership service is not difficult. Most advertise in business periodicals and newspapers and often are featured prominently in the charter section of national Yellow Pages. While most popular and available in North America, fractional services are available in many other parts of the world. Note that fractional providers are considered to be private operators in the United States but are considered commercial operators in many other countries.

It is important to have the fractional representative provide comparisons of his or her company's services with other available options, including charter and whole ownership. These comparisons must include both financial and service related features. Particularly important are comparisons that show cost per hour over a range of utilization amounts, ideally between 50 and 400 hours.

Details. The major expenditure associated with fractional ownership is the value of the fractional share of the aircraft itself. Ranging from $500,000 to $20 million, depending on the aircraft type and fractional share, this expense entitles the fractional owner to the rights, benefits, and obligations of any owner of a major asset, albeit for just a fraction of the full aircraft. The fractional owner may depreciate his or her share of the aircraft, as would any other full aircraft owner, to the full limit of the value of his or her share. Along with this privilege comes the obligation of owning the aircraft, that of keeping the aircraft

Fractional Flight Hours per Share

Share	Flight Hours
$\frac{1}{16}$	50
$\frac{1}{8}$	100
$\frac{1}{4}$	200
$\frac{1}{2}$	400
Full	800

airworthy and sharing the asset with the coowners. Accomplishing these obligations is taken care of under the several agreements signed between the fractional owner and provider, the principal ones being the management, joint-ownership, and interchange agreements entered into at the time of the purchase.

Fractional owners are subject to additional charges above the stated monthly management fee and hourly flight charges, including the following:

- Extraordinary maintenance, handling, and administrative fees may be applicable depending on the nature of a specific flight or the condition of the aircraft.

- Providers are permitted to raise their standard monthly fees based on external indices, such as the consumer price index.

- While normally adequate hull and liability insurance is provided under the provider's contract, war risk liability insurance may be required to be purchased at the owner's expense.

- Early contract termination (normally less than the specified 5-year minimum) will allow the owner to sell the aircraft to the provider at a predetermined value, less a marketing fee.

While all of these items are specified in the several contracts the owner is required to sign, some require careful examination to determine their applicability.

Note that the owner's specific aircraft may never be made available to him or her due to the complex scheduling required to run a large fractional operation. However, the same type of aircraft will be supplied from the provider's stable of aircraft, if available. If the appropriate aircraft is not available, a similar type of aircraft will be supplied from an aircraft charter operator under contract to the fractional provider. These charter operators may not operate to the same standards of service specified by the fractional provider, however.

As with charter operations, the fractional provider supplies a transportation service subject to many variables. Therefore, the fractional owner should know what is being provided in terms of technical, administrative, and service quality. A number of consultants are available to evaluate fractional providers to ensure their compliance with terms of the contract, national aviation regulations, and service quality; they may be found through national and international aviation associations dealing with business and charter aviation.

Managing It

One of the greatest difficulties fractional service users report is managing the available number of flight hours specified in the service agreement. Each participant is provided a certain number of hours under the contract, according to the amount of fractional share purchased. A one-eighth share will receive 100 hours under the contract at a specified hourly cost, ranging between $1000 and $7000, depending on the type of aircraft involved. If this number is exceeded, most providers supply additional hours "borrowed" from subsequent years of the contract, up the limit of the contract, normally 5 years. When the total number of contract hours is reached, supplemental hours may be purchased, but at up to three times the normal contract hourly rate.

Similarly, it is possible to trade up or down into larger or smaller aircraft. If the owner's contract is for a midsized-cabin aircraft and a large-cabin aircraft is desired for a specific trip, this is possible by trading a multiple of 2.5 (or more hours) in the midsized aircraft for 1 hour in the larger aircraft; if a smaller aircraft is acceptable, tradedown provisions are also permissible. Upwardly mobile tradeoffs can rapidly consume the annual allotment of program hours. Therefore, it is prudent to program and track available hours to ensure that they are not exceeded early in the contract.

This may be best accomplished by channeling all requests for use through a single person or office to track hours used. If a variety of people/offices are permitted to use the service, an allocation of time for each group may be necessary to control the expectations of those using the aircraft. This office also should coordinate closely with the financial function of the company responsible for paying the fractional provider's invoices to ensure that the conditions of the contract are complied with.

IN-HOUSE AIRCRAFT

This is the most popular of all forms of on-demand air transportation. Perhaps the reason for its great popularity is the level of control provided to the company or individual using the service. These forms of control include

- *Schedule.* The personnel setting policy for use of the aircraft exercise total and ultimate control over who uses the aircraft, where it goes, and when it returns. Priorities are set, trips are evaluated on their merits, and the "winner" is assigned the valuable transportation asset.

- *Aircraft type.* The aircraft or combination of aircraft that best suits the operation has been selected carefully by the user. And if user needs change over time, changing aircraft is relatively easy.

- *Personnel.* Finding and hiring the best manager, pilots, aviation maintenance technicians, and schedulers may be difficult, but with proper assistance, they should prove best suited for user needs.

• *Policies and procedures.* Every flight operation needs well-founded, mature poli-cies and procedures to guide department administration, operations, scheduling, and maintenance. Within the regulations governing flight operations, whatever a company wants in terms of policy and procedure can be theirs for the asking—no compromises required.

• *Cost.* Flight operations normally have wide latitude in controlling their costs but must have direction from the company to ensure that concomitant safety, quality, and reliability goals are met. Companies operating their own aircraft have the ultimate level of control over expenses.

• *Quality.* Although sometimes a secondary consideration, service quality is quite important to many companies. The ability to travel in a style of their choosing, whether strictly utilitarian or opulent, rests solely with the dictates of the users.

So it's all about control—control over the various aspects of the operation, be they tech-nical, financial, or service-related. Companies having their own in-house flight departments, fully managed and controlled by company employees, have the best chance at getting the flight operation they desire. If they do not get it, they have no one but themselves to blame. The factors just mentioned should serve as guiding principles for companies establishing a flight department. While it is easy to get caught up in the technical aspects of aviation, it is the basic elements of any process or operation that are important.

Beginnings are important. We will start the process by assuming that the processes mentioned in Chap. 2 have been accomplished:

• Air transportation analysis completed

• Basic type of aircraft selected

• In-house flight department chosen

As mentioned earlier, a comprehensive checklist for a flight department startup is shown in Table 3.1.

Finding the Right People

Since aviation, especially aviation involving turbine-powered aircraft, is a complex and specialized proposition, the first step in establishing a flight department is to hire or appoint a flight department manager. Hiring a knowledgeable and experienced individual to start the operation makes good sense. If a person with little aviation experience is given the responsibility to purchase an aircraft, establish an operating base, and hire aviation personnel, he or she may easily miss some important aspects of the operation. Without extensive expe-rience in the field, the person making such choices will be relying on a variety of individuals to advise him or her on the various aspects of the operation. While a variety of opinions may be valuable in determining the various aspects of the operation, a cohesive view of the end result should be formed and built by the person who ultimately will be responsible for the flight department; that person will be designated the flight department manager. A good compromise is to hire a manager and contract with a flight department management consultant to provide perspective and a view of industry best practices in the process of establishing the department.

The Leader/Manager. The aviation or flight department manager is the key person oper-ators should rely on to establish and maintain their flight operation. This is the person who must live with the operation over time, direct its growth, and make policy corrections as the operation progresses. Therefore, this person should be given full responsibility and authority for the operation; without this level of control, the degree of success in establishing and maintaining the operation will be less certain. Choosing the manager/leader of the flight operation is quite important.

Finding the right person can prove difficult if the right objectives are not provided for this individual. Unfortunately, most operators rely on their instincts in finding the right individual, depending on a person's aviation credentials to determine his or her fitness for the job. Running a flight department is no different from running any other venture; however, having a modest amount of aviation experience can help the process. Yet companies frequently are blinded by extensive aviation qualifications and experience possessed by individuals who do not have credible leadership or management skills.

Experience has shown that the best *managers* make the best flight department managers. While this may sound obvious, companies seldom heed its simple truth. Too often aviation personnel with little management training or demonstrated management experience are thrust into positions of control and power; while some survive, and a few even thrive, many are doomed to failure because they are not predisposed to being managers and leaders.

While tradition has placed pilots at the head of flight departments, an increasing number of aviation maintenance technicians have been filling the top slots. Again, it is the experience, training, and preference of the individual that make him or her a candidate for the top job, not necessarily his or her specific type or depth of experience. And once the flight department has been established and has grown in complexity and function, managers with little or no aviation experience have been placed successfully as aviation department managers.

The lead pilot chosen for the operation, whether manager or not, should be experienced in the type of aircraft to be acquired by the flight department. Additionally, 3000 total pilot hours is the normal minimum requirement for the principal pilot in startup flight department; 1500 hours of PIC should be required as well (PIC time means time spent actually flying an aircraft). The pilot also should have least 500 hours in the class of aircraft to be used, e.g., turboprop or turbojet, and preferably be type-rated (a specific pilot rating required for certain sophisticated aircraft) in the actual type of aircraft to be operated, with 100 to 200 hours of pilot time in type.

While titles may not seem important, they make a difference in pay and prestige for individuals. Typically, a startup flight department operating a single aircraft with just two or three total employees designates a chief pilot as the head of the operation. This individual takes care of all aviation functions from hiring people, to selecting contractors, to flying the aircraft—he or she instantly becomes a jack-of-all-trades. Granted, the range of management duties is somewhat limited, but leadership and management skills are important to the success of the operation. Larger flight departments use an aviation or flight department manager in recognition of the additional number and range of duties required as a department grows in number of aircraft, employees, and functions. Flight department managers traditionally are paid 10 to 20 percent more than chief pilots for a given type of operation, based on title alone.

In addition to a solid background of training and experience in management and leadership, operators should look for the following traits in the person they choose to run their flight department:

Curiosity.   The manager must be interested enough in new concepts and ideas to be able to go beyond his or her aeronautical realm and find out what makes the company function. It is this thirst for new knowledge, to understand what goes on at headquarters and at the company facilities, that facilitates the learning and absorption process. Without it, the transition from aviation person to executive is hard, sometimes boring work and probably will never be completely effective. Once the manager has made the transition, holding onto this characteristic will serve him or her well for years to come.

Vision.   The ability to see beyond the airport boundaries, beyond the company's current product line, and to see new applications for corporate transportation will accelerate the transformation to executive status. The willingness to explore new ways of doing business and to be able to connect disparate elements of the entire corporate function will make the new executive more valuable for both the flight department and the company as a whole. And unlike our eyesight after age 40, our *vision* actually should improve with age.

Commitment. Working long and hard for more than just the aviation function but also to make that function the best possible asset the company has will cement the new manager's position in the upper reaches of the company. Working with the travel, disaster preparedness, and marketing departments, for example, to help perfect those functions demonstrates an understanding of corporate priorities and a willingness to support them. If properly acquired, this trait will grow with time as well.

Innovation. Working with the company travel agency to coordinate (or even consolidate) its functions with the flight department schedule, prepositioning flight crews at other locations to accommodate long duty times, and instituting zero-based budgeting for the flight department show an innovative and agile mind. And if these efforts are coordinated properly within the company, the resulting changes undoubtedly will attract favorable attention. Innovation thrives on new experiences, fresh approaches, and a wide range of interests.

Marketing. The manager should realize that he or she always must be selling the company product and the benefits of his or her department and making the right people aware of the value of

Flight Department Manager Duties[4]

• Provide on-demand air transportation services for the aircraft operator.

• Develop and institute department policies and procedures that will accomplish the department's mission safely, effectively, and efficiently.

• Prepare and administer an annual operating budget.

• Establish procedures for aircraft use and scheduling.

• Maintain contacts with user personnel to ensure proper service.

• Regularly advise users on the status and requirements of the aviation department.

• Devise and use metrics with which to measure department performance.

• Prepare short- and long-range plans that include user and departmental objectives.

• Develop and train subordinates.

both in appropriate measure. Market analyses and implementing strategies are essential to this effort, too. Indiscriminate selling to either the inside or outside world may be a waste of effort; more important, the right audience is not getting the benefit of the sales pitch. The tendency to explore markets can be developed.

People power. With a bit of luck, executives realize the value of people long before achieving their grand status; just in case they made it all on their own, they have an important lesson to learn. Peers, subordinates, and seniors—they all have the power to make, break, or outlast the person with authority. If the manager always invests time, faith, and effort into the people reporting to him or her, life certainly will be easier, if not more successful.

It's really a management job—flying the company airplane is just an occasional perquisite!

—EXPERIENCED FLIGHT DEPARTMENT MANAGER

Where does one find Mr. or Ms Right? Surprisingly, in the same places that all good employees are found, through diligent search and effort. Here are a few places to start:

- *Word of mouth.* Other companies having flight departments in the area should be able to supply a number of recommended individuals through their networks.

- *Online.* A number of aviation personnel and specifically flight department Web sites are available that list a variety of occupational types by experience, location, and specific qualifications.

- *Aviation placement firms.* Several aviation placement firms exist worldwide that specialize in finding all levels of pilots, technicians, and administrative personnel for flight departments.

- *Advertise.* Advertisements placed in aviation periodicals such as *Flight International, Business & Commercial Aviation, Aviation Week,* and *Space Technology* often yield substantial numbers of qualified individuals.

Other Personnel. Many flight departments are able to commence operations with just the aviation manager or chief pilot. If an aircraft requiring just one pilot is used, no other personnel are required immediately. However, support personnel within the company are always required to perform financial and administrative functions. Table 3.4 provides a hiring checklist.

More Pilots. If the aircraft is to be operated by a single pilot, the flight department personnel complement is complete once the manager is in place. However, many aircraft require more than one pilot, based on the regulatory requirements for specific aircraft types. And even though only one pilot may be required by regulation, many operators choose to operate with two pilots as an increased safety factor, especially for aircraft operations in high-density flying areas surrounding major metropolitan areas. More than the minimum number of pilots to crew the aircraft may be required depending on how the aircraft will be used and the tempo of operations (see Chap. 4).

An experienced aviation person should need little additional experience in finding an additional pilot through existing or local aviation networks. If specific types of individuals or qualifications are needed, aviation placement firms or aviation periodical advertisements probably will suffice.

> *Pilots and technicians should be selected primarily for their potential to bring value to the company, not just because they possess good technical skills.*
>
> —EXPERIENCED AVIATION MANAGER

Aviation Maintenance Technicians (AMT). Many small flight departments with just one aircraft depend on outside sources for required maintenance and inspection of the aircraft. Normally, the local fixed-base operator (FBO) will supply traditional nontechnical support services such as aircraft positioning (towing), fueling, and cleaning. Additionally, minor aircraft discrepancies relating to tire pressures, light bulb replacements, and minor adjustments may be available through the FBO AMTs. With this arrangement, major inspections and maintenance traditionally will be accomplished by an aircraft repair station or service center for the specific type of aircraft operated. These facilities may not be located where the aircraft is based, however.

There are advantages of having an AMT on staff. Not only is this person able to comply with required inspection and maintenance procedures for the aircraft, but he or she is also able to ensure that the aircraft is kept in top condition and that maintenance services are available when needed (see Chap. 7). Guidelines for finding a good AMT include

TABLE 3.4   Flight Department Hiring Checklist

What do you want?
- Develop a *detailed* job description
- When do you need the employee?
- What compensation package can you offer?
- Look beyond technical qualifications:
  - Interpersonal skills
  - Supervisory potential
  - Administrative capabilities
  - Ability to fit flight department/corporate culture
  - Personal presentation (appearance, demeanor)
- What corporate human resources rules apply?

Finding them
- Networks—company, business, aviation
- Ask employees to help
- Corporate human resources
- Headhunters/professional search firms
- Advertise in business and trade publications

Selection
- Screen résumés carefully—ask for references
- Work with human resources on the process:
  - Requirements
  - Procedures
  - Forms required
  - Compensation levels
  - Applicable legal issues
  - When can a job offer be made?
- Develop interview questions beyond the technical aspects:
  - Customer service orientation
  - Time demands of the job
  - Ability to integrate with flight department team
  - Administrative skills (speaking, writing, organization)
  - Job/promotion expectations of the candidate
  - Corporate/flight department culture and values
- Schedule interviews with people inside/outside the department
- Develop a practical knowledge/skills test for pilots/technicians
- Ensure understanding of job demands, compensation, benefits
- Request FAA violation history check for pilots/technicians
- Draft *detailed* job offer specifying compensation and job description, for clearance with human resources

---

- Aviation maintenance technician/engineer licensed by the national regulatory authority
- At least 1 year (ideally 2) working on the same class of aircraft
- Specialized training for the type of aircraft operated (may be provided after hire)

The AMT's duties include

- Performing maintenance and inspections in accordance with manufacturers approved methods and techniques
- Keeping abreast of and maintaining a current working knowledge of the procedures, parts, and tools needed to perform maintenance and repair work on the company aircraft
- Complying with the manufacturer's technical data, national regulations, and applicable safety rules

- Being responsible for strict adherence to the inspection system employed for the assigned aircraft
- Shipping, receiving, and inspecting aircraft parts

Director of Maintenance Duties

- Ensure that all maintenance operations are conducted safely
- Provide guidance and direction for those assigned to the maintenance section
- Maintain the company aircraft in accordance with the manufacturer's continuing airworthiness instructions, federal aviation regulations, and the highest standards of airworthiness and appearance
- Assist with flight department planning issues, including budgets
- Ensure that maintenance personnel are properly qualified and trained for their assigned duties
- Maintain adequate spare parts and consumable inventory
- Contract with vendors to provide maintenance services as needed
- Ensure that the hangar and associated facilities are properly maintained

The first AMT employed is also normally designated the director of maintenance in recognition of his or her managerial role in ensuring that the aircraft is maintained properly. The director of maintenance reports to the aviation department manager and is responsible for maintaining department aircraft in accordance with the manufacturer's standards and regulatory requirements. Obviously, the director's managerial responsibilities will be minimal with just one technician on board, but such abilities should be considered when employing the first person in this category.

Others. While a variety of personnel, including line service, aircraft cleaners, receptionists, and schedulers, may be required for a flight department, only the scheduler is required for most flight departments. The others come as the department grows in size and function, but the scheduler is the required regular interface between the flight department and those who desire transportation.

The scheduler receives requests for transportation in the aircraft, recording details of desired trips for the passengers. This person may not be devoted full time to the scheduling task but rather may be the full-time secretary or administrative assistant for a highly placed executive within the company, traditionally the principal or CEO. The scheduler's duties are essentially a collateral duty for this type of person but a good fit given the position and function of his or her immediate superior.

This person does not necessarily have to be particularly aviation literate because the little knowledge he or she requires is learned easily for most routine scheduling tasks. It is important, however, for this person to be familiar with company and personal operations and personnel at middle management and above. The scheduler deals with the principal's family members, top-level employees, and customers on a regular basis and must be customer-oriented and aware of appropriate service levels for the passengers using the aircraft.

Eventually, the scheduler may devote his or her full time to the scheduling task and coordinating the internal functions of the flight department with those of the operator. This is a normal evolutionary process emerging from increased numbers of aircraft and operations.

A full-time scheduler/flight coordinator can prove quite beneficial to any flight department because of the organization's dynamics. Typically, the pilots, technicians, and flight department manager are deeply involved in a wide range of detailed operational tasks.

However, these tasks are often fragmented and highly compartmentalized, taking these individuals away from the hangar for significant periods of time or denying them the big picture of the total operation. The scheduler is normally the only person who stays at the hangar and provides a central point of information and reference. Since these tasks require good people and organizational skills, the transition to a full-time scheduler should take these factors into consideration.

Collateral Duties. There once was a time when all a corporate pilot did was show up 1 hour before takeoff time, fly the trip, and then retire gracefully to his or her abode to await the next scheduled trip or the beep of the dreaded pager. However, an increasing number of flight departments are tapping the many talents of their pilots, schedulers, and AMTs for additional duties that are not related directly to their primary job descriptions.

Scheduler Duties

- Scheduling travel for company passengers on the company aircraft
- Scheduling ground transportation and accommodations for both flight crew and passengers
- Coordinating aircraft operational information with pilots and AMTs
- Logging flight times and keeping department flight records
- Keeping passenger manifests and logs for all flights
- Providing flight crews with a flight plan, and manifest
- Arranging for catering services and FBOs

The advent of the collateral duty probably came to us from military aviation, where no squadron member escaped with just the single task of flying or fixing aircraft. These additional duties were given in recognition that a subsidiary task needed doing and a warm body was needed to accomplish it. To a greater degree, however, the military realized that its drivers and maintainers would not receive the training and experience necessary to accept increased responsibility and become more knowledgeable of the big picture of the many aspects of running the store. The same forces are at work in corporate aviation today, particularly with the demands to be leaner and more efficient.

An informal survey of department managers shows that most of them were not elevated to their position by chance, but by demonstrating their administrative and managerial abilities through collateral assignments. At the other end of the spectrum, the chances of being retained during a downsizing are enhanced if the individual has shown that he or she can do more than fly and fix aircraft.

Collateral Duties

Training	Flight information planning
Safety	Budget/financial
Automation support	Catering
Aircraft type specialist	Standardization
Reports	Flight/maintenance records
Purchasing	Publications

Instituting collateral duties may meet with some resistance in established departments, but chances are that if the right people are chosen for the other duties, they will welcome the chance to show their stuff. Most departments have individuals who are interested in computers, flight planning, the intricacies of specific aircraft, and administrative matters. Ask them what their hobbies are—hobbies are a good indicator of what people will be good at.

The big payoff in having collateral duties is that the added involvement of these people will make the department work better and should develop a more satisfied employee. And since the department managers only have so much time to give to the job, more work will get done. Finally, the jobs of pilots and mechanics will be easier to justify to corporate management when their collateral duties are added to their job descriptions. See the Appendix for collateral duty job descriptions.

Basing the Operation

Where to base an aircraft is a critical decision if full advantage of the aircraft is to be taken. The reason the operator will acquire an aircraft is to have ready access to on-demand transportation. Convenience for passengers should be a major factor in determining where to locate; however, the airport closest to corporate headquarters or the principal's home may not be the right location. A careful balance must be struck between competing factors when selecting an airport (see the following sidebar).

Note that selecting an airport has been placed ahead of the section on aircraft acquisition. This is done because the size and facilities available at the selected airport may figure prominently in the type of aircraft to be used. Actually, selection of the airport and the aircraft should be done almost simultaneously to accommodate their mutual features and restrictions.

Once an airport has been decided on, an operating location at that airport must be found. Typically, a startup flight department hangars its aircraft and bases its pilots at a suitable FBO at the airport. Considerations for selection of a FBO include

Airport Selection Considerations

- Passenger accommodations
- Aircraft facilities
  - Hangar space
  - Maintenance
  - Fueling
- Flight crew office space
- Amount of aircraft traffic
- Noise restrictions
- Runway length
- Instrument approaches available
- Operating fees
- Security
- Type and quality of airport management

- Cost
- Maintenance availability
- Access during nonworking hours
- Passenger facilities
- Security
- Fuel availability/cost
- Aircraft storage/maintenance facilities
- Crew accommodations

Using an FBO's hangar may require the company aircraft to be moved unnecessarily during repositioning of other aircraft, exposing the company aircraft to the possibility of damage. Security of the aircraft while it is in an FBO's hangar is a potential problem as well. Despite the FBO's best efforts, it is difficult to ensure total access control over either the hangar or the individual aircraft. While this is not a common problem, the potential for vandalism, theft, and sabotage is possible in an unsecure hangar. Therefore, one's own hangar or one shared with a limited number of tenants is preferable for security reasons.

Buying or building a dedicated hangar may be a good investment once it has been determined that an airport is a good fit with one's operation. This capital expenditure may prove quite affordable once life-cycle costs are compared against the renting alternative. Additionally, the resale value of hangars is usually quite good. Airport land use restrictions and covenants should be investigated carefully prior to building because land/structures reversion provisions in airport leases are common.

Ideally, flight and maintenance crews should be provided with office, working, and storage space within the same hangar where their aircraft is located. Using space leased from an FBO makes this difficult because such space is normally limited. Crews often share office space with other corporate operators or work out a combination of their homes and the FBO crew lounge. Since theirs is a nomadic existence under normal circumstances, providing them with dedicated office space should be a priority consideration when basing an aircraft.

If aircraft maintenance is to be performed by the FBO, it is preferable for it to possess an repair station certificate/authorization from the national regulatory authority, appropriately rated for the type of work needed for your aircraft. If company personnel will be used to perform maintenance on the aircraft, arrangements must be made with either the FBO or other leasing authority to perform the maintenance. Provisions also must be made for tools, parts, and ground support equipment storage.

Whatever aircraft storage and servicing options selected, there are liability issues to be considered. Whether there is a potential for a claim between the FBO, airport, lessor, or colessees and the company, this liability should be examined carefully by corporate risk managers and/or corporate counsel. Appropriate types of insurance should be secured to protect the company from potential liability concerns.

Acquiring the Aircraft

Once the decision has been made to acquire an aircraft, several issues must be resolved:

- Aircraft type
- Purchase or lease
- In-house personnel or outside management

All these issues are too difficult for the layperson to address and may be too difficult for an experienced individual who will head the flight department. These issues can be addressed by aircraft manufacturers, brokers, or acquisition consultants. Each brings some bias to the decision process; therefore, it may be desirable to approach several and solicit advice and actual bids. Lists of such resources are available from the *World Aviation Directory* and business aviation association in the country of residence. In the United States, the General Aviation Manufacturers Association (GAMA), the National Air Transportation Association (NATA), the National Aircraft Resale Association (NARA), and the NBAA are good sources. The best method of selecting an aircraft purchase advisor is a word-of-mouth recommendation from a trusted associate or other company operating the type of aircraft desired. Yet this valuable advice only provides a single data point in what should be a comprehensive search. See the sidebar "Aircraft Acquisition Advisors" in the section entitled, "Owner/Employee-Flown Operations," earlier in this chapter.

Aircraft Selection. The air transportation needs analysis should have narrowed the choice of an aircraft to just a few. However, the final decision may be difficult given the conflicting advice and sales information provided by manufacturers, brokers, and consultants. Often company executives or family members who have some familiarity with aircraft they have flown in will further narrow the choice. The final decision must be contingent on the decision maker taking a demonstration flight in the actual aircraft to be purchased. And don't forget to take spouses along for the ride, too, if they are to be regular users of the aircraft.

New versus used, turboprop versus turbojet, cabin size, interior amenities, ability to operate from short fields, and resale value are but a few of the variables that will have to be addressed during the selection decision process. A number of opinions from operators of the candidate aircraft are very useful in the process.

Reference materials to assist with the aircraft selection process are available from *Business and Commercial Aviation* (Annual Purchase Planning Handbook, usually the May issue), Conklin and deDecker Associates (aircraft performance comparison and cost evaluations), and individual aircraft manufacturers.

Once the analysis has been completed and provisional selection made, some judgment must be exercised in selecting an aircraft. If the analysis indicates the ideal aircraft to be a small turboprop, but the principal or CEO clearly likes jets, a modest entry-level jet may be a wiser choice. Certainly both types of aircraft should be suggested as solutions to the identified air transportation needs. And if a prominent passenger is mildly claustrophobic, a medium to large jet may be a better choice than a more economical small one. Finally, do not forget, again, the preferences of spouses of the primary passengers; more than a few aircraft acquisition decisions have been made based on interior amenities and the size of the lavatory.

There is no "right" aircraft for any individual or company. More than several types will be adequate to meet their needs; final selection is not too different than selecting an automobile or a house. The big difference between these more common items and an aircraft is its complexity and price; expert assistance is needed. And more than one voice should be heard in the process. See the sidebar, "Considerations When Acquiring an Aircraft," earlier in this chapter.

Unless you have vast experience with the type of aircraft to be purchased, a prepurchase inspection should be done. There are too many hidden limitations, restrictions, costs, quirks, skeletons, and anomalies associated with a corporate-type aircraft for the uninitiated to be familiar with. Just because an aircraft is presented with a "fresh" set of inspections does not necessarily mean that the aircraft is in good shape; experienced eyes must make that determination. A prepurchase inspection should be performed by an *expert* specializing in the *particular type* of aircraft to be acquired. The inspector's report should address most of the preceding considerations and come with a guarantee or warranty against unknown or unanticipated surprises regarding the aircraft. To qualify the potential inspector, ask essentially the same types of questions you asked the dealer/broker. Finally, the prepurchase inspector should have no conflict of interest with regard to owners, operators, manufacturers, brokers, dealers, or the like.

Purchase or Lease.　　This decision goes more to the realm of the accountant than to the aviation expert. The capital debt structure and philosophy of the company or principal will be the main determinant for this decision, although brokers, manufacturers, and financial institutions may provide alternatives and insights that could affect the decision.

Leasing may be the most attractive option to an operator new to on-demand aviation because it may afford the opportunity to evaluate an aircraft over a relatively short term without making a long-term commitment. However, financial and tax considerations should be used as a primary factor in making the lease-purchase decision. In addition, a wide variety of creative leasing schemes is available that may combine the best features of both purchase and lease methods.

And whether or not you are well-heeled enough to write a check for the purchase price of the aircraft, it is a good idea to use or obtain the advice of a finance company or bank familiar with aircraft purchase/lease. Their knowledge of markets, aircraft values, resale values, title issues, insurance, and other paperwork items make their counsel invaluable. While their caution exercised in the purchase process may seem unwarranted, the time taken up-front may save grief later.

Aircraft Markets. At any one time, a number of preowned aircraft are on the market. Popular aircraft are scarce and command a premium price; unpopular aircraft are plentiful and are subject to heavy price negotiation. The point is that the aircraft market is constantly changing, driven by financial, regulatory, technological, and preference factors. Therefore, market timing is important for both new and used aircraft. Markets awash in good, low-time aircraft will cause all prices to soften and be subject to negotiation, even those of new aircraft. Conversely, if the aircraft to be purchased is in tight supply, an acceptable one may not be available, regardless of price.

The advisors selected in the purchase process will be reacting to these market features; their advice must be evaluated carefully to get the best possible deal. And if the market for the type of aircraft desired is bad at the time the decision to acquire is made, a short-term lease of that type or charter may be used to wait for better times.

Insurance. Before commencing any type of flight department operation, insurance should be obtained. That is, before any aircraft lease or purchase agreement is signed, an insurance binder must be in hand. This includes insurance for both aircraft operations and the facility at which it will be based. If the aircraft is leased, or if a lien is attached, the lessor or financial institution will stipulate certain insurance limits to be carried for the aircraft; the base facility (hangar) probably will not be included in this requirement.

As with so many other issues holding significant financial consequences, several quotes should be obtained for the insurance. This process also will provide an education about the components and provisions of aircraft insurance. However, before the search for insurance begins, your risk manager, facilities director, or legal counsel should be consulted regarding risk and insurance philosophy. Table 3.2 provides an aircraft insurance checklist. An Appendix to the *NBAA Management Guide Appendix* also contains an excellent primer on the subject of aircraft insurance.

At a minimum, two quotes should be obtained for initial insurance coverage and every 3 years thereafter to ensure that the company is getting adequate coverage at the best possible price. The flight department manager should become sufficiently familiar with aviation insurance terms, coverage, and fees to act as a consultant to a risk manager or legal counsel on aviation issues. This often can be accomplished by tapping the manager's network of fellow managers or by going to a number of broker/underwriters to become familiar with the desired information.

Father/Son Handoff Expands the Fleet

An Oklahoma entrepreneur built a drilling equipment business in the 1970s and 1980s by specializing in niche well support equipment. The successful business soon discovered the virtues of on-demand air transportation and acquired a Westwind jet to support its business. The Westwind was replaced by a Learjet Model 35, and it, in turn, was replaced by new Lear 60. The entrepreneur's son joined the business and learned to fly. As the son took over more of the business, the father found other pursuits that occasionally began to take the Learjet away from the business. The son bought a CitationJet to fill the gap, which he regularly pilots along with the company pilots. The son finally encouraged dad to release the Lear 60 to the company and to get his own aircraft.

MANAGEMENT COMPANY

Under this arrangement, an aircraft management company provides all personnel and services required to operate an owner-supplied aircraft. This method of aircraft operation is often used by companies new to aviation or those not wishing to become involved in the aviation department management process itself. In essence, an aircraft is "given" to the management company to operate for the owner as a turnkey operation.

The management company charges a monthly fee and provides personnel, training, a base of operations, passenger scheduling, and aircraft maintenance services. Salaries, benefits, fuel, hangar rent, aircraft maintenance, and other operational costs are all collected by the manager and passed through to the owner, usually with no markup. These comprehensive services relieve the aircraft owner of most of the responsibilities of aircraft operation.

Hundreds of aircraft management companies are available worldwide, ranging from the giants that have hundreds of aircraft in their stables to the very small operators who may be, in reality, small charter companies engaged in management activities as a sideline or complement to their main activities as charter operators. This is so because many charter operators "borrow" aircraft from corporate flight departments when the company is not using the asset for use as a charter aircraft. The management-charter symbiosis works to the advantage of both the charter company and the corporate operator if the asset is managed properly.

The use of a managed aircraft for charter services reduces the owner's scheduling flexibility because charter trips scheduled in advance make the aircraft unavailable to the owner for last-minute trips. The additional aircraft utilization created by the charter trips accelerates the aging process on the aircraft and exposes it to users who may not treat it as kindly as will the owner. Attempting to regain major portions of the fixed expenses associated with aircraft operation may prove difficult unless the charter revenue is substantial. In attempting to increase charter revenues, the aircraft becomes less available to the owner; if this method is chosen, a balance must be struck between availability to the owner and desired revenue levels.

The services provided by management companies are valuable, yet the act of outsourcing these services reduces the company's control over policy, procedure, costs, and desired quality levels; the management company introduces an additional level of control and a filter to use of the asset. While many of the technicalities and complexities associated with operating an aircraft become the responsibility of the management company, full understanding and appreciation of available options may not be possible—the management company may recommend expediency over cost control or service levels. However, the use of management companies has increased in popularity within the past few years, principally as a method for aircraft owners to rapidly enter on-demand air transportation with little of no knowledge of the subject.

These companies may be found at most airports featuring significant numbers of either charter providers or corporate operators. The Yellow Pages in large metropolitan areas are a good starting point. The *World Aviation Directory* contains a comprehensive listing of charter operators and management companies.

The Contract[5]

The instrument binding the aircraft owner to the management company should be a comprehensive and detailed contract that sets out the duties and responsibilities of both parties. Efforts to incorporate precision and completeness in the contract should leave little room for interpretation or complaint between the parties. In addition to normal concerns of services rendered in return for a fee, legal and liability considerations also must be included to protect both parties.

For instance, it must be made clear that the management company is simply providing management services and not transportation. There can be substantial adverse national regulations and tax consequences if the management company is determined to be providing transportation services to the owner. In the United States, the FAA focuses on which party has "operational control," and the IRS looks to which party has "possession, command, and control" of the aircraft. Factors such as who employs and/or controls the pilots, who controls the scheduling and availability of the aircraft, and who procures the aircraft insurance are all relevant.

Liability considerations are important to both parties because each has obligations and responsibilities based largely on what is contained in the contract. Issues to be covered should include

- Insurance requirements
  - Applicability—operations and geographic coverage
  - Aircraft hull and liability
  - Personnel injury (worker's compensation)
- Rights of subrogation and breach of warranty
- Management company's standard of care
- Liability for losses caused by negligence, misconduct, etc.
- Hold harmless or indemnification provisions.

If the aircraft and associated personnel are to be used for charter flights, additional provisions must be included:

Management Company Contract Issues

An enumeration of services to be provided must be included:

- Identification of the aircraft and its equipment
- Operational, administrative, and financial policies and procedures to be used
- Scheduling practices, especially when the aircraft is used for charter as well as owner personnel
- Aircraft maintenance and inspection program to be used and who will perform the work
- Employment and supervision of the flight and maintenance personnel
- Rights of both the management company and owner for hiring, reviewing, and firing personnel
- Minimum experience levels for each employment category
- Personnel training requirement
- Personnel exclusive use (optional)
- Alcohol and drug testing requirements

- Management company responsibilities normally include
  - Obtaining necessary certifications and approvals to operate
  - Obtaining the owner's prior authorization for all charter flights
  - Ensuring that the crew meets regulatory qualification and training requirements
  - Drug and alcohol testing program
  - Invoicing of charter customers for transportation and applicable taxes
- Owner responsibilities normally include
  - Making the aircraft available for certification and training flights
  - Paying the cost of any aircraft modifications required for charter qualification
  - Paying certain expenses related to initiating and maintaining the aircraft on the management company's charter operating certificate
- Additional considerations include
  - The formula used for allocating charter revenue and expenses between the parties
  - Specifying which party is responsible for bad debts from charter customers
  - Ensuring management company "possession, command, and control" when it operates the aircraft for charter

- Allocating applicable taxes
- Building in performance measures/reports

Because of the complexity and liability considerations of the management contract, an attorney experienced in these matters should be consulted prior to finalizing any agreement with a management company.

Performance Measures/Reports

An aircraft management contract is typically a lengthy and complex document that concentrates on who is responsible for what and the associated legalities. Yet the company initiating the contract should have a method of ensuring that it is getting what it pays for and that components of the services are received at the best possible price. Table 3.5 presents a list of fee/expense elements associated with aircraft management operations. In subsequent chapters these same performance measures and report formats will be recommended for in-house and other types of on-demand operations, but they are just as important to the recipient of managed services.

The management company is at a distinct advantage in procuring and passing through the many expenses required to operate the client's aircraft. The manager is the expert; the client knows little about aeronautical issues, especially the financial aspects. Yet a very important subset of the management services supplied should be in obtaining the best possible deal for the client. Yet how are clients to know, given their relative naiveté on the issues?

Therefore, a series of reports and insights should be supplied to the client outlining the efforts the management company has made to obtain the best possible price on parts, fuel, training, cleaning services, etc. Anytime a new or different article, commodity, or service is purchased by the manager for the client, an explanation should be supplied. Table 3.6 provides a list of suggested reports.

TABLE 3.5 Typical Aircraft Management Company Fee/Expense Elements

---

Fixed management fee for each aircraft
All other fees associated with this contract are normally passed through to the client with no markup. These may include but not be limited to

- Direct (variable) operating costs associated with aircraft operation to include
  - Fuel—contractor-provided/controlled fuel to be supplied at best available prices
  - Maintenance (nonscheduled and scheduled)—provided at preferred shop rates
  - Aircraft parts—best negotiated price
  - Engine overhaul and parts reserves/insurance programs
  - Landing/parking/hangar fees
  - Catering
  - Flight crew expenses
- Indirect (fixed) costs associated with aircraft operations to include
  - Salaries for a negotiated number of pilots, flight attendants, schedulers, aviation maintenance technicians, and aircraft cleaners, as applicable; other personnel costs must be approved by client
  - Aircraft Insurance
  - Required or approved training for core client personnel
  - Flight information and aircraft maintenance publications
  - Aircraft flight planning and aviation weather information systems (pro rata share if used by other management company clients)
  - Hangar rental/aircraft movement and cleaning services
- All other legitimate fees/charges associated with client aircraft operations (must be submitted to client for approval)

TABLE 3.6 Suggested Aircraft Management Company Reports

The management company should maintain databases and devise reporting systems to prove compliance with the terms of this contract and to inform the client about general aspects of flight operations and financial activity. These reports should be provided to a designated employee in the company within 10 days after the end of a reporting period and should include:

- Monthly flight activity—company and charter
  - Date
  - Aircraft
  - Origin
  - Destination
  - Duration
  - Passengers carried
  - Crew members
  - Significant remarks
- Monthly flight crew utilization—normal and contract pilots/flight attendants
  - Date
  - Origin
  - Destination
  - Flight and duty times—company and other use for normal crews
  - Training activity
- Monthly maintenance activity
  - Routine inspections
  - Significant maintenance actions
  - Unusual unscheduled maintenance
  - Upcoming scheduled maintenance activity
- Monthly expenditures—list all expenses associated with the operation and maintenance of the aircraft and flight crews
- Irregularity reports—any irregular event required under national air charter operating rules (Federal Aviation Regulations Part 135 in the United States) and any event in which a passenger is inconvenienced or makes a negative comment about a flight to a flight crew member or other contractor employee will be made verbally to the client company aviation representative within 24 hours of occurrence
- Ad hoc reports—operational and financial databases should be sufficiently comprehensive to provide on-demand ad hoc reports requested by the company

---

JOINT OWNERSHIP

Under this arrangement, two or more persons and/or companies become registered joint owners of an aircraft. One of the owners employs and furnishes the flight crew, and each of the owners pays a share of the charge specified in an agreement. Administrative, financial, and operational details of the aircraft operation usually are assumed by the owner employing the aviation personnel. Otherwise, this type of operation is quite similar to the more traditional in-house flight department. The principal advantage is in having another company share the fixed costs of the aircraft, which, depending on utilization, may comprise one-half the total aircraft expenses.

This type of operation is normally considered legal in most countries; however, tax considerations in some jurisdictions may make the arrangement less attractive than other types of ownership and control.

This method works well when the owners, normally two, use the aircraft infrequently and at times that complement one another. For instance, a company may use the aircraft mainly during the week for business trips, and the coowner may use the aircraft primarily for personal purposes on the weekends. Scheduling conflicts may be the main problem area for these arrangements. A preexisting relationship between parties or an intimate knowledge of the other's business operations is almost mandatory if a peaceful and long-term joint ownership is to be enacted.

Selection of a common aircraft type is an important first step for the partners in establishing their operation. While casual investigation of several types of aircraft by principals may prove an adequate method of choosing the type, an independent air transportation analysis of each party's needs should be conducted. A good fit for the aircraft to the parties' requirements is important to getting the agreement off to a good start. Further, basic policy issues of how long one party may keep the aircraft on the road, will company personnel be permitted to use the aircraft for personal use, and scheduling priorities must be discussed prior to deciding what aircraft will be purchased and where it will be based.

A detailed joint operating agreement is essential part of a successful joint-ownership operation. Scheduling, priorities, and conflict-resolution methods should be worked out and tested before the final agreement is signed.

Issues to consider:

- Duties of the managing partner
- Compensation for managing partner
- Payment procedures/considerations
- Recordkeeping responsibilities
- Scheduling procedure/conflict resolution
- Administrative and operational controls/standards
- Tax considerations
- Command, control, possession issues—legal and operational
- Risk management/insurance

> *Successful aircraft joint-ownership operations are like a good marriage—give and take makes it work.*
>
> —Experienced joint-ownership party

The advantages and disadvantages of taxes, depreciation, and liability are shared by the partners. Control over all aspects is shared by the owners, somewhat diluting the ability of any partner to dictate all elements of the operation. Yet the shared-ownership aspect usually provides motivation to create and maintain a high-quality flight operation. Regular communication between those controlling aircraft operations and the partners is a critical element in a successful joint-ownership operation.

OTHER METHODS

Interchange and time-share methods were mentioned in Chap. 2 as methods of supplementing existing in-house, managed, or joint-ownership provisions. These two methods permit a flight department to temporarily augment its fleet by reliance on other flight departments' aircraft. Yet specific provisions must be instituted to achieve a legal and equitable agreement. Note that these methods may not be practical in all countries.

Interchange is an arrangement whereby an owned aircraft is leased to another entity on a permissive basis in exchange for equal time in that entity's aircraft when needed. No charge or fee is made for this service except that a charge may be made not to exceed the difference between the cost of owning, operating, and maintaining the two aircraft. This method requires that each party own his or her aircraft and exchange his or her aircraft on an hour-for-hour basis.

A time-share agreement means an arrangement in which a company leases its airplane with flight crew to another person, and up to twice the direct operating expenses of the aircraft may be charged.

Detailed agreements must be signed by the parties to protect them and to ensure that one another's obligations and privileges are fully understood (see NBAA Web site for suggested agreement formats). Tax and liability issues must be specifically addressed. Perhaps most important is an understanding that specifically provides scheduling, cancellation, and conflict-resolution procedures.

REFERENCES

1. National Business Aviation Association. *2002 NBAA Compensation and Benchmarking Survey.* Washington: National Business Aviation Association, 2002.

2. NBAA Tax Resources: Carriage of Elected Officials and Candidates; available at *www.nbaa.org/member/taxes/carriage.htm.*

3. NBAA Tax Resources: Empty Seat Use of Employer Provided Aircraft; available at *www.nbaa.org/member/taxes/personalempty.htm.*

4. National Business Aviation Association. *NBAA Flight Operations Manual Workshop Notes.* Washington: National Business Aviation Association, 2000.

5. *NBAA Guidelines for Aircraft Management Agreements.* Washington: National Business Aircraft Association, 2001.

CHAPTER 4
RUNNING THE BUSINESS

IT REALLY IS A BUSINESS

Too many flight departments view their activities as being principally aviation-related and not business- or service-related. It is all too easy to get caught up in the technical and, yes, the romantic aspects of flying to the exclusion of the more mundane yet practical aspects of running a business. Those depending on the flight department for services are more pragmatic about them and find it hard to understand the technical appeal of aviation as a subject unto itself.

Many flight departments are run like an executive taxi service or as the principal's personal limousine. Unfortunately, they see their mission as a very narrowly defined activity that requires few of the traits of an actual business. These departments are lulled into feeling that they provide an on-demand service to whomever may call for it, with little regard for the concept of other essential service functions. Marketing, sales, profit and loss, customer service, product development, and research and development are the essentials of normal businesses and many business units within large corporations. These "you call, we haul" departments are missing a major and essential portion of their activity, that of considering themselves as a complete self-contained business unit.

Businesses are marked by certain characteristics. They

- Have a product to produce and sell
- Market the product
- Have customers who use their product
- Receive compensation for their product
- Exercise control over all aspects of the enterprise
- Anticipate and respond to market forces and trends

Certainly, flight departments have a product—on-demand air transportation—and customers—passengers—but do they work under and accomplish the remainder of the business indicators? Unfortunately, for many flight departments, the answer is no.

Marketing, control, and response to markets are not usually pursued by flight departments because, for the most part, the department enjoys a monopoly status in the executive transportation field and is protected from competition from outside agencies. So why bother with these unnecessary features not germane to flying airplanes? Because the privileged, protected status now enjoyed may evaporate with a changing passenger base and less profitable times.

The flight department must be run as a business, a venture that will stand on its own because dependence on artificial factors and protections constitutes false hope for better times. In essence, the flight department is a small business or business unit that must stand alone.

Whether it makes a profit is immaterial; it must make *sense* to the powers requiring the service. Ideally, the flight department manager must act as an entrepreneur or a small business owner to ensure the life and future of the venture. There has to be a sense of ownership not only for the manager but also for the members of the department. The first step in ensuring the success of the venture is to be sensitive to the needs and concerns of the customer.

Successful flight departments are run as a business, with a service to be provided as the product of their labors. They look toward being both effective at what they do and efficient as well. To do this, they employ accepted business and management practices, especially those used by the company or person for which they work. It is this mindset that allows them to become integrated into their principal's or corporate structure and to measure their performance as a service. This allows them to become a part of the larger organization and still let them do what they came to do in the first place—operate aircraft.

Flight departments are often isolated from their parent organization because of their need to be located at an airport. They are further isolated from the company by the autonomous and technical nature of their operations. Some flight departments are considered to be the private domain of a privileged few, often as providers of transportation perquisites. These factors tend to promote further isolation and concentration on technical aspects of aviation, often to the detriment of business-support concepts that should be driving them.

Human resources, information technology, risk management, and accounting all fulfill essential support roles for their companies—the company could not exist without their services, either in-house or outsourced. Why shouldn't company flight departments be considered as important or essential? In many companies they are, but achieving this institutional status has taken many years and much effort to achieve. The key ingredient of these institutional flight departments is that they have become an integral part of the company, actively following company strategies and providing *transportation solutions* to help the company achieve its goals and objectives. In short, it is a true business orientation that allows flight departments to become fully integrated, whether they work for an individual or a company. Successful flight departments provide high-priority transportation services to their clients; they just happen to use aircraft instead of some of some other form of transportation.

Flight departments normally operate as follows:

- A demand or request is placed on the department for a trip.
- Feasibility for the trip is determined (operational issues).
- Availability of a flight crew and suitable aircraft is determined.
- The trip is confirmed and scheduled.
- Detailed trip information is gathered and disseminated.
- The trip is flown.
- Flight information is recorded and stored.

In order for this procedure to be accomplished, a structure must be in place that will make the process as routine as possible. Policies, procedures, and recordkeeping systems must be available to accommodate a variety of actions performed by the department. Personnel must be in place to perform the required functions within the structure. All these items (and more) must be devised and implemented to make the department run with some semblance of order and discipline.

ORGANIZATION

Flight departments are generally semiautonomous organizations owing to their location and technical complexity. However, since the goal of the flight department is to be fully integrated with the parent organization, a strong link to it should be cultivated. Typical corporate flight department reporting seniors and the rationale for these choices are listed in Chap. 3.

The department organization should be both functional and flat. That is, the three principal functions within the department—administration, operations, and maintenance—should be represented by key individuals; their relationship should be quite close, with little intervening bureaucracy. Figures 4.1 and 4.2 show typical flight department organizations, keyed to department size.

FIGURE 4.1   Typical small flight department organization.

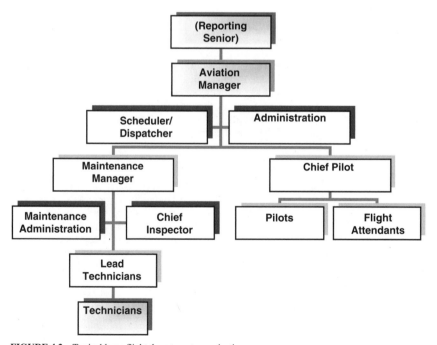

FIGURE 4.2   Typical large flight department organization.

Note that in smaller departments, an aviation manager is generally not needed; instead, a chief pilot is used to manage the operation. This is typical of single-aircraft operations. Also, reporting to the chief executive officer (CEO) or principal allows the chief pilot to have direct access to the individual who can both appreciate the flight department's value and provide necessary support. In this size department there may or may not be an aviation maintenance technician. If assigned, this person takes care of all aircraft maintenance duties, except when large inspections are undertaken or specialized maintenance is required; in such cases, either contract employees are hired to assist or the aircraft is sent to a service center.

In larger flight departments, a manager is designated to serve as the focal point of the aviation operation and to supply most of the administrative and financial expertise for the group. The chief pilot is used to provide operational expertise and represent the interests of pilots and flight attendants. Similarly, the maintenance manager is usually an experienced technician who has demonstrated administrative, leadership, and managerial skills to enable his or her segment of the organization to operate effectively and efficiently. Typically, the chief pilot acts as a pilot in command (PIC) in one or more types of assigned aircraft, flying somewhat less than a normal line pilot due to administrative and management duties associated with the job. While maintenance managers remain qualified as technicians, they are not often used for actual maintenance and inspection duties in large flight departments.

Other administrative, financial, operational, facilities, and ground support personnel may be assigned to provide specialized services to larger flight departments. All personnel, regardless of classification, should be provided with a detailed written job description to ensure that they understand what is expected of them and to coordinate their tasks with others in the department. A few job descriptions are listed in Chap. 3; a more comprehensive set may be found in the *NBAA Management Guide.*

SCHEDULING

The scheduling function within the department may be thought of as the point of sale or ordering point. The availability and capabilities of the department (the marketing function) are known among the principal passengers—through the joint efforts of both the parent organization and flight department agents. Now a customer must place a demand on the system for it to perform its primary function, that of providing on-demand air transportation service to the company. Therefore, the scheduling function is a critical link between passenger and flight department and should be treated as such.

Personnel

Schedulers in single-aircraft departments are typically administrative assistants assigned the collateral duty of scheduling the aircraft and its passengers. This person works closely with the chief pilot to ensure that as many passengers as possible can be accommodated, given the availability of the aircraft and limitations of the flight crews and maintenance personnel. This arrangement works well with some organizations because it places the administrative and decision burden on people outside the flight department. Conversely, this feature may mean a loss of control for the flight department and, more important, a loss of contact with people within the company or principal's organization who may be politically useful to the department. At best, keeping the scheduling function within the administrative structure of the parent tends to isolate the flight department from the company, denying it useful information and contacts.

In larger departments, a dedicated individual is normally located with the flight department to both schedule and coordinate all departmental operations. Some large flight departments use dispatchers to assist flight crews with the operational planning process and schedule flights and passengers as well. Weight and balance, route and weather planning, crew duty time limitations, and air traffic control (ATC) and airport restrictions must be known and accommodated by this person. While all operational factors ultimately are the responsibility of the PIC, the scheduler/dispatcher can make his or her task easier and provide a independent source of critical information. The shared responsibility of pilot and dispatcher in airline operations has become an accepted practice that yields economic, operational, and safety benefits; the same partnership is possible in corporate flight operations. Some of these dispatchers hold dispatcher licenses issued by the national regulatory authority.

Policy

Passenger scheduling policies must be devised and published to provide prospective customers with information regarding use of the aircraft. These measures should be published in a company memorandum or on-demand air transportation policy and procedures document (see Appendix) and authorized by the principal or high-level executive within a company. In some organizations, these issues are contained within a subset of the department operations manual specifically prepared for use outside the department itself. These company aircraft procedures manuals provide potential passengers with the guidelines for aircraft usage and procedures for scheduling them. See Chap. 3 for a more complete discussion of the aircraft use policy document.

Employees above certain levels or specifically named positions within the company may be authorized to use the aircraft. These individuals either may have scheduling authority or may have to seek that authority from an even fewer number of executives within the organization. Sometimes a single individual such as the principal's or CEO's assistant may act as the de facto scheduling authority, only deferring to the boss in cases of conflicts. A few principals and CEOs prefer to authorize all aircraft use as a matter of control and information about business operations. Priority to use any aircraft or a specific aircraft usually follows hierarchical lines, with juniors deferring to seniors.

Use by nonemployees or those outside the principal's family, whether they are customers or potential customers, family members of employees, political candidates, or friends, should be addressed in detail within the policy to preclude misunderstandings and to protect against potential liability concerns. Customers or potential customers normally are not a concern; however, many companies stipulate that a company employee be present in the aircraft anytime a nonemployee is on board. Family members and friends should be specifically authorized to travel on board a company aircraft by a corporate sponsor and may be subject to tax considerations for the individual or sponsor. [The Internal Revenue Service (IRS) rules concerning this usage are complex; see the *NBAA Management Guide* and other National Business Aviation Association (NBAA) tax publications.] The decision to use the aircraft for nonbusiness purposes should be well documented in use policy documents considering the tax consequences of this usage.

Procedure

A formal procedure should be developed to accommodate the passenger scheduling needs of the company. This procedure is normally tied closely to the aircraft usage policy and promulgated throughout the company. The procedure may include provision for informally checking on the availability of an aircraft but always should require the person requesting

Scheduling Elements

- Name of person making the request and authorizing the trip
- Trip purpose
- Dates of trip by segment (leg)
- Destinations—by address, nearest airport, if possible
- Passengers (by leg)
- Chargeback authority
- Ground transportation
- Catering desired
- Special information (unusual baggage, medical concerns, special ground handling requirements, etc.)

the trip to provide certain information in writing (facsimile, e-mail, or linked computerized scheduling system are the normal methods) to confirm the request.

After scheduling information is received, the scheduler will research aircraft and crew availability, suitable airports and flight-based operations (FBOs), and special considerations (ATC and airport slots and restrictions, airport hours of operation, noise considerations, etc.). Once it has been determined that the flight is possible, it should be placed on the flight schedule and confirmed with the requestor in writing, preferably by a detailed trip confirmation sheet. If the trip is routine, the scheduler may be allowed to schedule the trip without further consultations within the department. In some instances, the department manager or chief pilot is the only individual who can schedule a trip and assign a specific aircraft or flight crew. These individuals retain this right to ensure that they maintain operational command and control of each flight.

After the trip is authorized, a trip sheet is prepared providing both requestor and flight crew with information required for the flight.

Trip Sheet Elements

- Trip dates
- Crew names
- Aircraft assigned
- Departure times, by leg
- Destination airports
- Passenger manifest, including lead passenger
- Catering
- FBO/fueler
- Ground transportation—passengers and crew
- Accommodations—passengers and crew

Designating a lead or principal passenger on the trip sheet is useful for the flight crew. This is the person with whom the crew communicates concerning the conduct of the flight while enroute regarding schedule and passenger changes. This person should be provided with information on how to contact the flight crew at any time during a trip, regardless of the length of layover or location.

Scheduling Software

Many small flight departments create, modify, and maintain their flight schedules, using a simple spiral-bound monthly planning book or dry marker white board. This system appears to work well for these departments, yet the many inevitable changes made to scheduled flights prior to departure test the erasing and communications skills of the scheduler. Thus only the scheduler has a completely up-to-date copy of the schedule; others, including the chief pilot, rely solely on the scheduler for changes to flights made prior to departure. Further, dissemination of accurate schedules to flight crews, maintenance personnel, and other company personnel is made more difficult under this method.

Flight scheduling software is available that not only keeps the schedule up to date but also captures virtually every detail of the flight, before and after, in a database. This type of software provides flight operations management features for the entire department by scheduling, tracking, and reporting on all operational activities of the organization. While many people consider this software a luxury, especially for smaller operations, a long-range view of what it can do for the department should be investigated.

As a trip is "built" by the scheduler, a number of details must be captured and tracked through a number of inevitable changes occurring prior to flight. Having passenger, flight crew, aircraft, airport, and FBO data preloaded into the software greatly speeds the process. The schedule can be made available online to anyone possessing proper access to the system, making multiple and invariably inaccurate versions of the schedule held by several people unnecessary. Passenger confirmation and trip sheets and flight logs are prepared easily from the database electronically or on paper. After the flight, flight times, corrected manifests, trip fees, chargeback information, and pilot flight log data are captured in the database, completing the planning/recording process.

Perhaps the best feature of the software is its array of standard management reports available at the touch of a few computer keys. These reports (see the following sidebar) can be used to provide essential management information for both flight department and company personnel to determine the best methods for supplying on-demand air transportation services. Without these reports and their underlying database, most flight departments do not measure important elements of their operations, thereby depriving themselves of essential management tools. At some point in each flight department's existence, a call will come for an analysis of some feature of its operations; deriving any of the reports listed in the sidebar manually, using paper flight schedules and logs, involves much tedious effort and may yield results of questionable accuracy. While some operators may be reluctant to purchase this software because of the costs involved, it inevitably proves to be a good investment over time for all flight departments.

A number of software programs are available that should suit just about any flight department's needs. Since these are detailed and complex systems, a significant amount of research should be invested in determining the right type for your operation. *Business & Commercial Aviation* magazine occasionally reviews this type of software and the NBAA Web site Products and Services Section (*nbaa.org/prodsvcs*) lists manufacturers.

Flight Scheduling Software

- Provides accurate schedule data
- Allows a variety of individuals to share rapidly changing data
- Promotes a professional image with passengers
- Generates important management reports
- Reduces administrative load
- Provides an operational information database

Flight Operations Software Reports

- Aircraft utilization
- Flight statistics
- Destination/city-pair summaries
- Flight crew utilization/flight logs
- Chargebacks
- Passenger utilization/load factors
- Fuel usage/costs
- Department expenses
- Operational performance measures
- Total department activity

International

International flights require additional planning and consideration because of the different regulatory, economic, and cultural environments in which the aircraft will be operating. Interaction with the passengers becomes more detailed and intense, requiring precise itineraries, airports desired, and information regarding country entry procedures. The scheduler and flight crew normally work as a team to ensure that all required information, clearances, handling requirements, and planning data are assembled in a timely manner. The key to a successful international flight is complete, in-depth planning that provides for contingencies. Most important, the passengers must be made aware of the additional measures to be taken for international trip planning and the closer tolerances required for the operational aspects of the trip.

If a foreign destination is not visited regularly, a flight planning/aircraft handling service should be employed to reduce the number of variables and unknowns associated with such a trip. International flight plans, weather briefings, preferred routings, overflight permits, regulations, fuel service and payment provisions, visas, and ground transportation requirements are best handled by those who provide the services on a daily basis. The vagaries of international travel in corporate aircraft are too unpredictable and consequential to be performed by the uninformed.

Flight crews and the scheduler must receive international operations training from an experienced individual or training vendor. Even though an international trip planner/handler is employed, flight department personnel must have certain elementary background information about international regulations and procedures to safely and predictably plan and conduct the flight. Since international rules and procedures change frequently, periodic recurrent training on international subjects is also a must.

ADMINISTRATION

Administrative practice provides the foundation on which management is accomplished. Without structure, management becomes a hit-or-miss proposition because the elements of predictability, standard procedure, and control are not present. Moreover, these practices regulate and direct the flow of work within an organization. Without some measure of administrative process, paperwork becomes unmanageable, reporting structure is muddied, feedback concerning essential operations becomes nonexistent, and chaos sets in.

Administrative practices within the flight department depend heavily on established administrative procedures employed by the principal or company. While this is not to say that the department has no flexibility in devising its own procedures, the need to fit into an existing administrative structure is essential. Moreover, following established elements of administrative practice will facilitate the department startup process. Requesting assistance of the parent's administrative personnel will help new operations and provide valuable contacts within that structure for establishing operations.

Each of these sidebar issues should have some procedure associated with it. Most established organizations have procedures in place that will accommodate most of the elements listed. Internal departmental procedures will have to be established addressing the remaining elements to produce a good fit with the parent administrative procedures.

Administrative Practice

Policy, process, and procedure (the three Ps) are the means by which actions are accomplished within any organization; they are the lubricants and channels by which work is accomplished. Administration is the umbrella under which the three *P*s combine and interact. Many organizations maintain massive volumes delineating administrative practice, some to good effect and some counterproductive. If the stated procedure is obscure, overly complicated, or in conflict with a related procedure, not only will it will not work properly, but it also will create confusion and frustration for the employees attempting to use it. The same is true for the administrative practices of the flight department. If a procedure does not make sense, is cumbersome, or conflicts with another, it will create confusion and discord.

While most procedures should be written and recorded in a easy-to-retrieve format to facilitate use and avoid misunderstanding, some simple procedures may exist as a body of unrecorded common procedures known to all within the department. Regardless of the level of utility or formalization, all procedures should be reviewed for applicability, relevance, and effectiveness on a regular basis.

Administrative procedure must serve some purpose and contribute to the efficiency and effectiveness of an operation or task. If the reason for a procedure is, "That's the way we have always done it," "I don't know, but accounting wants it that way," or "The boss wants it that way," the procedure is probably a burden rather than a useful procedure. The biggest question to ask about administrative practices is, "What will the procedure do to enhance the operation?" If a valid answer results, then the procedure probably has some utility. Administrative procedures that are simple, understandable, and easy to accomplish will be better received and practiced than those that are complicated, obscure, and cumbersome.

Finally, the fewer procedures, the better. Integrated or linked procedures accomplishing more than one goal at a time are better because they are more user friendly, and the commonality of data put into the procedure will ensure greater accuracy when compared at some point downstream.

Flight Department Administrative Elements

- Communications
  - Methods/technology
  - Process
  - Content
- Control
  - Processes
  - Overall records management
  - Reports
- Personnel
  - Qualifications
  - Staffing requirements
  - Hiring
  - Salary actions
  - Evaluating
  - Terminating
- Information management
  - Production
  - Storage
  - Control
- Financial
  - Purchasing
  - Billing
  - Bill paying
  - Budgets/variances

Developing Practices

If a relevant procedure exists within the parent organization, it should be used rather than developing an ad hoc one. However, if the procedure is inappropriate or cumbersome for use by the flight department, steps should be taken to change it. The best way to accomplish this is to approach the person responsible for the procedure (sometimes difficult; be

Fuel Receipt/Invoice Process

- Purchase fuel (pilot)
  - Receive receipt
  - Attach receipt to flight log
  - File flight logs and trip receipts
- Receive receipt (administrator)
  - Verify trip/fuel purchase information
  - Enter fuel data into database
  - File receipt
- Receive monthly invoice (administrator)
  - Locate applicable receipts
  - Verify invoice charge with receipt
  - Authorize invoice payment
  - Send invoice to accounting for payment
  - File copy of invoice
  - Discard receipt

Typical Administrative Procedures

- Operations
  - Scheduling—passenger, aircraft, crew
  - Postflight recordkeeping—aircraft, crew, passengers
  - Training
- Maintenance
  - Scheduled maintenance planning
  - Discrepancy control
  - Maintenance recordkeeping
  - Parts inventory and control
- Accounting
  - Expenses
  - Purchasing
  - Budgeting and variances
- General
  - Personnel
  - Facilities
  - Crisis management

persistent) with *questions* regarding the purpose and impact of the procedure. Only after the true purpose of the procedure or practice has been determined can it be criticized objectively and suggestions made for its improvement.

Original or department-unique procedures should be developed with the assistance of those who will have to carry them out. Consensus regarding a practice is desirable but not necessary, however. The manager may have to hear all arguments regarding competing procedures and make a decision regarding the most desirable.

Once a practice or policy has been devised, it should be revisited from time to time to evaluate its continued applicability and usefulness. Organizations are littered with practices that once had meaning and relevance but have since become obsolete. Purging these administrative dinosaurs will streamline the operation and please the employees.

The actual design of the administrative practice should be done using actual, not theoretical, processes. Too often the procedure is designed around the ideal method rather than an in-place, realistic one. Once an actual process has been traced throughout its life cycle, enhancements may be added. A useful method of dissecting a process is by using bulletized lists or flowcharting techniques. This affords the designer a graphic view of the entire process, allowing a full picture of the critical and not-so-critical events. The previous sidebar provides an example of a fuel purchase receipt/invoice handling process.

Note that each step in the process requires an individual to complete the action. It should be clearly understood who in the department is responsible for each action, and preferably, a backup person should be designated to ensure that the action is completed regardless of the status of the principal individual.

The processes listed in the "Typical Administrative Procedures" sidebar should be devised by the individuals expected to accomplish them and recorded in department administrative policy and procedure manuals so that all personnel understand and appreciate the process.

TALKING WITH THE FOLKS DOWNTOWN

Wars are fought over it. Marriages are ruined because of it. Governments are toppled as a consequence. Differences in cultures and cultural expectations are perhaps the strongest split known to humanity because a gulf, nay, a chasm, exists between the backgrounds and very birthright of the parties. Thus it is with many aviation departments and *all others* within the parent organization.

The very nature of the flight department sets it apart from the administrative, financial, marketing, manufacturing, and human resources types at headquarters. The location of the flight department at an airport and its unique tasking tend to make the rest of the company view it as unique, sometimes mysterious, and always different. These are the people who fly the principal, the president, and senior staff to "important meetings" in Bangor, Los Angeles, and Paris. These are the people who are always "on a trip" when needed to answer questions about expense reports, budget variances, or annual reviews. Just who are these people, anyhow?

Don't laugh; the flight department is an enigma to most people within the organizations it serves and destined to remain so if the department manager does not make a real effort to dispel these myths and become an integral part of the company team. More important, the flight department must start working with these folks downtown if it is to realize its full potential or even survive as a part of the larger organization.

Organizational Conflict

The difficulty lies in both the aviation personnel and *all others* understanding and appreciating one another—accounting versus aviation, human resources versus the pilots, lawyers versus everybody. Each discipline comes with its own set of values, expectations, and arcane language. The whole process of understanding between parties is more an exercise in foreign relations than organizational development. However, aviation may as well be the one to make the first step because it has the most to gain. Yes, flight departments come and go, but finance, administration, and human resources go on forever.

The Downtowners

Essential	Good to Know
The chairman/president's office	Planning
Accounting/finance	Disaster preparedness
Budget	Environmental
Purchasing	Industrial safety
Payroll	Marketing/sales
Accounts payable	
Human resources	
Administration	
Property management	
Risk management	
Legal	
Security	

Everyone has had misunderstandings with the aforementioned departments.

- Accounting wants to know why the flight department has exceeded its monthly mainte-nance budget by 300 percent, and you cannot make them understand what the APU air-worthiness directive is all about.
- Legal will not sign off on the hangar lease because of the airport reversion clause.
- Human resources wants all the annual appraisal form blocks filled in even though the mechanics do not do half the stuff listed for a "refinery technician" (which is how they are classified) and environmental does not know what to do with the used MEK.

The natural tendency is to throw up your hands, say *they* do not understand, and ignore the problem. Unfortunately, this will only go on for so long. Even the chairperson cannot pro-tect his or her air force forever from an irate comptroller.

Basically, all these warring entities are on the same team: the company. They are sup-posedly a part of a team that is working for a common set of goals and objectives. Granted, this fact is difficult to discern much of the time. How to break the impasse? Simple, talk it through.

Every department within an organization wants to do well and to look good. Accounting wants to get its variance reports out on time, human resources wants to get the retirement plan questionnaires back and compiled, and purchasing wants all outstanding purchase orders reconciled. And you want to get your flights out and back on time. These are all very different functions, but they all work toward a common goal—to make the company achieve its operating targets and place of prominence in the industry. The problem is that everyone is too narrowly focused on his or her own interests and goals. What we have is a failure to empathize and communicate.

Get Them on Your Side

They do not understand aviation, and you probably do not understand much of what they are trying to accomplish. It is like transitioning to a new aircraft or flying to Europe for the first time—all of what is encountered is strange and does not make much sense. After a while, though, you begin to understand the new system, its language, and its culture. You may not agree with it or want to do it for the rest of your life, but you can understand it and can work within its confines. You may even like or at least admire some of what you see.

Since the flight department has the most to lose, the first move belongs to the flight department manager. Approach the appropriate people in the departments that mean some-thing to you and ask for their assistance. Yes, ask for help. People normally respond well to requests for assistance in a field they know something about. Show an interest in their work, empathize with their problems, and offer to help where you can. Pursue the relation-ship if its appears fruitful; find another contact if not. Learn their language, find out what is important to them, start thinking in their terms, and cultivate a mentor or at least a coach. Invite them out to visit the hangar, show them around, take them to lunch, and ask for their help again. Tell them what is important to you and the flight department; talk in terms of supporting the corporate mission, of common goals. Build a mutual admiration society; bridge the cultural differences.

Before you start, think of what the other people want, of what motivates them. At the most basic level, we all want to feel secure—secure at home and at work. Beyond this ele-mentary need, people need to feel that they are a part of a group, an integral part of a team working toward some worthy common goal. Moving on to people's higher needs, they want to feel that they are respected and that their efforts are appreciated, not so much that they receive a special award but merely to have somebody say, "Good job." The final step in the motivation chain must come from the individual himself or herself. Self-actualization or self-fulfillment represents the employee's personal concept of high value for the work in which he or she is engaged. These items constitute Maslow's hierarchy of needs (see Chap. 5), which has stood the test of time in the workplace. It is important to note that for self-fulfillment to be possible, *all* the lower needs must first be met.

Helping your target audience satisfy their needs will take time. However, the investment will be well worth it. Enlist the aid of other flight department members, especially your secretaries, administrative assistants, and schedulers, because they work closely with many sections of the company. Assign them tasks and goals to establish contact and build relationships with significant players within the parent hierarchy. Encourage mutual visiting and sharing of resources, where possible. Do not overlook the pilots and technicians as sources of contact with the downtown crowd either. This is an essential element in their professional development and must be pursued by them early in their careers. And if they have been assigned collateral administrative duties within the department, these "outreach" activities are a natural for them.

It may be desirable to create situations where a group of the downtowners are invited to the hangar for a formal presentation concerning the flight department, its aircraft, mission, and operations. A tour of the aircraft and facility, a presentation about your mission, and a frank discussion of your needs and aspirations will go a long way toward establishing firm communications links and bridging the cultural gaps that exist between the flight department and "them." And provide a catered lunch, too.

Making House Calls

However, suppose that "downtown" is 300 miles away? Headquarters may be at some location remote from your airport, forcing you to do all your business via remote control. This complicates your task of establishing good relations with your "support staff" but is by no means impossible. If opportunities do not present themselves to allow face-to-face visits with the people who count, they must be manufactured. Request opportunities to discuss long-range plans, budgets, department restructuring, plans for the new hangar, or salary administration with the appropriate people at headquarters. Getting the right people to visit the hangar may be more difficult to accomplish but will be more effective than your visit to them. These are legitimate activities for the flight department manager and should be honored. Granted, this means an investment of the department manager's time, but much is at stake.

In your effort to become aviation's good will ambassador, do not forget the helpers on the other end either. The secretaries and administrative assistants who schedule the aircraft for their bosses can make or break the flight department. Without their understanding and support, their bosses will have a difficult time in thinking well of the department; secretaries are true gatekeepers and opinion molders. Why not a special day at the hangar for just the secretaries?

On your way to establishing good relations with those who can help the cause of the flight department, you also will be selling the concept of on-demand air transportation. This is something that all members of the department always must be aware of and engaged in. The position of the flight department is tenuous enough; you need all the support you can get in making the company believe that aviation is a real support function. These relationships will further that cause.

In the largest sense, you are building a support staff within the greater organization. Instead of having those departments make demands on your department, enlist their aid in helping you to achieve your departmental goals. This is possible, but remember, there is a cost. It takes an investment of time and effort to show that you understand their needs and

An In-House Operation Pays Off

A financial services company that specialized in providing initial stock offering services to customers had regularly used aircraft charter services during the busy first days of an offering. The charter aircraft were used to transport company executives and clients to visit investment firms in an effort to generate interest in the new offering. In doing so, the aircraft was used to good advantage, often visiting three cities in one day and ten cities in a week.

After a year of working to find a charter operator that could be flexible enough to accommodate the last-minute and often-changeable nature of its requirements, the firm retained a consultant to determine the best course of action. In a short period of time, the firm was operating its own Lear 45 aircraft, often for its own travel needs rather than those of its clients. Not only was it able to control the aircraft's schedule, direct operating costs became less expensive once the company passed the 250-hour annual usage point.

are acting as an integral part of the larger group. The payoff is too good to pass up: Wouldn't it be great to get an annual budget or personnel request through on the first try?

Cultural differences can be bridged. The creation of your very own people-to-people program within the company definitely will help to get the flight schedule accomplished. And don't forget to say "Thank you" often.

FINANCE AND ACCOUNTING

The aviation department manager probably spends the second largest amount of his or her nonaviation time on financial matters—the largest amount of time spent is, or should be, on personnel matters. Financial matters equate to resources, resources that make the difference between a struggling, barely-able-to-get-by department and one that achieves excellence with a measure of style. Therefore, the manager spends much time on financial issues just to stay ahead of the other cost centers within the organization that vie for available resources.

Each of the items shown in the financial processes sidebar are equally important and must be kept in balance if the department's goals and objectives are to be met.

The knowledge of basic accounting and finance practice and processes is essential to managing these affairs within the department. Without this knowledge, the manager is at the mercy of those within the system who do know and appreciate financial terms and practices. Perhaps the best way to learn or to brush up on this field is through an individual working in the larger organization's accounting department, preferably one who will be involved directly with the flight department accounts. In

Basic Financial Processes

- Planning
- Budgeting
- Recording
- Controlling/tracking
- Justifying

this manner there should be some mutual exchange of information about the participant's specialties, thereby enhancing the communications process between the two departments. This exchange should not stop with the flight department manager either. Other members of the department with direct financial interests, notably the director of maintenance, parts handlers, and secretary, should establish their own relationships with accounting personnel.

A key issue in working with expenses, budgets, and accounting in general is that the accounting department must be able to process the purchase orders, invoices, bills, and credits and provide operating divisions with reports in a timely manner if management is to be able to properly control financial matters. If invoices are held and not processed and paid for weeks at a time and/or if journal and variance reports are not released until 2 weeks into a new month, then managers are always far behind real time and never sure of where they stand with their vendors or the budget. The accounting process is a two-way street; if the accounting department expects adherence to financial policies, then it must cooperate with operating divisions by providing accurate and timely information.

Basic Accounting Practices

- Purchase supplies and equipment
- Pay invoices
- Reimburse personnel expenses
- Verify invoices paid in a timely manner
- Receive consolidated reports of purchases and expenses (journal)
- Receive reports comparing planned with actual expenses (budget variance)

Taxes

Taxes, be they federal, state, or local, can present even the most astute accountant or tax attorney with a bewildering thicket of arcane statutes, conflicting regulations, and tax law precedents. If tax laws are difficult for the experts, then the flight department manager has almost no hope of comprehending these confounding rules and regulations. However, department managers should be aware of the rudiments of the laws to protect themselves and the parent organization.

Basically, the flight department must keep a record of all flights made, providing at least the date, departure and arrival points, names of passengers, and whether the passengers were employees *and* whether they had a business purpose for the flight. If the passenger is not an employee or an employee without a business purpose, information will be needed regarding the reason for the flight or relationship to an employee or the company. These are just the basics for the flight department and the company; a more comprehensive treatment of the subject may be found in the *NBAA Management Guide*. At a minimum, managers should be aware that there are significant implications to the issues shown in the sidebar.

Tax Issues

- Nonbusiness use of employer-provided aircraft
- Affiliated company group use of aircraft
- Carriage of elected officials
- Interchange agreements
- Spousal travel
- Joint ownership of aircraft
- Flight department companies
- Time-sharing companies
- Personal use of company aircraft

Financial Planning

Planning as a stand-alone subject is covered later in this chapter, but since planning is an integral part of the budget cycle, it will be mentioned briefly here as it applies to the financial process. Some flight departments consider financial planning for budget purposes to be the process of adding anticipated annual inflation to last year's budget to arrive at the numbers to be submitted for next year's budget. This so-called incremental budgeting robs the manager of what can be a valuable tool to be used in achieving departmental renewal and progress. This "lazy man's" way of performing an unpleasant task will not allow the department to move forward, to incorporate new features, or to get rid of obsolete or inefficient processes.

Corporate strategic and short-term plans should be studied to determine the direction and goals of the company as whole. If the departmental goals do not fit into and support the organization's plans, the budget process will be difficult. By supporting the stated desires of the parent group, the department can show that it is a member of the team, willing to subordinate its desires to the greater good and be a full contributor to the joint effort.

In helping the company or principal achieve short-term goals, however, the concept of reaching both the parent and departmental long-range goals also must be considered. For instance, if an immediate company goal is to reduce capital expenses while supporting a long-term goal of expansion into a foreign country, the department must find a means to begin flights to the target country even though the aircraft currently available are inadequate to the task. A potential answer may be the short-term lease of a long-range aircraft to support the short-term goal while achieving the long-term goal as well.

The planning process should include as many people within the department as possible. Their particular view of the overall operation should be valuable because of their experience and expertise. Moreover, engaging them in the process will make them feel a part of the team. However, this planning process should be carefully controlled and not merely a far-reaching brainstorming session to see how the department can be expanded regardless of need. Rather, the planning process should begin with a careful look at existing operations to determine desirable and undesirable elements with an eye toward improvement. This introspective look at operations should include an investigation of whether the departmental goals are being met with regard to both effectiveness and efficiency. Only after this examination of current operations should the discussion of future needs be opened.

The object of the planning process is to develop realistic goals that can be met within a specified period of time. The normal tendency is to focus principally on short-term goals to the detriment of the long view. A well-integrated set of long- and short-term goals that fit into the corporate view of the future should form the basis for a realistic and easily justified budget. To be of real value, goals must be quantifiable so that progress toward them may be measured. Merely saying that the department will have a goal of improved customer service probably will not be achieved because no performance factors have been assigned. However, a goal stating that the semiannual passenger satisfaction survey will yield 10 percent more passengers describing service as good or excellent is something that can be quantified and progress measured toward reaching it.

Budgets

A budget is an extension of the planning process that restates short-term goals in financial terms. The budget takes an abstract concept such as providing on-demand air transportation and gives it the detailed resources necessary to bring the concept to reality. Unfortunately, most people do not view the subject in such lofty terms. Rather, they look at the budget-building process as a tedious, no-win game played for the benefit of the accounting department and the budget itself as a tattle-tale device that can only show the

PLANS INTO ACTION

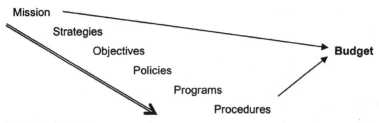

FIGURE 4.3   Budget concept.

boss that they are not performing well. These negative stereotypes have arisen in large part from a lack of understanding of the budget process and what it can mean to the department in terms of resources to be gained. Figure 4.3 illustrates the importance and utility of the budget as a means of converting plans into action.

If viewed and understood properly, the budget can be used to the advantage of the department—to help it obtain the resources it needs and look good in the process. However, the basic language of finance and accounting must be understood and appreciated first. As stated previously, this is best accomplished by finding a member of the accounting department who is willing to take on a student—you—in the pursuit of practical accounting and finance knowledge.

There are two types of budgets that the flight department will use: operations and capital. The operations budget sets forth expenses and revenues (if any), providing a breakdown by detailed accounting categories. Budgets are usually made up for a 12-month period designated the *fiscal year*. This may not necessarily conform to the calendar year but may fit a convenient period from an accounting and taxation standpoint. A simple flight department operations budget is shown in Fig. 4.4.

Note that the expenditures are broken down by variable and fixed costs. Variable costs are incurred only when the aircraft flies, e.g., fuel, maintenance, and reserve for maintenance items (e.g., engine, auxiliary power unit, and thrust reverser overhauls) and crew expenses. Fixed costs are incurred whether the aircraft flies or not, e.g., salaries, hangar rent, training, etc. Where possible, the budget should provide separate variable costs for each aircraft assigned to better account for the operating costs for each aircraft.

Depreciation.   Depreciation expense, sometimes included in flight department operating budgets (not shown in this example), recognizes the fact that from an accounting standpoint, a capital asset (property or device possessing value) has a finite life span and therefore loses value over its life span. When its useful life has expired, only its residual or resale value remains. The decreasing value of the asset is recognized over its accounting life as a fixed expense. Flight department personnel must be aware of depreciation provisions to more fully appreciate its effects on budgets and other accounting features.

It is important to note that there are two types of depreciation: tax and book. *Tax depreciation* refers to the tax consequences of reducing the taxable value of the asset over a minimum period of time specified by tax authorities, as few as 5 years for a corporate aircraft; at the end of the taxable depreciation period, only a small residual value, often as little as 10 percent, remains. *Book depreciation* refers to the actual decrease or increase (appreciation) in value of the asset during the intended period of use by the company. In practice, the book value of a popular aircraft after 5 or even 10 years of use may actually be greater than its purchase price.

		Flight Hours per Year		
Cost Item		250	450	600
Variable/Direct Costs				
Fuel (price x gph)	$550	137,500	247,500	330,000
Maintenance				
Labor (hrs/flt hr x rate)	$112	28,000	50,400	67,200
Parts	$99	24,750	44,550	59,400
Engine Reserves				
Restoration allowance	$210	52,500	94,500	126,000
APU/Reverser Overhauls	$27	6,750	12,150	16,200
Landing/handling fees	$14	3,500	6,300	8,400
Crew Expenses	$135	33,750	60,750	81,000
Catering/supplies	$40	10,000	18,000	24,000
Total Variable Costs	**$1,187**	**$296,750**	**$534,150**	**$712,200**
Fixed/Indirect Costs				
Crew Salaries/Benefits	$175,000	175,000	175,000	175,000
Hangar	$5,500	5500	5500	5500
Aircraft Insurance	$43,000	43000	43000	43000
Training	$33,000	33000	33000	33000
Flight Planning/Weather	$3,500	3500	3500	3500
Flight Publications/Data	$4,500	4500	4500	4500
Other fixed				
Total Fixed Costs	**$264,500**	**264,500**	**264,500**	**264,500**
Total Costs		**$561,250**	**$798,650**	**$976,700**
Total Cost Per Hour		**$2,245**	**$1,775**	**$1,628**
(Per hour cost savings)			-21%	-27%

FIGURE 4.4   Sample annual operations budget.

Practical Budgets.   All of this effort requires the cooperation of many people within the company, beginning with the CEO and ending with just about every employee who has a goal to reach. It is the budget-cycle process that links the diverse organizational groups in their competition for the resources that will enable the company to complete its mission and, hopefully, make a profit. However, the means by which the cycle is completed, the financial accounting system, must be capable of completing all the stated tasks in a timely and accurate manner. Without a sufficiently fast and accurate system, the budget cycle will not function efficiently enough to be of value as a forecasting and measuring tool. For example, if the accounting department cannot enter information concerning obligated expenses in a timely manner to enable monthly reports to be sent to the operating departments by the tenth of the following month, the operating managers have no up-to-date information regarding their financial performance and progress toward their goals.

If this process cannot be accomplished in a reasonable period of time, the flight department may be forced to keep its own books or maintain a running total of expenditures by accounting category to ensure that it does not overspend the allocated amount. This double book-keeping inevitably leads to discrepancies between the department's and accounting's systems and is a time-consuming, extra task that robs the department of productivity. However, this may have to be done as a defensive measure to ensure compliance with the budget.

Are Budgets Necessary?   A significant number of flight departments, mostly small ones, are not required to submit budgets. This is largely due to the CEO or principal absorbing the operating expenses within the general and administrative budget, a segment traditionally having sufficient elasticity to absorb large variances.

Flight departments operating under this system may consider that they have an open-checkbook fiscal system and are not fully responsible for what is spent. While most managers/chief pilots do not abuse their stewardship, this form of fiscal nonmanagement can lead to both abuse and poor management. Without being accountable to a budget, it is also difficult, if not impossible, to measure efficiency and productivity.

The real downside to this method is that the munificent CEO will not be there forever, and when the new person takes over, there may be some uncomfortable questions asked about flight department expenditures and the relevance of the department in assisting the company meet its goals.

Thus, for the sake of good management practice and anticipating the need to one day show value, building and living within a budget is a good idea, regardless of whether the boss wants one or not.

Building the Budget

Each year companies begin the budget cycle by setting forth general budget goals that flow from their long- and short-range plans. These goals may be expressed as a desire to increase sales or profits by a certain percentage or to decrease expenses by absolute amounts or percentages of individual budget line items or the entire budget. By the time these budget goals (actually mandates) have reached the flight department, several layers of additional detail may have been added to the original broad goals, thereby adding further constraints to an already constrained budget.

A budget worksheet is usually provided that shows the previous year's budgeted and actual expenditures. Spaces are provided for the budget request for the upcoming fiscal year by budget line item as designated in the accounting department's chart of accounts. It is important to have the proper level of detail in the chart of accounts that supports the actual types of expenditures used by the flight department. Accounting departments sometimes force flight departments to use codes that have existed within the company as a consequence of its line of business, including truck heavy maintenance, small craft repairs, machinery maintenance/overhaul, and sales training. If these classifications are used, it will be difficult to determine where the department's funds are expended. Therefore, flight departments should insist that their own unique terms be placed in the chart of accounts. Table 4.1 shows a sample flight department chart of accounts.

Note that this is a very generalized statement of expenses. When building the budget, actual categories should be used to estimate expenditures and then subtotaled to match the broader classifications listed in the worksheet. A more detailed chart of accounts for flight departments may be found in the *NBAA Management Guide.*

TABLE 4.1   Sample Chart of Accounts

Variable/Direct Expenses	Fixed/Indirect Expenses
Fuel	Salaries and benefits
Maintenance	Pilot
Airframe	Maintenance
Avionics	Administrative
Engine	Part-time employees
Parts/material	Facilities maintenance
Contract services	Support equipment maintenance
Engine overhaul reserves	Contract services
Catering	Training
Flight crew expenses	Flight planning/weather services
Fees—landing, parking, etc.	Utilities
	Administrative/office
	Insurance
	Aircraft
	Hangar
	Taxes

The major factor driving budget estimates for the upcoming year is the estimate of annual usage of the aircraft, expressed as flight hours. While flight hours will not directly affect the fixed-cost portion of the budget, it will do so indirectly. For example, if aircraft utilization is expected to increase appreciably, additional pilots and aircraft maintenance technicians (AMTs), training, and maintenance facilities may be required, thereby increasing both variable and fixed expenses. Figure 4.4 incorporates this relationship in the budget worksheet, showing management that increased utilization reduces unit costs by significant amounts.

It is tempting to just add the value of inflation to each worksheet category and be done with it. However, such an expedient might prove harmful to the department if upcoming but obscure expenses are overlooked in the process. Moreover, if justification for an expense category is requested, it will be difficult to defend the inflation method of budget estimation. Assumptions for continuing and new expense items are very important, particularly when it comes to budget justifications. Therefore, a budget analysis method for each significant expense category should be devised and used to give the preparer a basis for justifying either existing or new requests. Such methodology is invaluable when the inevitable budget revisions are requested. A sample of one such method is shown in Fig. 4.5.

While it is not necessary to provide an analysis for each category of expense, it will provide a useful record of the assumptions and factors used in reaching a decision regarding a particular budget request item. This is particularly true when the reason for an estimate is needed for future reference.

When building a budget, the standard methods of budget estimation and justification used by the parent organization should be followed carefully. Failure to understand the process probably will require resubmission of the budget request, bringing unwanted attention to the department. Further, a contact within the accounting department will prove very useful when questions concerning budget policy or procedures arise. Moreover, discussing budget philosophy and corporate strategy concerning the upcoming fiscal year with the flight department reporting senior should yield valuable insights.

Capital Budgets

This type of budget recognizes that certain purchases have long-term value or the ability to create value for the company. Machinery, buildings, furniture, computers, and aircraft fall

Account_____   Account Number_____   Date_____

Budget Period _____

Previous Level _____

_____

Assumptions

_____

_____

_____

Analysis

    Month   Event   Impact

    _____   _____   _____

    _____   _____   _____

    _____   _____   _____

    _____   _____   _____

    _____   _____   _____

    _____   _____   _____

    Overall Impact

_____

_____

Justification

_____

_____

_____

FIGURE 4.5 Sample budget analysis worksheet.

into this category. Because of the ability to create or enhance value for the company, the object is assigned a finite life over which it is expensed. Therefore, if an aircraft is purchased new, it may be assigned a tax life of as little as 5 years and may be expensed over that period, leaving just a residual value at the end of the period (see "Depreciation," on page 4.17).

Capital budgets are important for flight departments because they are not considered a part of the annual operations budget. In essence, the capital budget is a separate budget used for buying permanent, major assets. It is a way of obtaining a new hangar, ground support equipment, aircraft equipment upgrades and interior refurbishments, support vehicles, and furniture essentially off-budget—the normal operations budget, that is. However, the capital items must be justified and put into competition with other capital item proposals made by the rest of the company. And if the company is to realize some value from the money it invests, it must be capable of producing some measurable benefit for the company. Sample justifications are shown in a subsequent section.

Any major purchase or expense should be reviewed by accounting for possible inclusion in the capital budget. Removing major items, especially unanticipated items, from the operations budget will make the department appear more in compliance with the planned expenditures and enable it to gain needed items.

Any action that increases or extends the value of a capital asset should be capitialized. The examples mentioned earlier easily meet those criteria; some maintenance actions also meet the criteria, although they may not be readily apparent. Engine, thrust reverser, and APU overhauls fall into this category because service bulletins and other improvements are incorporated during the overhaul process that may extend or improve the value of asset. Make sure accounting knows about these features; it may be able to recapitalize the asset.

Controlling/Tracking Budgets

The budget is just a plan for spending money. It contains no method of ensuring that the plan is carried out or how actual expenses compare with the original estimate. Therefore, a method of comparing monthly expenditures with budgeted estimates known as *variance reporting* is used by most companies requiring budgets. An example of a segment of a variance report is shown in Fig. 4.6.

Note that the effect of a higher or lower expenditure for a single month may be quite different from the effect on the year-to-date section. For example, in Fig. 4.6 the salaries expense for the month of April was 2 percent less that the budgeted amount, but because of some overbudget expense in the previous 3 months, the net effect on the year-to-date section was 10 percent more than budget. And the large overbudget maintenance expense in April does not look as bad when spread over the 4-month period.

A method used to level out large unbudgeted expenses for departments that occasionally have unexpected expenses is the *moving-average variance*. This adds the current-month expense with the previous 11 months and divides by 12 to show the effect of the expense over a long time period. This is particularly helpful for the maintenance section, which may have large, unexpected expenses relating to nonscheduled maintenance items. The purpose of this method is to show the effect of spreading the current-month expense over a long period of time.

Division: Administrative				Department: Aviation			Month: April 2003	
	April				**Year-to-Date**			
	Budget	Actual	Variance	%	Budget	Actual	Variance	%
Salaries	56,250	55,000	(1,250)	-2	250,000	275,000	25,000	+10
Maintenance	25,000	140,000	115,000	+460*	100,000	195,000	95,000	+95
(12 mo. av.	*25,000*	*32,500*	*7,500*	*+30)*				

* Note: $105,000 one-time engine repair on N123 due to foreign object damage

FIGURE 4.6   Budget variance report example.

Note that the reason for the large monthly variance has been footnoted on the variance report. This is important to preclude questions concerning the variance. Preferably, the reason for a potential variance should be made known to the flight department manager, his or her reporting senior, and the accounting department as soon as it is known. Nobody likes surprises, especially large monetary surprises.

Budget Justification

When budgets are being built, large variances are anticipated or received, or new budgeted items are contemplated, a justification statement may be required to accompany the other budget documents. This is merely a detailed description of the item or service to be purchased along with an explanation of its purpose and utility. Why do you want it? How strongly do you feel about it?

The justification should contain, at a minimum, the following items:

- Background
- Prior expenses
- Current situation
- Assumptions
- Proposal
- *Detailed* justification
- Benefits

An example of a detailed justification is shown in Fig. 4.7. This level of justification may not be necessary; ask the boss what level of justification is appropriate.

Division: Administrative   Department: Aviation   Date: 5-12-03

Item: Purchase One Stellar Model 8346 Spectrum Analyzer

Cost: $57,500 New

Useful life: 5 years

Application: Repair aircraft electronic equipment.

Justification: Aviation Department must send unserviceable aircraft electronic equipment to vendors that may require 2 day shipping/processing time. This causes the department to maintain much rotable (spare) equipment, now valued at $235,000.

The spectrum analyzer will complete the electronics repair suite at the Aviation Department's facility. This completed suite will allow in-house technicians to save an estimated $11,000 per year in repair costs and reduce the rotable equipment by an estimated $110,000.

Alternatives:
1. Continue to use the vendor services at $32,000 per year to repair spares.
2. Purchase a used analyzer @ approximately $23,000. This option is undesirable due to the lack of needed features contained in the new equipment.

FIGURE 4.7   Sample budget justification.

PERSONNEL

The members of the flight department are its most important asset. Their expertise and willingness to perform are its real treasure. Without those attributes, the department is, at best, a mediocre group of aviation personnel. Their willingness to perform, or motivation, must be properly channeled and shaped if a high-quality product is to result. The channeling or directing function leads to the concept of teamwork—equally important as motivation. If the people all act independently and without regard for one another, however well they perform, the result may be chaos rather than a smoothly running organization.

The artform for the aviation department manager is to successfully direct and channel the efforts of assigned personnel to form an effective and efficient team of professionals that will provide high-quality air transportation services to the company. This artform is called *leadership*.

It is impossible to cover all aspects of personnel management in a book of this nature; therefore, the aviation department manager should have some formal or practical supervision and/or management experience and training prior to accepting the job. Many supervisors/managers have learned their craft on the job, but the mistakes made in the process are largely avoidable with some planning and forethought. Some issues are more important than others, however. The first step is to hire the right people.

Hiring

There is normally an abundance of well-qualified pilots and AMTs in the job market at any given time. In times of expansion and prosperity for corporate aviation, the best qualified people are not as apparent or available, but they are there. However, a wallet full of Federal Aviation Administration (FAA) certificates and years of experience do not ensure that any individual will work well in your operation.

The culture of the company and the department dictate the required personality of the prospective employee, not the proper certification and experience. Perhaps the greatest

Hiring Process

- Know what you want: detailed job description, experience levels, ability to perform collateral duties, etc.
- Work closely with the company human resources department—their experience and insight is essential.
- Verify former employment and education.
- Check with the FAA Information Management Section (AFS-624, Box 25082, Oklahoma City, OK 73125) for possible airman certificate violations.
- Let the candidate interview with at least three (preferably five) people, including one or two managers outside the department.
- Fly with or observe the candidate perform maintenance functions.
- If possible, employ the candidate on a part-time basis prior to making the permanent hire decision.
- Hire for the long-term. Is this person 20-year material?
- Make sure the candidate fully understands the job being offered.

difficulty in finding the right employee is to determine the corporate and departmental culture and then find a match for those characteristics. If the company is mature and well structured, a less formal, free-spirit personality may not fit well. Conversely, if the company is in its entrepreneurial stage, this type of personality may prove a good fit.

Take the time to fully evaluate candidates for employment. Consider using the items listed in the accompanying sidebar (see also Fig. 3.7).

Motivation

Perhaps more than any other single personnel management skill, the leader's ability to motivate is the single factor that will get the most and best work out of people. Motivation creates an internal incentive within a person to accomplish a task at hand. Instilling and maintaining this incentive should be a primary job of the manager. Another issue is understanding what factors contribute to job satisfaction (see the sidebar).

Motivation comes from realizing that the job being done is essential and has value. Instilling motivation requires that the employee understand

- The mission of the company and flight department
- Where he or she fits in the organization
- The importance of their job

While there are no guarantees, if these factors are considered as guiding principles, the chances of having a productive, happy workforce are high. It may not always be possible to approach each tasking with all these tenets in mind; some jobs just are not fun. However, if the concept of motivation is kept in mind constantly, employee performance should be high.

Positive Job Factors

- Respect shown by management and peers
- Good pay (not necessarily high pay)
- Opportunity for self-improvement
- Perceiving that the job is important
- Opportunity to do interesting work
- Latitude to accomplish the job without excessive direction

Good managers and leaders show respect for the individual. If the individual is made to feel that he or she is an important part of the overall operation, that his or her opinion counts, and that his or her welfare is considered in every action concerning his or her employment, then that person will be a relatively happy member of the team. When management practices respect for the individual, other components of good personnel management should follow. The concept of respect will tend to promote fairness in scheduling and compensation, opportunity for advancement, positive reinforcement for a job well done, and some slack when the employee makes a mistake.

The quality of a person's life is in direct proportion to their commitment to excellence, regardless of their chosen field of endeavor.

—VINCE LOMBARDI

Communicating Expectations

Nobody likes surprises, particularly on the job. If complete and detailed expectations of job performance are not provided (and updated regularly), a worker will be constantly surprised by the tasks assigned. Job descriptions, task briefings with completion standards included, and *regular feedback* concerning performance are essential items to be communicated to every employee.

If an organization's employees are its most valuable asset, then they must be maintained and upgraded so that the organization continues to realize a return on those assets. Getting the new person to a point of full productivity may take 6 months or more; this is a major task that should pay handsome dividends in the long term. With this concept firmly in mind, develop an initial *asset investment plan* for the new hire.

Most managers have figured out that while technical competence is an important aspect of a person's job qualifications, in the long run it is the person's ability to work toward common goals, to interact effectively with people, and to provide value to the organization that count the most. (These are the real reasons you hired the person, aren't they?) To get the new person started in the right direction, he or she must know what the company's values are, what product or service it offers, and what characteristics in people the organization prizes most. These elements constitute the organization's culture, that elusive but essential descriptor of what makes it unique. If the new hire has a good understanding of what constitutes the corporate culture, he or she also will understand what is expected of him or her.

New Hire Checklist

- Discuss expectations (write them down)
- Introduce/reinforce organizational culture
- Provide department orientation
- Devise a training plan
- Articulate policies
- Set standards
- Describe the evaluation process/set goals
- Constantly evaluate and comment on performance
- Introduce to peers and their work
- Train to proficiency

Many companies hold periodic new employee orientation sessions covering the contents of the employee manual, what the company produces, and how to get around within the corporate structure. Flight department employees should be required to attend these sessions; they provide essential information and begin to provide the basis for the culture they are joining. Additionally, it is up to the employee's supervisor to continually reinforce cultural norms and customs—this is important.

Everybody wants to know if they are doing their job well or not; allowing either excellent or poor job performance to go unnoticed constitutes poor supervision. Waiting until the annual employee performance appraisal to praise or chastise is a waste of employee resources. A frequent word to correct, redirect, or praise a person's work is all that is normally needed. This is just one more manifestation of the important feedback function of management.

Communication is a two-way street, too. The employee must be encouraged to provide feedback regarding the task and related expectations. Without his or her input, communication is incomplete.

Performance Evaluation

There was a time when a pilot showed up, flew the trip, did not spill the boss' coffee, and went home to wait for the next go 'round. As long as he or she did not bend metal or egos, the pilot's job was secure, and the cost-of-living increases continued. The same was true for the maintenance technicians: Keep 'em flying with a minimum of fuss, and the job "spoke for itself."

During these halcyon days, the concept of a periodic employee evaluation for aviation department personnel was considered at least superfluous and at best mildly demeaning. These were professionals—they were above something so crass as an attempt to evaluate their highly developed skills.

Alas, the folks in human resources now insist on at least an annual evaluation of each employee's performance, be it the custodian or the executive vice president; even the chairman and president receive one (at a board meeting). However, how do you evaluate something so strange as a pilot? Maintenance technicians are easy; they are the same as any other mechanic, right?

Experience has shown that pilots do not quite fit into the manager category, nor do they entirely fit into the technical professional group. And aviation maintenance technicians (AMTs) are different enough from steam plant workers to warrant another look at performance measurements.

Pilots and technicians are highly paid not only to demonstrate a high level of skill in the aeronautical environment but also to stay within the legal framework of the many rules and guidelines provided. Should they be evaluated on a level of technical performance that is at once a standard and excellent as well? If they do not measure up to the high standards of technical competence required of them, they probably should not have the job. So what is left to evaluate?

Most of us want to be more than just a success, but an *artistic success* to boot. Evaluations, therefore, should look at the margins of excellence, at the increments of performance that set one apart from one's peers. There is always a better way to accomplish a task, to please the customer, to add icing to a well-prepared cake.

The real value of communicating performance information is to give the person being evaluated a means to improve and continue to contribute to the success of the flight department. This means deciding on mutually acceptable improvement goals and developing a way to accomplish them. And most people like to walk away from an evaluation with a sense of direction and beginning anew.

Do not forget to cut human resources in on these great ideas.

Employee Evaluation Factors

- Judgment (the right decision at the right time)
- Efficiency (saving the company money)
- Resourcefulness (getting the job done in difficult circumstances)
- Potential for increased responsibility (ability to manage)
- Interpersonal skills (keep the customer happy)
- Team orientation (working well with others)
- Communications skills (*listening,* speaking, writing)
- Willingness to go the extra mile

Human Resources

Flight and human resources departments often endure strained relationships due to the isolation and uniqueness of the company aviation branch. As far as human resources is concerned, the flight department works out of a nontraditional, often distant location and communicates precious little information regarding its activities. The flight department may be heard from only when something is wrong with an employee's vacation balance or pension contribution. From the flight department's point of view, human resources always wants something: a performance evaluation, a pension election verification, or attendance at a boring lecture.

The uniqueness of aviation personnel makes job classification and salary administration a problem for human resources. Pilots are neither technicians nor managers, yet they share certain attributes with these occupations. Aviation maintenance technicians seem like automobile mechanics or machinery workers, yet they too do not quite fit existing job classifications. The receptionist/secretary/scheduler/accounting clerk composite person present in many departments defies all comparison. All this makes fair compensation for department personnel difficult and sometimes contentious.

The answer to all these problems is better communications. If both parties understand what the other's needs are, then most problems will become manageable if not nonexistent. The flight department manager should become quite familiar with the director of human resources and visit his or her office regularly. Additionally, a single person within the department should be assigned the duty of handling all human resources issues so that a mutual understanding of various situations can be fostered.

Detailed job descriptions will assist with both job classification and compensation issues. Human resources must understand the high degree of training and experience and mandatory certification required of aviation personnel; this is an education process to be performed by the flight department manager. Human resources also must be challenged to conduct pay comparability surveys for flight department personnel or to participate in industry salary surveys.

Human resources and the flight department may never fully understand one another, but open communications and a good-faith effort by both groups will work wonders.

Career Development

Most flight departments devote a majority of their training and personnel development time and money to technical issues. Initial, upgrade, transition, supplementary, and recurrent training on specific equipment or other aviation issues is purchased to ensure that the department is current, competent, and safe in producing its primary product, on-demand air transportation for the parent organization. Many managers consider this training an investment in safety and efficiency for the department.

Beyond these basics, however, many pilots, technicians, dispatchers, and schedulers may have a greater potential value to the department and company in nonaviation pursuits. Early development of latent organizational, administrative, leadership, and management skills in people will pay dividends later in the individual's tenure with the larger organization. And most people respond well to new opportunities and challenges if they are delivered in a considered, nonthreatening manner. This is particularly important for flight departments where upward mobility is limited due to the small size and specialized nature of the work.

Most career development occurs by providing an employee with some degree of initial training and then letting the person put theory into practice on the job. With sufficient nurturing, coaching, and observation, most adequately motivated people will master a new task within a reasonable period of time. Motivation is a key concept in performance; if an employee cannot see the value of the new task, he or she seldom will perform well.

It takes some effort on the manager's part to link what needs to be done with who can do it. Sometimes the employee volunteers; sometimes a "volunteer" must be found. The discovery of a desire and talent in an employee belongs in part to the manager and his or her people-reading skills and in part to the employee himself or herself; the link is the artform. However, the process is usually a rewarding one for both the manager and the employee.

A series of different jobs that stretch the employee's capabilities in increasingly responsible positions should lead to a person who is able to lead and manage when the opportunity to fill new positions comes available. In large measure, this sequence of development is really self-development. Development should be encouraged in all employees.

It may only be chosen by a few, but all should be afforded the opportunity. See "Collateral Duties" in Chap. 3.

Small departments have a problem in growing their personnel, but the successive assignment of collateral duties, increasing levels of responsibility along the way, has the same effect as a formal development program. Pilots or technicians who are given the opportunity to plan, budget, handle vendors, work with human resources, and assist in the training of others are well on their way to being ready for a more responsible job when it comes available. The next job does not necessarily have to be within the flight department either. A small number of talented individuals "go to corporate" when the opportunity presents itself. Has the flight department lost a member, or has the company gained a manager who fully appreciates the value of corporate aviation?

Ideally, each manager always should be training a replacement. This should not be viewed as a threat but as a means to fully exploit the talents of every member of the department. Here are a few ways of going about it:

- Get to know each employee beyond his or her job description; all employees have hidden talents.

- Seek opportunities to delegate tasks to subordinates that will give them a chance to succeed.

- Provide management, administrative, and leadership training for the most promising employees.

- Let your boss know who you are developing and why—the boss can help.

- Only give an employee as much as he or she can handle, yet everyone needs to be challenged.

- If a department member does not handle an assigned task well, find out why and redirect his or her efforts and talents.

There are many ways of investing in employees; career development may present the best return on the investment.

Leadership

- Leadership is the glue that binds an organization.

- Leaders do the right things; managers do things right.

- Leaders are those with the ability to get other people to do what they do not want to do and like it.

- Leaders maintain the organization's vision.

Leadership

All the items shown in the preceding sidebar may be true and have stood the test of time, but leadership may be the single most important characteristic possessed by the head of the department. This is true even if the department consists of just one airplane and two people. The leader is the person with the foresight, vision, and responsibility to carry out that vision for the organization.

Notice that the terms *manager* and *leader* are not necessarily interchangeable. The "Leaders do the right things; managers do things right" statement tells the story. Leaders motivate people; managers channel the motivation. The military found out the hard way that the management training that it invested in its officers during the 1960s and 1970s did not necessarily translate to the needs of the battlefield. Managers thrived in Washington; they did less well in team-oriented, goal-directed stressful situations that required a *leader*.

Every organization needs a leader, someone with the vision to see beyond the horizon and to get people to march toward that unseen goal. Once the team is started in the direction of the goal, managerial qualities are needed to make sure that everybody gets there with some degree style and efficiency. How does one learn to be a leader (few are born with the requisite qualities)? Fledging leaders traditionally are tested in the crucible of increasing responsibility and team tasks. They are asked to accomplish things that involve *people*. Accomplishing goals through people is the mark of a leader.

Is leadership necessary in the flight department? Definitely! Try accomplishing goals without it.

PLANNING

We all make plans, consciously and subconsciously—retire by age 55, buy a house in 5 years, pick up a bottle of milk on the way home. Plans define our lives, provide direction, and communicate intentions. Unfortunately, most people do not communicate their plans well to others who may be directly involved or be able to help. Flight departments are also victims of this deficiency, often to their detriment.

Plan the flight, fly the plan.

—ANONYMOUS

Mission Control

Mission statements have less to do with how well you see who you are as they do with how clearly you see where you are going. Every organization has a vision, a concept of where it fits into the grand scheme of things and, most important, a sense of direction. The statement may not be memorialized on parchment and framed in prominent locations around the building, but every employee should know what that vision is and *live* it every day.

The statement of vision may only exist in the head of the top person in the organization and not be a particularly well-formed statement either. However, it is he or she who must be the "keeper of the flame" that constitutes the reason for the organization's existence. This is true for the each unit within the organization, too.

The flight department not only must have a view of how it fits into the overall scheme of things, but also it must have its own sense of direction and worth. The aviation department manager or chief pilot must conceptualize, develop, nurture, and *communicate* the vision to every person within the flight department. The vision statement becomes the daily reason for wanting to come to work and the rallying cry for which superior performance and customer service are delivered.

Unfortunately, many vision statements are grandiose, unrealistic, and unattainable. Because of this and the fact that whatever vision statement that comes from the top is frequently poorly supported at all levels,

Missions

- "At Avis Rent-A-Car, our business is renting cars; our mission is total customer satisfaction."

- "[Boeing strives] To be the number one aerospace company in the world and among the premier industrial concerns in terms of quality, profitability, and growth."

- "The mission of Southwest airlines is dedication to the highest quality of customer service delivered with a sense of warmth, friendliness, individual pride, and company spirit."

- "The mission of the flight department is to provide safe, reliable, and efficient on-demand air transportation to our employees and customers."

these statements are held up to ridicule and largely ignored. The key to making the statement work is to make sure that it reflects reality and is supported by all management levels *on a daily basis.* Without this level of support and dedication, department members will view the statement as just another dream delivered from on high. Management not only must talk the talk but also must walk the talk.

The vision statement must be well-focused, simple, and realistic. It should not be a wish list; it must be rooted in terms of attainable and well-defined issues. It should answer the following questions about the department:

- Where does it fit within the company?
- How does it want to be seen by the company and by other departments?
- What dreams does it hope to realize?
  - Where are we going?
  - What are our goals?
- What reputation will it establish?
- Where do you intend to be positioned in your industry?
- What desired standards of excellence will be used?

No department is too small not to have a vision statement. Without it, the employees will use their own values and standards, but most important, they will not all be working toward the same goal. Without it, wherever the department goes is just fine, for it has no sense of direction. Importantly, a view of the organization's destiny is needed before launching any plan.

The Plans

Large companies used to live and die by their plans—strategic, operational, contingency, backup, 5-year, 10-year, long-range, short-range, near-term—all had their place in corporate life. No move to the future was attempted without ensuring that it was done in accordance with the applicable plan or plans; plans ruled the corporate course. Changing a plan was difficult and regularly encountered resistance from the corporate hierarchy or bureaucracy. Carefully measured change within the planning process was the key to stability and predictability for the company. Alas, those days are a part of corporate America that have gone the way of jobs for life, gray flannel suits, and unlimited expense accounts.

The flight department manager of a large multinational company recently told me that the company's long-range planning horizon was *1 year* and that operational plans only extended to 6 months. He laughed at the idea of aligning the flight department's plans with those of the company. The flight department purchased, outfitted, trained for, and began operating a large-cabin aircraft in less than 3 months

Plans

Strategic:

- Long-range
- Examines contingencies
- Open-ended
- No timeline

Operational:

- Specific
- Detailed
- Timeline
- Resource-specific

as a consequence of an emerging corporate interest in Asia. His comment: "How can you plan when the program changes on a daily basis? I haven't heard of a strategic plan around this place in years."

Welcome to the world of *Future Shock* and *Megatrends*. Corporate America has learned to use rapid communications and comprehensive information systems to gain a competitive advantage. In doing so, corporations have had to become agile and flexible not only within their traditional markets but also within unrelated markets as opportunity presents itself. Smart companies do this within a broad planning framework that may read more like an extended mission statement than a plan. The less insightful companies become reactionaries to the winds of change, altering course at the whim of a few and making it difficult to keep following their lead. Regardless of the disdain for strategic plans in some quarters, such plans are still a good idea because they bring future *possibilities* into clearer focus.

A basic strategic plan that looks out to a 3- to 5-year horizon containing broad objectives and alternative courses based on possible economic, market, or environmental moves seems to be the plan of choice. The big difference between this type of plan and those of previous times is their inherent flexibility; major changes to the plan are possible in as little as *1 day* due to the very responsive processes built into the plan.

Operational plans are inherently shorter term and are more specific, containing milestones and resource requirements (see sidebar). Strategic plans should be used to create operational plans—this creates planning continuity within the department and the company.

Regardless of your company's plans and planning processes, the flight department should have a basic but flexible plan ready to accommodate what the company may need, short of going to the moon. It need not be elaborate, but it should be heavy into "what ifs," looking at possible alternatives to changing demand, destination, and capacity needs. Some thoughts:

Plans for the Flight Department

Strategic:

- Air transportation analysis
- Aircraft replacement and refurbishment
- Long-range budget projection
- Facilities

Operational:

- Annual training plan
- Scheduled maintenance
- Flight schedule
- Projects
  - Vendor selection
  - Fuel purchase plan
  - Equipment purchase

- Confer with the flight department's reporting senior on a regular basis, attempting to gain a sense of what the corporation is planning to do.

- Sensitize flight department personnel and friends of the department to listen for trends and possibilities that may affect its future. But do not take every scrap of information as gospel; rumors abound in times of change.

- Devise a 3- to 5-year plan incorporating aircraft capability and service life, potential upgrades, and personnel considerations. Share it with the boss and revise in at least annually (see Fig. 4.8).

- Ensure that major changes within the department are made in accordance with "the plan." Making changes outside the planning framework will invalidate it; change the plan, and then act.

- Draw as many members of the department as possible into the planning process; they can implement change better if they understand it. Be ready for what the company may want.

Action	2003	2004	2005	2006	2007
Personnel					
Hire	AMT	Scheduler		(Pilots)	(AMT)
Upgrade	Pilot		AMT		
Aircraft					
FMS	Upgrade				
EGPWS	Install				
Eng ovhaul			Both		
12 yr. insp.		XX			
Paint		XX			
Interior		XX			
Replace				Analysis	Purchase
Additional			Analysis	-?-	
Facility					
Offices		Add			
New hangar				Analysis	-?-

FIGURE 4.8 Sample flight department plan.

FLIGHT DEPARTMENT PERFORMANCE

One accurate measurement is worth a thousand expert opinions.

—GRACE MURRAY HOPPER, REAR ADMIRAL, U.S. NAVY

A popular maxim taught in business schools states that if a process or product cannot be measured, it cannot be controlled or managed. Thus accurate measurement of business processes relies heavily on a series of yardsticks designed to provide management with information that can be used to control the business. Corporate flight does not escape this need.

Whenever chief pilots and aviation department managers congregate, the subject of operating costs is usually a staple of conversation. It seems that their reporting seniors want to know how well their flight department stacks up in relation to other departments. Compensation, maintenance, fuel, and overhaul costs are all subjects of interest. Everyone wants to know how well they are doing compared with their peers. However, these measures may not tell the real story of performance in the flight department. The real question should be, "Am I operating efficiently and effectively?"

Most departments dutifully provide monthly compilations of raw data to headquarters that describe their operations. Typical measures provided are shown in the sidebar.

While these numbers provide a measure of activity within the department, they say little about how efficiently or effectively these feats have been accomplished; they are merely statistical measures of the flight department's response to demands levied on it. They do not describe how well the department used its resources.

Flight Department Monthly Statistics

- Flight hours
- Miles, trips, and legs flown
- Passengers carried
- Load factor
- Direct costs
- Cost per hour/mile/seat-mile

Efficiency versus Effectiveness

Efficiency is usually measured as a ratio of output to input for a given activity. Efficiency asks the question, "Is a given action being performed with minimum effort/resources?" compared with the concept of effectiveness, which asks the question, "Is this product or service fulfilling the organization's mission adequately?" The two concepts are different but complementary. You may be providing aircraft services very inexpensively, but in so doing, the flights may be late or delayed—efficient but not effective. Conversely, the flights could be always on time but done so at great expense—effective but not efficient. Thus the two concepts must be considered together to provide a complete picture. Some judgment must be used in applying these values:

- How much value does the boss place on efficiency as opposed to effectiveness?
- What is the corporate culture regarding this issue?
- What means should be used to measure these issues?

Ratios

Most organizations examine efficiency and effectiveness in both financial and productivity terms. Ratio analysis is a well-developed and respected method of measuring performance. This methodology reports key factors as fractions or percentages of one another. For example, simply looking at profits after taxes is a single data point that gives no indication of how profitable the company is. However, if profits after taxes are divided by assets, a figure known as *return on investment* (ROI) is generated. If a company had $1 million in assets and made a $150,000 profit after taxes, it would have an ROI of 15 percent. This number either could be compared with some other period in the company's history or could be compared with an industry average. If last year's ROI was 10 percent but the industry average is 20 percent, things are improving but perhaps not enough. ROI is just one of many financial indicators used to determine corporate health.

Similarly, the production department compares hourly output of goods produced with the number of employees required to accomplish it to arrive at an *employee productivity ratio*. Service providers may determine how many customers an employee can serve per hour. Whatever the measure, the key is a comparison between two related variables.

The most rudimentary ratio-analysis tool used by flight departments is aircraft costs per hour, mile, or seat-mile. This figure is derived by taking total operating cost for a particular aircraft and dividing it by either total hours, miles, or seat-miles flown over the same period. This should be further broken down into direct and indirect operating costs to provide a more detailed appraisal of operating efficiency.

A number of other measures of either efficiency or effectiveness are available to flight department managers (see Table 4.2). Carefully consider which measures are relevant for your department and organizational culture. Certainly, they all do not have be tracked or portrayed to headquarters, but one or two key measures of *relative performance* should be used to show management that the flight department is concerned with efficiency and effectiveness. For example, if the maintenance hours per flight hour have increased by 30 percent over the previous 12-month period, there may be some hidden factor that should be investigated further. At the most elementary level, the aircraft could just be getting older, or the quality of replacement parts could be substandard. More telling may be that the personnel turnover in the maintenance section has been so high that the department has been left with only minimally experienced technicians who may require more time for troubleshooting and understanding the systems. Without these numbers and trend information, it will be difficult to justify a replacement aircraft or higher salaries for the technicians to improve their retention.

TABLE 4.2   Flight Department Performance Measures

Efficiency
- Cost per flight hour/mile/seat-mile
- Fuel used per mile/hour
- Maintenance cost per hour
- Maintenance personnel hours expended per flight hour
- Scheduled flight time versus actual flight time
- Budgeted versus actual expenditures
- Crew productivity (trips/hours per crew member)
- Passenger versus ferry/maintenance flights

Effectiveness
- On-time performance versus delays
- Dispatch rate (trips flown versus trips scheduled)
- Trip denials (trips accommodated versus schedule attempts)
- Load factor (passengers per leg/segment)
- Time saved for passengers—total/ratios
- Aircraft/crew availability

Tracking It

A means of tracking and recording the necessary data to generate these ratios must be devised. While it is possible to generate some of these numbers with paper records, a calculator, and a stubby pencil, the easiest and in some cases the only way to accomplish this is via a computer. Some departments have generated relatively sophisticated tracking and recordkeeping programs in-house, but most companies use the report writing capability of off-the-shelf proprietary computer software designed specifically for the scheduling and operational data records of on-demand flight department operations. Choosing the proper software for your operation is an important choice; suffice to say that the software capabilities should be evaluated carefully to ensure a good fit for your operation. Many of these programs have features that may not be necessary or serve your operation well. Some software may not be able to generate the data and ratios you want. Ask for an extensive demonstration and ask other flight departments who use the software for their appraisal before you buy (see Chap. 3).

Comparisons

Once the desired ratios are generated, they must be compared with other reference points to be meaningful. A common method used is to compare this information with that of a previous time period. Comparison with the previous month or quarter may not be realistic, given seasonal anomalies or aircraft availability. However, comparison with the same month or quarter in the previous year may be more realistic. For the long view, companion of the current period ratio with a moving 12- or 24-month average of that ratio is probably most useful. This method smoothes out the short-term perturbations associated with periodic data and presents the values with greater perspective.

The other means of comparison is by using values generated by other, similar flight operations. Accurate and up-to-date information of this nature is often difficult to obtain, however. Some of it is available from the *NBAA Compensation and Benchmarking Surveys,* aircraft manufacturers data, and consultants' proprietary information (see "Seeking a Better Way," on page 4.43).

Presenting the Information

What do you do with the information once it has been generated? The results of these calculations should be shared with both department personnel and corporate management, although the same information may not be appropriate for both groups. Let management know the "big picture" items such as cost per hour, load factor, cancellation rate, etc. There is some risk of providing them with too much information, more information than they can understand or appreciate. For example, does management really want to know how productive the flight crews are, i.e., how many trips/hours/days/days away from home the crews fly? Probably not until it comes time to reengineer, resize, or downsize. It may be helpful to track these numbers internally for just such an eventuality.

Again, absolute values without a means for comparison will have little meaning for the nonaviation manager viewing the reports. Such a manager must be led to understand the significance of the information through displayed trends and comparisons with other flight departments and aircraft types and even airline travel. Graphic displays are also impressive and helpful in understanding performance information. Some companies have developed sophisticated measures of executive time saved per trip, nights away from home averted, and additional conference and work time afforded by use of a private aircraft setting versus a less conducive airliner. Any efforts in this area may be useful in keeping utilization high and your job secure.

Information versus Data

Note that the term *information* has been used instead of the term *data*. This usage is intentional to denote the difference between a large number of unrelated facts (data) and facts that have been collated, analyzed, and presented in a fashion that will prove useful and are designed to *inform*. Merely providing line after line of trip detail and passenger manifests will do little to help the nonaviation manager assess performance. This detail may be provided to selected users to be used as a permanent record for their files. Accounting may need this level of detail for tax purposes, or the president may want to scan the previous month's flights to determine who is using the aircraft and to correlate these data with other pertinent business details. Whatever the reason, there should be an explicit, stated purpose for providing high levels of detail to recipients outside the flight department.

The members of the flight department should be privy to just about all measures of performance and levels of detail. The performance ratios and other measures will give them a means with which to measure their individual performance and as a team. This information, in turn, can be used to motivate them through goal-setting. The judicious use of information always provides real value to you and your department.

Perhaps the best yardstick for measuring performance is to use comparisons with previous time periods. However, cost alone does not tell the full story. A set of standard performance measures should be devised for your operation based on the corporate culture and standard internal policies.

No one number can tell you how well the department is performing. It is the rational assessment of a combination of measures valued by your company that tells this story.

Reports

What does the boss do with this prized information? How is it used? Does it tell him or her how well the flight department is accomplishing its mission? Does it provide information on how well the department uses its resources or its efficiency?

Unfortunately, many organizations do not ask these questions. As a consequence, flight department reports become self-perpetuating monuments to poor information management. The usual answer I get when I ask why a monthly report is sent to headquarters is, "We've always done it."

Regarding the sidebar, which one does your boss want? The second and third bullets seem to be the ones bosses *should* wish to see. Alas, bullet number four seems to take the prize in most cases.

In reality, the boss should want to see how well the department is *performing.* On-time departures, dispatch rate, number of denied trips, load factor, and cost per mile are all performance measures that may warrant management's attention, including

---

Why a Report Is Needed

- Management information—quick data used to make decisions

- Trends—system values are tracked for significant change or straying outside preset limits

- Exception reporting—something unusual happened, good or bad

- Idle curiosity—What's happening?

- Prediction—What will happen? (really a forecast or plan)

---

management *within* the department. Ideally, these performance measures are tied to goals and objectives set at the beginning of the year that reflect accomplishment of the department's mission.

The point is that merely flying hours, reaching destinations, and carrying passengers do not necessarily mark achievement of the department's mission, which should be to support the on-demand air transportation needs of the company (hopefully defined somewhere).

Suppose that the company really just wants to have an airplane available to go to random destinations on short notice and does not really care about *efficiency?* Obviously, the company cares about *effectiveness* (dispatch rate, on-time departures, completed missions) but not necessarily such items as hourly direct costs, crew productivity, or maintenance hours per flight hour. OK, then just tell the company how *effective you are* using the appropriate measures.

If management wants the traditional hours/passengers/gallons measures, at least give them data from previous measurement periods so that they can see a trend. This information ideally can be displayed in a graph or series of graphs to provide quick visual recognition of possible trends.

Trends can be powerful indicators when tied to relevant issues. Suppose that flight hours have been decreasing steadily over the past 6 months. What does this indicate? It simply may hide the fact that the aircraft has endured a series of major unscheduled maintenance episodes and that a number of frequent flyers have been transferred to another division— be careful, the data may belie true causes.

Ask the boss what he or she wants, what measures of performance make a difference. Better yet, ask the boss how he or she uses current reports; what *information* does he or she receive from them. If the boss is honest, you can then help define what he or she believes really makes a difference within the flight department. Then report it. Figure 4.9 presents a sample report.

Do not forget your own needs within the department. Specialized reports regarding crew duty days, expenses, and maintenance personnel hour reporting may be important within the department and be of little use to the remainder of the company. Remember, in order to manage the operation effectively, ensure that you have the information you need in a form that is of use to you. And do not forget the rest of the department—let them know how the department is performing by sharing some or all the reports generated with them. Once they see what's good and not so good about the operation, they can help make it better.

	April 2003	**April 2002**	**Difference**
Hours	45.5	37.0	+23%
12 Months	552	441	+25%
Trips	19	15	+27%
12 Months	260	190	+37%
Passengers	41	44	-7%
12 Months	506	588	-14%
Load Factor	2.2	2.9	-24%
12 Months	2.0	3.1	-35%
Dispatch rate	100%	94%	+6%
12 Months	98%	96%	+2%
Demand met	91%	100%	-9%
12 Months	94%	98%	-4%
Cost per hour	$855	$902	-5%
(12 months average)			

Highlights

- 300 hr inspection conducted over third weekend
- Windshield half replaced due to inflight fracture @ $43,000
- Joe Weil completed recurrent pilot training
- Safety audit completed – report due end of month

Upcoming Events

- All hands CPR/BBP training in May
- 600 hr inspection due October – four day down time
- Technician recurrent training in June for Harry Smart
- Passenger secretary/admin assistants familiarization in June

FIGURE 4.9   Sample flight department monthly report.

Flight Department Evaluation*

Never mistake motion for action.

—ERNEST HEMINGWAY

The priorities for most flight department managers usually come down to two big ones: safety and keeping the boss happy. Having achieved these on a daily basis (you hope), the same majority of operators turn to the more mundane, unglamorous tasks of ensuring that the fundamentals of the department work well enough to support its principal goals. It is these details that determine how well the department performs.

---

*This material originally appeared as an article in *Aviation International News,* February 2000.

These details assume primary importance when a review of the flight department is conducted either internally or by a third-party contractor. Flight department self-audits tend to review policies and procedures that ensure compliance with national regulations, maintenance programs, and company directives. A more comprehensive view of the department—an outside audit—examines management, organizational, customer service, and efficiency issues. The end result of both types of investigations answers the question, "Is the department safe, and does it comply with applicable regulations and policies?" Ideally, an outside audit goes one step further and yields an answer to the question, "How well-managed and efficient is the operation?"

In answering these questions, it is important to know what issues will be investigated. If the audit is done internally, department personnel simply may generate a checklist that looks at just the regulations. Table 4.3 shows such a list for the U.S. Federal Aviation Regulations (FAR). Others expand this to include standard procedures, administrative or operational, as well. When a company's internal auditors get involved, administrative and financial issues are added to the checklist to prove compliance with company procedures.

Contract auditors who specialize in flight department operations probably will use a detailed list of operational, administrative, and procedural items that encompass the normal

TABLE 4.3   Regulations with which to Comply

The Essentials*

Certification: Pilots and Flight Instructors
  61.3   Requirement for certificates, ratings, and authorizations
    .23   Duration of medical certificates
    .51   Pilot logbooks
    .55   Second-in-command qualifications
    .57   Recent flight experience: pilot in command
    .58   Pilot in command proficiency check
    .63   Additional aircraft ratings

General Operating and Flight Rules
  91.7   Civil aircraft airworthiness
    .9   Civil aircraft flight manual, marking, and placard requirements
  .103   Preflight action
  .171   VOR equipment check for IFR operations
  .203   Civil aircraft: certifications required
  .213   Inoperative instruments and equipment
  .403   General (maintenance)
  .405   Maintenance required
  .407   Operation after maintenance, preventive maintenance, rebuilding, or alteration
  .409   Inspections
  .417   Maintenance records
  .503   Flying equipment and operating information
  .513   Emergency equipment
  .519   Passenger briefing

Maintenance, Preventive Maintenance, Rebuilding, and Alteration
  43.3   Persons authorized to perform maintenance, preventive maintenance, rebuilding, and alterations.
    .5   Approval for return to service after maintenance, . . .
    .7   Persons authorized to perform maintenance, . . .
    .9   Content, form, and disposition of maintenance…records
  .11   Content, form, and disposition of records for inspections
  .13   Performance rules (general)

---

*A number of other regulations may apply depending on the operation.

day-to-day operational environment. The level of detail will vary with the contractor selected, but the list of items to be investigated usually will be lengthy (see Table 4.4).

The question on most aviation department managers' minds is, "Given that an audit is scheduled, how do I prepare for it?" In reality, very little can be done because these investigations rely on examining existing policies, procedures, and the records of accomplishment to determine the department's fitness. The time to prepare for an audit is sometime before it is scheduled, perhaps years, and not after the date is set. Here's the normal process.

The Basics.   An audit will explore the following features of a flight department:

• Standards and procedures used

• Adherence to those standards and procedures

• Methods of determining compliance with the standards and procedures

TABLE 4.4   Flight Department Audit Checklist

Administration
    Facility appearance and condition
    Passenger handling/facilities
    Flight planning procedures
    Catering
    Certificates, manuals, op spec*
    Passenger scheduling
    Financial status*
    Crew duty time management
    Dispatch and flight following
    Emergency/incident procedures
    Insurance coverage/certificates*
    Facility/aircraft security
 	
Flight operations
    PIC/SIC qualifications
    Pilot training program/records
    Cabin attendant training/records
    Flight operations manual
    Standard operating procedures
    Operational limitations
    Flight operations records
    Pilot proficiency monitoring
    Flight information publications
    Operational standards
    International operations
 	
Flight evaluation
    Flight planning
    Aircraft release/inspection
    Passenger handling/briefing
    Use of checklists
    Compliance with FARs/SOP
    Flying technique
    Crew resource management
    Flight records
	Safety management
	    Safety program contents
	    Designated safety personnel
	    Personnel qualifications
	    Safety awareness
	    Previous incident/accidents
	    Passenger safety
	    Industrial safety/OSHA compliance
	
	Aircraft maintenance
	    Manager/technician qualifications
	    Technician training program/records
	    Maintenance manual/procedures
	    Scheduled maintenance control
	    Inspection program approval
	    Quality control program/records
	    Aircraft discrepancy control
	    Deferred maintenance procedures
	    Aircraft maintenance records
	    Computerized records tracking
	    Controlled manual procedures
	    Parts inventory, inspection, control
	    Vendor selection procedures
	    Fueling procedures
	
	Maintenance processes
	    Work flow/job assignment
	    Turnover procedures/logs
	    Compliance with FARs/SOP
	    Use of reference documents
	    Parts control
	    Inspection process
	    Records procedures/control
	    Cleanliness/organization
	    Tool control

*Applies to charter operators only.

Taken individually, these elements provide the foundations for a good flight department. When all are brought together under a corporation that truly believes in on-demand aviation and a department management that uses good leadership principles, excellence is very likely.

Standards. Standards come in all shapes and sizes: regulations, aircraft manufacturer's continuing airworthiness instructions, company policies and procedures, and best industry practices. The regulations should be as well known as the contents of the manufacturer's maintenance manual. These basic rules are the foundations of any flight operation; these come first and are the principal determinants of compliance and safety.

Company policies include such diverse items as the care and feeding of passengers, crew duty times, takeoff weather minimums, recording aircraft discrepancies, and scheduling. To be communicated effectively to corporate management, passengers, and flight department, all this information should be in writing and published, normally in the form of a flight operations manual. This manual should be comprehensive and serve as a central reference work for all concerned with corporate flight operations (see the *NBAA Management Guide*).

The final category of standards looks at best industry practices, i.e., policies and procedures shown to be successful when used by similar flight operations. While comparison with unwritten standards may seem unfair at first, most flight department managers want to know how they stack up against similar departments. Being introduced to new ideas and concepts in this manner is one way to be exposed to other ways of running an operation and to compare one's operation with others considered to be "best in class."

Doing It. Having all the processes and procedures on paper is one thing; doing them is another. This phase of the audit looks at how well run the department is and how well members comply with their own rules and methods. Confidential interviews with all department personnel are normally employed to determine levels of compliance, management style, and morale; an experienced interviewer can soon tell whether what is on the books is actually happening within the department. Observation by the auditors of daily work operations and on jumpseat rides in the aircraft complete the process of determining whether a department is really "walking the talk" and not merely "talking the talk." Incidentally, jumpseat rides are normally an optional feature of audits and are designed to see whether crews follow their own procedures and not to assess how a crew flies the aircraft.

Recording It. Audits are really about records. The only way an investigator can really determine whether department directives are being accomplished is through written records.

The records shown in the sidebar will be examined in detail for compliance with standards, inconsistencies, and obvious "pencil whipping" (fraudulent entries). If present, more subtle record manipulation will be revealed during interviews with department personnel—people love to tell virtually everything they know when given the opportunity.

Flight Department Records

- Flight schedules
- Completed flight logs and passenger manifests
- Flight crew duty time
- Flight crew currency
- Training received
- Aircraft maintenance records
- Personnel qualification and employment
- Financial

Who Asked for It?

An increasing number of flight departments integrate audits into their normal management process. That is, they conduct an audit of their operation on a periodic basis, normally every 2 or 3 years. This provides management with trend information to determine performance and ensures that management remains abreast of best industry practices through the use of a third-party auditor.

Perhaps the most frequent cause for initiating an audit is a situation such as adding or exchanging an aircraft, expanding the department, or an external influence causes the flight department manager or chief pilot to become curious as to how his or her operation compares with the rest of the pack. Inherent in such a move is a desire to improve the performance of the department.

Occasionally, the flight department corporate reporting senior or other senior corporate officer will request an audit. This may stem from a desire to see how the department compares with other corporate operations or to determine whether the department is safe and in compliance with the regulations. Less frequently, a safety-related event or internal dispute within the department will cause a corporate officer to seek an outside view of the operation.

Good, well-kept records support one another, forming an interlocking story of the department's activity. Poor records lack this interdependence, displaying gaps and inconsistencies that are difficult to explain. Most important is a bullet-proof system of recordkeeping procedures that uses parallel inputs to edit and substantiate other entries.

While records may make the department and its managers appear to be doing a great job for their companies, the real reason to maintain good records is to prove compliance with standards in case of an accident or incident. The FAA, the National Transportation Safety Board (NTSB), insurance companies, and lawyers will pour over operational and administrative records in minute detail to determine whether the operation has missed an important mandatory compliance item. Good records provide an excellent form of insurance in case of a mishap.

Putting It Together.   As noted earlier, if all the basic elements of the flight department come together under enlightened managers, excellence can happen. This excellence will be readily apparent to the auditor/evaluator soon after arrival, too. Flight department personnel normally exhibit a high level of confidence and pride in their operation. However, if poor teamwork or morale problems exist, these features will become readily apparent to the evaluator during the personnel interview process. These intangibles are an important part of the audit for the investigator. While they may not be manifested by letter-perfect recordkeeping or high standards that have been set, they are an indication of the real performance of the department.

Thus, is it possible to prepare your department for an audit? Yes, but the preparations should have started years ago. However, this should not delay initiating an audit; valuable lessons can be learned because the report received will provide a means of charting a path to a better operation. More important, resolve to profit from the experience by getting all hands involved in working to improve the department once they have read and absorbed the report.

Saving Money

While many flight departments are not required to submit or live under a budget or otherwise attempt to economize on any aspect of their operation, doing so is good management. Even if the boss does not care, the flight department manager should care about saving a buck just because it is a subset of being efficient, doing more with less. Granted, those who do not have to may not squeeze a nickel until it screams, but there is virtue and a sense of personal accomplishment when you strike a good deal. Whether it is saving $50,000 on a 12-year inspection or 15 cents on a gallon of jet fuel, doing so makes one feel like something good has been achieved.

The boss may not ask for the most efficient operation, but efficiency and cost savings are time-honored means of measuring success of any operation. Why not see how efficient you can be?

There are three major expense categories in flight departments that may yield the greatest savings: fuel, maintenance, and personnel compensation. Concentrating on these areas makes the most sense if significant savings are to be realized. See the sidebar for ways others save money in these areas.

Money-Saving Ways

Fuel:

- Build your own fuel farm
- Buy bulk fuel and store it at the FBO's facility
- Join all fuel savings/purchase programs
- Always call ahead to ask for a discount at FBOs
- Use cruise control and track optimization techniques

Maintenance:

- Use in-house technicians to perform most maintenance/inspections
- Initiate long-term agreements with maintenance vendors
- Join a maintenance/parts insurance program

Compensation:

- Conduct/subscribe to compensation surveys
- Provide bonuses/profit sharing to keep annual salary increases to a minimum
- Use contract personnel during times of high demand

SEEKING A BETTER WAY

Several years ago a large forest products company set out to discover the best way to operate a flight department. To accomplish this, the company assembled a team of four managers and a corporate officer to tour the flight departments of companies with similar corporate product lines and geographic diversity. Over a 2-week period, the team visited the flight departments of four large forest products companies around the country to determine who accomplished their air transportation tasks better than the rest.

To the investigation team's surprise, it discovered that their company measured up pretty well in relation to those they investigated. However, they did find that there were interesting and innovative ways of performing common tasks that could incrementally improve their own operation. The team allowed that while the exercise was revealing, it could have accomplished as much through a continuing systematic internal analysis of its own operation coupled with an eye to seeking new ways to do things; finding new ways to do things probably could be accomplished through networking with other companies' flight, human resources, and accounting departments.

Optimizing

The team had stumbled onto what has become one of the hottest techniques to improve performance in the business world—best practices. While the team may have done it the hard way, it set out to seek the holy grail of optimizing business processes. Note the term *optimizing*—there probably is no "best" means to accomplish tasks within your operation. What may be best for others may not fit your company's culture, department size, staffing level, mission, etc. Therefore, seeking to find a "silver bullet" that will make the entire operation run like a top may be quixotic and naive—most companies have found that incremental and continuous improvement is a more practical and achievable goal for the long term.

The search for best practices is a type of *benchmarking*—the continuous process of comparing your operation with other organizations' outstanding practices and processes. Benchmarking employs data points, or performance measures, to determine quantitatively what constitutes better and, perhaps, best in any task or field of endeavor.

All this effort focuses on process, a series of interrelated activities that produces an output or result. The concept of process is important because it is the small subfunctions that, when taken together, constitute an organization's total activity. Understanding one's own processes is an essential prerequisite to the search for best practices. Without a full understanding of the minute components of your processes, it will be difficult to compare them to others'.

For example, if your scheduling operation is restricted to a limited number of passengers and is handled over the telephone with passengers' secretaries and recorded in a desk calendar, it is difficult to compare it with a flight department serving a large passenger base using online database scheduling methods. However, certain aspects of the larger system, such as trip-confirmation procedures, may be applicable to yours.

Know Thyself

Prior to looking outside for an improved practice, have a good understanding of your own and the underlying reasons why those practices have been used over time. Doing so may not be as difficult as you may think. First, define which processes are critical to your operation. Having determined which processes (listed in the following sidebar) are essential, each process should be mapped or flow-charted to show how it works. Then the assumptions and policies that underlie each process should be listed to support the depicted system. Finally, describe/show how these processes link to and interact with related processes. For instance, passenger scheduling is, at a minimum, linked to aircraft, crew, and maintenance scheduling; flight schedule production; chargeback accounting; and recordkeeping—flow-chart or describe these interactions.

The principal benefit of this exercise will be to help you better understand what you do on a daily basis and to see how all the processes fit together. This approach constitutes an internal audit that will form the basis for improvement. In many cases, the display will provide ready insights into wasteful, inadequate, redundant, or poorly linked processes. Chances are that before you go outside the hangar, you will already have discovered better practices on your own.

Asking for help from your company's process control engineers and benchmarking and planning groups to assist with your internal audit should provide helpful insights into your operation. These people have the opportunity to observe a wide variety of processes that may provide you with useful information about how quite different operations within the company accomplish similar processes. For example, scheduling passengers and employees for training or contracting for outside aircraft and high-tech machinery maintenance may be similar enough to yield useful techniques for the flight department. An internal search for best practices or benchmarks inevitably uncovers useful ideas that may be used for improvement, regardless of your company business.

Outside Help

Information about how others run flight departments is readily available from a variety of sources. Perhaps the simplest way is to ask a peer from a neighboring flight department; most people want to talk about their operation, but more important, they want to see how their activity compares with that of others. This is the fuel for flight crew conversations at the FBO as they await the return of their passengers or the topic of technicians' talk in the service center's break room. Unfortunately, the majority of this talk centers on salaries, technical aspects of the equipment they operate, or their number of duty days.

These settings offer great opportunities to find out how others schedule passengers, budget, conduct training, and offer superior customer service. Therefore, all flight department personnel should be attuned to the benchmarking and best practices needs of the organization. If they know that critical department practices and process are under consideration, they can perform a valuable information-gathering function. Then, once sufficient input is gathered, small groups of employees can evaluate and discuss the newly found ways of doing business to determine whether there is a better means of accomplishing common processes.

Flight Department Processes

Understand the market:

- Customers
- Economic/business environment
- Competition

Establish/maintain resources:

- People
- Budget
- Aircraft
- Facilities
- Company support
- Administration

Provide service:

- Scheduling
- Flight operations
- Maintenance
- Customer service

Control:

- Planning
- Performance measurement
- Feedback/corrective methods

More formal best practices searches include visits to similar facilities, attending seminars and workshops, using consultants and industry sources, and formal investigations of single processes in dissimilar industries. Visits to similar facilities can be as simple as spending a few hours at another corporate operation at a nearby airport or as involved as traveling to a distant location to observe an admired facility for a matter of days. NBAA and other industry seminars and workshops offer an excellent source of ideas from both the presenters and fellow attendees; more important, contacts made at these meetings add to your network of "experts" on whom you may call in the future for ideas. Consultants can provide both anecdotal and hard evidence of best practices, offering a wide spectrum of methods from which to choose. Industry sources of hard data include operational and financial data from the *NBAA Compensation and Benchmarking Survey,* Conklin and de Decker aircraft cost and performance materials, and operation-specific custom benchmarking data offered by companies such as Aviation Research Group U.S.

Finally, search outside the aviation world for best practices used by other industries and communities. Heavy truck maintenance scheduling is not dissimilar from aircraft maintenance scheduling, and charging trips to passengers may be more like assigning costs for corporate information services than you would think. Therefore, cast your net wide when seeking better ways. But don't stray too far from home—your own company probably has many processes similar to your own; look in your own backyard before going far afield.

All That Glitters Is Not Gold

Initial efforts at both internal and external benchmarking inevitably yield many attractive new processes and modifications to your existing processes. However, which ones will really work in your operation? Again, knowing your organization from department to the board room is an indispensable part of evaluating new processes. Unless you understand your corporate culture and what its basic values are, you probably have less that a 50 percent chance of implementing new practices that will satisfy either you or the chairperson.

Are there sufficient resources to implement the change? Will the change destroy a balance with other work processes? Will additional effectiveness, efficiency, or value result from the change? These are important questions to ask of yourself and others when contemplating change. Have doubts? Wait awhile and reconsider.

Implementing change should be a shared process. If you have found what you consider a best practice, share it with your staff, peers in the company, and your boss. Let them become used to the idea and help with the evaluation process. If there is universally great resistance to the concept, it may be an idea whose time or place is not right. If only spotty resistance is evident, try for more solid support from those who favor it, and perhaps go further afield for additional support. If you really believe in it, give it a try—conviction and commitment are important.

The Payoff

In a recent meeting of directors and managers from a variety of Fortune 50 manufacturing, financial, and consumer companies, 92 percent of the participants reported that internal benchmarking had enhanced their company's productivity. Nearly 60 percent of these companies had resources specifically dedicated to benchmarking, and 52 percent used a formal benchmarking model. Further, 80 percent said that increased product/service quality, decreased cycle time, and reduced costs were derived from external benchmarking.

While increases in productivity may be difficult to measure or slow to be realized, the important point is that your operation is striving to improve constantly, to look for better ways to accomplish your mission. Inherent in this activity is a positive attitude and vision of the future that will serve any organization and its people well. There may be a better way. . . .

IMAGE OF THE DEPARTMENT

It is the perception of value received that will cement the position of the flight department within the company.

—INSIGHTFUL CFO

How is the flight department perceived within the company? More to the point, how do the executives who fly as passengers regard the department? The department can have a spotless accident record, a 100 percent dispatch rate, be the model of efficiency, and still be held in low regard by those who use its services. It is image that creates the perception of a customer rather than substance. The actual practices and performance of the department must come first, but its image will make or break it.

Advertising the Department

Many flight departments pride themselves or their anonymity and obscurity. "We just get the boss from A to B with the minimum amount of fuss—I stay away from downtown as much as possible" is often the mindset of the department manager. Staying out of the lime-light has its benefits in terms of presenting a smaller target for the bean counters and efficiency experts, but hiding your light under a bushel may bring an equal number of negatives.

A flight department may provide transportation to a limited number of executives within the company and have a very low profile as a consequence. Only the highest eche-lons of the company *and* the financial department know and perhaps appreciate the value of reliable on-demand air transportation. This exclusiveness often provides an inviting target not only for the bugeteers during financial droughts but also for other operating divi-sions of the company that are looking for cuts in all area except theirs.

The flight department is as much an integral part of the company as is manufacturing, research and development, and human resources. It provides a valuable service and con-tributes to the bottom line as much as or more so than other segments of the business. This must be portrayed to the rest of the company in terms that demonstrate value and service orientation. If you make your point to enough people, there will be less tendency to view the flight department as an inviting target for elimination when senior management changes or the company-wide crunch comes.

Without a broad base of support within the larger organization, the vagaries of the business world may make the aviation func-tion tenuous at best. Service must be con-sidered in terms of the entire organization, not just the few senior executives afforded the privilege of on-demand air transporta-tion. It is the ability of the flight depart-ment to actively and significantly support the core mission and goals of the company or principal's group that produces value. Without the concept of the flight depart-ment producing value in the minds of a majority of the decision makers, the days of the employees who work at the airport may be numbered.

Start your image campaign with the boss. Tell him or her your desire to make the organization more aware of the flight department and, if appropriate, to make the aircraft available to a wider range of employees. Be prepared with some posi-tive suggestions concerning this wider role within the company (see the sidebar). Then begin your marketing campaign.

The valuable side effect to the exercises listed in the sidebar is in enhancing your knowledge of and appreciation for the orga-nization you support. And the more you know about that organization, the more ways you can find to make the flight department useful to it.

Be prepared for a negative reaction from the principal or CEO who is protective of his or her perquisites and may not want other personnel using the aircraft, no matter

Marketing the Flight Department

- Create multistop trip packages for sales and marketing that minimize their time away from home and save money too.

- Hold a field day at the airport for administrative assistants and secre-taries of executives to acquaint them with the operation and scheduling procedures—throw in lunch, too.

- Work with the communications department to provide a story in the company newsletter about the flight department and its people.

- Apprise key departments about the rapid-response capabilities of the aircraft in supporting critical-failure scenarios.

- Let finance know about your cost-saving efforts in parts procurement, maintenance, training, and fuel pur-chases.

- Create and deliver a transportation efficiency and effectiveness presen-tation for junior executive training courses.

- Provide aerial observation flights for site selection and survey teams.

how much sense that makes. And these individuals may be protective of their people's travel budgets, wanting to use all available funds for research and development or marketing. The manager can still initiate some of the preceding measures without necessarily drumming up new passenger business. Regardless of the intent of internal advertising, it should have a positive effect on internal working relationships with those people who can make life easier or more difficult for the folks at the airport.

NBAA has produced a number of excellent brochures depicting a variety of utilization strategies for corporate aircraft, and they are available for the asking or from the NBAA Web site (*nbaa.org/library*).[*]

Customer Orientation

You may think you are in the aviation business, but the aviation department is really a "service provider." Aviation is just a means to get to the organization's real product. Granted, providing safe aircraft that are maintained and flown by good people is certainly important, but these really form the basis for the delivery of the real product—*air transportation service*. As a service organization, customer satisfaction should rank at the top of your priority list.

Many flight department personnel assume that a routine, minimum-turbulence, on-time flight that terminates with a smooth touchdown will keep the "customer" in back happy. But is this really true? What are the passengers' expectations regarding corporate air trans-

---

Customer Focus

- Make all personnel aware on a continuing basis that the department is customer-oriented.
- Conduct a written or in-person survey of all your regular passengers to determine their desires and perceptions of the service regarding flight department services. Include the passengers' secretaries and administrative assistants in the survey, too.
- Provide customer service training for key flight department personnel.
- Institute a standardized flight crew flight briefing and debriefing procedure for passengers.
- Provide incentives for flight department personnel to find ways to improve service.
- Discuss customer service at all departmental meetings.
- Evaluate department personnel on their level of customer service.
- Provide several briefings each year regarding flight department mission, operations, and scheduling procedures for passengers and their assistants.
- Encourage informal contact between flight department and corporate support personnel to find out what the company thinks about your service and to communicate your service orientation to them.
- Find ways to measure passenger satisfaction on a regular basis.

---

[*]National Business Aviation Association, Washington, DC: *Face To Face, The Real World of Business Aviation* (1999), and *Business Aircraft Utilization Strategies* (1999).

portation? Are they comfortable with the scheduling, boarding, briefing, catering, delay, communications with the flight crew, and ground transportation procedures? Just because they have never complained does not mean that they are pleased with the service. And what works for one passenger may not work for another.

Get closer to your customers. Find out what their expectations are. Have *them* define a superior level of service for your department. Contacts with your frequent flyers are probably brief and cursory at best, and they are probably thinking more about business than the quality of the service when speaking with you. Communications with your less frequent patrons is even less substantive. Therefore, a regular, focused effort to determine the desires and attitudes of your customers is needed.

More important though, each member of the flight department should be customer-oriented. They should be thinking in terms of *service* in addition to their technical specialty. They should be thinking of ways to deliver a better-quality product to the customer. They should be attempting to make every customer contact a pleasant and positive experience. In short, the entire department should become *customer-caring.*

Just because you get them there in one piece does not necessarily mean that good service was provided. Complacency regarding the customer may bring unwelcome surprises.

Customer Surveys

The flight departed on time, proceeded smoothly, and landed ahead of scheduled time (thank goodness the limo driver was there early). The return trip went equally according to plan and was blessedly uneventful. The CEO obviously was preoccupied as he left the aircraft at home base. He barely mumbled a "Good-bye" as he rushed to his waiting car. Another good flight, right? Or was it?

Who's to know whether your customers like the service they are receiving? Is the chairperson's ritual, "Great flight—thanks," a good measure of what he or she really thought about the flight? Or is your boss, the chief financial officer (CFO), regularly saying that he or she hears nothing but good things about the department providing you with meaningful feedback? What about the things he or she does not hear? And does he or she tell you everything?

Many departments take these random comments as the true measure of how well they are performing. However, taking these comments as an indicator of performance is rather like your simulator instructor saying, "Great flight!" and nothing else after a particularly sweaty LOFT ride. You naturally want more details to know what was really good about your performance, what was average, and what needed work. To begin with, you have a good idea where you were rough and where you excelled; you want those self-assessments verified by the instructor. However, you also know that in the heat of battle, you may have missed some performance items that require some comment. Unexamined performance adds little to experience.

Therefore, how do you determine how well the department is performing with regard to passenger service? Flight departments use several methods to get their customer's opinions about the level of service they are receiving—voluntary comment cards, written surveys, informal sessions with selected passengers, and formal interviews with all passengers who are company employees.

Voluntary comment cards are usually take the form of 3 × 5 or 5 × 8 inch postcards and are either found in seatback pockets or handed to passengers as they deplane. These cards may ask the respondent to relate his or her experiences regarding specific aspects of the service: timeliness of the flight, courtesy of flight and ground personnel, quality of catering, cleanliness of the aircraft, and availability of their favorite reading material. General comments regarding the quality of the service and suggestions for improvement also may be solicited.

Unfortunately, this form of feedback rarely yields substantive comments regarding service rendered. First, few people, especially at the level of your passengers, want to take the time to focus on the details of their transportation. Second, they have little outside experience in on-demand air transportation with which to compare their experiences. Last, few people want to give their honest views about levels of service for fear of being considered a "bad guy." Instead, they tend to give glowing reports, with responses migrating toward the "Outstanding" end of the answer spectrum.

If you run a shuttle operation or fly large quantities of customers, a service-level response card may be the best way of getting information from passengers about your operation. However, ensure that you be specific about what you want to know, going beyond, "Was your flight a pleasant experience?" Role playing with passengers you know well or with friends and family should yield well-focused questions that go to the core of your operation.

Before attempting to find out what passengers think about your operation, it may be well for you to determine what level of service you intend to provide. Without creating service standards, it is difficult to determine how well you are doing and to tell your passengers what level of service they should expect. These standards might include the following:

- All flights will be fully prepared for departure 15 minutes prior to scheduled departure time.
- A standard list of beverages, snacks, newspapers, and periodicals is available for every flight.
- Passengers always will be escorted to and from the aircraft by a flight department employee. Their baggage always will be taken to the aircraft for them.
- Flight details (destination, estimated time enroute, weather, etc.) will be provided to passengers prior to each flight.

Creation of these standards will provide performance targets for flight department personnel and, if published, tell passengers the level of service they are to expect. Not only will this tell passengers what to expect on each flight, it also will demonstrate an exceptional level of care on the part of the flight department. Further, articulation of services to be provided will create a level of expectation for passengers, allowing them to know what to expect on each flight.

The personal touch seems to work best when soliciting information about flight department service. This is especially true with senior executives. They have little time (or patience) to fill out forms, particularly for a service they have come to take for granted. A few well-chosen questions about how they perceive the flight department, presented in the proper setting, will show that you care about what they think and want to improve the service. Such interviews not only gather useful information, but they also serve as a tool to advertise your desire to deliver a superior level of service.

While your passengers are on board and enroute, they are an attractive potential captive audience—just stroll back into the cabin, sit down, and start asking questions, right? But remember, many passengers consider their time aloft as their own private time and do not want to be disturbed.

Instead of intruding on their time and to underscore the importance of your mission, set up a formal appointment with them to "discuss their air transportation needs and performance of the flight department." Schedule the meeting for 15 minutes; this is short enough not to intrude on a busy schedule. If the passenger wants to talk longer, so much the better. Attempt to schedule the meeting in the passenger's office to put him or her at ease and to make the appointment easier to get. Alternatively, suggest the meeting be held immediately following the passenger's next flight in your office or the passenger lounge. In this way, the interruptions will be minimized and flight details will be fresh in the subject's mind.

Take notes during the interview, and then take the time to fully record the details of the session after its conclusion. Records of these interviews will provide strong evidence of the department's performance (hopefully good) when it comes time for performance reviews and for considerations about future directions for corporate aviation.

Another source of information about passengers' attitudes is their administrative assistants or secretaries. There is little about their bosses' lives that these supporting players do not know, both good and bad. While they are generally discreet in releasing information, they usually have their bosses' best interests at heart and should pass on what they have overheard about the flight department. These individuals often hear very detailed information about flights that can be quite useful in validating or improving department performance. Bumpy rides, warm soda, stale sandwiches, lack of information about flights, and missing newspapers all seem to get funneled through these important support staff members. They will be glad you considered them important enough to be asked, too.

How often should you seek information about your department's performance? Ideally, a continuous flow of feedback from the customer is ideal, but this may not be practical. At least once a year your frequent flyers should be interviewed; however, informal updates could be solicited every 6 months. Your less frequent flyers also should be queried regularly, although not as often. Remember, just asking shows that you care. How often should you care?

Once you have this valuable information about your customers, how should it be used? Summaries of the interviews should be kept in a central location, normally in the original paper note form for continuing reference. If there are sufficiently large numbers of passengers to make a paper record impractical, set up a simple database that captures the essential

What to Ask

In your one-on-one interviews, ask specific questions that require more than just a "yes" or "no" answer. After a few warm-up questions, try questions like these:

- What was your most notable trip with us last year? Why?
- What aspects of corporate aviation provide the best value for you?
- Are the aircraft available to you frequently enough to meet your needs?
- Are the aircraft adequate for your needs (size, range, speed, cost)?
- What can we do to make your trips more productive (equipment, scheduling, timing, etc.)?
- Are there other employees or customers who could benefit from the corporate aircraft?
- Have you ever felt anxious or concerned about something that happened on a flight?
- Did you experience any aircraft delays last year? Did you appreciate why the delays occurred?
- What would you like to know about the aircraft or their operation?
- What can we do to make you time airborne more productive or pleasant?

elements of the interviews. However, the real reason for finding out what your customers think is to ensure that you are delivering at least your predetermined standard of service and to improve, where possible.

Therefore, set up a system that evaluates the customer comments in terms of service delivered. Once it has been determined whether standard levels of service are being provided, what items can be improved on? What is important and not so important? Share this information with both your reporting senior and the entire staff of the flight department. Assuming that most of what is in the report is good, the department's reputation goes up within the company, and valuable feedback is provided to your employees. Dramatizing the results of the interviews for department personnel will provide both a morale boost and targets for improvement.

Regardless of the questions asked, do ask. Not knowing what the people think may be hazardous to your career longevity.

The Tools

Perhaps the best-selling tool is a well-motivated marketeer/salesperson. If the desire to promote your product is there, it will get done. However, to help you demonstrate value, you must provide concrete examples of how your way of doing things is superior. Ask your corporate marketing staff; they know how. But first, know what you are selling.

NBAA's *Travel $ense* travel analysis software provides you with the ability to show actual value and competitive advantage of corporate aircraft over air charter or the airlines. This computer program steps you through the many variables involved in travel analysis and presents solutions in a graphic and easy-to-understand manner. This software may the best sales tool available to you because it presents practical, realistic examples of transportation solutions in business terms. Without it, you will have to do a lot of research and calculator punching.

What to Sell

Are you really selling seat-miles? Or air transportation? Well, yes, but in doing so, it is like selling the shoe sole (practical) instead of the entire shoe (style and protection). In reality, you are selling

- Solutions
- Opportunities
- Access to new markets
- Efficiency
- Security
- Confidentiality
- Success
- A time machine
- Assistance
- Possibilities

Presentation

Once you have your research complete and have your corporate beneficiary on board, practice your sales pitch to someone below the decision maker's level but also within the chain of command leading to that person. Once you have that person's blessing (and support), take your show to the decision maker.

Presentations are all the same. They

- Define a problem
- Discuss alternative solutions
- Provide the best possible solution (yours).

They always speak in terms of the person being sold, never in the presenter's terms. They present *potential value,* not savings or profit or glory. They create a picture of success; they create possibilities.

The Sale

After you have convinced the subject of the value of the product, you also must "ask of the order." Without his or her OK to proceed with your idea, nothing changes. Therefore, you must say, "I would like to schedule the marketing team's trip for the second week in February, on a not-to-interfere basis with priority executive trips." Without this request, nothing will happen.

Marketing and selling are a continuous process, a never-ending attempt to promote the value of your operation. And this is a job not just for the flight department manager but for all members of the department. The potential benefits of the department can be communicated from the scheduler to the CEO's secretary, from the maintenance manager to the person who handles the flight department's accounts, and from the chief pilot to the human resources supervisor.

Without an active marketing program for the flight department, it may be in jeopardy of falling victim to the budget axe or the whim of a new chief executive. Times change; the flight department must be ready to go with the flow and adapt to survive and thrive.

Selling 101

Selling is a universal technique. That is, one technique isn't used for selling cars and another for encyclopedias. Certain techniques common to most great salespeople have been cataloged and made the subject of innumerable books and seminars. Here are a few:

- Know your product—what do you have to offer?

- Know your prospect—what do they do; what do they need?

- Be a good listener—you'll never know their needs if you are talking.

- Speak in terms of the prospect's success—you can solve their problems.

- Ask for the order—nothing happens until something is sold.

- Be persistent—Rome wasn't sold in a day.

- Practice, practice, practice—try your spouse—there may be the greatest challenge.

THE SMALL FLIGHT DEPARTMENT

The week started out typically frantic: Test fly the aircraft before a "revenue" trip Monday afternoon; budget variance meeting on Tuesday; renegotiate the hangar lease; find a solution to the continuing scheduling screwups in the president's office; get a replacement body for the trusty copilot's vacation; lobby for a secretary; and get the landlord to work on the balky hangar doors and get rid of the rats. And it all has to be done by the one, the only, department manager, chief pilot, head bottle washer, namely, you. Thus the joys of the small flight department.

Approximately four-fifths of NBAA members have just one aircraft. This means that there are a lot of small operations that work with between one and three full-time individuals and contract out the majority of their services. These departments must be efficient, flexible, and creative just to survive; they must have their priorities in order and run a tight organization.

The key to this organization is its head. Whether the title is aviation department manager, chief pilot, or grand vizier, this person must have a Swiss army knife collection of management, people, technical, and organizational skills. This individual should be comfortable with independence and unilateral decision making. Moreover, he or she probably prefers this organization to a more structured and bureaucratic one; self-reliance is a prized characteristic.

The manager sits at the crossroads between the parent organization and the flight department. This is an important role because the expectations of both organizations may be unrealistic or biased. If the passengers think that their one-airplane airline should be available 24 hours a day, 7 days a week, it is up to the flight department manager to help set more realistic expectations regarding availability. Conversely, if the department thinks the pilots should be treated differently by the finance department for processing travel claims, then this impression should be tested by communicating with the person in charge of travel claims. More important, the flight department manager becomes the aviation expert and spokesperson for the parent organization and is charged with the role of conveying the proper expectations about the department to users.

A number of the topics covered in this section have been covered in a different manner in previous parts of this book. However, the unique structure of the small flight department often demands a slightly different treatment of some aspects of the job. Thus this section will attempt to provide a different perspective on some of the more critical issues associated with operating a flight department.

Communications

Getting the word out (and back) correctly becomes a major role of the department manager, whether it is aircraft capabilities and limitations, the daily flight schedule, hangar rent, recurrent training, pilot hiring, or equipment upgrades. The skill with which the manager presents the case for aviation and negotiates for the items needed to run the department well in large part determines the degree of success the department enjoys. If the parent organization never hears from the department or hears from it only when it needs something, it will suffer. If the manager makes an effort to become an integral part of the larger organization, the chances of the department prospering increase markedly. Do not forget to cultivate the communications habit among all department personnel; managers always needs a communications backup and all the salespeople they can get.

Typically, the small department manager reports directly to a high-level executive within the company or the principal and takes marching orders only from that person. An administrative assistant or executive secretary usually takes care of day-to-day scheduling issues, leaving the flight department to operate unfettered by a range of conflicting demands made by a variety of potential users of the aircraft. If the flight department is fortunate, it will have either a full- or part-time secretary/scheduler/all-purpose person to help with the administrative workload.

Personal Preference Drives Purchase

A dot-com company founder made it big, sold the company at the right time, and now "works" at helping promising inventors, philanthropy, and enjoying his family. Early on he realized that the airlines could not serve his diverse and changing needs. He bought a quarter share of a Hawker 800 aircraft under a fractional program and was pleased with the result.

Over time, he realized that the 200 hours per year available to him under the factional contract was insufficient for his needs. Further, he wanted to see the same faces in the cockpit for every flight and to have greater control over all aspects of the operation. After 2 years with the fractional company, he bought his own Falcon 50, hired a flight crew and aviation maintenance technician of his choosing, and is building a hangar for the aircraft. It seems to be working.

Support Staff

The other usual player in a small department is typically a copilot or combination copilot/mechanic. This person also has to have a broad-based bag of skills to complement that of his or her boss. And since this may be the only other person in the department, he or she is often given "everything else" by default; there is nobody else to give "it" to. But is there?

Successful small departments have developed a support staff within the parent organization to help them with their many tasks. Instead of remaining the remote and mysterious people at the airport who fly the boss around, the clever departments have recruited company personnel to do their work for them while they fly. These departments have done so by communicating well with the principal's office, human resources, finance, and administration departments to make them appreciate their unique role within the company. By asking questions, learning to appreciate the other's roles within the company, and establishing a friendly relationship with the important departments, the flight department has gained allies and a support staff to assist it with its functions.

The relationship of the flight department manager to the senior executives and principal's supporters may prove advantageous is securing support from the larger organization. These executives can open doors for the flight department that normally may take long hours of effort to open through normal channels. However, realize that potential support staff may resent the high level attention provided to the mysterious folks at the airport. The solution to this is usually to make a special effort not to appear special or untouchable but to identify with the overall goals and objectives of the company. If your potential supporters see you as team members instead of prima donnas, your access to them is much easier.

However, even with a great support staff, there is still much for the flight department to accomplish. Maintenance providers, hangar landlords, fuel salespeople, aircraft cleaners parts vendors, catering suppliers, recurrent training companies, and janitorial services all make demands on the flight department's scarce time resources. This is where good organizational and prioritization skills are essential. There is often too much to do for the given amount of time in which to accomplish it; something has to give. If the support staff cannot handle it, then it is up to the flight department to do it.

Again, the smart flight operators get the vendors and suppliers to help them. Instead of figuring out what the scheduled maintenance plan, costs, and alternatives will be for next year, ask potential maintenance vendors to do it for you as a part of the bid process. Get the caterer to analyze the previous year's consumption and provide a quote for a structured catering plan for the next year, including periodic deliveries and restocking catering supply cabinets. Arrange with the landlord or janitorial service to conduct a monthly inspection of the hangar to take care of minor maintenance items before they get to be major items. These and other suppliers of goods and services should be providing *full service* and not just face-value service; make them work for you and become involved in your operation.

An invaluable means of support may lie within that personal computer sitting on your desk. The flight department management software available today can tie scheduling, trip planning, budgeting, invoicing, maintenance, and personnel files together into one tidy package. Communications features available on this software tie you to the boss's office, accounting, and the flight planning/weather provider, too. Sure, it takes some getting used to, but once you become accustomed to its idiosyncrasies, you may never go back to paper and the mail. Seriously, the computer revolution has taken the corporate aviation world by storm, proving particularly beneficial to the resource-strapped small department. The personal computer may become your most useful "staff member." And let the software vendor set up your desired program for you.

Networking

Since the experience and knowledge base for the small department is relatively small, a network of other flight departments is essential to finding the best deals and for assistance in time of need. If another flight department on the field can recommend a maintenance or parts vendor from its own experience, this is valuable information. Word-of-mouth recommendations made by someone who has a similar operation will save you much time and effort in searching for a vendor on your own. And if you need a part, a special tool, advice, a copilot, or merely someone to commiserate with, your trusted network probably will pay immediate and bountiful dividends. Building the network may not be easy, particularly if you operate a relatively rare aircraft or are located at a small, remote airport with few corporate operators. Working with the aircraft manufacturer's customer service organization or aviation association should soon yield suitable networkers. Operators at airports that are normal destinations for your department are candidates for your network, too. If you get to those facilities more than once every 2 weeks or so, they may be able to provide mutual services and aid.

Networks may be formalized into time-share operations to create a mutual assistance pact when aircraft availability or heavy trip requirements become a factor. The ability to call a nearby operator and have him or her cover or back up an important trip not only keeps the stress level under control, but it also makes your organization more valuable and credible to management within your company. Naturally, time-share agreements are not to be entered into lightly, and they do require the involvement of lawyers, accounts, and senior executives (your support staff). However, do explore the possibilities of these mutually advantageous arrangements.

Cybernetworks are becoming popular among all flight departments, but particularly among small ones. Bulletin boards posted on business aviation Web sites provide a ready outlet for questions, opinions, and insights regarding everything to do with running the operation, including finding employees, vendors, foreign handlers, parts, and local hotels. The NBAA Airmail System is especially well used.

Think Backup

The one-airplane airline is out of business if its single aeronautical asset becomes unserviceable due to either scheduled or unscheduled maintenance. However, this need not lead to disastrous consequences. Scheduled maintenance should be scheduled to coincide with known slow travel periods for the normal users of the operation and well publicized in advance to preclude possible disappointments. Unscheduled maintenance is a bit more tricky but manageable. An arrangement with a local charter operator to provide short-notice backup for your flights is a good solution to the specter of a unserviceable aircraft. Operators on field are specially helpful because of their proximity and potential for short response times. Interchange and time-share arrangements (previously mentioned) are ideal ways to obtain a backup for your operations. However, creating a mindset among the regular passengers that an occasional trip may have to be delayed or canceled due to maintenance or weather is an essential part of the department manager's role, too.

Planning

One of the most important functions for the small operator should be that of planning for the future. Whether it be preparation for the heavy transportation requirements for the annual board retreat, equipment upgrades, augmenting the department with additional personnel, or planning for the purchase of the next aircraft, foresight and planning always should be in the mind of the manager. If not, events surely will overtake the operation, and the value of the department will be reduced and credibility lost. Credibility of the operation is probably the most important asset of the flight department; it must be protected. The manager must allocate a sufficient amount of time to look to the future, long and short term, to ensure the continued health of the department.

This planning must be linked to action through an individual who sets priorities properly and communicates well with all. The narrow range of assets available to the manager of a small flight department makes the ability to view the future in clear terms with priorities well formed absolutely essential. Obviously, the manager must not do this in a vacuum but must use all the assets available to him or her from the CEO down through the janitor to accomplish the mission.

The manager of the small flight department must be single-minded in dedication to the department's mission: Providing the best possible air transportation for the parent organization. If the manager really believes in this concept and is at least an adequate performer, the rest is relatively easy. Well, maybe not easy, but clear and well-defined. However, this is no different for a flight department manager of a department of any size, is it?

The greater thing in this world is not so much where we stand as in what direction we are going.

—OLIVER WENDELL HOLMES

CHAPTER 5
FLIGHT DEPARTMENT MANAGEMENT

While most flight department personnel have a good feel for what it takes to fly and maintain aircraft, they often have little appreciation for how to integrate those operations with other elements that go into running a flight department. Scheduling, personnel, reports, budgets, planning, communications, and control all have a significant impact on flight department operations but may be foreign concepts to the people responsible for running the department. In many ways, aviation personnel lag behind their corporate counterparts in knowledge of these essential elements because while the aviation people were focusing on the narrow disciplines of flight and maintenance at the beginning of their careers, the folks downtown were wrestling with budgets, human resources, planning meetings, and the like. The business folks *grew* into their management positions, whereas the aviation people were *thrust* into the world of management at some point in their careers. In other words, it is catch-up ball for the people out at the hangar.

Many people in corporate aviation have been exposed to the world of management through college courses, company training, military service, and jobs taken to feed their aviation habit. However, unless they were given the opportunity to put the principles they learned into practice soon after receiving their training, they probably soon forgot them. There also seems to be a common misconception that sound business and management principles do not necessarily apply to the world of aviation. Aviation personnel tend to get caught up in the technical and romantic aspects of flying and think that "all the rest" will take care of itself. Perhaps it is a matter of priorities, but management often receives short shrift in the aviator's world.

In many cases, the main reason that many flight department personnel are not ready for management positions is that they have not been tasked with other than aviation duties on their way up through the ranks. Flying and maintenance tasks may be all they have been expected to perform during their tenure. They may never have been given the opportunity to confront budgets, training plans, long-range maintenance planning, performance reviews, or aircraft replacement justifications. Moreover, because they were never given the opportunity to *learn* through these essential functions, they are unprepared for the giant step to management. Remember this as a need for your subordinates once you attain the lofty perch of manager.

The best executive is the one who has sense enough to pick men to do what he wants done, and self-restraint enough to keep from meddling with them while they do it.
—THEODORE ROOSEVELT

MANAGEMENT 101

Whether you have an MBA or are merely an ATP or senior aviation maintenance technician, it is a good idea occasionally to review the basic principles of management. By doing so, you will be providing yourself with a useful perspective for viewing your daily tasks in terms of a theoretical framework, one that may yield valuable solutions.

Manage

To direct or control the use of.

To direct or administer (a business, for example).

To direct, supervise or carry on business or other affairs.

The Basics

The dictionary definitions of *manage* in the sidebar are really quite complete; if they were followed, all management functions would be accomplished. It is interesting to note the Latin root of *manage* is *manus,* meaning "hand." The derivation comes from the use of one's hand to direct and shape events and perhaps even to coerce. The implication is one of control—of things, resources, processes, and people. The underlying thought is that one must be "in control" if management is to occur.

Most management writers list the following functions of management:

- *Planning.* What does the organization need to thrive?
- *Organizing.* How do you order available resources to achieve the goals?
- *Resource allocation.* People, money, and time.
- *Leading.* How do I get it all going in the same direction?
- *Controlling.* Am I really making progress, and if not, how can I change?

However, this can be shortened to just:

- *Planning.* Goal setting.
- *Execution.* Making it happen.
- *Feedback.* How are we doing? (See Fig. 5.1.)

Obviously, organizing, staffing, and leading must take place, but they really are subsets of execution. Regardless of how many elements are included in the management process, it is important to dwell on the point that it is not only a process but a *continuing process.* It

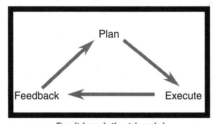

Don't break the triangle!

FIGURE 5.1   Essential management tasks.

is really a cycle of events that never ends. Projects, people, and other resources may come and go, but the process never ends.

Planning

Planning looks for a destination and a way to get there. If it is done correctly, planning involves looking for several ways of getting to a destination, for detours or new roads may be encountered on the way. This is the essence of strategic planning. Although planning was covered in Chap. 4, a slightly different view may be helpful.

Strategic planning looks at the long view, the big picture. It asks, "Where are we going as an organization?" and "What are the alternative means of achieving our mission?" The articulation of the ultimate organizational goal is known as the *mission statement*—"To make uncommonly good cookies and crackers" (Keebler Foods), "We rent cars" (Avis), or "We move money" (Brinks, Inc.). Organizational elements of the company should have a mission statement that supports the overall mission: "We provide safe and efficient on-demand air transportation to the XYZ Company."

The next level down in the process establishes goals or objectives needed to achieve the mission statement: For example:

- Achieve a minimum 99 percent dispatch rate for all passenger-carrying flights.
- Receive a least a 95 percent approval rating from passenger surveys.
- Acquire or build a new hangar by December 2005.

Note that these objectives are measurable but not necessarily concrete, real tasks. Note also that they do not state exactly how the objective will be reached.

Operational planning looks at the short term but still attempts to support the mission and objectives statements. For example:

- Replace the interior on the Gulfstream at the next 72-month inspection, scheduled for mid-2004.
- A 2-year training plan.
- The monthly flight schedule.

Note that some of these are long range and some short range, but they are all operational plans because they are concrete and measurable. In contrast with strategic plans, they address ways and means of achieving these shorter-range goals.

This planning must be done with full knowledge of what the parent company is doing about the future. If corporate headquarters is moving to another city within the next 2 years, it makes little sense to look for a new hangar at the current airport. Corporate plans and objectives are sometimes difficult to obtain, and it is frequently even more difficult to know what the latest plans are. Therefore, your network within the company is a vital source of information about what the latest plan is.

Execution

Once a plan is developed, the more practical aspect of making it a reality comes next. The elements of execution include

- *Problem definition.* What are we really trying to accomplish?
- *Standards development.* How do we know we are doing it right?

- *Resource allocation.* Where do I place available resources?

The problem definition stage is, arguably, the most important aspect of project execution. Without complete knowledge of the task at hand, many surprises are possible. Take some time on this one. Some action items include the following:

- Develop a *complete* task statement.
  - Is it a complete interior refurbishment or just upholstery?
  - Is this a good time to do the APU STC?
- List available resources.
  - Do I have to send a technician to oversee the refurbishment of the aircraft while it is at the service center?
  - Can I use my contingency fund, too?
- Define the project schedule or time to process.
  - Can we do the landing gear trunion replacement during the repaint?
  - Will this schedule provide enough contingency time to make the board meeting schedule?
- Develop alternatives.
  - If the aircraft is not finished on time, will the boss use charter?

Standards development seems simple enough on the surface, but what standards are in question? Time, quality, airworthiness, good operating practices, usage of people and money, or company policy? And why not standards you have developed for the department? If you do not designate standards and communicate them to your people, vendors, the company hierarchy, and *yourself,* it will be difficult to determine the quality of performance.

Examples:

- Materials used in the modification will be specified in writing prior to commencing the project.
- The project will be completed in four phases in accordance with the following schedule.
- Personnel completing the course will do so with a score of 5 or better.

Resource allocation simply means, "Am I using my available money, time, and staff to best advantage?" How you place these scarce commodities often makes the difference between success and failure. For instance, should you use your lead technician to babysit the Challenger during a major inspection at the service center or use him to train the new technician on the King Air? Or should you wait until after the European board meeting to send your best international captain to management school? Perhaps the best way to accomplish this well is to simply list the pros and cons side by side on a sheet of paper to make sure you consider all alternatives. And don't forget to include other projects on the same sheet that vie for the same scarce resources.

Feedback

Feedback and its natural partner, control, are the features that make the entire process work on a continuing basis. The ability to obtain timely, accurate, and germane input regarding a project or process provides a means to correct it if it is not going according to plan or schedule.

During the planning phase, feedback mechanisms should be developed to provide necessary information concerning the progress of the project. The most important aspect of feedback development is a means to measure progress, be it time, quality, quantity, or resources allocation. For instance, if no standards are set regarding dispatch rate for trips or costs per hour or passenger satisfaction, then performance cannot be measured. Similarly, if quality, time, and price standards for a TCAS installation are not defined for a vendor, success or failure can be questioned only with difficulty. Take the time to define standards so that feedback is possible.

Feedback must be timely and complete if it is to be of use in managing an ongoing process or project. And the time spent in developing the feedback should not be out of proportion to the payoff expected from the information received. Report systems design is a science in itself that will not be discussed here, but it is an integral part of the success of the feedback loop. (For more information, see Chap. 4.)

Once feedback is received, it must be evaluated and acted on if it is to be of value to the management process. If the 600-hour inspection is 2 days behind schedule or the training budget is overspent by 50 percent and it is only June, something must be done to get these or any other deficient projects back on track. This is when you should return to the planning and execution phases to see what alternatives are available. Can you hire additional part-time technicians to complete the inspection prior to the Aspen trip? Should you ask for additional training funds or delay the international operations training until next year?

It is this constant process of planning, execution, and feedback that spells the difference between a successful manager and one less so. It is attention to detail while not losing sight of the big picture that separates the good from the not so good. There is another dimension of the management process that cannot be overlooked—that of people doing the managing and work.

Management is tasks. Management is a discipline. But management is also people. Every achievement of management is the achievement of a manager. Every failure is a failure of a manager. People manage rather than "forces" or "facts." The vision, dedication and integrity of managers determine whether there is management or mismanagement.

—Peter Drucker

No Shortcuts

The greatest problem managers seem to have with the management process is shortcutting the system. Figure 5.1 uses a closed triangle to demonstrate the three-step process. However, there is a tendency to break the integrity of the triangular process once feedback has been received.

Let's say that a hangar is being built for the flight department. The foundation has been poured and structural steel support fittings anchored. A delay in receipt of certain steel components has opened the option of modifying the hangar structure to accommodate the shortage. If the manager makes a decision based on the need for expeditious completion, the integrity of the triangle has been violated. Any feedback should be considered first as a potential modification to the initial plan and not simply used summarily to modify the execution process. Doing so thwarts the original intent of the project and jeopardizes its ultimate utility.

The plan should be considered the driving force for any project or ongoing process. This is most evident when people disregard their organization's mission in favor of a short-term, visible goal that seems to make sense. For instance, if an operator opts to keep its 25-year-old aircraft despite its failing reliability and escalating maintenance costs, it may be ignoring the "reliable" and "efficient" segments of its mission statement. More important is the failure of a department to ensure that every action taken must consider safety as a primary consideration—this should be part of the primary plan for all flight departments. Never break the integrity of the triangle!

THEORIES OF MANAGEMENT

Within the framework of the basic management process, there are a number of theories that both describe the means to manage and further define management itself. These theories are numerous and sometimes conflicting; therefore, one must be selective in the use of these various theories. The theories described here are possibly the most popular that have arisen in corporate America and certainly the most enduring.

The Beginnings

As a consequence of the industrial revolution, there arose a desire to make work processes more efficient and effective. Late in the nineteenth and early twentieth centuries, the scientific approach to work and management took shape. Frederick W. Taylor's *Principles of Scientific Management* is the seminal work of the scientific management movement, which featured time and motion studies to achieve efficiency. Henry L. Gantt focused on the need for realistic work standards based on study and measurement. His work schedules, now known as *Gantt charts,* were widely adopted. Finally, Henri Fayol, a French engineer, worked on organizational issues and was the first to define management by its constituent parts (planning, organizing, commanding, coordinating, and controlling) in his 1929 book, *General and Industrial Management.*

Behavioral Approaches

As it became evident in the post-World War I period that time and motion studies were limited in achieving increased productivity, management theorists began to focus on the worker rather than on the work itself. Elton Mayo found that worker productivity is related to social and psychological factors as well as the work itself. He called in 1933 for managers to consider human relations factors, and people-management skills began the human relations movement in management. Chester Barnard concentrated on the need for effective managerial communication and motivation skills and emphasized that managers' real power comes not from their position but from acceptance of the workers. And perhaps the most famous behaviorist, Douglas McGregor, developed the concepts of theory X and theory Y in which pessimistic and optimistic views, respectively, of the worker are set forth. His 1960 book, *The Human Side of Enterprise,* introduced the corresponding theories of authoritarian and participative management.

Motivation theory has been and continues to be a major part of the behavioral approach to management. The theory states that workers will not willingly perform that which they are not sufficiently driven to accomplish. Abraham Maslow held that individual unsatisfied needs are the main source of motivation. He stated that these were hierarchical in nature from the most basic to the most mature; e.g., all lower needs must be present for the higher ones to occur. The needs are

• Physiologic/survival
• Safety

- A sense of belonging
- Ego status—self-esteem, reward systems
- Self-actualization—working for the sake of work itself

Frederick Herzberg took this theory one step further, stating that the first three needs must be present before any motivation (embodied in the two highest needs) could take place. In fact, without the first three, the employee would be dissatisfied.

Modern Theories

Theory Z management is based largely on Japanese approaches to management, which feature long-term commitment, worker-management cooperation and discussion, and decision making that relies on group consensus. The popular terms *quality of worklife* and *quality circles* are components of theory Z. This spawned total quality management (TQM), one of the hottest theories of the 1990s. TQM tenets include total quality control, continuous improvement, and quality improvement teams. All these were fathered by the quality guru, W. Edwards Deming, the man who transformed Japanese industry of the 1950s into the force it is today.

The cult of worker excellence and the ability to manage chaotic change in the workplace were popularized by Tom Peters and Robert Waterman in the 1980s. They developed a formula for determining excellence within companies and applied it to a number of companies to prove their point. Their book, *In Search of Excellence,* became a runaway best seller in management circles in 1982. Their central thesis of excellent firms involved the need for constant improvement and change. Subsequently, Peters' book, *Thriving on Chaos,* discussed the need to move from hierarchical management structures to more horizontal, fast, cross-functional, cooperative ones.

To meet the demands of the fast-changing competitive scene, we must simply learn to love change as much as we hated it in the past.

—TOM PETERS

Reengineering involves front-line workers performing complete tasks without departmental boundaries or supervisory checks dividing and slowing down the operations. While not a new theory (Toyota pioneered the basis of reengineering in the 1950s), its rediscovery has enabled corporations to take advantage of new technology in manufacturing processes by freeing workers from stifling organizational paradigms.

A single individual has lived, survived, examined, discarded, and added to virtually all these theories. Peter Drucker started as an economist and became a management consultant for General Motors during World War II. Since that time, he has devoted his life to the practice of management, writing scores of books on the subject, including my personal favorite, *Management: Tasks, Responsibilities, Practices* (Harper & Row, 1974). Drucker brings an enlightening mix of disciplines to the task of management, seeking to find a balance between the needs of the worker and the company.

Future Theories

Theories of management keep academics and consultants active and in business. However, their postulates serve as a useful way to view the world of work and the means of accomplishing it in an orderly and efficient manner. Each theory provides us with a different perspective on how to gain the best productivity from the worker and ourselves.

Undoubtedly new management theories will emerge that will expand our understanding of the phenomenon. In time, however, these too will yield to still newer paradigms. The point is to gain as much as possible from each theory without being totally taken in by its tenets. We have a tendency to unequivocally embrace hot new theories to the exclusion of other proven means of getting the job done. There never has been a complete and perfect management theory; there probably never will be. Use the theories as they come as aids, not ends unto themselves.

Managers do things right. Leaders do the right thing.

—WARREN BENNIS

Learning It

Obviously, this brief look at the theory and practice of management will not be sufficient to make you an ace. The best way to learn about management is to be exposed to its principles and theory on a continuing basis and then practice, practice, practice.

Local colleges normally have a variety of basic management courses available at night, and many companies conduct their own supervisor and management training in-house. Either of these is good to start with, but the company training may be preferable just because it gets you closer to company people. Knowing nonaviation company personnel will help you with your network of contacts and will teach you more about the corporate culture.

At the very least, read a book on the subject of management. The bookstores are full of them, some good and some not so good. You are probably better off reading the classic management gurus rather than studying the management technique of the month, which goes away almost as rapidly as soon as it came; the classics age well.

Management Reading

- Carnegie, Dale, and Associates. *Managing Through People.* New York: Simon and Schuster, 1978.
- Drucker, Peter F. *Management: Tasks, Responsibilities, Practices.* New York: Harper & Row, 1974.
- McGregor, Douglas. *The Human Side of Enterprise.* New York: McGraw-Hill, 1960.
- Peters, T., and Waterman, R. H. *In Search of Excellence.* New York: Harper & Row, 1982.
- Blanchard, Kenneth, and Johnson, Spencer. *The One Minute Manager.* New York: William Morrow, 1982.
- Walton, Mary. *The Deming Management Method.* New York: Dodd, Mead, 1986.
- *NBAA Management Guide.* Washington: NBAA, 1999.
- Virtually any *Introduction to Management* book or similar title found in a college book store.

Note that these are not new or trendy books—for a reason.

Once you have taken Management 101 or even 102 and read your book, do not stop there. Continue to take courses and read about the practice of management. The pages of *Fortune, Forbes, Fast Company,* and *Business Week* are filled with tales of managerial rights, wrongs, dos and don'ts, usually told in an entertaining fashion.

Your organization probably has its share of good managers and role models. Think about it: At least a few of your manager's must be doing something right to keep the organization afloat. Each of these good performers is a potential mentor or coach. Find the right person, and establish a relationship. They do not have to know anything about aviation; in fact, that quality is probably an advantage.

You Can't Get There from Here

A large consumer plastics products company in the Midwest employed a number of boutique manufacturers to supply it with specialty products. In many cases, these suppliers were located in rural locations not near airline-served airports. The ones that were near airline airports often received only infrequent service from commuter carriers. Design, engineering, purchasing, and quality control personnel needed regular access to the suppliers, so 30 years ago a small twin-engine piston-powered Piper Navajo was purchased to meet the need.

As the company grew, so did its need to access an increasing number of suppliers, distribution centers, and customer outlets. The single aircraft has become a fleet of four turbojets, each operating more than 400 hours per year in support of company needs. The long-time CEO is enthusiastic in his endorsement of company aircraft, saying, "For many of the places we need to go, you can't get there from here, but the company airplane can!"

MANAGEMENT SKILLS

Theories are great if nothing has to be accomplished. However, the object of management is to do exactly that: *to accomplish objectives in a productive and efficient manner.* Managers must develop and exercise certain skills to apply the theories in much the same manner as a pilot or technician does in the pursuit of his or her trade. Pilots need to understand the flight environment and have good hand-eye coordination, spatial relationships, and motor skills. Technicians must understand mechanical devices, be good troubleshooters, and have good motor skills. All these attributes become skills when applied to their trade. The same is true for the manager. Some of the skills needed include the following:

Communication. The ability to transmit one's ideas to others in a timely, clear, and concise manner is perhaps the most important skill for a manager. Moreover, if the manager cannot understand and appreciate what subordinates are saying, then true (two-way) communication has not taken place. It is said that at least half of communication should be spent listening and the other half thinking about what to say.

Written and oral forms of communication are equally important for management. The ability to express oneself clearly and concisely in writing is a particularly useful attribute. Memoranda, letters, performance appraisals, and budget justifications are all essential written communications that will recur with disturbing regularity; be prepared and practiced. The ability to say what you mean to individuals or groups is an essential mark of a leader and a manager.

Control and dissemination of information are forms of communication that also must be addressed. Everybody does not need to know everything you know, but some need to know more than others; knowing the difference is the artform.

Decision Making. This skill allows the manager to choose between alternative courses of actions, plans, and materials. Without it, nothing happens. Without the proper techniques of choice, the wrong things happen. This is an important skill that involves data gathering, analysis, and judgment skills as well. Only time, practice, and perhaps a good mentor will help the decision-making process.

Motivation. The ability of managers or, perhaps more appropriately, leaders to get people *willingly* to do their bidding is more art than science. Yet, without this skill, they will never get the most out of their people or accomplish the desired objective with speed and efficiency. Motivation involves understanding the human psyche and knowing what stimulates people into spontaneous action, i.e., generating action without manipulation. Group motivation is somewhat different from individual motivation; both should be mastered.

Time Management. This skill involves setting priorities and determining the proper allocation of personal resources in achieving the object of the priority. Self-discipline and the ability to see beyond a specific component of a task are also important. Work planning and delegation come into play for time management.

Conflict Resolution. Resolution of differences with superiors, peers, and subordinates is another artform that spells success for managers. The win-win approach to conflict resolution is always best, when possible. Communication skills are an important subset of this skill.

Group Dynamics. Small work groups, peers in meetings, and larger groups are all multiples that must be dealt with. Again, communication and motivation skills are subsets of group management that must be mastered. The interplay of people and human nature in the workplace reveals an infinite number of permutations and combinations. Understanding the nature of the individuals within the group is step one; understanding their individual motivations and ability to cope with change are important subsets of this effort.

Acquiring Skills

The appropriate skills can be encountered in the classroom, but they must be practiced to become a part of a manager's repertoire. A firm understanding of management theory is a useful prerequisite to the actual skills-acquisition process. Assignment of responsibility and authority to accomplish certain tasks are the usual means of gaining the requisite management skills. And the skills do not come overnight. Years, not months, of concentrated effort are often needed to master the rudiments of these essential skills.

The National Business Aviation Association (NBAA) has developed the Professional Development Program to help flight department personnel learn and appreciate the intricacies of management practice. The organization acknowledged the excellent job being done in flight departments to remain technically and operationally proficient but identified a need to strengthen knowledge and skills in management and leadership areas. Concentration on these areas was deemed necessary if sufficiently talented individuals were to be available to manage and lead the flight departments of the future. The NBAA board encouraged industry and an academic task force to develop a curriculum to be available through a variety of delivery methods and targeted to the needs of current and future aviation managers.

A survey of NBAA members indicated that management education is an unfulfilled need in the corporate aviation community. Survey results also were used to focus on four broad subject areas and to determine the overview, goals, and topics (performance objectives) under each of the areas. The NBAA-recommended skills represent essential areas of knowledge for aviation professionals. They were developed through consensus among educators and aviation managers. Here's what they came up with.

Aviation Management. Managing a modern corporate flight department requires an aviation professional to possess unique managerial skills; knowledge and expertise to properly manage significant capital resources, human resources, information resources, and the processes that create transportation value are essential. It is necessary to use these capabilities and standard management principles (i.e., plan, organize, staff, direct, measure, and control) to ensure that the department adequately supports corporate strategic objectives.

Leadership. Leadership can be defined as a process of influencing the behaviors and performance of individuals and groups to achieve the desired objectives, outcomes, and goals of an organization. Leading an aviation team that can interact smoothly and positively with its parent company in today's dynamic and highly competitive business climate is becoming increasingly important. This leadership program will concentrate on developing and practicing the skills and attributes necessary for the aviation department manager. These will include being effective in the motivation and inspiration of personnel, as well as appreciating the influence of strategies, structures, and corporate culture on high-performance teams.

Communication. Communication is the process of creating understanding between individuals or groups. The ability to communicate effectively is a fundamental element required for the successful operation of a flight department. Therefore, effective communication skills are those that maintain interpersonal relationships and facilitate completion of the aviation department's mission, goals, and tasks within the culture and framework of the organization.

Business Administration. In today's competitive business environment, the aviation manager is expected to effectively administer all aspects of the aviation department in line with accepted business standards and company policies. Therefore, a solid grounding in many business functions beyond direct aviation-related subjects will be required. Table 5.1 lists specific program objectives.

A number of academic institutions offer courses designed to provide the skills necessary to accommodate this curriculum and the needs of flight departments. The NBAA program goal is to develop a certification program for individuals that will assist them in achieving career goals in business aviation. Receiving the Certified Aviation Manager designation should make it easier for employers to choose flight department managers with greater surety and to provide better career opportunities for those who choose the program.

THE FLIGHT DEPARTMENT MANAGER AS A BUSINESS EXECUTIVE

Nobody in business aviation ever said, "When I grow up, I want to be a business executive." Executives do dull, boring things that fathers do all day: shuffle papers, talk on the telephone, and go to meetings—yuck! "When I grow up, I want to be a pilot and fly all over the world" or "I want to tear airplanes apart and put them back together."

And sure enough, this is how most of us got to where we are today, with a simple wish and the single-minded determination to achieve the goal of flying or maintaining airplanes. We chose the profession; it did not choose us. However, a select few of us not only did well enough at the aviation job, but we also were chosen for a position of leadership, authority, and responsibility and were given a position in management. And if we stuck with it long enough, a very few rose to the heights of flight department manager. In many companies, this means a director-level position—a business executive. From Cessna 152s to the big time in 20 years or less; this is no mean achievement. However, what does it really mean to be an executive?

TABLE 5.1   NBAA PDP Performance Objectives

Aviation management

- Develop comprehensive safety and security programs.
- Use goal-setting, motivational theory, measurement, critique, and conflict-resolution techniques to achieve department and company short-and long-term goals.
- Demonstrate completion of an air transportation analysis, and use it in an aircraft selection process.
- Develop and control department budgets, inventory, quality assurance processes, portable equipment, hangars, and fueling facilities.
- Manage an effective, efficient flight operation and the associated maintenance and dispatch functions.
- Understand and apply the professional standards for all aspects of aircraft maintenance.
- Implement and enforce the unique regulatory requirements dealing with hazardous materials.
- Operate an aviation department within the insurance and legal requirements of international, federal, state, and local regulations.

Leadership

- Foster a unified vision and strategic plan for the flight department.
- Recognize the fundamental concepts of leadership and supervision, and apply appropriate strategies for motivating flight department personnel toward implementing organizational plans and goals.
- Promote ethical and professional behavior in the corporate flight department through personal example and expectations.
- Improve interpersonal relations within the flight department and between the flight department and other corporate entities.
- Use the principles of individual and organizational behavior to develop high performance teams.

Communication

- Develop and use effective and appropriate forms of written communication.
- Plan and deliver effective and appropriate oral presentations to various audiences.
- Use communication to solve problems, make decisions, and resolve issues of importance, including challenges that occur within crew resource management (CRM).
- Influence others through the prowess of interpersonal communication.
- Communicate and work effectively with others in teams, committees, and small groups.
- Utilize a variety of appropriate communication technologies (e.g., e-mail, voice mail, and the Internet).

Business administration

- Develop policies and implement procedures to provide for efficient and effective department administration.
- Organize the flight department into a functional unit.
- Assess technology, equipment, and operational needs for the conduct of business.
- Understand basic economic and marketing principles as applied to the services of the aviation department and other air travel resources.
- Assess and understand transportation needs and desires of the company and its passengers so as to effectively identify the intangible benefits and value-added services provided by the aviation department.
- Value and communicate to appropriate corporate staff the impact of departmental decisions on overall company revenue and expense.
- Understand general accounting and financial principles.
- Understand fundamentals of business information systems and use typical computer applications in data and information management, word processing, decision support systems, and other applications in managing the aviation department.

The aforementioned leadership, authority, and responsibility are not bad descriptors for the occupation (see sidebar). It is usually a step above middle management and a step below corporate officer. It means increased prestige and perquisites and a bigger salary. And yes, executives do talk on the telephone, shuffle papers, and go to meetings. It means preparing budgets, planning for next year, hiring, firing, coordinating, defending the aviation function, and being called back from vacation when something goes wrong. Most of all, it means entering a foreign territory, learning the new language of corporate America, and crossing swords with MBAs and accountants.

The new flight department manager is thrust into a strange new arena, one that has little to do with airplanes, flight schedules, and making a slot time at National Airport. Not only is the entire weight of operational matters placed squarely on the department manager's shoulders, administrative, financial, human resources, public affairs, and marketing are heaped on for good measure. Yet these are just the details of the job. In a greater sense, the new executive must acquire or develop a larger view of the department's job. Moreover, he or she must gain an appreciation for the goals and objectives of the company itself.

No longer can such a person be interested in just making airplanes fly. His or her perspective becomes one of transportation, support, and helping to meet company objectives. Not only must he or she begin to talk to his or her fellow executives in these terms, he or she must *think* in these terms as well. We are talking transformation, metamorphosis, big change. However, just how does a person trained to fly or fix airplanes adapt and adjust to this strange new world?

If the system worked the way it was intended, the fledgling executive has been trained to assume the mantle of executive ever since he or she started with the corporate aviation world. Management training courses, night school, collateral duties, increasing amounts of responsibility, and assisting the flight department manager should have all happened to provide corporate management with an opportunity to observe the candidate manager under fire and to have provided the candidate with the necessary tools and experience to prepare himself or herself for the role. While this sounds good and very textbookish, reality is seldom so. The new manager is usually thrust into the new position suddenly, somewhat unexpectedly, with little notion of the real substance of the job.

If senior management has chosen well, the fresh-caught manager will have adequate management skills to survive a transition period and, more important, will have the potential to grow into executive material. If management has chosen badly, the department probably has lost its best line captain or head technician and gained a mediocre manager. Even with the proper background, there is always a chance that the new person will not make it; there are a lot of unknowns in any personnel move.

Flight Department Manager's Ideal Traits

- Curiosity
- Vision
- Commitment
- Innovation
- Marketing
- Appreciation of people power

The new manager can increase his or her chances of success as an executive by developing and nurturing a few simple personality traits. Those listed (and treated more fully) in Chap. 3 and the sidebar have stood the test of time. The best way to come up to speed in these traits is through a coach or mentor within the corporate hierarchy. Cultivate these individuals early in your corporate tenure. They can be your key to success.

There is a separate classification of flight department manager that has been gaining popularity in recent years, that of the nonflying or non-aviation-experienced manager. This type of manager is not flooding the ranks of department managers but is becoming a significant force within the community. Presumably, these individuals are chosen for their management and executive characteristics, so they have a head start in these areas prior to showing up at the hangar. However, just as the experienced pilot or maintenance technician must learn the management and executive ropes, the nonaviation type must learn the complex and arcane world of the airplane. Moreover, he or she must learn the unique culture and personal characteristics of aviation personnel.

Apart from the possible up-front resentment of the pretenders to the throne of department manager, the nonaviator must understand and appreciate the characteristics and limitations of aircraft and the standard procedures that attend a sophisticated flight department. The rules, regulations, and procedures that reside in a flight department can be daunting to the novice. And department personnel may not be terribly honest or forthcoming regarding the facts when the new person asks. One such new kid on the block likened his first few months on the job to an extended snipe hunt; reality and fantasy were difficult to separate.

Strangely, the naiveté of the nonaviator presents him or her with a great opportunity to test the mettle of his or her new charges by having them explain to him or her the significance and importance of all aspects of the aviation world. Sure, he or she will receive some bad information, but in so doing, he or she will soon find out who the bad and good guys are. The lack of bias and preconception the new manager brings to the job may just make up for his or her lack of aeronautical knowledge. A fresh viewpoint and outlook may be what the department needs to renew and improve itself. (Come to think of it, an experienced new aviation manager may want to take the clean-slate, challenge-existing-assumptions approach, too.)

The nonaviator must immediately rely on his or her lieutenants, the chief pilot and director of maintenance, if he or she is to survive. And this reliance should continue long after he or she has been in the job. By empowering these senior aviation personnel, managers free themselves to concentrate on the larger issues required of the executive. And because the aviation personnel are freed of the larger nontechnical tasks, they can concentrate on their areas of expertise. And this brings us back to the experienced aviator who has been designated the flight department manager.

This individual is at a disadvantage because he or she has to split himself or herself between the demands of remaining current in an aircraft or staying abreast of maintenance issues and learning the larger view of management within a large company. At best, the manager will be unable to keep his or her position as a full-time pilot on the flight schedule or to be involved in all maintenance planning decisions. At worst, he or she may have to give up these familiar pleasures entirely in favor of the executive life. The demands of running a complex, costly aviation operation may not allow much more than token participation in the aeronautical arena, and this may prove disconcerting to the individual or even unsafe because of a lack of proficiency. There are lots of flying and maintaining department managers in corporate aviation today, but each one of those individuals has had to make a conscious decision regarding the proper mix of aviation and management he or she chooses to undertake.

There will be times when the flight department manager longs for the simple life of 5-day road trips, night circling approaches, and a phase check that is days behind schedule. However, many have made the transition to the life of making an executive transportation system work in support of a growing corporation. The aeronautical and the administrative tasks do not necessarily have to be mutually exclusive in the manager's life, but for the company and department to benefit, the *executive* must choose the job with the vision and larger purpose. Certainly this is something we would not have picked when we started down this road, but it is something we can grow into.

TRAINING THE BOSS

Let's say that it has taken you over a year to train your current boss on the proper way to view corporate air transportation and to understand the intricacies of expensive pilot training, required maintenance inspections, and the need for pricey safety upgrades. Now he or she tells you with some pride that he or she has been promoted to executive vice president and that the flight department will report to a new face in his or her old job. While you are happy for him or her, you inwardly groan about having to convene Aviation 101 for the new person.

Fret not; herein lies an opportunity to train the new executive about the virtues and values of your stellar department. If this is done correctly, you will get the support you need and gain an important ally on mahogany row. So what is important for the new person to know? How will you present the flight department in the first meeting with him or her? First impressions count.

First, do not prepare a "here's how we fly airplanes and why the task is so difficult" presentation. Rather, present your operation as an essential service unit that provides *transportation solutions* to the "customers." Your presentation should be nearly devoid of aeronautical jargon so that you can capture the attention of the newbie in his or her language, that of business. Supply, demand, resources, value produced, efficiency, effectiveness, and market coverage are terms the new principal, chief financial officer (CFO), or vice president of facilities will understand. While some basic statistics regarding hours, miles and passengers flown, and attendant trends will prove useful in describing the operation, most of the presentation should stick to business terms and concepts.

The "aviationese" can come later as enhancements to the basic knowledge about what makes the flight department really run. Introducing regulations, continuing airworthiness, and operating limitations in the first session will only tend to confuse your potential benefactor. The items shown in the following sidebar are more appropriate.

Describing the Essence of Your Operation

- Company policies regarding how the aircraft are used
- The resources required to accomplish a trip
- Who the company frequent flyers are and where they normally go
- Previous year's activity—passengers, miles, hours, and trends, past and future
- Anecdotes about how useful/valuable the corporate aircraft have been for the company
- Anticipated future activity and company air transportation needs
- A plan to accommodate those needs
- Adequacy of existing resources
- Indicators of performance and passenger satisfaction
- Problems and opportunities

A *brief* presentation portfolio of backup information about the department should be prepared and left with the boss to provide essential facts about the department and its personnel.

Pictures, graphs, and tables will enhance the presentation. If you feel comfortable with the process or know someone who can help you, prepare a PowerPoint presentation to provide all the facts just listed. The visuals dress up a presentation and cement essential facts in your audience's mind.

This presentation is vital to your relationship with the new boss. If you can impress him or her with a high-level, business-oriented grasp of the flight department's role and position within the company, you will be off to a roaring start. If, however, you stumble through a detailed, minutiae-laden, and lengthy recitation of technical aspects of how to fly airplanes, you risk alienating the person who will be doing your next performance evaluation.

Never gave a presentation of this nature to your boss. It is never too late. If you wish, you can weave this type of overview of the flight department into your next pitch for a replacement aircraft, additional personnel, or a new hangar.

You will be constantly educating your new boss about aviation in general and the flight department specifically during your time together, but those first 15 minutes can set the tone for a good, professional relationship.

Prepare your presentation carefully, be prepared to answer detailed questions with backup information, and remember, breathe normally while you are speaking.

PREPARING THE NEXT GENERATION

Tom was new to the aircraft; in fact, he was new to civil aviation. He had just come out of the Navy, where he flew carrier jets and was used to firm touchdowns. While he had heard of a slight attitude adjustment prior to touchdown, the technique had eluded him in his initial tries in the Sabreliner. His arrivals were discussed by his fellow pilots but not to his face. No passengers had complained yet, but it was only a matter of time.

The chief pilot, Dan, decided to work on Tom's problem after a particularly tooth-jarring performance on a deadhead leg. He directed Tom back to the approach end, saying, "Let's work on the finer points of putting this beast on the runway." He first discussed attitude adjustment, sight pictures, and power-management techniques and then gently talked Tom through three additional landings. The light bulb came on in Tom's head on the third landing. Problem solved. Dan continued to provide advice and counsel to Tom until his civilian transition was complete and he had become a rising star within the department.

Think back—did you get to where you are today on your own? Did sheer determination, force of will, and innate talent put you into a cockpit or into a maintenance shop? If honesty prevails, probably not. We all owe somebody for their concern and attention to our fledgling plight, perhaps for even taking pity on us. More likely, pity did not enter into the equation for our mentors; rather, it was probably a desire to pass on a bit of their good fortune to another desiring to travel the same road they once did.

Mentoring

All this sounds terribly altruistic and good-neighborly, but there is a much more practical aspect to this mentoring—that of ensuring that every member of the flight department is as properly trained and prepared as is humanly possible. While Dan felt some sympathy for Tom's plight, he also realized that without attempting to help the new pilot's minor technique problem, that problem might become his problem, too, if left unattended. Altruism aside, the reputation and integrity of the flight department were at stake; Dan just put good personnel management principles into practice.

Should the task of mentoring always fall to the most senior people in the department? Consider the following: Jack had just joined the department as the junior technician in a six-person maintenance department. While he had some experience working on turbojets, his time on Citations was no match for the Falcon 900's sophistication and unique Dassault aircraft systems. Although he was paired with a more experienced technician, Jack was making heavy going of the Falcon's maintenance manuals during a hydraulic pump change. It was not his very experienced partner who came to this rescue but, until recently, the most junior man in the department. Tony, who had only been with the department for just 1 year, took Jack aside and led him through the intricacies of the Frankish references. Tony continued to share his meager knowledge with Jack until the point where they began to learn together.

Why did Tony help? He had the same problem less than a year ago and had instantly recognized the symptoms of Jack's predicament. He helped primarily out of sympathy for one who was traveling a similar road—the plight of a kindred spirit. Watching another's pain and predicament can be an uncomfortable and unsettling experience.

However, what of the rights of passage, paying ones dues, learning the hard way? We all had to do it, didn't we? Why not the new people? True, we cannot and should not interfere with the self-discovery process because some lessons learned on our own are the most valuable. However, there are limits. Aviation often has required its junior members to learn most of the best lessons for themselves. In doing so, those possessing the knowledge have had the pleasure of watching others climb the ladder of experience one rung at a time. In doing so, however, the organization probably has been slighted.

The mentoring process normally does not end with a single act of assistance. It often manifests itself as a long-term project for the mentor, providing insight and advice on a variety of topics over a period of months or even years. One act of providing advice does not constitute mentoring. In reality, mentoring is a special form of friendship between individuals, usually having some significant gap between their ages. However, as we have seen, the age gap is not necessary to the process—only the genuine concern of one more experienced for one who shows potential for his or her position and needs a word of advice from time to time.

Teamwork

Perhaps the ultimate form of mentoring is teamwork. If all members of the department work together toward a common goal, a form of cross-mentoring may take place.

Regardless of how experienced an individual is, there is always someone who knows more about a subject. The best example of this comes to us in the form of modern technology. What junior copilot cannot manipulate the flight-management system or electronic flight information system displays with an agility and understanding that leave the gray beards dazzled? The fresh-caught technician usually understands built-in test equipment, CD-ROM reference search engines, and electronics troubleshooting better than his or her seniors (who can still rib stitch and time a magneto).

Everyone possesses some advantage of skill, knowledge, or talent. Sharing that advantage with fellow workers is not just a nice thing to do. Doing so allows the flight department to meet its goals and perhaps to excel. Ideally, this expertise may be shared with not just one, but all members of a work group may share through formal or informal training sessions. Failing this, sharing one's expertise with fellow employees in turn will accomplish the same goal. Keeping a talent or skill to oneself serves no one well.

It has been said often that one of the primary jobs of the manager or supervisor is to train his or her replacement. While egos sometimes interfere with this process, this practice often happens by default rather than design. Preparing employees for leadership and management positions is an essential element of job progression for a department, an element best not left to chance. However, the process should not stop with management; regardless of position, the job of each department member is to ensure that the next generation, the freshman class, is progressing to the point where they someday may become seniors and carry on.

Universal Mentoring

Up to this point we have been talking about working within specialties, pilot to pilot and technician to technician. What would happen if pilots worked with technicians to solve a particularly troublesome discrepancies? Could an experienced scheduler help a pilot understand the intricacies of his or her job and thereby help him or her appreciate the important process of customer service? Could the chief of maintenance take the department's bookkeeper from accounting under his or her wing and help the bean counter understand and appreciate what was going on out at the hangar? Sure he or she could. So can you.

Wouldn't it be great if you couldn't tell the mentors from those receiving the assistance?

Mission

The primary mission of the flight department is to provide excellent service to its customers. To maintain the focus, everyone in the flight department should be prepared and eager to treat each customer encounter with a level of service that exceeds the recipient's expectations.

FLIGHT DEPARTMENTS IN TROUBLE

Seeing the warning signs preceding any major event often may be difficult. Frequently the indicators are subtle and inconsequential. A little bit here, a little bit there—they all add up.

Consider a failing engine. The subtle signs of impending failure are often overlooked during day-to-day flying. The slightly delayed light-off, slower spool times, lower oil pressure, transient vibration, higher climb and cruise ITT readings, and perhaps, strange noises. The individual indications normally do not tell the whole story, but taken together, they create a pattern of indicators that may spell trouble.

Therefore, the trick is to be alert for slightly abnormal indications and to look for trends and combinations of indicators. The point is that you have to be on the lookout for the subtle signs of trouble. If you wait until the more visible signs of trouble appear, it may be too late to recover.

Normal Operations

The boss sweeps by the flight crew on the way down the airstair saying, "Good job, guys." Or while waiting for the remaining passengers to show, the senior vice president for operations says, "I don't know what I'd do without the flight department." These and other brief passenger comments often form the primary performance feedback indicators for the flight department and, owing to their general nature, provide a favorable aura that may conceal more substantive and critical comments.

However, if the flight schedule is full and the boss is happy, what more could a flight department ask for? Under normal circumstances, not much. Unfortunately, anecdotal and nonquantified forms of feedback often lead to a false sense of security. Yet many flight departments blithely charge ahead, going through the motions of scheduling trips, flying flights, working with vendors, and so on without getting any substantive feedback from those who control their destinies.

Flight departments often are lulled into a false sense of security because of their closeness to the corporate hierarchy and because of their relative remoteness from the rest of the company. These features of a flight department's existence actually may prove to be negative rather than positive features. Regardless of the pros and cons, flight departments must be constantly alert for warning signs that may have negative consequences for them in the future.

What follows are just a few of the more common signs that I have observed in my consulting practice that may spell trouble for flight departments. See if you can identify with any of these.

Warning Signs

Few Supporters. This is the situation in which only the top three of four executives in a company regularly use the aircraft; others are sometimes invited to join the chosen few, but rarely. While this may be justified in some, especially entrepreneurial, companies, it provides the flight department with little opportunity to demonstrate its real value to the company. It would be like saying, "Human resources, accounting, and information services may only be used by the manufacturing division; research and development, administration, marketing and sales have to find the own services." This is not very practical or prudent.

The flight department needs all the supporters and cheerleaders it can get. When a downturn comes, or when new management takes over, broad-based support is essential for the continued good health of the aviation operation. And everyone in the company needs to know how valuable the flight department is, not just the chosen few permitted to use its services. Only continual interaction between flight department employees and personnel at all levels of the company will achieve this; a company network of believers is a necessity.

Decisions Being Made by Accountants. When top-level executives must defer to accountants and/or the finance committee of the board of directors, this usually means severe turbulence ahead for the department. Basically, this indicates that stringent cost controls are in effect and that each action taken by executives is placed under a fiscal microscope, giving the bean counters veto power over most corporate decisions. If no means of demonstrating the value of on-demand air transportation are available, at a minimum, utilization is sure to decrease. Worst case: The flight department is declared a nonessential perquisite and eliminated.

The antidote to this situation is to have developed a means for demonstrating value produced by the flight department and to have developed a database showing this feature over time. The NBAA's *Travel $ense* software is an ideal means of accomplishing this.

Little Interaction with Company. The flight department stays to itself, has little communication with the company, and relies on one or two people for information about the company. Taken by itself, this sounds like an ideal setup: Stay at the airport, fly airplanes, and leave the business stuff to the boss's secretary. However, flight departments traditionally have suffered from their isolation and lack of interaction with the company.

Basically, it's out-of-sight, out-of-mind. Only the select few passengers ever think about the aircraft and then just as a means of transportation, not as a valuable part of the company. News about company activities that could aid the flight department is lost, and the flight department rapidly becomes known as "those people at the airport." Worse, the broad base of support that sustains most departments is not developed, opening the door for the budget cutters and new management to question the value of the operation.

Too Much Negative Attention. The flight department reporting senior only wants to hear good things about the strange group that lives at the airport. The same is true for legal, human resources, information services, and finance. If the administrative and managerial overhead required to maintain the flight department rises to an unacceptably high level, a management company, fractional ownership, and charter become increasingly attractive alternatives for the company. Personnel problems (often the biggest negative), contracting faults, vendor difficulties, and unresolved financial issues are all examples of this phenomenon.

Good management and leadership will prevent little problems from becoming big ones that only corporate headquarters can handle. And timely interaction with the experts downtown can alleviate future problems that may get out of hand.

Reactive, Defensive, Head-in-the-Sand/Detached Bunkerism. What I am trying to get across here is that the flight department is acting as an autonomous entity with little interaction with the company. This disease sometimes infects flight department managers who believe that their "patron" in the company (chairperson, CEO, chief financial officer) is powerful enough to protect them, come what may. Alternatively, the flight department feels that it is remote enough to ride out any administrative or fiscal storm that may arise. In reality, the flight department manager may not be comfortable enough with business processes to enter the fray downtown. Therefore, he or she decides to ignore the process and continue to do what the department knows best—fly.

Unfortunately, patrons go as rapidly as they come, and businesspeople are persistent. Surprising as it may seem, the flight department provides a service that supports the company and is subject to common business practices and metrics. The flight department must be run like a business, just like any other supporting business unit within the company.

The Warning Signs

* Few supporters within the company
* Decisions being made by accountants
* Little interaction with the company
* Too much negative attention
* Reactive, defensive, head-in-the-sand department management
* Merger/acquisition changes
* Low utilization

Failure to do so will result in micromanagement from above, personnel changes, or worse.

Merger/Acquisition Changes. Merger/acquisition mania has been a fact of worldwide corporate life for years. Economies of scale, cornering markets, and tax advantages are all reasons for this phenomenon. With mergers and acquisitions come change, often in the form of downsizing and doing more with less. This may mean, at worst, the demise of the flight department or, at best, a reduction in size and possible relocation. The problem with these actions is that they may take years to accomplish, and during that period, the fate of the department goes largely unknown. Rumors are rampant, and the uncertainty level becomes an unwelcome adjunct to all operations.

Rather than hunkering down and awaiting your fate, become a part of the decision process. If you are being acquired, educate the new company regarding the advantages of corporate aviation; develop a plan that demonstrates value for the merged venture. If the new company already has a flight department, collaborate with it to provide a win-win consolidation of assets. If you are the dominant partner in the marriage, develop a plan to serve the other company as rapidly as possible. Most important, stay in touch with the movers and shakers in your company to gain information about and to influence the action.

Low Utilization. If the airplane flies two or three times a week, everybody seems is happy. However, when utilization falls to one or two times per week, will this be noticed until a definite trend has developed? Why the lower utilization? Have passengers found another way to travel? Is the company going through a slump? What's wrong?

Regardless of the reason, lowered demand for the flight department's services should be viewed with concern. As aircraft utilization falls below 250 to 300 hours per year, alternative forms of transportation may become more attractive/economical. A subset of this is that corporate management becomes concerned about the positioning (deadhead) rate, load factor, or fitting trips together in an effort to increase efficiency. Management may be missing the point of what the actual mission is for the aircraft; high deadhead rates and low load factors actually may be dictated by desired utilization patterns.

Do not wait for low utilization or corporate meddling to reach epidemic proportions; see the downward trend early, and work to reverse it. Normally, a little marketing effort with your passengers and potential passengers will either bolster declining flight hours or reveal a valid reason for lower demand. Strive to increase the two to three times per week to four to five times.

Bottom Line

The warning signs just mentioned rarely occur in isolation; several are linked to create complex situations that are often difficult for flight department personnel to detect. Therefore, regular objective reviews from both inside and outside the department are essential to the continued well-being of the organization.

Communications, poor and lack of, are the common denominator for all the warning signs mentioned. This applies to both communications within the department and with the company. Transmitting and receiving information is really job one for management personnel in any organization, especially highly specialized groups remote from the parent organization. Communicating must come before flying, administrating, financing, and managing.

The flight department should be considered a business unit that supports the overall goals and objectives of the company. As such, it must

- Stay closely connected to the company.
- Strive to be effective and efficient.
- Maintain a broad base of support within the company.
- Actively seek feedback that can be turned into service improvements.
- Look for early performance/status warning signs.
- Be run like a business.
- *Communicate!*

Flight department personnel must be constantly alert for warning signs that may threaten the future strength and viability of the organization. To do less may endanger not only the organization but also the career development of its occupants.

In every instance, we found that the best-run companies stay as close to the customers as humanly possible.

—Tom Peters

THE DEFINING MOMENT

You have been flying the boss around for 15 years, rising to department manager 5 years ago. The old man has treated you like a son, investing full faith and confidence in your powers as pilot and manager. Then one day on a routine flight, a pressurization controller fails, and the cabin altitude begins to fluctuate. The copilot correctly switches to manual pressurization but turns the controller the *wrong* way to stabilize the pressurization. Before you can say anything to correct the situation, the cabin altitude warning illuminates, and the passenger masks suddenly fall. A great furor and near panic besets the boss and his elite companions before you can get the flight deck squared away and put in a personal appearance to explain the presence of the rubber jungle of oxygen masks above the passengers' heads.

With control of the pressurization improved and calm in the cabin restored, the destination is reached without further incident. When the passengers deplane, the boss is ashen and strangely silent. A call from his administrative assistant the next day confirms that the incident is not over; a full report of the incident is requested, along with proposed remedial actions. The seemingly small incident begins to take on a life of its own—consultants, shouting matches with the manufacturer's customer service representative, and tens of thousands of dollars spent do not seem to yield a definitive solution to the problem. The boss and his assistants keep asking questions for which you do not have answers. Their confidence in you and the flight department begins to erode; you begin to have doubts about your future at the company.

Far fetched, you say? Too small an incident to bother the boss? Maybe, but this incident really happened. It took the department more than 6 months of hard work, under a cloud of suspicion, to regain a semblance of its old status in the minds of the company executives.

Attention Getters

Brief encounters with thunderstorms, icing, near midair collisions, aborts, and abrupt stops while taxiing are other examples of events that capture the attention of passengers. The attention-getting phenomena need not be as dramatic as these, however. Sustained moderate turbulence, strange noises from the aircraft's innards, or an autopilot bump can spook passengers. After some of these events, little can be done to restore the long-standing trust that has existed between the pilot and his or her boss. Regardless of the flight department's continuing stellar performance, there will always be a tinge of doubt in the chief passenger's mind. It takes a lot of living and positive actions to erase some memories; a single event has become a defining moment in the mind of the passenger regarding the flight department.

We all have had similar events happen to us. Some have become great negative happenings that shake the boss' confidence, and some are just glossed over as the price of air travel in "little airplanes." What makes the difference between the significant event and the insignificant? The difference literally lies in the mind of the individual; the important thing for the flight crew to realize is that a passenger has been seriously affected by such an event.

Being attuned to the sensitivities of your passengers will do a lot to keep you out of negative situations and also will help you to determine that such an event has happened. Our familiarity with unusual flight situations can desensitize us to the more normal concerns and fears of our passengers. Most turbulence, heavy rain, and icing are the facts of life for us but may prove worrisome for a passenger if it is sustained, unanticipated, or mixed with another unusual phenomenon such as lightning.

A Fast Way to Get into Town

Three ranching families living in a remote portion of Wyoming were all good friends and regularly socialized with one another. A constant complaint from adults and children alike was their relative isolation and inability to "see the big city." The heads of the households had a more pressing need to get to larger markets to sell their crops and cattle.

On a whim, one of the ranchers chartered a King Air to take the six adults of the families to Denver for the weekend to celebrate his wife's birthday. The weekend celebration was a success, but it also opened all their eyes to the convenience of a 90-minute flight compared with a grueling 7-hour drive.

Within months, the three families became joint owners of a used King Air, to be used for both business and personal purposes. Two of the ranchers became pilots and began to fly aircraft when their contract pilot was not available.

Educating

Good personal communications before and after the fact certainly will help to prevent negative defining moments and are a *must* after the fact. When people know beforehand of a potentially uncomfortable situation, their anxieties and fears are usually lessened. Passengers appreciate thorough, thoughtful preflight briefings concerning the weather, air traffic control (ATC) delays, and aircraft condition. Enroute updates are a must, too.

There are other opportunities to educate passengers about situations they may find unsettling. Flight delays and other waiting periods should be viewed as golden opportunities to educate and inform your VIPs about weather, aircraft performance, ATC operations, and safety features of the aircraft. Tell them how radar helps with convective weather avoidance, but also tell them about its limitations. Talk about forecast accuracy and how fast weather can change. Aircraft limitations with regard to weather, airport suitability, speed, and range are always of interest. Most people are curious and a bit apprehensive about the aviation environment; you can help them understand it.

Communicating (Again!)

What happens once lightning has struck, literally or figuratively? First, admit that it happened as soon as possible. Attempting to avoid or ignore the issue will only make your passengers more anxious. Briefly describe the phenomenon without attempting to hide or embellish any part of it. Merely acknowledging the event will go a long way toward heading off negative perceptions.

Make time after the flight to expand on your initial observations. Again, do not make up anything designed to placate rather than inform—your passengers usually will see these attempts for what they are. Express your own concerns and show that *you understand theirs.*

A personal visit or at least a telephone call to *all* affected parties on the next working day to further explain and *listen* to their impressions and concerns is essential. Offer to provide further information, background material, or expert opinions on the event. Most of all, show that you are concerned about their perceptions, however foreign or unreasonable they seem to you. ˙

During these calls, try to *read* the passenger's mood and attitude about the incident. Respond to that mood accordingly; if the passenger is still shaken, sympathize. If he or she is merely concerned, attempt to rationalize the event logically. If he or she is critical of your judgment or some other performance factor of the department, be a good listener and do not be defensive or evasive. Show the passenger that you can take criticism, but do not leave him or her with the impression that there is some inherent defect within your operation. Go to lengths to show that your department is the safest possible under the circumstances.

All these efforts could be described as psychological first aid. Once the trauma has subsided, scars may remain. Follow-up memoranda, more phone calls, and personal visits may be called for. Again, this is where you must read the situation correctly; further attention to the subject may be overkill and serve to highlight the situation rather than alleviate it.

It Only Takes Once

It only takes one close encounter with a thunderstorm, a gusty crosswind outside demonstrated limits, or a rogue engine or system to introduce you to the subject of negative defining moments. Landing short of your destination, diverting to a nearby field, or canceling a flight is often preferable to a slavish dedication to goal directedness and 100 percent mission completion regardless of the consequences.

It only takes one negative defining moment to get the boss thinking about the real need for a flight department; you should not be the precipitating factor in that thought process. You may not get a second chance. Make your defining moments positive ones. (See Table 5.2).

CORPORATE STAGES OF DEVELOPMENT

Like so many things in life, flight departments do not fit into neatly defined categories. Certainly such descriptors as big and small, domestic and international, single aircraft and multiple aircraft, and short range and long range are valid means of describing many flight departments. However, there are other more insightful terms that really tell the story of the mission of the department and how its aircraft are used.

The following descriptions reflect stages of a corporation's life cycle—its journey from birth to death or, hopefully, rebirth or absorption into another company. It is important for flight department personnel to think in these terms because they will have to creatively support these different stages if they are to remain viable. The department manager must be aware of the organizational changes and shifts sufficiently far in advance that the flight department can be positioned properly and prepared to *take advantage* of these impending metamorphoses. While a flight department providing personal transportation to an individual or family may not see such well-defined or dramatic changes over time, much of what follows should be kept in mind to prevent unwanted surprises. Figure 5.2 presents an overview of the stages and their effect on flight department activity.

Entrepreneurial Stage

This stage marks the birth and infancy of a company, run by a few single-minded individuals growing an enterprise. There is little planning or structure, only intense focus on well-defined objectives. Once the advantages of corporate flight are discovered, the chairperson or president may use the aircraft on more than 80 percent of its trips, often alone. If so, the flight department provides what is essentially a personal transportation service, pejoratively described as a "royal barge" operation. However, if the boss is a hot entrepreneur

TABLE 5.2   Customer Training Outline

Desired outcome: To sensitize flight department personnel to the needs of their customers and to develop good customer service practices within the department.

Part 1.   All personnel

- The concept of customer service—what it is and isn't
- Who are our customers and what do they want?
- What business are we in?
- What impresses people; what doesn't?
- Attitude, body language, and tone of voice
- Develop a service plan
- Measure service performance
- Work as a team

Part 2.   Flight crews

- The travel experience
- Appearance and body language, part 2
- Creating service expectations in the customer
- Safety and passenger apprehension
- What happens when things go wrong?
- The flight crew—passenger bond
- Role playing—dealing with the customer
- Making it better one flight at a time

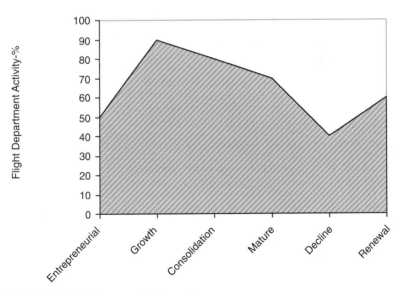

FIGURE 5.2   Flight department development stages.

having the capacity to generate 30 or 50 times his or her compensation and needing rapid, reliable on-demand air transportation to accomplish this magic, why not a royal barge?

This type of flight operation usually feels like it is on the cutting edge of company development, in on all the latest deals and acquisitions—it is a heady time for both senior management and the flight department as well. There is little predictability to the operation, only the promise of constant change and challenge.

However, it is a precursor to transition and organizational change as well. Entrepreneurs find it difficult to sustain this stage because, by its very nature, it is at once both introductory and transitory. The company will either graduate to the next stage of growth or be acquired by a larger company (and then graduate).

Growth Stage

As the company develops and matures, the need to provide primarily personal transportation for the CEO begins to wane as the principal's personal presence is increasingly required at headquarters to manage the burgeoning empire. This is a critical time for the flight department because of the reluctance of company senior management to use the boss's perquisite and because they do not know how they can justify use of the company aircraft. This is an important point for the aviation department manager to be aware of because it will be largely up to him or her to educate these managers regarding the value of corporate air transportation. The department manager must sell the concept of corporate aircraft usage to the next echelon as the company enters its growth or development stage. However, a perceptive—or prompted—boss may be the first to suggest that subordinates use the aircraft.

Suppose that the boss does not want to share his magic carpet with others in the company. This is a not uncommon development in the corporate world as the entrepreneur moves into maturity. Possible answers include purchasing another aircraft for everybody else, heavy use of charter aircraft, purchasing a fractional share, and sweet-talking the boss into letting a subordinate use the aircraft at times when the principal user is earthbound.

However, a significant number of flight departments never go beyond providing personal air transportation just for the boss. This may be intentional to restrict company size or simply possessiveness. Whatever the reason, this *is* the boss, and his or her wishes should be respected. It would not do any harm to plant the suggestion that others could benefit from using the corporate aircraft. Some homework and collaboration with other corporate executives may yield a solution to the sole-user dilemma.

Consolidation Stage

This is the period during which the organization considers its gains and losses and further development while consolidating its present position. This, too, is a critical time in a company's life cycle because the company's growth can easily plateau or even decline. However, the flight department is probably well entrenched and an integral part of the corporate culture at this stage of development. Opportunities for additional corporate acquisitions, both domestic and foreign, make the flight department particularly useful.

It is during this stage that a flight department's activity may peak. Traditionally, significant numbers of senior managers use the aircraft as a productivity tool and can justify it as such. Middle management should be encouraged to use the aircraft when possible through activities such as planned group sales, marketing, or production inspection team tours.

Mature Stage

This is a time when the company elaborates its structure, decentralizes, and adapts to its environment rather than creating it. Product lines are stable, and markets are well defined and, well, *mature*. This is usually a time of calm and stability for the flight department, relying on well-established tradition and culture to supply its passengers.

However, this also can be a period of transition for both the company and the flight department. Maturity can lead to stagnation or decline, conditions that eventually will require the company to restructure itself, to streamline itself in order to remain competitive. Flight departments become attractive targets for budget cutters during this stage. Therefore, this should be a time of intense planning, selling the benefits of the department, and search for additional uses and outlets for the aircraft.

Decline, Renewal, or Acquisition

These three options are virtually the only paths available to mature companies. All involve change, sometimes dramatic and radical. All will mandate some change for the flight department.

Decline usually means that a company can no longer compete in its chosen markets. Rising costs, lost market segments, and noncompetitive products will drive the company out of business unless a means of revitalization can be found. This is a time for seeking efficiencies and cost cutting for the flight department, but aircraft utilization usually declines, making the goal of economy more difficult. Declines sometimes can be only temporary setbacks and preludes to renewal, however.

Renewal means that the company has found a means to compete in its current market or, more likely, has found a new market in which to compete. These are heady and risky times for all within the company; the company essentially bets itself against the market. Corporate life takes on the characteristics of either the entrepreneurial or growth stages, with lots of activity to reach out and touch new markets and customers. The flight department's capabilities may be taxed to accommodate this new activity, but every effort should be made to respond. The CEO may not play prominently in this stage; instead, aggressive "young Turks" may form the nucleus of the group reengineering the company.

Acquisition by another company is a fearsome time for all, including the flight department. New cultures, values, and people change the workplace; people and concepts become surplus to the new effort. If the new company has never or rarely used corporate aircraft, the future of the flight department may be in jeopardy. There is not much to do to get out in front of this problem, except to preempt the new group with a presentation demonstrating the capabilities and advantages of corporate aircraft.

If the acquiring group has its own flight department, the resulting marriage of departments must be arranged carefully to preclude the inevitable clash of cultures. The different operating and management styles will cause some hard feelings and must be dealt with sensitively and promptly. Whoever is chosen to head the newly combined department must move quickly to evaluate the policies and processes of the two groups and devise a common set of rules and expectations. This should be a true merger of *ideas and cultures,* not just the imposition of a new system on the vanquished. Both sides must give something if the new group is to grow into a cohesive team.

Combinations

Does the president still use the aircraft 80 percent of the time *and* other senior executives regularly attempt to use it *and* project teams from marketing are vying for it too? This is a pleasant situation for the flight department because it spells job security, but it also means that the department will be running what are essentially three types of operations, often with just one aircraft. The department must tailor its operations to accommodate the desires of the company and realize that these differing demands must be met in slightly different ways.

Juggling a full schedule of diverse requests requires creativity and diplomacy to answer all requests adequately. Sufficient resources are often the answer to these problems, necessitating the use of charter aircraft, a fractional share, contract personnel, and creative scheduling. Eventually, these ad hoc solutions must be answered with more permanent ones, usually involving additional resources.

Whatever the nature of the operation, management personnel must be forward-looking and anticipate changes as far in advance as possible. It is important for the department manager to suggest solutions to upcoming corporate challenges rather than to be surprised by orders from higher authority. This is why the department manager must be an integral part of the company management team and not just the keeper of the assets at the hangar.

LESSONS LEARNED

Is there a perfect flight department?...I'm still looking.

Learning from our mistakes is a valuable but often costly experience. Working for the wrong boss/company, forgetting to put the landing gear down, and failing to acknowledge a spouse's birthday are definitely valuable learning experiences, but the cost may be high indeed. Unfortunately, there are too many mistakes, some too costly, for us to experience; learning not just from our mistakes but also from other people must be considered—there just is not enough time to make them all on our own.

Perhaps the best people to ask about mistakes are those who make it a business to observe and comment on the mistakes of others. These people may be teachers, counselors, or consultants who observe errors and attempt to provide perspective and guidance for those making them. Of course, the credibility of the observer/fixer is important—we have all received bad advice from those unworthy of the teacher/counselor name.

I make my living by, among other things, evaluating flight departments and charter operators against federal and company standards and best industry practices. As a consequence, I get to see a variety of flight operations: large and small, single-task and multimission, fixed and rotary wing, and single and multiple bases. As you may imagine, these run the operational gamut from excellent to unsafe and the managerial spectrum from super to couldn't manage their way out of a paper bag.

The good news is that the great majority of operations I visit are safe and try hard to get the job done effectively and efficiently. This is a tribute to the professionalism of the pilots, technicians, schedulers/dispatchers, and receptionists who make it all happen, for these individuals are sometimes not well led within their department nor supported by corporate headquarters.

Predictably, certain patterns of performance emerge when a significant number of operations are examined. Here are some common themes that separate the really great ones from the merely good and those that need work.

A Sense of Mission

Those departments that believe that their job is to fly airplanes for passengers who may occasionally sit in back may be setting themselves up for a fall. The operative expression in this job is *customer service,* not flying. First, *service,* then *transportation,* and then *aviation.* "*Safe, reliable, efficient on-demand air transportation for company employees and customers*" is the concept that must be internalized by all concerned within the flight department. The concept of a flying club that allows people to go along for the ride is a perversion of the main mission. And mission statements hung on walls in attractive frames and not lived on a daily basis only waste picture frames. Ya gotta live it!

Standards

Not surprisingly, the best departments have a well-developed and current set of administrative and operating standards. These standards reflect the actual operating policies and procedures used by the department and are not merely window dressing for the folks downtown or the insurance broker. These standards are memorialized in a flight operations manual that is well known and used regularly by all within the department. Scheduling, duty time, crisis management, standard operating procedures, and maintenance all have prominent parts within the manual; all the parts fit together into a well-thought-out set of guidelines and rules that leave little doubt in the minds of those who live by it. However, standards, no matter how good, cannot do the job without having a means of making sure that everyone is singing from the same hymn book.

Leadership

Without this critical element, all the rules in the world will not make an organization perform well. There must be a means of transmitting a vision of what the organization is all about to get people to follow the rules. If policies and procedures are merely enforced, the operation will lack spirit and a sense of direction that mark great organizations. Notice that it is *leadership* that is required and not merely *management skill*. Inspiration, a sense of direction, counseling, and a role model are the elements that separate the leader from the manager.

Management is obviously needed, but leadership wins in the end. Leaders already may be good managers, or they can get by with minimal management skills; managers often have a harder time becoming leaders.

Rapport with the Company

The best departments have good relationships with a variety of headquarters personnel, not just the secretaries of their passengers. Knowing where the company is headed and how it plans to achieve that progress is essential information for the flight department. Without this knowledge, the flight operation will never be prepared to support the company with its desired direction. In fact, it will always be behind its needs. Being able to chat easily with the chairperson or CEO may make the department manager feel like he or she is "in the know," but it may just mean that he or she can chat easily with the heavies.

It is detailed knowledge of the direction of the company or principal's interests with all their twists, turns, and changes that will adequately prepare the department manager for the future. The CFO and heads of research and development, planning, manufacturing, facilities, and human resources are the ones who are more likely to speak substantively of enabling events and timeline. The very top executives usually speak in terms of concepts, the big picture, and a sense of direction; their lieutenants have the details and make it happen.

Close connections with the workers in human resources, accounting, facilities, risk management, and safety by a variety of flight department employees will make the operation more knowledgeable and efficient. These company people are experts in their fields and can help the flight department run itself like the business that is really is.

Teamwork

This is an often maligned and misunderstood term that is the capstone of successful flight departments. This means everyone rowing in the same direction, helping where they can, pitching in when the tough work falls on just a few—these are all examples of people working under a sense of mission toward a common goal. Team members do not really care who gets the credit or glory—they all benefit from it. The secret to teams? Teams are formed and fostered by leaders and coaches.

Is there a perfect flight department? I doubt it, but I am still looking. Until I find it, I will continue to push the qualities listed above. And even the best departments cannot be best all the time, only during peak periods of well-focused effort. However, they can (and do) attempt to excel in everything they do. This probably will keep them in the good to very good category most of the time—not too bad a grade on a consistent basis.

Your task is to decide if my observations are valid and that I am credible. If so, you do not have to make all the mistakes of those who came before you. And even if you do not believe everything I have told you, you will be better off than you are now. You can't beat that.

Good management consists in showing average people how to do the work of superior people.

—JOHN D. ROCKEFELLER, JR.

CHAPTER 6
OPERATIONS

OVERVIEW

The essence of business and personal flight operations is providing on-demand air transportation services to the principals, the company, and their guests. While this sounds simple, there are many operational considerations to be made to ensure safe, reliable, and timely service.

The key word is *service*. In reality, the flight department is a service provider, similar to human resources, information technology, and other groups that support the company's or principal's mission and goals.

IS THIS ANY WAY TO RUN AN AIRLINE?

Your flight department probably does not possess an air carrier operating certificate, which is required to officially designate your operation as an airline. But wait, the International Commercial Aeronautics Organization (ICAO) definition of a *commercial air transport operation* (airline) is, "An aircraft operation involving the transport of passengers, cargo or mail for remuneration or hire."* Except for the remuneration or hire part, this sounds a little bit like your operation, doesn't it? In fact, the flight department is in reality a nonscheduled airline, carrying passengers on demand. Although the assets of the department may consist of a single aircraft and one or two people, it meets the practical definition of an airline, regardless of compensation.

Airlines carry people for hire. They determine what routes and destinations will sell, market those routes, provide the service, and collect fares. All this is conducted under the watchful eye of a national regulatory authority that provides a bewildering welter of rules, regulations, and standards. For instance, under U.S. law, the FAA Administrator must when issuing an operating certificate ". . . consider the duty of an air carrier to provide service with the highest possible degree of safety in the public interest."

Thus the Administrator uses a different standard for general aviation operations, that of merely "promoting safety." All this makes good sense, especially if you are a paying passenger. However, doesn't your organization have to pay someone to carry its passengers in its aircraft? What level of safety do these people deserve?

Most flight departments operate under their country's general operating and flight rules, based on International Commercial Aeronautics Organization (ICAO) Annex 6, Part II (in the United States, FAR Part 91). While there is a small section that applies higher standards to large and turbine aircraft, flight departments adhering to Part 91 in the United States and similar references in other countries operate in the same category as do small single-engine aircraft. Visual Flight Rules (VFR), no flight plan, 30-minute fuel reserves, special VFR,

---

*The U.S. FAR Part 1 definition of *air carrier* is, "...a person who undertakes directly by lease, or other arrangement, to engage in air transportation."

contact approaches, minimal training, and the ability to commence an instrument approach when weather conditions are below minimum values specified for that approach are all acceptable under Part 91. Yet it is under these less stringent rules that the broader classification of general aviation suffers under an accident rate as much as *20 times worse* than that for the airlines (see Chap. 8).

Accident Rates

Luckily, turbine-powered personal and corporate aviation's accident rate is very close to that enjoyed by the airlines; in fact, corporate aviation accident rates are usually better than those of the airlines in virtually all countries. Why, then, do turbine-powered business and personal operations enjoy such a good accident rate if they fly under Part 91 rules? The simple answer is that most flight departments self-impose rules more stringent than the general operating rules, often approaching and even exceeding airline rules. Flight departments voluntarily adopt more stringent regulations and policies in recognition of the fact that they hold themselves out to be a *desirable alternative to the airlines*. If principals do not think their aviation assets are at least as good as the airlines in terms safety and service, they probably would not keep the flight department. Thus, if a flight department is going to present itself as being at least as safe as the airlines, shouldn't it abide by most of the additional restrictions imposed on its money-making counterparts?

While many flight departments acknowledge this philosophy, they can be very selective in adopting stricter rules. Most departments impose takeoff minimums, recurrent training, and mandatory use of a checklist but usually avoid the sterile cockpit, no approaches to below-minimums airports, additional runway performance requirements, or elevated minimums for low-time captains. This is just a snapshot of the hundreds of operational, administrative, and maintenance restrictions and limitations imposed on the airlines. The question arises: Which restrictions will provide the greatest level of safety along with the least operational interference for my "airline"?

The next time a flight crew is waiting for passengers, crew members should dust off their regulatory handbook and turn to the airline section (FAR Part 121 or 135 in the United States) for a little research. Look to the following subparts for insights:

- Manual requirements
- Crew member qualifications
- Flight operations
- Dispatching and flight release rules

Once the limits and restrictions have been published in an airline's operations specification and operations manuals, some system has to be established to ensure compliance. The airlines have specific tasks imposed on their management personnel to "conduct safe operations and to ensure regulatory compliance." Moreover, airline management is required to "possess and maintain both the intent and ability to comply with" their regulations. In other words, they must have more than just good intentions regarding compliance; they must have some means for enforcing the rules.

Compliance

Airlines have extensive groups of inspectors to ensure compliance with their own rules and those of the government. Finally, the regulatory authority provides each airline with operations and maintenance inspectors to oversee these overseers.

The parallels to these airline measures within the flight department are often few and far between. Compliance with operations manual policies and standard operating procedures may be left up to the integrity of the individual and the leadership abilities of senior flight crew members and technicians. Even if these measures work fairly well, there is seldom any means to track compliance inspections or evaluations. The "good 'ole boy" and "professional colleague" network kicks in to protect the weak performers or blatant scofflaws. After all, there are *two* pilots up front, aren't there? And when was the last time we had an instance of maintenance error?

What keeps corporate aviation so safe if there is no surveillance mechanism to keep track of who does and who doesn't? The answer keeps coming up *individual integrity* and *professional pride*. To their credit, pilots, technicians, and schedulers in corporate aviation often perform safely and with excellence *in spite of* department management, policies, and procedures. The great majority of personnel in personal and company aviation want to do a good job, abide by the regulations, and make the company look good. This is fine for 98 percent of the population, but what about the maverick, scofflaw, or rugged individualist? These types may not generate the most accidents or incidents, but they probably generate the most gray hairs or loss thereof.

Perhaps the reasoning should be, "Can this department afford to rely on the absolute integrity and professionalism of every member all the time? What if somebody slips up or just has a bad day? Can we accept individual performance as insurance against mishaps, or should there be *system* in place to provide a last line of defense against human error?" This system should serve as a check and balance against human frailty and an uncanny affinity for Murphy's law.

The airline model contains all the right stuff: standards, limitations, surveillance mechanisms, and management systems. Flight departments opt to pick and choose among these to find what suits them. The trick is to pick enough of the higher standards to ensure safety and professionalism without jeopardizing the need for flexibility required in company and personal aviation. Unfortunately, some departments may choose combinations that do not have enough of the right stuff to make the system work effectively in terms of safety, standards, and service.

However, realize that what you are running is in fact an airline. If you are to continue to attract customers and operate safely, you must operate to some standard that exceeds Part 91. Thus, when it comes time to reflect on your operation, ask yourself, "Is this any way to run an airline?"

Regulatory Compliance.   The world of aviation is one of the most completely regulated activities in the world. With the possible exception of nuclear power, aviation interests have more regulations that any other industry. Even under a nation's general operating and flight rules (e.g., ICAO Annex 6, Part II and U.S. FAR Part 91) that govern most corporate flight operations, the regulatory burden is considerable (see Table 6.1).

Then comes the other federal agencies with their restraints. In the United States the Environmental Protection Agency (EPA), the Occupational Safety and Health Administration (OSHA), the Federal Communications Commission (FCC), and the Equal Employment Opportunity Commission (EEOC) were all once remote and nondemanding agencies, but now they are forces to be reckoned with on an increasingly frequent basis. These agencies often have state-level counterparts that impose a welter of sometimes confusing regulations that actually have little to do with aviation. State regulations often concentrate on workplace issues, particularly the protection of workers, and must be taken seriously to avoid unpleasant involvement with these agencies.

In addition to the government, the company usually imposes its own policies and procedures on both the aviation and administrative aspects of the operation. In many cases,

TABLE 6.1 U.S. Flight Regulations for Corporate Operations

Certification: Pilots and flight instructors
61.3 Requirement for certificates, ratings and authorizations
.23 Duration of medical certificates
.51 Pilot logbooks
.55 Second in command qualifications
.57 Recent flight experience: Pilot in command
.58 Pilot in command proficiency check
.63 Additional aircraft ratings

General operating and flight rules
91.7 Civil aircraft airworthiness
.9 Civil aircraft flight manual, marking, and placard requirements
.23 Truth in leasing
.103 Preflight action
.171 VOR equipment check for IFR operations
.203 Civil aircraft: Certifications required
.213 Inoperative instruments and equipment
.403 General (maintenance)
.405 Maintenance required
.407 Operation after maintenance, preventive maintenance, rebuilding, or alteration
.409 Inspections
.417 Maintenance records
Subpart F Large and turbine-powered multiengine airplanes
Subpart G Additional equipment and operating requirements for large and transport category aircraft

Maintenance, preventive maintenance, rebuilding, and alteration
43.3 Persons authorized to perform maintenance, preventive maintenance, rebuilding, and alterations.
.5 Approval for return to service after maintenance
.7 Persons authorized to perform maintenance
.9 Content, form and disposition of maintenance . . . records
.11 Content, form, and disposition of records for inspections
.13 Performance rules (general)

Hazardous material regulations (DOT)
Part 175 Carriage by Aircraft

---

these company-imposed rules are more restrictive and demanding than the government's regulations. Airfield limitations, higher instrument approach minimums for new pilots in command, minimum fuel requirements, duty time limits, and weather restrictions are common examples of these restraints. And even smaller companies have layers of regulations affecting personnel, accounting, administration, health, safety, and security. Although the flight department is usually located far from corporate headquarters, it is not immune from these strictures.

Achieving regulatory compliance is difficult enough for the regulators, but when the other official constraints are added, the problem takes on extraordinary proportions. Attempting to do this on a case-by-case or situational basis seldom works well, given the constant and pervasive nature of the regulations. And merely knowing and understanding all these regulations is almost impossible unless the primary mission of the department is sacrificed to the regulatory juggernaut. Clearly, assistance is needed.

Assistance can come from several areas: the parent company or contractors, regulatory agency personnel, and your own system designed to ensure compliance. The parent company also has to comply with many of the non-aviation regulations; therefore, it should already have procedures in place to accommodate many of these regulations.

For the ones the company does not track, efforts should be made through the department's network of flight departments to determine applicability and means of compliance. The agencies themselves can be of assistance if time and persistence are available for the inquirer. The fear of investigation from regulatory personnel who provide the information may be a factor, but not knowing the rules may be even more hazardous.

Developing a system to ensure compliance with the many regulations and procedures is a must-do item to avoid running afoul of our many watchdogs (see the sidebar).

You will not win many points by being in compliance with the regulations, but the thought of loss of points from noncompliance should be sufficient motivation to do the right thing.

Model Compliance System

- Determine what regulations apply to your operation (sometimes the hardest part).

- Know the applicable regulations or find/hire someone who knows them.

- Grow experts within the department who will be responsible for tracking specific regulatory areas.

- Ensure that there is a means for keeping up to date on the regulations.

- Develop a comprehensive record-keeping system to track your compliance actions.

- Devise a tickler system to highlight recurring compliance actions and reporting requirements.

- Conduct periodic audits or inspections of the areas affected by the regulations.

RISK VERSUS REWARD: CAUTIONARY TALES

The small West Virginia airport had not come to life when you and your copilot arrived to preflight the Citation. The fog was just turning gray when you groped your way to the aircraft, fog that appeared to allow less visibility than your personal takeoff minimum of one-quarter mile. Hope springs eternal, you remind yourself; the morning sun will quickly burn off the offending restriction to visibility—at least this is what you will tell the boss when he shows.

When his taxi creeps up to the fixed base operation (FBO), the fog may have gotten thicker instead of improving. The boss accepts his wait with mild irritation and collapses into a corner char, absorbed in the *Wall Street Journal*. Little has changed by 8:30 A.M., with the exception of the fog getting brighter when the boss asks, "When can we go?" You make all the normal excuses, predications, and qualifying remarks, ending with, "Maybe soon." His irritation is poorly disguised when he reslumps into his favorite corner.

The fog is perceptibly brighter at 9:30 A.M., but the prevailing visibility is still about three Citation-spans. The boss has resorted to cajolery: "Let's start up, taxi out, and see what happens—so we have to wait awhile at the end." Since this is hard logic to refute, you relent and do as suggested. However, when you arrive at the end of the runway, with clearance in hand, you can just barely make out the third runway light, hardly a quarter mile. Over your shoulder, the boss is looking, too. Sensing his irritation and impatience, you decide to go. The takeoff heaps untold amounts of adrenalin into your anxious body, but you are soon sailing above the thick white blanket. What's to worry about?

However, is this something that you should have done? Did you yield to pressure from the boss and jeopardize his life and others, including your own? Was what you did unprofessional? If you made this concession, will the boss want you to flout other standards and regulations, too?

Hold this thought.

Next situation: You arrive at the end to the runway and find that your left engine fire warning light will not test. After checking the self-test feature of the light, you resort to the minimum equipment list (MEL), which does not list this item as a possible deferral. Under normal circumstances, you would tell the passengers about the problem and taxi back for mechanical assistance. However, the boss has the chairman and three board members in back, all heading for a really big merger meeting. The weather is severe clear, the flight is short, and the mission is important. What to do?

With the rationale that the engines have been performing flawlessly for the past 1000 hours, you convince yourself and second in command that "We can go, just this once." The flight proceeds uneventfully, you deliver your precious goods, and you feel vindicated in your command decision. However, was it the right thing to do? What if a fuel line blew or a burner let go?

Overweight takeoffs, ignored second-segment climb restrictions, untrained copilots, squall line penetrations, and overflown inspection intervals are also common ways of cutting the corner, shaving the edge, and just getting by. Most of the time we get by, but sometimes we don't.

Departing in marginal VFR weather in search of an elusive air traffic control (ATC) clearance, an unstabilized approach to a slushy runway, and taking off with questionable equipment are situations that have made their way into the accident records. Was the rush worth the reward?

However, you may say, "If we didn't take some risks, we would often have to scrub a flight or delay it unnecessarily." "We are paid to know the difference between what's acceptable and what is not." "My job is on the line every time I fly—if I don't produce, I'll be history." Granted, but what price are you willing to pay for "producing"?

Every time we fly, we take risks. The very act of flying as a form of transportation involves risk—but carefully controlled risk. Aircraft certification standards, pilot recurrent training, airport maintenance, airworthiness requirements, and company restrictions all go into the risk/reward equation with the goal of reducing the outcome to an acceptable value. The large gray area that separates the acceptable from the unacceptable rests within the pilot in the form of judgment.

Critical Elements

The ability to weigh the critical elements of a situation and arrive at a reasonable and prudent decision comes with experience. As we build experience, we learn our limits and those of our aircraft and the environment in which we operate. Unfortunately, if we have been getting away with overly risky acts, those acts may someday catch up with us. Just because a pilot or crew has gotten by with a questionable act more than once does not mean that the decision to do so was either reasonable or prudent; it means that luck was once again on their side. The element of chance lies outside the risk/reward equation, unfairly biasing the outcome of our operational actions.

Relying on chance assigns our fate to the roll of the dice or spin of the wheel—betting your life and others while tightly holding Lady Luck's hand makes little sense. In doing so, you cast aside the thousands of hours and years of experience you have so carefully accumulated as a responsible, safe pilot.

However, when does carefully calculated risk stray into the realm of chance? This normally occurs when established standards and limits, published or not, are ignored or "shaved." If the Federal Aviation Regulation (FAR) says that you must see the runway environment before you can land on an instrument approach and you choose to interpret this as the well-known airport service road prior to the runway, you are taking a chance. If the company flight operations manual says no flying within 20 miles of a thunderstorm and you pass within 10 miles (hopefully, because you are upwind), you are taking a chance. If your personal resolve never to accept a night circling approach at a strange airport is cast aside, you are taking a chance.

Once standards and limitation are compromised, the path to other compromises becomes a slippery slope.

Attractive Awards

With risk hopefully comes reward as the motivating factor for risk taking in the first place. What reward is sufficiently attractive for operating outside a set of standards or limitations? Perceived job retention? Getting home to the spouse and kids? Looking good to the copilot? Are these really worth the effort?

When contemplating reward, consider the possibility that your boss may consider the more conservative course of action the right thing to do. The reward that comes with this eventuality is his or her increased trust and confidence in your judgment—something you can take to the bank. However, if your safety value system and that of your boss do not often coincide, it may be time to look for another job—one that will enable you to reach retirement without taking unnecessary risks. It's your decision—make it carefully.

The best flight departments practice their excellent standards every day.
—JOHN SHEEHAN, AVIATION CONSULTANT

FLIGHT OPERATIONS MANUAL

Most flight departments have a flight operations manual (FOM). Larger departments are more likely to have and use an FOM, whereas smaller (especially single-aircraft) operations tend not to have a manual or have one but seldom use it. Why don't all departments have, let alone use, a manual?

Answers to this question run the gamut from "We only have two people, so we don't need one." to "Its just more paperwork." Variations include "Everything we need is in the regulations or aircraft flight manual" or "We used to have one, but we never used it."

Some flight departments have an FOM just to meet an insurance requirement or association membership requirement. If these are the only reasons to have a manual, it undoubtedly will not be used. So why have a manual?

The FOM is primarily a communications device, a means for getting the word out about how the flight department will be run. Policies, standards, administrative and financial issues, and procedures to run the department in a logical, measured fashion are all items that should be communicated to members of the department but also to the principal or company as a whole. Secondarily, it sets standards and limits for the operation—items that all must know.

The contents of the manual should be used to set the overall tone for the operation of the department—to establish the culture in which all members of the department will work. If employees know what is expected of them regarding work performance, required paperwork, standards of conduct, and operating policies, they should be more accepting of them. Without these items in writing, the department is making up its procedures every time it performs an act, literally winging it. Without some form of reference, policies and procedures developed on the spur of the moment will become the norm rather than the exception. And with no set form of work policy, supervisors tend to vary their pronouncements to fit each situation as it arises—inconsistency surely will be the result.

Flight Operations Manual Preface

The XYZ Corporation operates its aircraft as a management tool to improve its efficiency and ability to compete in the marketplace by providing safe, available, and reliable on-demand air transportation.

The policies and procedures contained in this manual are consistent with management practices and philosophies of the company. The contents of this manual are to be followed in all cases unless extraordinary circumstances dictate otherwise. Any deviation from the procedures shown in this manual may only be approved by the aviation manager or me.

It is especially important for all passengers using our corporate aircraft to realize that for safety of flight reasons the operational authority of the pilot in command of a flight is absolute; this authority must not be questioned regarding flight operations. If there is some question concerning the pilot in command's actions, it should be brought to the attention of the aviation manager after the fact.

/signed/Chief Executive Officer

The FOM forms a contract between company senior management and aviation department personnel, a contract that provides the expectations of both the senior executive and the flight department. If the manual has been signed by the company president or principal, there will be little tendency for the passengers to abuse the privileges of the aircraft or to ask for something not permitted by the FOM. This is important when a passenger "demands" to go when the weather says no or when you are asked to go beyond your 14-hour duty day just so your passenger can sleep in his or her own bed.

A manual is as essential a part of a flight department's operation as is an aircraft flight manual, manufacturer's maintenance program, or company financial handbook. And developing (and updating) one is a valuable and productive experience. This raises the point of how should an FOM be developed. There are purveyors of generic one-size-fits-all manuals that merely insert your corporate name into the appropriate places of the computer program, put a nice cover on it, and ship it to you in the desired quantities for a bargain-basement price. Or departments have been known to borrow another company's manual and excerpt large portions of it for their own. Either process will yield, at best, a marginally acceptable manual, one that will be used seldom or provide adequate guidance for department members or the larger organization. A manual developed for a multiple-turbojet operation probably will not be suitable for the single-turboprop operator. This is so because of the order of magnitude of operations and differences in backup capability and tempo of operations are markedly different.

There are different sets of expectations for large and small operators, differing levels of administrative requirements, and differing methods of communications required within the department. However, the most important aspect of an FOM is that it should represent the actual operation of its department, reflecting the detailed procedures and processes used by its members.

Building It

Here lies the key to a successful manual, one that will be used by all members of the department and will be updated on a regular basis: It is the people who have to use the manual who must be its authors. Department members have developed their procedures through an evolutionary process, procedures for which they were responsible and with which they feel comfortable. If they are suddenly presented with a neatly formatted, bound volume that purports to be a description of how they do things, they initially may be curious enough to at least look at it. However, as soon as they come across something that does not ring quite true or, heaven forbid, a radical departure from reality, the manual is instantly suspect, suddenly alien. If too many of these inaccuracies are discovered, the manual is relegated to that part of the bookshelf reserved for the company personnel and style manuals.

However, if instead the members of the department are challenged to develop a manual that truly reflects their actual day-to-day operations, they probably will respond by developing a credible, useful document. They will do so because they are, for the most part, interested in their jobs and want to find ways to improve them. In large measure, the development of the manual becomes a process of discovery, questioning, and refinement: discovery of things they did not know they all did, questioning of existing procedures that may not be well founded, and refinement of long-standing procedures that need a bit of polish to make them truly exceptional.

The process becomes at once the first meeting of the standardization committee and an excellent team-building tool. Pilots and mechanics like to talk about what they do, share ideas, and compete for the best way for doing things. "Building" the manual is often a very positive experience for the entire department.

While most people think of an FOM as the sole domain of the pilots, the maintenance and administrative segments of the department must have their say as well. Like it or not, the department cannot exist without the entire team working together. Schedules and flight statistics have to be processed for the department to run properly, and without the maintenance function, the pilot's career would be short-lived indeed. Everyone within the department must have a clear understanding how all the segments fit together, or else chaos (even more than normal) will result.

The process of development is at least as important as having one, for without the full commitment of senior management and all department personnel, the mere fact of having an FOM is of little consequence and, perhaps, a wasted effort.

How to get started? The National Business Aviation Administration (NBAA) *Management Guide* has some useful guidance on the subject and a detailed outline of an FOM in it. The NBAA often conducts workshops on the subject of flight and maintenance operations manuals. And there are a number of consultants who specialize in providing development and drafting services. The best way to get started is to put all the department personnel in a room and tell them to list what policies and procedures they would like to see developed and published. There will be plenty of input.

Excuses, Excuses

What about the department that says, "We have been doing things the same way since I can remember—everybody knows the drill; why put it into writing?" First, if they have been doing it the same way forever, is it still the right way? The outside world changes with amazing rapidity. Shouldn't the flight department change along with it, at least in some issues? Second, will the same people be in the department forever? Are contract pilots or technicians ever used? Don't they need to know what the policies and standards are? And what should the folks downtown, the people at company headquarters who regularly deal with the department, know about its operation? Finally, can everybody really remember the way a certain issue was handled the last time it came up?

The preceding comments are not just for those departments who do not have a manual. They also apply to departments who have a manual but do not use it. This is probably the worst situation—to have a set of policies and standards on the books and not use them. This says, "We have a directives, but they are just for show and do not apply to our real operations. We must be flexible in meeting our operational requirements and can't be tied to strict procedures." Variations on this are the selective use of portions of the manual. Use the rules when they suit the situation, and ignore them when they are inconvenient or are overly restrictive. Examples of this might be that although the manual states that non-type-rated pilots will not fly in the left seat, an individual pilot in command (PIC) may allow his or her second in command (SIC) to fly in the left seat on deadhead legs. Or the manual states that once any part of landing gear actuation system integrity has been broken, it must be inspected by another technician, but because it is 2 A.M. and you are the only technician at the hangar, just this once I will return the aircraft to service without the second set of eyes looking at it.

I often hear the comment, "We don't use that procedure anymore because we got the new aircraft" or "The new chief pilot likes us to do it a different way." OK, use the new procedure, but change the manual to reflect the new procedure. Even a single instance of ignoring a standard operating procedure (SOP) or policy will lessen the power and utility of the manual. Once the first exception has been made, others will come easily.

Changes

Changes do not have to be a big production either. Approach the chief pilot or chief of maintenance with the suggestion and see what they say. Ideally, they will refer it, formally or informally, to a number of other department employees for comment. If they like it, the change is as good as made. However, the change must be put into writing, normally as an interim change, and approved by the department manager and distributed to everyone within the department. Then, once a year, all the interim changes should be incorporated into the manual along with other changes made during the annual review of the document. Yes, to keep the FOM relevant and up to date, it must be examined annually.

Annual reviews should be accomplished by a small group of individuals from a variety of disciplines within the department. A review need not take long; only a discussion of items requiring change needs to occur. If the document has been used actively during the year, a list of prospective changes should have been collected and will serve as the review committee's agenda.

Active use of the manual throughout the year is the key to keeping the department aligned with its contents. In many departments, the FOM forms a centerpiece for the entire operation. When any unusual situation crops up, the first move to resolving the issue should be to the FOM. "What does the ops manual say?" should be the words heard when an operational question arises. Enforcing and reinforcing this tendency are a prime responsibility of management. Managers must be the keepers of the flame if the manual is to be respected and used. The old phrase "Use it or lose it" applies in spades to the FOM.

Every Situation?

What should be included in the manual? While the simple answer is "Whatever you want," a more detailed answer is difficult. The manual should reflect the operational culture of a flight department and contain all items necessary to safely and effectively run the department. The usual main headings include administration, operations, and maintenance, but a lot can be included under these headings. The real answer to this question is, "Whatever it takes to standardize all aspects of the flight department and to effectively communicate those policies and procedures to both department personnel and corporate management" (see Table 6.2).

TABLE 6.2   Flight Operations Manual Topics

This list of suggested topics is taken from the *NBAA Management Guide.*

I. Administration
  A. Mission/objectives
  B. General policies
    1. FAA enforcement actions
    2. Smoking
    3. Alcoholic beverages/drugs
    4. Medical fitness
    5. Interaction with media/press
    6. Security
    7. Insurance
  C. Organization
  D. Job descriptions
    1. Aviation department manager
    2. Chief pilot
    3. Captain
    4. Copilot
    5. Flight attendant
    6. Flight mechanic
    7. Director of maintenance
    8. Technician
    9. Aircraft handler/cleaner
    10. Scheduler
    11. Secretary
  E. Personnel
    1. Appearance
    2. Records
    3. Primary and collateral duties
    4. Use of part-time personnel
  F. Pilots
    1. Authority of pilot in command
    2. Qualifications
    3. Training
    4. Contract pilots
    5. Pilot currency
    6. Duty time
    7. Physical fitness
    8. Alcohol/drug policy
    9. Flight evaluation
  G. Aircraft maintenance technician
    1. Qualifications
    2. Duty time
    3. Training
    4. Physical qualifications
  H. Crisis planning
    1. Organization
    2. Notification
    3. Information gathering
    4. Initial actions
    5. Communicating the crisis
    6. Records
    7. Participation in the investigation
    8. Media

I. Charter operations
    1. Company policy
    2. Qualification of operations
II. Operations
  A. Safety
  B. Control of flights
  C. Scheduling
  D. Basic operations
    1. Dispatch release
    2. Airworthiness
    3. Flight crew member duties
    4. Flight plans
    5. Operational reports
    6. Maintenance test flights
    7. Positioning flights
    8. Aircraft noise policy
  E. Passenger relations
    1. Policy
    2. Crew duties
    3. Authority of pilot in command
    4. Schedule changes
  F. Limitations
    1. Airports
    2. Weather
    3. Aircraft
    4. Crew
    5. Hazardous material
  G. Standard operation procedures
    1. Policy
    2. Crew assignment
    3. Basic crew responsibilities
    4. General
    5. (Specific)
  H. Abnormal operations
    1. Emergencies
    2. Terrorist hijacking
    3. Accidents/incidents
  I. International operations
    1. Training
    2. Qualification
    3. Planning
    4. Documentation
    5. Security
III. Maintenance
  A. Purpose/mission
  B. Basic policies
    1. Airworthiness
    2. Inspection of work performed
    3. Airworthiness status documentation
    4. Controlled publications
  C. Airworthiness release
    1. Postflight
    2. Release document

TABLE 6.2   Flight Operations Manual Topics (*Continued*)

D. Scheduled inspection and maintenance	I. Aircraft fueling
1. Maintenance programs	J. Maintenance test flights
2. Work assignment	K. Checklists
E. Unscheduled maintenance	1. Accident/incident
1. Discrepancy reporting	2. International operations
2. Deferred discrepancies	3. Flightcrew evaluation
3. Work assignment	L. Forms
4. Recording work performed	1. Manifest
5. Returning aircraft to service	2. Flight log
F. Vendor selection	3. Abnormal operations
1. Approval process	4. Airworthiness release
2. Approved vendors	5. Maintenance discrepancy
3. Major work	6. Deferred discrepancy
a. Request for proposals	M. References
b. Evaluation of proposals	1. Advisory circulars
G. Aircraft maintenance records	2. NTSB Part 830
1. Responsibility	N. Telephone numbers
2. Record entries	1. Flight department
3. Computerized tracking system	2. Company
H. Aircraft parts	3. Emergency
1. Ordering	4. Government
2. Receiving	5. Associations
3. Inspection	
4. Inventory control	

How long should it be? Small departments probably can get by with as few as 10 pages for starters; large departments may need as many as 100 pages. Again, the answer is whatever it takes to get the word across clearly and concisely to those who need to know. The first edition of this masterpiece should be just the beginning of the living document that reflects the changes that occur within the department. The first edition may become a collector's item but should pass out of fashion.

Does the manual have to cover every situation that may be encountered by the department? No, because it cannot possibly cover all situations. However, it can provide policy guidance that will form the basis for sound, safe, and consistent decisions. If the concepts of safety in all operations, high levels of service to customers, and value provided to the company are emphasized throughout the manual, what to do in unusual situations should come easier to all concerned. See Table 6.2 for a list of topics for a flight operations manual suggested by the NBAA.

Singing from the Same Hymn Book

Perhaps the best reason to have and use a manual is to use it as the basis for determining how well the department is performing. If you do not perform actions consistently, how can you measure performance? That is, if you do the same things differently every time, there is no standard from which to measure.

The expression "singing from the same hymn book" comes to mind when considering the need for a viable FOM. It is hard enough to get the congregation to sing at all, let alone with the right words and notes. And if they have not grown up with or helped to develop that hymnal, they may not sing at all. Getting the "congregation" to sing from the same hymn book can make some beautiful and powerful music; the same is true for a flight department.

International Standards

In recognition of a worldwide need for an international business aviation operations standard, the International Business Aviation Council (IBAC) has developed the *International Standard for Business Aircraft Operations (IS-BAO)*. The primary purpose of the standard is to promote the harmonization of quality operating practices for business aircraft operations on the international level. It constitutes baseline requirements that operators should apply in structuring and staffing their flight departments and planning and conducting their operations. Implementation of *IS-BAO* by operators also may serve to satisfy certain national regulatory requirements applied by countries and their civil aviation authorities (CAAs).

The standards are developed to be applicable primarily to operators who operate multiengine, turbine-powered, pressurized aircraft. They are flexible in nature and can be adapted readily to other types of aircraft. Operators remain responsible for ensuring that all applicable national requirements are met.

Flight departments that adopt the *IS-BAO* code of good operating practices have the option of having the company registered with the IBAC. To be registered, the flight department must arrange for a third-party audit by an IBAC-accredited auditor. Flight departments that successfully demonstrate compliance with *IS-BAO* will receive a certificate of registration from IBAC that is good for 2 years, after which the department must be audited again.

STANDARDS FOR LIFE

Aviation is arguably one of the most regulated activities within the United States. Perhaps nuclear power may be more regulated, but aviation regulations occupy a significant chunk of the rules bookshelf. However, only a few of the rules speak to technique or operational procedures. Certainly the rules that apply to not flying below the glideslope in a turbojet aircraft or exceeding 250 knots below 10,000 feet brush lightly against procedure but have little to do with how the aircraft is operated in the sense of technique.

The government rightly leaves most issues of operational procedure to the operator; it is his or her rules that govern the detailed operation of the aircraft, planning for flights, caring for passengers, and maintaining operational records. However, not all operators have specific operational procedures for their crew to operate under. The air carriers, large air taxi operators, and some corporate flight departments have detailed SOPs carefully crafted and placed in their flight operations and standardization manuals, and most of them insist on adherence to them. However, some operators, particularly corporate operators, either do not specify SOPs or fail to demand compliance with them.

Needing Them

So why do we need SOPs? Don't we train in a high-fidelity simulator every 6 months, fly with the same crews day after day, and have an enviable accident record? Why SOPs for *professionals?*

- Pilot did not arm speedbrake or call for landing checklist.
- Did not inspect wing for ice.
- Did not extend flaps/slats after engine start.
- Did not use autobrake for takeoff.
- Initiated rejected takeoff above V_1.
- Engaged in nonpertinent conversation during a critical portion of the flight.
- Did not divert to nearest airport after dual generator failure.

Altitude Alerter Procedure

On receipt of a newly assigned altitude, the

- Pilot not flying (PNF) will read back the altitude and set it in the altitude alerter, point to it, and repeat the altitude.
- Pilot flying (PF) will point to the alerter and state the altitude observed in the window.
- PNF will note any discrepancy.

These items are all actual errors noted in National Transportation Safety Board (NTSB) aircraft accident reports. While they address errors in judgment, forgetfulness, and haste under pressure, they all show a failure to adhere to some SOP. Whether an SOP existed is not relevant; failure to use one indicated that the crew was winging it, making it up as they went, going by the ad hoc checklist.

In a notable wintry air carrier takeoff abort/overrun accident, the NTSB found that, among other significant factors, a probable cause was the flight crew's failure to comply with checklist procedures to turn on the pitot/static system heat, which resulted in ice blockage of the pitot tubes. The erroneous airspeed that resulted (indicated airspeed never exceeded 54 knots) from this failure was not acted on or an abort begun until the actual aircraft speed was 5 knots in excess of V_1. The NTSB listed 11 deviations from the airline's checklist procedures before it got to the actual causes of the accident. The abort due to an almost nil airspeed indication was not initiated until 34 seconds after the takeoff roll commenced!

Stabilized Approach

The following conditions must be achieved when the aircraft is within 500 feet of the MDA/DH on an instrument approach or the terrain on a visual approach:

- *Navigation guidance:* Within one dot deviation or 5 degrees.
- *Lateral guidance:* Within 200 feet of the runway centerline.
- *Vertical speed:* Less than 1000 ft/min descent.
- *Airspeed:* Ref. $-0/+10$ knots.
- *Landing checklist:* Complete.

If these conditions are not met, *a go-around or missed approach must be executed.*

So what happened? Other pilots who had flown recently with the accident crew described them as "perfectionists in performing checklists." "The captain did everything by procedure and explained what he wanted" and "One of the first officer's greatest strengths as a pilot was his attention to detail on checklists." However, the cockpit voice recording did not include an "Airspeed alive" or "80 knots" callout or a challenge/question from the pilot flying. If it can happen to this caliber of crew, what is possible with a crew that either has no SOPs or chooses to ignore them?

Research has found that in crisis situations human beings revert to early learning or *rote experiences.* However, if the individual has no rote to revert to, what is there to fill the void? Early learning? In a Cessna 150? Perhaps if the pilot's early learning had included a set of procedures and an iron-clad adherence to checklists and procedures, these accidents may not have happened.

Significantly, both the Flight Safety Foundation's Controlled Flight Into Terrain and Approach and Landing Reduction studies found that flight crew deviation from SOPs or lack of an appropriate SOP were major causes of accidents within the study.

Predictability

Many pilots resist SOPs because they perceive that rigid procedures may take away valuable prerogatives that could be used in an emergency situation. And they may confuse procedure with technique, believing that SOPs rob them of their ability to manipulate the controls or plan an action that will result in a superior outcome. Also, some pilots just do not like being told what to do for every little detail. Perhaps it is checklist/SOP backlash, but some pilots believe that they have a better way and want to be left alone to do it *their* way.

Whatever the reason, valid, well-thought-out procedures bring an air of predictability to the cockpit, one that serves as a tacit communications device between the crew members. Better still, they bring a wealth of knowledge and experience to the crew that normally would be unavailable. Best of all, they provide a standard against which performance may be measured; if you do not do it the same way each time, how can you detect what went wrong?

The military and the airlines learned long ago that "creativity" in the cockpit led to disastrous consequences. Standardization, coupled with enlightened training programs, excellent manuals, and a system of checking crews against the *standard,* dramatically reduced accidents and incidents. Even in the demanding environment of flying off aircraft carriers, the Navy was able to reduce its accident rate by more than half in just a few years of applied standardization. However, the airlines and the military rapidly discovered that *all* levels of the organization must buy into the program if it is to work. And lip service is insufficient when it comes to something as critical as adherence to SOPs.

While you may fly with the same individual every day, SOPs create expectations between the two of you that form the foundation of preflight and cockpit communication. If you fly regularly with more than one person, the SOPs are an essential part of the cockpit routine. And if you fly with contract pilots, the SOPs give the temp an idea of what to expect and make him or her a full participant in the process instead of a student to be trained.

Development

Procedures must be developed in a measured and rational manner, too. Arbitrary or whimsical procedural changes are soon seen for what they are and either winked at or ignored completely. Standards must be based firmly or reason and experience, tested, and validated.

Everyone must be singing from the same hymn book as well. There must be a departmental FOM, one that is up to date and adhered to by *all* participants. The one that was developed for the Jetstar in 1971 may not be of much use with the GIV. The training manual you got from the contract trainer is good, but it is not yours. You have to *own* the procedures as a department; somebody else's will not do.

Using the Flight Safety or Simuflite's procedures as a starting point is not a bad idea; these companies see a lot of training cycles go through their simulators and a fair amount of mistakes made. However, just about every department does it slightly differently from the way you learned it in the simulator. Because of this, take the time

---

Sterile Cockpit

Flight crew members may not engage in, nor may any PIC permit, any activity during a critical phase of flight which could distract from or interfere with the proper performance of any flight crew member's duties. . . . critical phases of flight include all ground operations involving taxi, takeoff, and landing and all other flight operations conducted below 10,000 feet, except cruise flight.

to carefully evaluate everything contained in the airplane flight manual, operations manual, and contractor's training manual. You may not want to use it all or find that some things are missing.

Developing SOPs is a joint venture, too. Every pilot should have a chance to comment on and discuss draft SOPs unless regulatory issues or hazardous conditions dictate otherwise. If consensus cannot be gained on a certain procedure, the chief pilot should act as the tie-breaker.

Procedure or Technique?

How far do you go with SOP? Should you have a procedure for eating the box lunch or going the lavatory? While some flight departments do, you may feel that this is a bit extreme.

Making sure that the cockpit is configured properly and that certain aircraft performance goals are met at a given point in time or space should determine whether a procedure is required. Telling pilots precisely when to set approach flaps or how to plan for an alternate may infringe on their technique sensibilities, creating an aversion to all SOPs. Make this a subject for discussion when developing your department's FOM. Guidance can be found in other department manuals, your training vendor's texts, and FAA Advisory Circular 120-71, *Standard Operating Procedures for Flight Deck Crewmembers.*

Checking Up

Takeoff Aborts

The following conditions will constitute the only conditions warranting an abort after 80 knots and prior to V_1:

- Engine fire
- Engine failure
- Loss of directional control
- Deployment of thrust reverser or ground spoiler

Then there must be a means of ensuring that *all* flight crew members follow SOP to the letter. If adherence to SOP is never tested, the concept will wither and die. If no one ever checks to see if pilots are using the manual, then inevitably the standards gradually will become less so. Eventually, procedural anarchy or entropy will occur.

Line check programs are standard features of airline and charter life. They are designed to ensure that all SOPs are adhered to and that the crew acts as a crew, not just two individuals occupying the same cockpit. These do not have to be terror-filled, punitive or threatening events either. Ideally, in corporate aviation they should be a relaxed learning event for the flight crew, an opportunity to show that they know or clarify what is required under the SOP. Some departments conduct biennial flight reviews in which there is no pass/fail stigma attached to the ride, only the opportunity to hone skills.

Make it happen:

- Discuss the procedures.
- Gain consensus.
- Write them down.
- Revisit/revise the SOP regularly.
- Ensure that it is used.

You will be glad you did.

OPERATIONS

The subject of operations contains many subsets; virtually all activities to do with the actual process of scheduling through flying the flight and delivery of the passenger are a part of the operations process. While it would be tempting to address every subset, this book is not long enough, nor would every issue covered be applicable to all departments. What follows are a number of subjects that seem to be of universal interest within flight departments.

Dispatch Control

Whether the flight department comprises a single aircraft or a fleet, some method of dispatch control should be used. This means that a conscious decision is made by competent authority to fly a trip, and the necessary steps are taken to support that decision. Some companies only allow flights to depart, including positioning and training flights, once a written schedule has been prepared by the department manager, chief pilot, or other competent authority, and proper company authority has been informed. These measures are for the protection of the flight crews and the company, to ensure that a flight release has been made by proper authority. Ground personnel are kept informed of the flight's progress at every stop and trained to conduct a communications search if the flight is overdue.

Trained dispatchers are used by large flight departments for this control and tracking function. The department secretary or, in small companies, the president's secretary may fulfill this role. Someone on the ground must know where the aircraft is at all times and be responsible for monitoring its and the flight crew's activities.

Setting Limits

Aviation regulations, airplane flight manuals (AFMs), and insurance policies are replete with limitations that form a structure in which all aircraft operate. While these items may appear to be overly restrictive in some cases and certainly comprehensive, they may not cover everything necessary to ensure safe operations for your department. The FARs,

Mr. Fixit Travels in Style

A large manufacturer of window glass fabricating equipment introduced a radical new technology that was embraced enthusiastically by its customers. Unfortunately, operational problems with the new equipment soon had customers clamoring for technical support to solve equipment breakdowns. The manufacturer had qualified technicians available but often could not reach its customers in less than 2 days because both manufacturer and customer often were not located near airline airports with adequate service.

In an effort to support the company's largest customer who was having significant problems, the chief executive officer (CEO) dispatched the best technician in the company King Air. The technician reached the plant site hours after the call for help was received and had the machine back in operation before the end of the day. As a result, the company aircraft is now used on a priority basis for what the CEO refers to as "911 calls."

Limits/Restrictions/ Standards

• Takeoff and landing weather minimums

• Airports—size, facilities, instrument approaches

• Severe weather operations

• Fuel—planned and minimum landing

• Inoperative equipment (beyond the minimum equipment list)

• Flight crew

  • Pilot currency
  • Health and medical certification
  • Low time in type and less experienced pilots
  • Flight and duty times
  • Multiple aircraft qualifications

• Training

• Aircraft noise and noise abatement

• Passengers, baggage, and cargo to be carried

AFM limits, and insurance provisions under which corporate aviation operates are designed as minimum standards and generalized limits. They do not refer to specific flight crew, weather, or operational situations that may require additional attention and, ultimately, limits.

For example, while the AFM may state that the aircraft may operate into an airport of a specific length under certain wind and weather conditions, many flight departments set minimum runway lengths (and widths) for their aircraft types to ensure an additional margin of safety. Similarly, they may restrict less experienced pilots in command (PICs) to higher takeoff and landing weather minimums or even longer runways until they reach some level of experience in the type of aircraft to which they are assigned.

Devising additional limitations should be done carefully and in response to a real or anticipated condition that could create a hazard or administrative failure. Overly restrictive limitations or restrictions may unnecessarily reduce the operational effectiveness of the department and engender the ridicule or animosity of department personnel.

Flight Crew Scheduling

The safety, efficiency, and reputation of a flight department's operations rest in large part on the performance of the crews assigned to fly individual trips. Therefore, care should be exercised in what may at first be a process that involves only the practice of rotating crews equitably through the schedule. The morale of the crews and resulting passengers' perception of the department are often at stake during the scheduling process. The tendency to allow this process to become routinized should be resisted.

A scheme should be devised to both equitably and logically assign crews to trips (see the following sidebar).

The tendency to assign crew parings without regard to the personalities involved sometimes may create situations that are either potentially hazardous or result in unnecessary friction between crew members. While the personalities of the crew members ideally should not enter into the scheduling equation, incompatible crew parings should be examined and dealt with. In small departments where there are few possibilities to avoid certain parings, the individuals must be counseled and the problem resolved by their supervisor to ensure safe and professional operations. In larger departments where multiple crew qualifications allow some crew flexibility, the temptation to allow some custom paring should be resisted as well; the problem inevitably will worsen. Custom parings are also unfair to the other crew members because their scheduling flexibility is reduced.

Custom parings may be justified when considering the experience levels of crew members, however. Paring the newest co-pilot with the just-qualified captain may not be a good procedure. While both are undoubtedly qualified, the combination of two junior pilots may not be good judgment.

Standby status for flight crews is a fact of life for corporate pilots because the true value of the corporate aircraft is its on-demand feature. However, there should be some rational, predictable considerations applied to this status. Two-pilot flight departments have little choice regarding their standby status, often being considered to be on duty 24 hours a day, 365 days per year, responding to a pager as the primary source of trip planning. Some small departments have devised duty schedules with their corporate management that allow them to take half or full days off from responding to trip demands. More frequently, a single crew member is given scheduled time off, and a contract pilot is put on standby is his or her stead. Alternatively, a charter company offering a suitably short response time can be alerted to accommodate the company's potential needs during a crew

> ## Flight Crew Scheduling Considerations
>
> • Rest and duty time limitations
> • Crew paring—senior/junior and experience in type mix
> • Senior/primary passenger preference
> • Pilot currency requirements
> • Seniority
> • Nights away from home base—short and long term
> • Experience and upgrade requirements
> • Scheduled time off
> • Personal preference (when possible)

standdown. Larger flight departments often have the flexibility to provide crew members with scheduled days off and should integrate these into the schedule as a matter of course.

Multiple aircraft qualifications for individual pilots is a subject that has generated some controversy. There is no regulatory and usually no insurance restriction limiting the number or type of aircraft in which an individual may act as PIC. However, the complexity of today's aircraft and the recurrent training demands placed on pilots beg for a limit to the number of aircraft a pilot can safely keep fresh in his or her brain. The industry norm for number of turbine-powered (includes turboprops) aircraft a pilot can operate as PIC appears to be no more than two. Mixing aircraft categories (airplane and helicopter) becomes more complex, yet a number of companies allow pilots to operate as PIC in at least one turbojet and helicopter simultaneously. Regardless of types or categories, many companies require a certain number of hours per month or quarter for a pilot to remain qualified as PIC and sometimes semi-annual recurrent training in *all* types.

Flight Crew Duty Time Limits

This topic is the subject of much discussion and debate in the on-demand aviation community. The unpredictable nature of corporate aviation operations is both a blessing and a curse: blessing for the passengers who enjoy on-demand air transportations and curse for flight department managers and crews because of their inability to provide structure and predictability to their lives. However, the controlling element in determining duty time is safety. Whatever determinants are devised, the manager always should ask himself or herself the question, "Can the flight crew perform its mission safely, given the crew members' rest history and the nature of the current mission?"

Corporate aviation duty and rest practices vary widely because of the diverse missions within the community. Duty time limits usually fall into the range of 12 to 18 hours, with a common average being 14 hours. Type of operation, number of legs, length of legs, and availability of day rooms (for rest) are all variables that are used to alter and modify these numbers.

National Aeronautics and Space Administration (NASA)/Flight Safety Foundation studies[1] have provided guidance to corporations seeking flight and duty time limits for their crews. Their recommendation for two-pilot flight crews is a maximum scheduled time of 14 hours of duty and 10 hours of flight time and a minimum of 10 hours rest between duty periods.

Factors that may be considered in refining the duty time equation include total flight hours in a duty period, number of legs flown per day, and length of legs. A 14-hour duty day that includes 4 hours of scheduled flight time is quite different from one with 8 hours of planned flight time. Some departments adjust the duty day based on the number of flight hours over 6 scheduled hours. Similarly, a duty day consisting of seven planned legs is probably more tiring than one with just two legs. And 30-minute legs are more demanding that 3-hour legs if flight time is to be accounted for. Certainly, all these factors have some bearing on the duty time issue; however, none of them has to be used, or they can all be used to modify duty time limits.

A full, if confusing, appreciation for the full dimension of the flight and duty time dilemma may be had by consulting U.S. FAR Part 121, Subparts Q, R, and S, and Part 135, Subpart F. After reading these arcane regulations, the reader may conclude that simpler is better when considering duty time limits.

Rest time for corporate aviation usually varies between 8 and 14 hours, with 10 hours being the norm. Again, the variables of consecutive duty days, type of duty day, and availability of rest facilities enter into the rest time equation. The cumulative effect of three consecutive 14-hour duty days can be impossible to fix with even fully allocated 10-hour rest periods; therefore, some cumulative duty time limit should be imposed, such as no more than 55 hours in 5 days. Ideally, a 24-hour rest period is usually provided at least once every 7 days.

While air carrier rest and duty times are inviolate, some flexibility must be built into those times used for corporate aviation. Canceling a flight because a crew member may run over his or her scheduled duty time by one-half hour may not make sense if the aircraft, weather, and crew are in good shape. Therefore, the authority to extend duty times or contract duty times once the flight has begun by some finite amount, usually not more than 2 hours, may be given to the flight crew as a consensus decision. The ability to alter these times should be used sparingly, or the standards will be undermined.

More problematic are the difficulties posed by ultra-long-range aircraft operations, often capable of flying for 14 hours or more. Augmented crews (three or more pilots), double crewing, and enroute crew changes are all means of dealing with what may become a 24-hour duty day. No clear guidelines are available for these operations at the time of this writing. Suffice to say, caution is a prime consideration when contemplating very long duty days because operations in foreign airspace are usually more challenging than domestic flying.

How Many Pilots?

While many business and corporate aircraft require two pilots to fly under the national authority's certification regulations, more than two pilots often are required to safely and effectively run the operation. Scheduled time off; flight, duty, and rest time limits; and administrative and training duties all work to take away from the time available to pilots in flying trips on a continuing basis.

Too often single-aircraft operations require their two pilots to be on call 24 hours a day, 7 days a week in anticipation of a last-minute or pop-up trip. While these pilots may have a significant number of days off each month, none may be planned; all occur just because the aircraft is not scheduled. This uncertainty regarding one's ability to have a predictable life is the principal compliant within the corporate pilot community and ranks high on the reason pilots leave such demanding operations.

The natural consequence of not having enough pilots is the necessity to hire a day or contract pilot to fill in for one of the two full-time pilots who must go to training, wants to take a vacation, or gets sick. While many contract pilots are well trained and experienced, the last-minute nature of getting a fill-in pilot does not lend itself to being highly selective. Unfortunately, the pilot chosen for the honor of filling in for a day may be only minimally qualified in type, not current, and has little idea about company standard operating procedures (SOPs). Consequently, the company PIC spends an inordinate amount of time briefing the contract pilot and overseeing his or her performance—hardly an ideal circumstance.

The answer to this uncomfortable situation? Hire at least one more pilot. How many pilots to hire? Use the NBAA pilot staffing formula as a baseline to determining the number of pilots required (see Table 6.3).

Some companies use 1.5 crews (3 pilots) per aircraft as a rule of thumb to estimate the number of pilots required. This would only apply to aircraft flown not more

Considerations Regarding Number of Pilots Required

- Number of aircraft operated
- Company flight time and rest considerations
- Aircraft hours per year
- Number of concurrent trips
- Number of trips that keep the pilot flying for a number of consecutive days
- Number of trips overnight (RONs)
- Number of night flights
- Vacation policy
- Training policy
- Manager/pilot ability to fly a standard amount

TABLE 6.3 Sample Calculation of Number of Pilots Required (NBAA)

Description	Calculation	Totals
Number of Days Pilot Needed		
Work days per pilot	52 weeks per year × 5 days per week	260
Days not available	• Vacation: 15 days	−41
	• Holidays: 11 days	
	• Sick leave: 5 days	
	• Training and physical examination: 10 days	
Subtotal of days not available		
Total days available for duty	260 days − 41 days	219
Number of crew seats (if two per aircraft)	2 aircraft × 2 pilots per aircraft	4
Number of operating days per year	7 days per week	365
Number of flight crew days per year	4 pilots × 365 days	1460
Number of pilots required (rounded up)	1460 flight crew days required/219 days available	7
Estimated Pilot Hours per Year		
Estimated number of flight hours per year	—	850
Number of flight crew seats	1 aircraft × 2 pilots	2
Total number of pilot hours	850 flight hours × 2 pilots per flight crew	1700
Duty/flight ratio*	3 hours duty/1 flight hour	3
Number of duty hours per year	1700 pilot hours × 3 (the duty flight ratio)	5100
Total hours available for duty	219 days × 8 hours per day	1752
Number of pilots required (rounded up)	5100 duty hours per year/1752 hours available for duty	3

*This ratio assumes that a pilot spends at least 3 hours on duty for each hour in the air. The duty time includes preflight, postflight and ground time. The ratio could vary for a company that often requires long periods of waiting between flights on the same day.

than 400 to 500 hours annually with an average number of overnight stays. It is essential to customize pilot requirements.

Consideration should be given to hiring part-time or temporary flight crews, especially during vacation periods and heavy travel times. However, any part-time or temporary pilot should meet experience and proficiency requirements for full-time pilots, as outlined by the company. They must be familiar with the flight department SOPs, aircraft checklists, and crew callouts. Importantly, they should exhibit the same levels of professionalism and deportment required of full-time crew members.

Checklists

"List complete, ready to go," says the copilot. You taxi into position with the ever-present question, "Are we really ready?" Not that you distrust your trusty copilot, a fellow captain and cockpit companion of many years, events, and escapades, but does the checklist contain everything you really need to be safe for this takeoff and was the copilot's recitation and review of the sacred items thorough and complete? Philosophy aside, you always execute your own private killer list—parking brake, trims, spoilers, flaps, igniters, and anti-ice.

Checklists are made to back up the all-too-fallible human memory. Certain controls must be set correctly within the aircraft to accommodate upcoming or existing conditions. All is well until we forget or misset or set the wrong control. The consequences of such boo-boos may be minor—no engine anti-ice without visible moisture is not a big thing. However, an attempted takeoff on a contaminated runway with the parking brake set is a disaster in the making.

Dire consequences come in many forms: Neglecting to set the altimeter to a local setting on the way down may net you a violation from ATC when you level off 500 feet low. Failing to turn off the seat belt sign in smooth air during cruise may bring embarrassing queries from treasured passengers. Forgetting to set the flaps correctly prior to shutdown may bring good-natured gibes from your ground crew. Not lowering the landing gear may create a settling sensation late in the flare followed by unusual noises.

Every pilot has a favorite checklist story: Failing to shut down engines, turn lights on at night, missing pressurization needs, and securing all generators at an inappropriate time all make for good war stories around the pilot lounge. However, many of these stories could have led to more disastrous consequences had the circumstances or checklist item been a bit different. Many times we fail to realize the real purpose of the checklist and how to use it during different phases of flight. More important, there may be a lack of understanding among crew members as to the appropriate use of the checklist. First, why checklists?[2]

We're All Human.   The need for checklists is an acknowledgment of a common human failing that prevents us from remembering long or involved/complicated sequences of actions required to consistently produce predictable outcomes. In other words, we forget. However, pilots and nuclear power plant operators are not the only ones who need assistance in remembering; Day-Timer and Palm Pilot would be out of business if all of us could remember what comes next. Aircraft operating checklists are part of the total discipline that goes into safe, predictable aircraft operations whether the platform be a Tri-Pacer or a Citation X. We use checklists because we do not want to forget important items of aircraft operation.

Verify or Do?   There are different ways of using checklists that sometimes escape mention among crews. For instance, the challenge-and-reply or challenge-response methodology is the most popular method of checklist employment. However, does this mean challenge, *verify,* response or challenge, *do,* response? In the first case, the person responding to the checklist has done all or most of the items before calling for a particular segment of the list, whereas in the second case, the responder is waiting for the challenge prior to completing the associated action. The verification method is most common for normal checklists, whereas the do-list method is used for abnormal or emergency lists to ensure and make doubly sure that an action is taken and that it is the right one too. Is this clear among your crews?

What about silent checklists, where the pilot not flying (PNF) notes the accomplishment of each item in sequence and reports completion of that checklist segment to the pilot flying (PF)? Is this method allowed for certain segments at *all* times? Consistency is the key. If the checklist is normally challenge and reply but the PF (or PIC) curtly orders, "Complete the list to yourself..." only during times of high workload, does this satisfy the purpose of the checklist?

Short Circuits in the Process. Perhaps the biggest problem with checklists is being distracted from completing the listed items once the list is started. Either the list is never completed or, more insidiously, it is resumed after skipping one or more items. The culprits? Malfunctions, traffic watch, ATC communication, studying approach charts, and radar monitoring. Each of these items somehow demands greater or more immediate attention than does completion of the checklist. These events should raise alarms in the minds of aircrews because of their distraction potential.

Next in line for checklist subversion is complacency. It is the seventh leg of the day and the 22-item taxi checklist begins to blur into the background—"All of the items were set properly at shutdown, why would they change?" Or forgetting to initiate the descent or approach checklist may catch the cockpit crew napping or unaware. Reciting the checklist from memory is another favorite method of accelerating the checklist, especially for short segments such as takeoff and landing. However, doing so undermines the entire rationale of the checklist—why bother?

Checklist holds are another way to lose you way through a critical sequence of events. ATC demands, aircraft configuration changes, malfunctions, and operational delays create natural stopping points in the checklist litany. But how do you know to restart the list.

The most insidious of all checklist faults may lie in not hearing the words, "[Segment] checklist complete." This statement should spell the end of one chapter of aircraft operation and signal that there may be another phase of flight requiring another checklist segment close behind it. Inquiring whether a particular checklist segment was completed should trigger real concern in the mind of the cockpit crew—doing it all over again may be the only way to resolve the question.

Designing a Good One. Checklist design figures heavily into efficient and effective checklist usage. Are there too many items on the list? If certain items were left off the list, what would be the effect on safety and security of the aircraft and its passengers? Should there be a turnaround checklist for quick turns? Is the checklist unambiguous; i.e., does it call for a *specific* setting, not just "Checked and set?" Are all items in the proper sequence, i.e., one that follows a logical flow? If your answers to these questions leave you in doubt, consider changing your checklists to the point where they make sense for your operation, fitting your operational culture and philosophy as stated in your flight operations manual (FOM).

Many regulatory authorities permit operators not required to hold an aircraft operators certificate to modify the normal portions of the manufacturer's checklist without notification. Most authorities will not permit modification of the manufacturer's emergency checklists without approval. If in doubt, check with your regulatory authority.

However, the most important issue regarding checklists is the discipline to consistently use them during all phases of flight. The aircraft checklist is an integral part of a *system* of references, procedures, and actions designed to safely and efficiently operate a specific aircraft. Removal of this essential part of that system invites error, mistakes, and potential disaster.

The Tyranny of Automation

Are cockpits becoming overautomated or overly sophisticated? Are cockpit crews becoming overly enamored with the new bells and whistles appearing in cockpits? Are flight crews drawn to new automation features because of their Nintendo appeal?

These questions have been and will continue to be debated hotly in flight departments and airlines around the world because of an increasing number of accidents and incidents associated with automation. However, manufacturers continue to automate and refine automated devices within the cockpit. Obviously, the people who build, certify, and buy these devices believe that automated systems are beneficial to the operation of modern aircraft, but is there an answer to this supposed tyranny of automation?

Problems. Automation-related incidents are common knowledge because of their increasing frequency of occurrence. They fall into several broad categories, including

- *Data-entry errors.* The KAL 007 shoot down is the most notable of these errors that pits the crew member's accuracy and spell-check skills against a device, usually a flight management system (FMS) entry key pad, that is unswervingly faithful to whatever it receives. A more common occurrence is entering the wrong altitude in an altitude alerter.
- *Monitoring failures.* Missing an FMS message, annunciator signal, or FMS page or mode change is a common fault under this scenario. Not knowing what to look for or how to find it is the principal cause.
- *System workarounds.* You cannot get the darned thing to do what you want, so you find a clever, albeit dangerous, way to "fool" the machine into getting it to do what you want. For instance, entering manual top-of-descent locations into the FMS to alter the computed points may yield other, unwanted effects.
- *Mode misapplication.* Autopilot vertical speed being selected instead of indicated airspeed or Mach number is a common fault. More insidious is working with a very complicated system that yields unsuspected or unanticipated effects such as the recent Airbus crashes involving engine control and instrument approach effects.

These faults rarely occur in isolation or without contributing factors. Haste, inattention, fatigue, distraction, and other system factors may begin the sequence of events that leads to the incident. As with virtually every type of accident, automated or not, it is a *combination of failures* that leads to the ultimate end result. In the final analysis, this means that there are inadequate checks and balances available to the crew to detect and interrupt the fault chain. Awareness, judgment, and good SOPs most likely will serve as chain breakers.

Some of the conditions that may lead to unsafe conditions in advanced-technology aircraft (or just about any machine) are

- *Mode awareness.* Operating in one mode when you think you are in another—heading hold instead or nav track, vertical speed instead of indicated airspeed hold, or fuel computed to an intermediate point instead of destination. Mixing a desired effect with an improper mode (or unknown/unanticipated mode) is the root cause.
- *Situational awareness.* Where am I, where am I headed, and where do I want to be? Navigational errors are popular consequences of lack of situational awareness. This may stem from too much attention to an aircraft problem or automation device. More that just a few seconds attention to a nonaircraft attitude or nonnavigational problem will rapidly put the crew out of the picture.
- *Systems awareness.* Electrical, hydraulic, and fuel systems may be complicated, but under normal circumstances, the automated systems manage them quite well. However, poor monitoring or knowledge of systems and their automated masters may lead the

unwary crew astray. Failure of electrical or hydraulic systems and fuel exhaustion are common consequences.

- *Increased heads-down time.* Automation may demand so much care and feeding that both crew members spend uncommon amounts of time ministering to the devices that are supposed to relieve them of routine chores. Result? No one is minding the store. Aviating, navigating, and communicating are sacrificed to undivided attention to the little black boxes. And nobody is looking outside the cockpit for other traffic. (TCAS has not solved all midair collision problems just yet.)

- *Overdependence on automation.* No system is infallible, even those that are designed to detect failures in other systems. Certain subtle or insidious failure modes may allow unexpected events to occur. Fuel balancing computers and navigation system comparators are examples of automated systems that can lead us astray when they malfunction.

- *Interrupted crew coordination.* When an automated system requires or captures the full attention of both pilots, the stage is set for disaster. The object of crew coordination and crew resource management is a system of checks and balances designed to help the crew to complement each other. When this link is compromised, the team is dissolved, and the two crew members become a single entity; it is as if one crew member leaves the cockpit.

Solutions. The antidotes to these faults all address human frailties and shortcomings in much the same manner as aviation safety practices have evolved over the past 100 years. Perhaps they have a new spin to them because of the automation devices involved, but they still address awareness, training, SOPs, and crew coordination.

- *Awareness.* Sure, we all know of the hazards associated with automated cockpits, but how often are we lulled into a false sense of security by these marvelous and clever devices? Although the analogy may overstate the case, it is almost like a human's relationship with a domesticated wild animal; the animal is usually friendly but has the capacity to bite when least expected.

- *Training.* Do all crew members receive initial and recurrent training in all installed automated systems. And are *all* modes operation and potential pitfalls practiced and explored? If the training is received on part-task or computer-assisted training devices, do these devices adequately replicate the system's interface modes and faults as they do in the real aircraft.

- *Standard operating procedures.* Good SOPs can solve many automation problems if devised (and revised) to reflect actual operating conditions *and* practiced by all crew members. Typically, there will be one or two crew members who are more "creative" than others and devise their own SOPs. The result may not be chaos, but the lack of predictability for the remaining crew member greatly diminishes the effect of the checks and balances afforded by having another set of eyes (and brain) monitor the principal's actions. Instituting good SOPs and ensuring their use is one of the principal challenges of modern flight department managers.

- *Crew coordination.* When an aircraft is certificated by the regulatory authority, considerable time is spent in determining whether a second crew member is required based on anticipated cockpit workload. If it is too much for one, the mandatory minimum is raised because the aircraft's systems are so complex and the dynamics so rapid that one person cannot handle it all. The introduction of increased amounts of automation has done little to change the certifying authority's opinion about the need for a second crew member on modern turbojet aircraft. The second person is there not only to divide up a large number of tasks; that person is also there to serve as a backup to the pilot, share the tasks, and serve as a safety and systems monitor. If there is a second person present, ensure that he or she is being used for the intended purpose.

The concept of pilot as monitor has been popularized in the joke stating that aircraft eventually will be crewed by a pilot and a dog, the pilot to monitor the automated systems and the dog to bite the pilot if he or she touches anything. The second pilot does not have to bite—a word will do.

Aircraft Airworthiness

ICAO and most countries' regulations require the PIC to determine that the aircraft he or she is about to fly is airworthy. This means that the aircraft inspection, life-limited items, and airworthiness directives status are current in accordance with the manufacturer's inspection program and applicable regulations. Additionally, any aircraft discrepancies should have been cleared by an aircraft maintenance technician (AMT). Unfortunately, all these items are often delegated to the AMT caring for the aircraft, leaving the pilot clueless about these critical airworthiness elements. A system should be devised to formally communicate these items, preferably in writing, to the pilot (see Chap. 7).

Aircraft Discrepancies.   It is often said with tongue in cheek that aircraft discrepancies only occur on the final leg home, never on an outbound leg, where the discrepancy might ground the aircraft. This miraculous occurrence certainly keeps the department's reliability rate high and provides the pilots with more flight time, yet in the process, the FAR Part 91 inoperative equipment rule may be stretched to the breaking point.

Handling aircraft discrepancies is a highly individualized process in flight departments. Some flight departments never write down a discrepancy for fear that an inquiring regulatory inspector will discover an "open" discrepancy and issue a violation. Still others insist that all squawks be committed to writing, no matter how minor. These are the departments that usually have a well-developed deferred discrepancy procedure to accommodate the minimum equipment list (MEL) too. Most flight departments come down somewhere between these two extremes, often recording only "downing" gripes.

Those departments that do not get much practice writing up discrepancies depend on verbal communications between pilots and technicians to convey the news about aircraft airworthiness. While this may work well for operations that have just one flight crew and one technician, when these numbers grow, communication regarding aircraft fitness begins to suffer. There is much to be said for maintaining a permanent record of aircraft discrepancies and, perhaps the most important element, their write-off by the technician. Without this final detail, the pilot may not be certain of the aircraft's airworthiness status.

Recording discrepancies provides a complete communication between flight crew and technician. The technician understands the discrepancy, and the flight crew members are apprised of the status of the discrepancy, either repaired or deferred in accordance with the FARs.

Ideally, a maintenance technician will meet each returning aircraft to discuss discrepancies with the flight crew. Whether this happens or not, the need for complete and legible discrepancy write-ups is essential to a safe and efficient flight department operation.

Noise[3]

The handwriting is on the wall. Public sentiment is strongly against perceived aircraft noise, regardless of the provisions within ANCA [Airport Noise and Capacity Act]. As a community, business aviation must fly neighborly. It's good business, and it is a necessary ingredient for acceptance of all forms of air transportation.

—J. W. Olcott, NBAA President

Noise is usually regarded as unwanted sound—sound that disturbs our routine activities or peace and quiet and perhaps causes a feeling of annoyance. Which sounds are noises is obvious to each listener, and he or she has no need to measure it. It is there, and it is bothersome. But those who work to abate noise, to minimize its effects, or to develop quieter vehicles need to measure noise. And this is not an easy task.

While there are many measurements and rules controlling aircraft noise, it is the perception of noise that determines the effectiveness of these measures in the mind of the public. Therefore, it is important to plan and fly our aircraft in such a manner, consistent with safety, that will leave little doubt in the minds of our neighbors that we are aware of their noise sensitivities and attempt to mitigate the effect of our noise each time we fly. It is also important to actively work with local officials and community groups to educate them regarding our operations and to listen to their concerns about both noise and safe operations around their homes and businesses.

Noise Rules of Thumb

- 45 dB is perceived as background noise.

- 65 dB day-night level (DNL) is the acceptable average sound level for airport areas.

- 100 dB is the noise of a heavy jet takeoff from 1000 feet.

- 3 dB is noticeable to most people.

- Adding two like sounds adds a 3-dB increase.

- Double or half the airport operations are ±3 dB.

- 10 dB sounds twice as loud or twice as quiet.

- Double or half the distance equates to 6 dB.

- Using DNL, 1 night flight equals 10 day flights.

Measurements. Noise is measured using a logarithmic scale. For example, if the noise power doubles, this would be a 3-dB change; if the power goes up by a factor of 4, this would be a 6-dB increase; for an increase of 10 times, the decibel change would be 10 dB, and for 100 times, 20 dB. One can see that a logarithmic scale compresses the measurements and makes them appear to be less than they actually are. When you hear someone say that it is only a 3-dB increase in noise, this means that he or she doubled the noise power, and you probably will notice it, particularly at night when the ambient noise is quieter. During the day, especially in an urban setting, it may be harder to distinguish a 3-dB increase.

One additional factor is also important in measuring a sound environment—the occurrence of sound events during nighttime. People are normally more sensitive to intrusive sound events at night, and the background sound levels are normally lower at night because of decreased human activity. Therefore, a penalty may be added to sound levels that occur during night hours to include these factors. By convention, a 10-dB penalty is added to sound levels occurring between 10:00 P.M. and 7:00 A.M. the following morning. The 24-hour average sound level, including this 10-dB penalty, is known as the *day-night average sound level* (abbreviated DNL). This 10-dB penalty means that one nighttime sound event is equivalent to 10 daytime events of the same level.

Many airports maintaining stringent noise-control programs actively monitor aircraft departures and arrivals using sophisticated noise-measuring equipment and analysis tools. These systems consist of a number of remote monitoring towers capable of sensing not only noise levels but also spectral data. The analyzer is normally set to detect an event when the sound pressure level (SPL) reaches 65 dBA and records an event when the SPL remains at or above 63 dBA for a number of seconds. These recorded events are then later correlated with radar flight track data obtained from the Federal Aviation Administration (FAA) to determine whether the noise source was a specific aircraft event or a nonaviation event.

Gridlock Solved

A large multinational company based in the Chicago area was plagued by the fact that company executives could not readily get from one location to another in the area due to heavy road traffic. A 15 mile trip undertaken during the wrong time of the day could take more than an hour.

An experiment using a chartered helicopter led to the acquisition of a five-passenger helicopter capable of flying in most weather conditions. The 15-mile trip rarely takes more than 10 minutes, except when the ceiling and visibility necessitate an ATC clearance; even then, 25 minutes is tops for the trip. One of the frequent flyers estimates that the helicopter saves him 5 to 8 hours a week. The way he puts it: "The helo gives me an extra day per week."

Operators whose aircraft are determined to have exceed prescribed noise limits are notified of their violation and warned, fined, or restricted from future operations.

While U.S. business aircraft operators are most familiar with noise restrictions at popular airports such as Teterboro, White Plains, Van Nuys, and Orange County, hundreds of airports around the world are governed by sometimes very complex noise restrictions, including surcharges for noisy aircraft. The *NBAA Airport Noise Summary* and the Boeing Airport Noise Regulation Information Web site (*www.boeing.com/commercial/noise*) attempt to list worldwide airports that maintain noise restrictions and procedures.

Abatement. Turbojet aircraft operators must accept responsibility for operating their aircraft in such a manner as to reduce the noise impact to the lowest practicable level. Noise abatement procedures should be made part of the routine in operating aircraft in and out of all airports.

Aircraft operators also must take the initiative and responsibility to obtain all pertinent information on the local noise abatement policies followed at any airport they currently use or expect to use in the future. Noise abatement requirements for specific airports may be found in national Aeronautical Information Program (AIP) documents, individual airport Web sites, or the Boeing Airport Noise Regulation Information Web site.[4] Each of these procedures first must be evaluated for their level of safety for the aircraft being operated and existing weather conditions; always err on the side of safety when considering noise abatement procedures.

Many large aircraft manufacturers provide noise abatement procedures in the airplane flight manual, and these should be followed when possible. Alternatively, the NBAA has developed a generic noise abatement program for use with aircraft not specifying these procedures.[5] These procedures should be used whenever possible to be a good neighbor to those living near airports.

Helicopter Operations

The operational flexibility of rotary-wing aircraft provides a great advantage to some corporate operations. However, this same flexibility gives rise to more ad hoc operational characteristics and less control over their operations. While the corporate helicopter safety record is good, the number of incidents within this community remains high for the amount of operations.

Suggested Helicopter Operating Standards to Include in the Operations Manual

- Minimum experience levels for pilots
- Landing site restrictions
- Minimum altitude/speed restrictions
- Flight following
- Passenger manifest control
- Weather operating minimums
- Required fuel reserves
- Night flying restrictions
- Passenger handling procedures
- Special/additional maintenance requirements
- Special safety procedures/precautions

The independent and largely unmonitored nature of these operations makes the use of experienced pilots a necessity. The lack of a flight plan and short leg lengths for most flights contribute to the ad hoc image of helicopter operations. This, coupled with the ability to operate into unprepared landing sites, makes helicopter operations a candidate for closer monitoring and controls. Therefore, additional standards and limitations unique to helicopter operations must be devised to ensure that sufficient guidance is available to pilots.

Passenger control in and around helicopters presents special problems due to the nature of operations, especially at remote sites. Boarding and discharging passengers with the rotor turning should only be allowed if the passengers are accompanied by an experienced person who can guide them away from danger areas. Once aboard, ensuring that seat belts and doors are secure is often difficult, given the configuration of the interior and other duties of a single pilot.

The unique capabilities and short flight duration of helicopter operations may require different management techniques from those used in fixed-wing operations. The Helicopter Association International and International Oil and Gas Producers offer operational and management guidance for rotary-wing operations.

Chartering Aircraft

Flight departments go to great lengths to give their companies the best possible service in air transportation. Scheduling, management, maintenance, crew training, and equipment upgrades are all given a high priority to ensure safe, efficient, and reliable service for the customer. This level of service usually builds a level of trust and confidence between members of the flight department and their passengers, one that serves them both well. However, what happens when the boss has to get to an important appointment and a department aircraft is not available?

Of the two possibilities, airlines and charter, the charter option is often considered preferable. The service is in theory similar to that provided by the flight department, and there are certainly plenty of on-demand air taxi companies available, with more than 3500 operating certificates current in North America alone. However, is the service similar, and if it isn't, what are the implications for the flight department?

If one of your corporate executives is exposed to a charter company that does not stick to the prearranged schedule, shows up with a old, dirty aircraft, gives an unnecessarily rough ride, and does not show the proper courtesy, the executive undoubtedly will be unhappy. While this should make him or her appreciate your operation, it may turn him or her off to all on-demand air transportation. High-class passengers expect the same level of service whether you provide it or some outside agency does; the effect to the passenger should be the same. If it isn't, the passenger is unhappy.

Many flight departments consider providing *all* on-demand air transportation their responsibility, not just that provided with their own assets. Some go to great lengths to make the operation appear the same to their passengers, arranging for an aircraft similar to theirs and putting one of their pilots in the right seat of the chartered aircraft (that pilot must meet the air taxi operator's requirements and be named on its certificate). As a minimum effort to ensure high-quality charter transportation, the flight department conducts an evaluation of the charter operator.

This does not need to be a full audit, but a check to see that you are receiving something above the minimum mandated by the FAA. The effort will require some background research and a brief visit to the operator. Some items to check for in a prospective charter operator include

- FAA FSDO for certificate actions against the operator
- Experience levels of the director of operations and maintenance
- Type and physical condition of the aircraft to be used
- Flight hours in type and within the last 90 days for the crews to be assigned
- Type and frequency of training for flight *and* maintenance crews
- Type of maintenance and inspection program used
- Inspection, airworthiness directive, and life-limited components status records for the aircraft to be assigned
- Reputation of the operator among other flight departments and his or her peers
- Competitiveness of the operator's charter rates
- Would you allow your family to use the operator?

The fact that you are asking these questions should tell the prospective operator that you expect superior service; he or she has lots of competition (see also Chap. 3).

Knowing the Regulators

The average flight department chooses to avoid any voluntary interaction with the national aviation regulatory authority responsible for their activities. They are generally viewed as the "police" and, as such, are not subject to normal interaction, social or professional. In fact, some flight departments go for years, even decades, without seeing or hearing from the regulators in any capacity. And when the interaction comes, it may be something as dreaded as a ramp check, wherein the basic aircraft and pilot certificates are checked for their existence and validity. (Most flight crews survive ramp checks without hassle or fines.)

However, what happens if there is need to contact the regulator in some official capacity, such as to obtain a minimum equipment list (MEL), ferry permit, or major repair authorization? Not knowing the inspectors and administrative personnel at the local office [FAA Flight

Standards District Office (FSDO) in the United States] when you need something from them can be a disadvantage. Knowing an experienced and accommodating operations or airworthiness inspector who knows your operation can be a big help when time is short and the stakes are high. Something so mundane as the need for an interpretation of a regulation or provision in an inspector's handbook will be eased greatly if you can connect a voice with a face at the regulator's office.

There may be some not-so-accommodating inspectors at the local regulator's office, but their reputations usually precede them, and they can be avoided. While you do not have to become best friends with your local government representative, you should take time to introduce yourself and other key personnel within your department. The investment of your time may later prove beneficial.

Training

Initial and recurrent training in specific aircraft types employing vendors approved by the aviation regulatory authority has become a routine feature of corporate flying. Often this is mandated by insurance requirements, although the frequency and type of training in large part have been borrowed from airline practices. The regulator's requirements for currency and recurrent training are minimum requirements and are normally exceeded by employing high-quality training vendors.

Flight. Virtually all initial and recurrent flight training is performed in a sophisticated flight simulators, certified to replace the actual aircraft in most training operations. The frequency of recurrent training is an often debated topic within private and business aviation. Most insurance requirements (and NBAA corporate membership) specify at least annual recurrent training. Many companies have adopted the airline practice of requiring recurrent training at 6-month intervals, employing both ground and simulator training at all sessions. For pilots qualified in more than one type of aircraft, an attempt is made to get them to recurrent training in each type at least annually. Before any decisions are made concerning pilot recurrent training, the requirements of the company's insurer should be noted.

Line Checks. The real question to ponder considering recurrent flight training is, "What are the proficiency levels of the pilots?" Perhaps a low-time pilot may need more training than the more seasoned senior just to make up for lack of experience. Perhaps a high-time captain flying multiple aircraft types needs more just to stay abreast of the differing characteristics of the various aircraft. The concept of training to proficiency has been around for many years and is employed by most training vendors, but the real issue may be, "How long does the individual remain proficient?" The only way to determine this is through objective observation and testing of individuals. That is why the airlines use line checks at intervals after recurrent training has been accomplished.

Ideally, line checks should be conducted at least annually by the chief pilot or individuals responsible for standardization or training. The object of the line check is to determine if the pilots follow the regulations and company policy, are proficient in normal aircraft operations, and exhibit good crew resource management techniques. Because persons performing the line check need to concentrate on observing the flight crew, they should not act as a crew member during the check but should function as an observer and be seated in the jumpseat.

If the line check is satisfactory, the flight crew should be given a comprehensive debriefing on the details of the flight and their performance recorded in their training records. If either crew member's performance is unsatisfactory, he or she should be provided with training to remedy the unsatisfactory portions of the flight and rechecked.

Flight Department Training

General:

- Management
- Company administrative courses
- Finance/budgets
- Environmental controls
- First aid/CPR
- Fire fighting
- Industrial safety
- Security
- Personal development (academic)
- Customer relations

Operations:

- Aircraft initial/recurrent
- Crew resource management
- International operations
- Emergency evacuation
- High-altitude physiology
- Survival
- Weather radar
- Cabin emergencies
- Scheduling/trip planning

Maintenance

- Aircraft initial/recurrent
- Powerplant initial/recurrent
- Specific systems
- Maintenance resource management
- Troubleshooting
- Avionics
- Manufacturer's seminars/workshops

Ground. Unfortunately, many flight departments consider recurrent training in specific aircraft to be the only training necessary for their flight crews. Training should be viewed not just as a means of satisfying an insurance requirement or preparation for specific events but as a concept to be used in the growth of both the department and the individual. Training should be considered an investment in the future of the company and the people who will be used to gain that future. When training is provided for an individual, it sends the message that you place a high enough value on his or her services to invest in him or her.

If you need further convincing or justification for training, note what the air taxi and air carrier operators have to accomplish for training other that aircraft-specific pilot training. Since you consider the level of your services at least as safe and efficient as that of a charter operator, the training required of that operator should be the minimum level you specify for your operation.

To be effective, the department's total training requirements should be set forth in a 2- or 3-year plan that both schedules and budgets these activities. Without a plan, there is little opportunity or incentive to get people to the proper training. And if training is not in the budget, the chances of it happening are even slimmer.

Preparing to Train. The need to be constantly refreshed about routine and not-so-routine systems and procedures has become an article of faith for personal and business flight department personnel. Executives, insurance companies, and even associations have recognized the value of such training to the point where it is expected and made mandatory through a variety of mechanisms.

However, once crew members or technicians leave the hangar for recurrent training, what are the expectations levied on both the individual and the training organization regarding that training? Most managers do not give the subject much thought—they have executed a contract with a reputable training organization and are sending a trusted employee to reap the benefits of the contracted services. What more could one ask?

Attitudes Toward Training. Those of U.S. who have been to recurrent training more than once know that there are many ways individuals approach the experience.

- "Something I gotta do."
- "Ho-hum—more V_1 cuts at Denver."

- "I have some questions about engine and FMS operation."
- "I'm going to ace every simulator session and do all the enhancement exercises."

Somewhere within this spectrum of expectations lies the preconceived notion of each recurrent training participant. What determines where each participant lies within this continuum is largely the self-motivation and curiosity of the individual. However, should it be left up to the individual?

The safety and professionalism of the department are at stake here. And training costs the company in terms of productive time lost and fees paid for the service. We make sure we get our money's worth for maintenance, upgrades, and FBO services. Why not for training? We create administrative, financial, and operational expectations for our employees to follow in the form of standards and limitations. Why not expectations for the training experience, too?

Expectations. For people going for their first or second recurrent training session, most will approach the experience with the anticipation that they will learn something they never knew before. In general, they go ready to absorb whatever they can about the aircraft or subject at hand. It is when they have been a few times that the anticipation level decreases and a sense of duty regarding the experience emerges. However, this need not be the case if the individual is properly prepared to accept what is offered.

Prepare the individual for the experience by asking him or her the following questions:

- What would like to know more about the aircraft or procedures associated with it? Do you fully understand the electrical bus transfer and load-shedding system? Have you done a circling approach in winds above 20 knots lately? Are you up to speed on the new FMS software changes?

- What training enhancement sessions would you like to receive? Training providers offer a variety of additional subjects that are available to participants that go beyond the normal recurrent subjects. These subjects occasionally may be substituted for normal syllabus subjects, too.

- At what skill level do you expect to perform during the ground school and simulator sessions? Could you pass the FAR Part 61.58 proficiency check on the first simulator ride? Could you pass your ATP check ride again on the first simulator session?

- Are you prepared for the experience? Have you reviewed your regulations, AFM, technical manuals, and SOPs so that you can hit the ground running on the first day of training?

- What do you expect to come home with as a result of the recurrent training? What will you have gained that will make you a better pilot/flight attendant/technician?

Training is an investment that benefits the department, the individual receiving the training, and everyone within the department. Make sure that you invest wisely and prepare individuals to profit from the investment.

International Operations

Performance characteristics of modern corporate aircraft have made most of the world accessible to today's flight departments. This, coupled with the rapid expansion of the global economy, has caused a significant increase in the amount of international operations for corporate aircraft in recent years. Intercontinental flights have become commonplace.

Since the aircraft flies the same, regardless of the nationality of the airspace in which it operates, the only differences between domestic and international trips are in-flight procedures and ground handling. Therefore, preparation for the flight is key to the success of the mission. And experience has shown that the amount of planning and *backup* planning that goes into the trip is directly proportional to the success of the trip. Backups are important because of the many surprises one is likely to encounter when operating outside a familiar environment and culture. The *NBAA Management Guide* contains a comprehensive international operations checklist that provides a useful way to begin the planning process.

If a foreign destination is not visited regularly or has insufficient facilities, a flight planning/aircraft handling service is normally used to reduce the number of variables and unknowns associated with that destination and enroute structure. International flight plans, weather briefings, preferred routings, overflight permits, regulations, fuel service and payment provisions, visas, and ground transportation requirements are best handled by those who provide such services on a daily basis. The vagaries of international flight are too unpredictable and consequential to be performed by the uninformed.

Those who have never flown in foreign airspace or oceanic routes should know that the differences are sufficiently large to be bewildering or at least confusing. Several corporate aviation training vendors provide excellent introductory courses for international operations that are well worth the time and cost. Additionally, the NBAA produces an annual International Operations Conference that provides a wealth of essential international operations information. Finally, the quarterly *NBAA International Operations Bulletin* (*IOB*) is a must-read source of current official and anecdotal information about flying overseas.

Companies conducting a large number of international operations often develop a separate international operations manual, providing additional and unique administrative, operational, and maintenance procedures.

Airports[6]

Airports always seem to be there in the background with few issues to concern users. Since airports normally are operated by municipalities and governed by federal, state, and local laws, issues regarding the airport rarely arise. Certainly issues such as access badges, perimeter security, and disposal of toxic substances are always present, but mostly as minor issues not materially affecting one's flight department.

Inevitably, issues that will significantly impact business aviation do arise. Operational and capital funding, user fees, noise impact, wetlands and wildlife concerns, operating curfews, and land use compatibility are among the more popular issues confronting both users and airport operators alike in recent years. Each of these issues is capable of severely restricting operations or closing an airport permanently; these are serious issues that cannot be ignored.

Unfortunately, airport users hear little of these issues that may significantly restrict their airport access until they are well advanced. Users customarily only become aware of forces affecting their access when they have become a real threat: Legislation has been introduced, funding measures have been approved or disapproved, or studies have been initiated that will lead to unwanted conclusions. Traditionally, users become aware in the eleventh hour and scramble to catch up and become advocates for their position in the debate. Often these last-minute stands are ineffective because of the force of hardened public opinion, credible evidence presented, and significant political pressure. These situations can be avoided with a little foresight.

Many threats to airport use come from outside the aviation community. These threats often may be defused by early action with local government or community groups. The investment of one's time in airport issues is time well spent.

If an airport, user, and community partnership can be formed that will address the needs of all members, the future of the airport will be bright indeed. Each airport user should become an advocate for the airport and its operations.

Involvement.   Sooner or later each airport user will become involved in airport affairs, willingly or unwillingly. Why not preempt the process and become involved in a structured and timely manner? Doing so will reduce the number of surprises associated with the airport and provide knowledge of the players who will become the advocates and, perhaps, adversaries on specific issues.

Forming or joining an existing airport support group is highly desirable for individual users and the surrounding community. This support group will be able to deal with emerging issues, educate the community regarding airport benefits, and set the record straight about aviation issues.

Organization. User groups normally form the core of airport associations. In some enlightened associations, airport management is an integral part of the association.

While business aviation needs may be unique among all airport users, a more powerful and diverse group will be formed if *all* airport users are included in the group; this includes nonaviation users. If

Airport User Group Goals

• Timely and accurate communications about airport issues

• Improve relationships with airport management and community leaders

• Understanding of community needs and concerns regarding the airport

• Education of politicians and community leaders about the benefits of aviation and the airport

• Promotion and preservation of desirable features of the airport

• Actions to improve airport operating conditions

an issue specific to business aviation interests arises, subsets of the total organization may be readily identified from among the full membership to provide a more focused approach.

To realize the benefits that aviation provides for our nation, airport management and aircraft operators must work together.

—J. W. Olcott, NBAA President

SECURITY

Security always has been important to business aviation operations due to the nature of the missions and types of passengers involved. The need to ensure both the confidentiality and security of on-demand air transportation operations has figured prominently into the rationale for engaging this type of transportation. Not only are the reasons for a trip sensitive to the future of corporate operations, but the embarked company executives also hold great value for the ability of the company to continue operations and grow to meet market forces and opportunities.

Terrorist activities have become a pressing issue for all types of transportation and must be accounted for in daily planning and execution of flight schedules and facility activities. Like safety, security is a mindset, a culture that must be cultivated within the organization.

Security is a complex and highly specialized activity requiring background and expertise not resident in most flight departments. For this reason, a security audit is recommended for all flight departments, regardless of activity level or aircraft type. Parent companies often have security departments that may be able to perform the audit. Constantly changing threats make the receipt of current security information important as well. Table 6.4 presents a security checklist.

While most flight departments or even parent companies do not have the expertise to deal effectively with the many aspects of security, common-sense adherence to the principles contained in the sidebar on page 6.37 should cover most "normal" security threats.

TABLE 6.4 Flight Department Security Checklist (NBAA)

Area	Response
People/processes	
Passenger manifest	Accurate and accessible manifest required for all trip legs.
Company aircraft	Only company personnel and authorized guests/vendors, identified in advance, are allowed access.
Luggage	Passengers or flight department members must maintain positive control. Must be matched to specific passenger.
Photo IDs	Crewmembers must display at all times
Establish "security" champion role	
Security plan	Developed, maintained, and periodically exercised.
Emergency response plan	Developed, maintained, and periodically exercised.
Aircraft	
Preflight	Check lavatories, baggage compartments, and all cavities for unauthorized people or objects prior to every departure.
Servicing (other than home base)	A flight crew member must be present at all times when the aircraft is being serviced (fueling, catering, etc.).
Servicing (at home)	A flight department member must be present at all times when the aircraft is being serviced (fueling, catering, etc.).
Aircraft's security system (other than home base)	Locks and alarms used whenever aircraft is unattended.
Facilities	
Facility perimeter security	Effective fencing, lighting, and security patrols to ensure access is limited to those individuals that have a right and need to be there.
External gates and doors	Closed and locked at all times; positive access control for all external doors/gates.
Hangar doors	Closed when area is unattended.
Storage (inside and outside) areas	Secured, positive access control for all storage areas.
Access control management system for keys and passes	In place.
Passengers', vendors' and visitor's identity	Confirmed and authorized prior to allowing access to facilities and aircraft; picture ID checked for unknown visitors/vendors.
Visitors	Escorted when in a secure area.
Emergency phone numbers	Posted prominently by telephones/adequate phones or "panic buttons."
Destination facility security	Confirm; preference for those meeting NATA security guidelines.
Information	
Security training	Required for aviation department members.

International security issues should be handled by security professionals who have access to current intelligence and threat levels.

Like safety, good security requires a dedication paralleling safety for an organization. A secure and safe environment begins at the top of an organization that provides a supportive culture for these essential features.

NBAA Best Security Practices for Business Aviation

People and processes:

- Require an accurate and accessible passenger manifest for all trip legs.
- Only company personnel and authorized guests, identified in advance, are allowed to board a company aircraft.
- Passengers or flight department members must maintain positive control of luggage.
- Positively identify all luggage and match luggage to specific passengers (color-coded bag tags can be helpful).
- Crew members must display photo IDs.
- Establish a security champion role (much like the safety champion's role).
- Have a security plan specific to your location and operation.
- Develop, maintain, and exercise an emergency response plan and its associated resources.

Aircraft:

- Check lavatories, baggage compartments, and all cavities for unauthorized people or objects prior to every departure.
- A flight crew member must be present at all times when the aircraft is being serviced (fueling, catering, etc.) at locations away from company aviation facility.
- A flight department member must be present at all times when the aircraft is being serviced (fueling catering, etc.) at home.
- Use the aircraft's security system (locks and alarms) whenever it is unattended away.

Facilities:

- Ensure home facility perimeter security with effective fencing, lighting, security patrols (as appropriate), gates, and limited-access areas.
- Ensure that external gates and doors are closed and locked at all times.
- Require positive access control for all external gates and doors.
- Close hangar doors when that area is unattended.
- Secure all key storage areas (food and liquor, parts and tools, etc.).
- Have an access control management system for keys and passes.
- Confirm the identity and authority of each passenger, vendor, and visitor prior to allowing access to facilities and aircraft.
- Accompany all visitors away from secure areas (visitor lounge, etc.).
- Require a picture ID of any unfamiliar or unaccompanied visitor or vendor.
- Post emergency numbers prominently around facility.
- Ensure easy access to phones or "panic buttons" in various facility locations (break room, hangar bay, etc.).
- Confirm security of destination facilities—showing preference for those meeting or exceeding National Air Transportation Association (NATA) guidelines.

Information:

- Require that aviation department members participate in security training.
- Maintain a security information program.

PROFESSIONALISM

Business and personal aviation enjoy an excellent reputation and safety record. Importantly, the safety record is comparable with that enjoyed by the major airlines. The significant part of the comparison is the differences between corporate and airline operations.

Operating out of smaller, often uncontrolled airports, some without precision approaches, and with a minimum maintenance staff, these operations are less fortunate than the larger scheduled carriers who enjoy these refinements. Most significant in comparing these operations, however, is the lack of support staff that the airlines enjoy. Meteorologists, dispatchers, avionics technicians, and many more specialists back up airline crews in the thousands every working day to provide an in-depth coverage of all aspects of air transportation operations. Without this expert support staff, flight and maintenance crews have to fill the void.

Thus, how is the high level of safety achieved, given the shortcomings of personal and business aviation? The motivation of the flight and ground crews is obviously the answer. Motivation may come from a fear of losing one's job and the challenge of a highly technical task or a truly professional approach. The goal of safety is the same; how you get there makes a difference.

Job Security

If job security is the motivating factor for conducting safe operations, chance alone may rule the outcome of flight operations. Anxiety over one's job brings with it a narrow, miserly view, one that shuts out other important aspects of a complex operation. The blinders of apprehension may cause the flight crew to press on to a destination when fuel is low and the weather down or maintenance crews to rush a job because of a misguided sense of service for the customer. Fear also may cause the release or acceptance of a marginally airworthy aircraft for the same reason. However, the main problem with fear as a motivator is that it may achieve a short-term goal for the wrong reason; e.g., get the aircraft to its destination at all costs because my meal ticket depends on it. And job security concerns may cause an individual to be constantly looking over his or her shoulder; constantly "checking his or her six" may cause him or her to run into something.

Technical Challenge

The second possible motivator, the challenge of flying and maintaining an aircraft as an interesting technical task, appeals to many flight department personnel. Call it the video game effect or just the love of a challenge coupled with the desire to achieve mastery of electronic/electromechanical gadgetry, most 8-year-olds have been captured by this familiar effect ever since electricity was invented. This desire to master a machine creates a positive motivating factor for both maintenance and flight crews regardless of whether that mastery is the right thing to do at the moment. Flight crews sometimes view a simulator ride as a very expensive video game instead of an opportunity to seriously practice abnormal flight procedures not available in the aircraft. And taking an aircraft component apart just to see what makes it tick can be great fun for a technician, but it may not do much for aircraft availability.

The danger in this motivator lies in the narrow view of the task at hand. If the task is to score as many game points as possible by getting to the destination in the shortest possible time with the least fuel burn and the smoothest ride, important supporting factors will be left out. Is the weather adequate for this goal? Is the crew proficient and sufficiently well rested? And is the proper task fine-tuning the auxiliary power unit fuel control to perfection or is it to merely to ensure that it starts every time? In other words, is the task driving the situation or is reason, logic, and aeronautical wisdom?

The Professional Approach

This leaves the professional approach as a possible motivating factor for corporate flight operations. But what is professionalism? The dictionary defines it as "professional status, methods, character, or standards." Suffice to say, the central motivator behind the professional is a desire to perform well *just because the profession demands it.* This implies discipline, judgment, adherence to a set of standards, and a high degree of self-motivation—the desire to perform well *for its own sake.*

The professional comes by his or her attitude through rigorous training, an apprenticeship period where skills are tested and validated, and a final period where responsibility is accepted for performing critical tasks. Along the way, the professional must constantly evaluate all aspects of his or her specialty for PC (*professional correctness*); without constant evaluation of his or her performance, job security, technical challenge, and other misdirected motivators detract from the main goal—safety.

Good example, mentoring, and a strict sense of inner discipline will lead to the desired degree of professionalism. Leadership from the top of the organization will cultivate, nurture, and maintain this desired attitude. An important feature of an individual's quest for professionalism is that the aspirant is constantly in a position to provide a good example of proper conduct to both peers and subordinates. And the professional always should be learning and teaching.

Perhaps the most important feature of professionalism and its corollary, "safetyism," is the environment or culture in which the individual is placed. If that environment is professional, disciplined, standardized, and scrutinized for excellence, the individual must conform or be ostracized. The maverick rarely can survive in a professional environment.

This culture must pervade the entire organization. If it is just practiced by the technicians and not the pilots, professionalism to any degree may not survive. This is not to say that if professionalism is weak in other areas of the department, it cannot still be practiced by the few. Aviation enjoys its own sense of professional excellence and maintains high standards of performance through peer pressure and review; the "band of brothers" can prove to be harsh critics. The real answer to a professional environment lies with proper departmental leadership.

The aspect of *character,* prominent in the definition of professionalism, is also as important as any other part of this discussion. If a person has adequate inner strength and a sense of ethical conduct, professionalism will be a natural consequence of those characteristics.

Corporate aviation has achieved its enviable safety record because of its professionalism, dedication to standards, and self-motivation. However, since the safety record is still imperfect, there must continue to be a dedication to excellence. Constant improvement must be the goal.

The professional works to the highest standards—his own.

—ANONYMOUS

REFERENCES

1. Flight Safety Foundation, Special FSF Fatigue Countermeasures Task Force Report, *Final Report: Principles and Guidelines for Duty and Rest Scheduling in Corporate and Business Aviation.* Alexandria, VA. Flight Safety Foundation, 1997; available at *http://flightsafety.org/member.cfm?redirect* = http://flightsafety.org/pubs/fsd_1997.html.

2. See also *Human Factors of Flight-Deck Checklists: The Normal Checklist,* NASA Contractor Report 177549, NASA Ames Research Center, CA,1990.

3. Excerpts from *NBAA Airports Handbook.* Washington: NBAA, 2002.

4. *http://www.boeing.com/assocproducts/noise/airports.html.*

5. *http://www.nbaa.org/noise/.*

6. Excerpts from *NBAA Airports Handbook.* Washington: NBAA, 2002.

CHAPTER 7
MAINTENANCE

One of the axioms of golf states, "You drive for show and putt for dough," implying that the glory goes with the first activity and the critical substance of the game goes with the second. The same is often said of the difference between flying and maintaining in the world of business and personal aviation.

The real essence of this type of aviation is having an aircraft ready when somebody wants to go somewhere. The pilots are supposedly always available via their pagers, but what about the aircraft? If it is not ready to go virtually all the time, the basic reason for having the aircraft is compromised. The aircraft may be officially out of service for certain periods of scheduled maintenance, but even then, it is usually understood that the aircraft can be returned to service within an hour or two and put on the line for a trip.

The point is that the maintenance function is quite critical. The boss does not understand aircraft dispatch rates of 99.5 percent; anything less than 100 percent represents unsatisfactory performance in his or her eyes. Passengers kept waiting for an hour while last-minute work is performed on the aircraft are not particularly understanding of the vagaries of mechanical performance or the stringent airworthiness requirements placed on their aircraft; getting to the destination in a timely manner is all they understand.

However, the most important aspect of good maintenance is safe operations. The complexities of modern turbine-powered aircraft are bewildering to the layperson and challenging to the aviation maintenance technician (AMT). Yet all the critical aircraft components have to be working all the time for the department's safety record to have even a chance at 100 percent. The trust and responsibility given to the maintenance crew are great, and they have proven to be well-placed. The maintenance safety record for professionally flown on-demand air transportation is near perfect.

Mission

The mission of the maintenance department is to provide airworthy aircraft, available when needed, at a reasonable cost. We are committed to inspect, maintain, and repair our corporate aircraft to ensure their safe operation and maximum dispatch reliability.

All this serves as preface to the fact that the maintenance function is very important and should be treated as such. The predominantly superior performance of aviation maintenance departments tends to make continued aircraft airworthiness look easy, something to be expected. However, it all comes at the cost of the hard work of dedicated professionals. Constant attention to and recognition of these efforts should be expected as well.

CONTRACT OR IN-HOUSE MAINTENANCE

Most airports have some form of aircraft maintenance available for personal and business flight operations. Be it a technician working independently, a fixed-base operator (FBO), or an approved maintenance organization/repair station, there is usually some form of maintenance available. Therefore, the question arises, should the department perform its own maintenance using company employees or an outside (contract) vendor?

The decision is not as clear-cut or simple as it seems. Every maintenance operation has its limits—work beyond its technicians' experience levels, tasks that require special tools, or processes or jobs that would keep the aircraft in an unserviceable condition for too long due to the nature of the work to be performed. Therefore, virtually all in-house maintenance departments must seek outside assistance at some time during the life cycle of the aircraft. However, the same is true for even the most capable and experienced FBO or repair station. The point is that regardless of the source of most maintenance, no one group can do it all.

To be airworthy, an aircraft must conform to its type certificate as well as be in a condition for safe operation.

—FAA ORDER 8700.1, *GENERAL AVIATION OPERATIONS INSPECTOR'S HANDBOOK*, CHAPTER 180

However, an experienced maintenance crew can perform most of the work required for the continued airworthiness of an aircraft. Given the right set of circumstances, the reliability, quality, and expenses involved may be superior to using an outside agency. Conversely, some operators find that contracting for all maintenance makes sense. An informed decision between the two requires a sharp pencil, knowledge of maintenance practices, and some hefty intuition.

Contract Maintenance

Contractors may perform maintenance under two different sanctioned methods: an individual aircraft maintenance technician's (AMT) certificate (license) or under an air agency certificate known as an approved maintenance organization (AMO) or aeronautical repair station. While there are many capable individual AMTs working on corporate aircraft, it is difficult to beat the advantages of a repair station. A properly certificated repair station has the advantage of written minimum personnel qualifications, supervisory methods, quality control programs, and a higher level of surveillance from the national regulatory authority. Further, the depth of personnel and experience for a given task are usually greater for an AMO. And if this organization is chosen for its expertise in specific types of aircraft, it should provide a higher level of service, if not confidence in its labor.

All this is not to say that non-AMO/repair station sources should not be used. However, the relative levels of experience and expertise possessed by the repair station should produce an advantage for that method over that of the individual technician. However great the advantage of the repair station, it should still be investigated prior to use. Table 7.1 presents some vendor selection guidelines.

Vendor Monitoring

When an aircraft is undergoing maintenance at a contractor facility, close contact will be maintained with that facility to ensure that the contracted work is performed completely, to high quality standards, and in a timely manner. Whenever possible, a maintenance technician will accompany the aircraft and monitor the work performed.

Regularly used vendors will be monitored for compliance with national regulations, manufacturers' standards, and good operating practices on an ongoing basis.

TABLE 7.1   Vendor Selection/Relations

Selection process
- The right facility for the job—Are they familiar with your
  - Aircraft type
  - *Specific* job requirements
- Cost
- Availability
- Reputation
- References for specific tasks/aircraft types
- Visit/audit the facility
- Corporate purchasing/legal clearance

Request for proposal
- Be specific about work to be performed
- Specify work/completion standards (usually those of the OEM)
- Specify worker qualifications/experience levels
- Require milestones/completion date(s)
- Include recourse provisions

Quality quotes from vendor
- Date of completion (and milestones, if applicable)
- Separate quotes for each requested task
- Warranty information
- Tax information
- Consumables/parts cost breakdown
- Administrative/certification/engineering costs
- Labor rates by employee/skill type
- Handling/storage/shipping/hazmat charges

Working relationships
- *Always* send a technician to oversee major work
- Review induction work order
- Participate in induction inspection
- Identify a *single* vendor contact for all communications
- Define/discuss when you will need to be called
- Define quality expectations—parts, hardware, cleanliness, etc.
- Delivery/paperwork inspection (must have provisional invoice)

Follow-up
- What's good, what's not—provide feedback in writing—always!
- Final invoice inspection
- Warranty claims

Seek to establish a lasting relationship with the vendor.

Potential contractors should be visited prior to work being performed. During the visit, interviews with key personnel (not just the owner) will yield useful information regarding the station's level of expertise and experience on the type of work to be performed. Ask to see personnel qualification and training records, observe typical work in progress, and inspect parts ordering, receipt, and issue procedures. However, the true test of a vendor's capability is customer satisfaction; call several recent customers chosen at random from the organization's files to see if they were pleased with the service they received.

Like so many other service provider decisions in life, the provider's reputation and word-of-mouth recommendations associated with it probably will provide you with the best sources of information. However, this choice must be tempered with your individual values and expectations. While cost should be a major consideration in the selection process, quality and reliability of the work preformed should rank at least as high.

Questions for Prospective Vendors

- How long have you been in business?
- How much experience do you have with my type of aircraft?
- What type and amount of initial and recurrent training do your technicians receive relative to my class and type of aircraft?
- Describe the process you use to obtain spare parts for aircraft? (Quality and price are important.)
- Do you use written work orders and provide a detailed breakdown of work completed on your invoice?
- Describe the warranty you provide for both labor and parts.
- Provide the names of three recent customers flying my type of aircraft to use a reference.

Contract Maintenance

All maintenance and inspection functions performed on company aircraft will use in-house resources whenever possible. When time restrictions, resident expertise, or tooling are a limiting factor, only vendors approved by the chief of maintenance will be used.

Vendors will be selected based on their Federal Aviation Administration (FAA) certification status, reputation, work history, and pricing policies. Although the cost of the work to be performed is an important factor, the most significant measures of suitability are the value and quality that corporate aviation receives.

Before any work begins with an outside contractor, ensure that a clear understanding exists (in writing) regarding the type and scope of work to be performed, including completion dates for individual tasks. Additionally, there should be a written agreement regarding the responsibilities of the vendor delineating actions to be taken when unusual items are found during the course of work and items that will extend the period of work performance. Specify that statements of work completed and invoices must contain sufficient detail to determine the type and amount of work performed and the parts used in performing it. Finally, the work performed and parts used should be subject to a written warranty.

All this applies whether the work is performed by an individual technician or a repair station. Setting up these procedures with a prospective vendor may require some effort the first time but will pay dividends later if the relationship continues.

A considerable amount of time will have to be allocated to scheduling, coordinating, and communicating with the vendor. Therefore, the director of maintenance, maintenance coordinator, or a designee will have to carefully integrate his or her maintenance oversight duties with his or her regular tasks if the relationship is to work correctly. If this is done properly, the flight department maintenance contact may spend many hours marrying department requirements with the capability of the vendor. If the coordinator is inexperienced in the field of maintenance, the learning curve in this new role will be quite steep.

In-House Maintenance

As stated earlier, an in-house capability will never permit all maintenance to be performed within the department. Nondestructive testing, component repair, many powerplant procedures, and avionics are examples of maintenance functions beyond the capability of most departments. However, most scheduled and nonscheduled maintenance should be within the capability of in-house personnel.

Proximity to an aircraft service center or major repair station may be a good reason to have in-house maintenance personnel, too. If the maintenance contractor is even a half-hour flight away, the inconvenience and wear on the aircraft just to get it to where it can be worked on may be more trouble than it is worth. And what happens if the aircraft cannot be flown to the vendor's site?

Having reasonably high experience levels of department technicians is critical to efficient and effective maintenance practice. AMTs working on sophisticated turbine-powered aircraft need both general and aircraft-specific training and experience to be truly effective. Without this background, performance of required tasks may require excessive amounts of time.

If an in-house maintenance capability is chosen, the type and level of work to be performed should be decided on. If just routine, low-level scheduled and nonscheduled tasks are to be performed, minimum staffing and experience levels will be required. This will be accompanied by the need to select appropriate vendors for higher-level, nonroutine tasks. If a comprehensive self-contained capability is desired, staffing and equipment requirements grow accordingly, with a corresponding reduced need for contractor support.

In-house capability may be supplemented through the judicious use of outside sources of information and advice there for the asking. Manufacturers' representatives and customer service personnel are often available to assist their customers with a wide range of services. Such services are normally free of charge and only a telephone call away. A strong local network of other technicians and repair station personnel, particularly those who operate similar aircraft, often will provide answers to difficult questions and yield some on-site advice. These methods should be exploited by the operators choosing in-house maintenance to enhance their capabilities.

I believe that one of the greatest advantages of having your own technician is for the times when someone else is working on the aircraft. Having your own person monitor the work being done on the aircraft is a service you should always have. This is a management and oversight job that will guarantee you getting the best parts, skill levels, and service when someone else is doing the work.

Good technicians have the ability to save their own wages every year by ensuring that outside work is done economically and correctly and that best prices are obtained on parts and services. This is especially true for more "mature" aircraft. If your maintenance costs run, say, $500 per hour, there are a lot of savings to be had in a 500-hour year.

In the final analysis, however, it is all about quality and control. How much does your company want?

Reasons to Send Your Technician with Your Aircraft to a Maintenance Vendor

- Sends a strong message to vendor regarding a desire for quality
- Ready point of contact for vendor
- Keeps downtime to a minimum
- Excellent training resource for the technician
- Ensures quality control
- Saves money

ORGANIZATION

While organizations may seem to be the same, regardless of the size of the flight department maintenance operation, significant differences arise.

Small Flight Departments

Small maintenance sections (generally two or fewer technicians) have little difficulty devising an organization because of the relative simplicity of their operation. A single AMT may seem to have the easiest task of getting organized, but because of lack of backup and depth, there are organizational factors to consider.

Just because a maintenance section has few people does not mean that there are not valuable resources available to them that will make their job easier, more productive, and more accurate. One or more of the pilots within the department may be assigned to assist the maintenance section during heavy work periods, especially if those pilots have either an Airframe and Powerplant (A&P) certificate or some maintenance management experience. Part-time or vendor-supplied technicians and semiskilled and apprentice personnel should be considered when developing an organization. All these additional resources may be used to good advantage during heavy work, vacation, and training periods. They may be considered a part of the maintenance organization if written controls and limitations are specified for their work and adequate supervision is maintained. Aircraft insurance policies and the insurance broker should be consulted to determine the legal limits placed on non-A&P and nondepartment personnel. Further, regulatory authorities strictly limit the privileges of nonlicensed maintenance personnel.

Larger Flight Departments

Larger departments should be organized to make the most of their collective and individual talents. The object of a well-organized department is to form a team that exploits the best features of all members of the section. While there should be definite divisions of work designated by job descriptions, there should not be so much compartmentalization of tasks that there is insufficient task overlap to allow individuals to cover for those who may be not present. Similarly, there should be as few as possible supervision and management levels within the section to allow for free communication and coordination of tasks without having to deal with an excessive bureaucracy.

Departments operating larger or more than two aircraft will require additional personnel, including some or all of the following:

- Maintenance department manager
- Chief inspector/quality control inspector
- Lead technician
- Crew chief
- Avionics technician
- Parts clerk
- Records clerk
- Aircraft line service technician
- Aircraft cleaner

All these titles may not be necessary for every department, but the functions will be required. Again, some of these functions may be performed by vendors, or they may be assigned as collateral duties for section personnel.

Quality Control Teams Make Time

A large mail-order clothing retailer located in the Midwest used its two Learjets to good advantage by transporting company executives on a variety of high-profile missions. The executives' busy schedules effectively precluded other employees, including middle managers, from using the aircraft.

As the company grew, its requirement to conduct quality control inspections on manufacturers placed an increasingly heavy burden on its inspection teams to maintain the same level and frequency of inspections. Further, manufacturing facilities were moving offshore in increasing numbers, making the inspection schedule more difficult to maintain.

The head of quality control finally determined that the inspection schedule could not be maintained without hiring an additional 15 inspectors. The vice president of manufacturing was dedicated to maintaining the quality of the products but did not want to put an additional burden on his already stressed budget.

As an experiment, one Learjet was assigned to transport a quality control team on its scheduled rounds to determine the time savings involved, if any. To the surprise of all concerned, the team's productivity was doubled for domestic visits and tripled for Central American and Caribbean visits.

The two aircraft now are used more than 75 percent of the time by quality control, marketing, and audit teams—top-level executives often use the airlines or charter.

PERSONNEL

As with other sections of the flight department, attracting and retaining properly experienced personnel that can fit into the organization's culture are essential parts of ensuring a high-quality operation. Chapter 3 listed basic guidelines for finding the right people for the maintenance section of the department. They are repeated here for convenience. In deciding the number of technicians, it is important to know how much time the aircraft will be at home base; if it is always on the road, it will be difficult for in-house personnel to adequately maintain the aircraft. In a related matter, extensive foreign operations may dictate the need for a technician to travel with the aircraft, further taxing personnel left behind to maintain aircraft remaining closer to home.

The first AMT hired normally will be designated the director of maintenance, regardless of the size of the flight department. Because this person may head the maintenance section as it grows and gathers more technicians, he or she should exhibit some leadership and managerial abilities in addition to being a good technician.

The director of maintenance reports to the director of aviation (aviation department manager) and is responsible for maintaining department aircraft in accordance with the manufacturers' standards and regulatory norms [Federal Aviation Regulations (FAR) in the United States]. Duties include

- Ensuring that all maintenance operations are conducted safely.

- Providing guidance and direction for those assigned to the maintenance section.

- Maintaining the company aircraft in accordance with the manufacturers' continuing airworthiness instructions, FARs, and the highest standards of airworthiness and appearance.

- Assisting with flight department planning issues, including budgets.

- Ensuring that maintenance personnel are properly qualified and trained for their assigned duties.
- Maintaining adequate spare parts and consumable inventory.
- Responsibility for contracting with vendors to provide maintenance services, as needed.
- Ensuring that the hangar and associated facilities are properly maintained.

AMTs are responsible for ensuring that the work performed on department aircraft is done in accordance with regulatory standards and good operating practices. Their duties include

- Performing maintenance and inspections in accordance with manufacturer's and FAA-approved methods and techniques.
- Keeping abreast of and maintaining a current working knowledge of the procedures, parts, and tools needed to perform maintenance and repair work on the company aircraft.
- Complying with the manufacturers' technical data, FAR, and other applicable safety rules.
- Being responsible for strict adherence to the inspection system employed for assigned aircraft.
- Shipping, receiving, and inspecting aircraft parts.

Guidelines for finding a qualified AMT include

- Aviation maintenance technician/engineer licensed by the national regulatory authority
- At least one year (ideally two) working on the same class of aircraft
- Specialized training for the type of aircraft operated (may be provided after hire)

As with all other department personnel, technicians should be hired for their ability to become a member of the flight department *team*. Interpersonal skills, a service orientation, communications ability, and overall ability to get along with their fellow workers must be considered as important, if not more important than their technical skills. See Appendix E for a list of performance criteria considered important by the National Business Aviation Association (NBAA).[1]

Most small flight departments exist with one or two AMTs and no other personnel to assist with the maintenance work. As the department grows, other specialties are added to the maintenance section (see "Larger Flight Departments," on page 7.6).

Determining the proper number of technicians to employ for a flight operation is difficult due the variety of operational modes and tempos of operations for various departments. Basic factors in determining this include

- Type and number of aircraft
- Flight operations tempo
- Aircraft hourly utilization
- Dispatch reliability expectations
- Amount of contract (vendor) maintenance used

This last factor is probably the most important feature in determining the number of technicians required. If all scheduled maintenance, including minor inspections, is performed by outside maintenance vendors, then few technicians will be required to perform routine dispatch and unscheduled maintenance. If, however, a flight department attempts to perform all but the most major inspections in-house and expects technicians to be present for each launch and recovery, then additional technicians will be needed. As a starting point, see Table 7.2 for the method recommended by the NBAA.[2]

TABLE 7.2   Sample Calculation for Maintenance Personnel Required (NBAA)

The following formula is provided for determining the number of maintenance personnel required. A constant of 4 work hours of maintenance per 1 hour of aircraft flight is used. Each company can revise this number as necessary. The other constant is 1577 maintenance hours a year per person.

- Work hours per year per maintenance technician: 2080
  (52 weeks per year × 40 hours per week)
- Subtract hours not available:
  Vacation: 120 (15 days × 8 hours)
  Holidays: 88 (11 days × 8 hours)
  Sick leave: 40 (5 days × 8 hours)
  Training: 80 (10 days × 8 hours)
- Subtotal of hours not available: 328
- Hours available for duty: 1752 (2080 hours − 328 hours)
- Nonproductive time: 175 (10 percent of 1752 hours) (Nonproductive time includes training, breaks, and cleanup time.)
- Total maintenance hours available: 1577 (1752 hours − 175 hours)
- Maintenance work hours per one flight hour: 4
- Estimated flight hours per year: 850
- Estimated maintenance personnel hours needed: 3400 (4 maintenance work hours × 850 flight hours)
- Number of maintenance personnel needed (rounded):   2 (3400 maintenance work hours/1577 work hours per year)

MAINTENANCE OPERATIONS

A number of maintenance functions are required of a flight department, common to all types of operation, regardless of size or type of aircraft flown. Understanding and preparing procedures for these processes will make life easier for the flight department and will make the maintenance section more efficient and effective.

Airworthiness Determination

In the United States and most other countries, the owner/operator of an aircraft is responsible for maintaining the aircraft as prescribed by regulatory authority. Moreover, each pilot in command (PIC) must determine that the aircraft that he or she is about to fly is airworthy. A formal maintenance release is required for airline operations to communicate the state of airworthiness between maintenance personnel and the pilots. Yet, in most corporate aviation operations, the actual determination of airworthiness is delegated informally to maintenance personnel, with no formal list of the items constituting an airworthy aircraft provided to the flight crew prior to flight. Therefore, the PIC normally reviews the disposition of a few recent aircraft discrepancies prior to conducting a preflight inspection and flying away.

Ideally, a flight crew briefing is provided by the director of maintenance or other technician regarding the airworthiness of the aircraft. However, there also

Airworthiness Release

The aircraft inspection, life-limited items, and airworthiness directives status are current in accordance with the manufacturer's inspection program and applicable FAA directives.
/signed/AMT

should be an independent means for the flight crew to ascertain the inspection, life-limited items, airworthiness directive, deferred maintenance, and discrepancy status of the aircraft. This is usually accomplished by placing a discrepancy, inspection, and life-limited items status sheet in the aircraft maintenance (discrepancy) log for the benefit of flight crews. Alternatively, a formal aircraft postflight form completed by an AMT could contain a statement attesting to the aircraft status (see the sidebar). A portrayal of this and the maintenance control process is shown in Fig. 7.1.

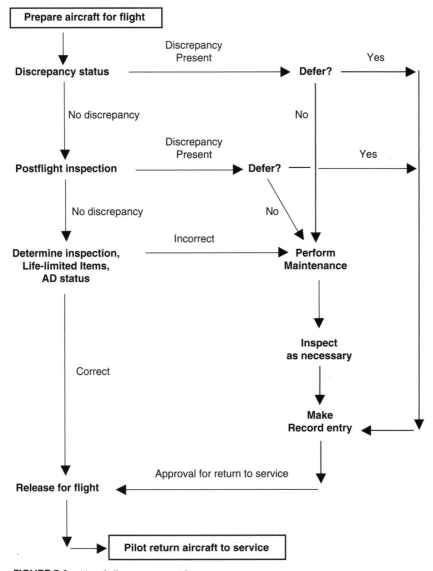

FIGURE 7.1   Aircraft discrepancy control process.

Maintenance Planning

All aircraft, particularly turbine-powered aircraft, are required to be inspected at regular intervals, and certain components must be inspected or changed when time limits are reached. Inspections may range from simple visual inspections of external components to complex inspections involving high-technology nondestructive testing methods. They may require only minutes to perform or weeks for major inspections. All these items must be scheduled to fit into the aircraft's operational schedule so as to disrupt its utility as little as possible. Maintenance planning is a critical part of the entire flight department's operations and should receive sufficient attention outside the maintenance group as well as within.

The task of maintenance planning or scheduling usually falls to the director of maintenance, who must coordinate the desired work with the chief pilot, aircraft schedulers (and indirectly, with potential passengers), vendors, and in-house work force. This work is complicated by the fact that some required inspection and removal items are predicated on calendar and some on flight-hour requirements. Simple 36-month inspection requirements may be difficult to coordinate with a 600-flight-hour inspection interval because it is not easy to determine on what day the 600 hours will have been reached. Computerized maintenance record tracking systems can assist with the planning process by projecting estimated flight hours onto calendar requirements to reach a comprehensive view of an inspection and replacement schedule.

If a vendor is to perform a scheduled maintenance action, an additional scheduling variable is introduced, that of the availability of the vendor to perform the action. Care should be taken to ensure that the vendor has the proper type and amount of labor available to accomplish the desired work in the minimum time possible.

Scheduling maintenance must be done in coordination with the department manager/chief pilot and the scheduler if proper customer service is to be realized. A scheduled maintenance plan should be devised and published for flight department personnel to alert them to expected dates of inspection and maintenance items based on anticipated utilization rates. If this schedule interferes with required aircraft use, adjustments may be made to accommodate them. Importantly, these dates must be updated continually to reflect both utilization rate changes and varying demand for the aircraft.

Scheduled Maintenance

The director of maintenance is responsible for scheduling required maintenance items a minimum of 12 months in advance of significant inspections and life limited components replacements. This schedule will be coordinated with director of aviation and the aircraft scheduler and updated as necessary.

Maintenance Control

The functions of anticipating airworthiness requirements and dealing with discrepancies that render and aircraft unairworthy are the principal tasks of the maintenance control process. This function ensures that required maintenance is accomplished on aircraft and that the aircraft is only released for service in an airworthy condition. The function is usually performed by a single individual who acts as a work and paperwork controller to designate what work is performed at what time and by whom and then finally ensures that the work is accomplished by monitoring the flow of paperwork. The function is considered important enough to often be performed by the director of maintenance.

The maintenance schedule is used to trigger inspections and time-controlled item actions, whereas aircraft discrepancy reports are used to initiate repairs. In large maintenance departments, work orders are commonly used to both initiate actions and determine their progress toward completion. Only after the work has been signed off and inspected should the aircraft be released to other work or approved for return to service. Ideally, when required maintenance has been completed, a maintenance release process will certify that the aircraft is airworthy and ready for service (flight).

Discrepancies

The principal source of maintenance actions outside of scheduled maintenance comes from aircraft discrepancy reports. These written reports may be received from either AMTs who have discovered the fault while working on or inspecting the aircraft or from flight crew members who have discovered a fault during flight. These discrepancy reports should be recorded on a suitable form that provides not only a section for recording the fault but also a companion section to indicate maintenance actions taken to correct it. Dates and signatures should be required for both sections (see Fig. 7.2).

Aircraft _____   **Time in Service**_____   **Cycles**_____

Discrepancy		Corrective Action	
Pilot	Date	Technician	Date
Part # off	# on	Part S/N off	S/N on

Discrepancy		Corrective Action	
Pilot	Date	Technician	Date
Part # off	# on	Part S/N off	S/N on

FIGURE 7.2   Sample aircraft discrepancy record.

Aircraft discrepancy recording and control are important functions within the flight department. A complete discrepancy and corrective action log provides both flight and maintenance crews with a complete record of a recent airworthiness history of the aircraft. Further, the corrective action taken section of the log may be used as a portion of the official aircraft log.

Many flight departments have instituted a procedure whereby an AMT is designated to meet every flight on its return to base. This procedure allows the flight crew to explain the written discrepancies and discuss them with maintenance personnel to ensure that a complete communication has taken place between the writer and the person who will correct the fault. The procedure provides another opportunity for maintenance and operations to interact, furthering good working relations between the two.

It is important for pilots and technicians to understand that the act of recording and clearing discrepancies is a critical communications process essential to the safety and performance of the flight department. Complete, comprehensive, and legible entries are important to the process. Most important, *all* discrepancies must be recorded and properly cleared by authorized personnel—verbal or Post It note discrepancies are not adequate.

If a discrepancy affecting the airworthiness of the aircraft cannot be corrected prior to the next flight, the aircraft minimum equipment list (MEL) should be consulted to determine whether the aircraft may be flown with the discrepancy outstanding. If possible, the discrepancy should be deferred using approved procedures and recorded as such. Although general aviation operators may defer discrepancies until the next scheduled inspection, an anticipated correction date for the discrepancy should be specified for planning and control purposes.

The MEL is used infrequently in most flight departments and therefore should be subject to training and discussion by both flight crews and technicians. Additionally, the technician responsible for ensuring that the maintenance technical publications are up to date also should check the currency of the master MEL (MMEL) at least quarterly.

Minimum Equipment List

If you operate turbine-powered aircraft, with certain exceptions, it should be covered by an MEL. Granted, if *everything* of consequence on the aircraft is operable for *every* flight, an MEL is unnecessary. However, credibility regarding perfect aircraft reliability falls into the same category as the Tooth Fairy and Santa Claus.

For the United States, FARs covering inoperative instruments and equipment essentially state that everything has to work on the aircraft prior to flight unless specific procedures are taken. In the case of turbine-powered aircraft, this almost always means using an MEL issued to a specific operator and aircraft.

Obtaining an MEL is usually as easy as downloading the master MMEL from the FAA Web site, presenting it to your local Flight Standards District Office (FSDO), and receiving an FAA letter of authorization (LOA). The combination of the MMEL and the LOA serves as a legal MEL, constituting a supplemental-type certificate (STC) for your aircraft and permitting you to fly it with certain equipment inoperative.

Once the LOA is issued, you must develop a procedures document stating what specific action flight and maintenance crews will take to accommodate allowable inoperative equipment. The aircraft may be operated under the provisions of the MEL while those procedures are being developed. The MMEL and the LOA must be carried aboard the aircraft along with records describing inoperative equipment.

Notification of revisions to the MMEL will be sent by the FAA. If installed equipment is not covered in the MMEL, you must apply through the FSDO for modification to your MEL or for an amendment from the FAA Flight Operations Evaluation Board (FOEB).

The MEL provides operators with greater flexibility by permitting an aircraft to be operated with certain types of installed equipment inoperative. Once pilots and maintenance technicians have studied and understand its provisions, the MEL allows for legal operation despite minor malfunctions.

Maintenance Away from Home Base

When air aircraft becomes unairworthy while away from home base, flight crews should consult with the maintenance manager or chief inspector via telephone concerning possible courses of action.

Minor discrepancies not requiring extensive aircraft-specific knowledge may be corrected by an aircraft maintenance facility where the aircraft is located. The company maintenance representative responsible for selecting the maintenance facility should be familiar with the facility, but if this is not possible, at a minimum, the facility should possess an FAA repair station certificate.

Resolution of major discrepancies or scheduled heavy maintenance away from home base may require the presence of one or more company AMTs to oversee the work performed. However, an aircraft maintenance facility having experience with the aircraft type should be considered adequate to perform the required work if the previously stated criteria are met.

Aircraft Maintenance Reference Materials

Reference materials required by the manufacturer's maintenance program and FAA regulations are required to be kept complete and current. Each manufacturer publishes a document that provides the current editions of and changes to its technical publications. This should be used to determine the currency and completeness of the airframe, powerplant, accessory, and appliance manuals required for department operations. Additionally, all FAA-required publications, including applicable airworthiness directives, advisory circulars, and regulations, should be kept current via FAA document checklists.

A system should be devised to ensure that these publications are kept up to date on a continuing basis. Ideally, an individual will be assigned to the task and review the controlled publications on a monthly or quarterly basis. This process may be handled most easily by subscribing to a service that will keep the documents up to date. This is particularly applicable to microfiche and computer media (CD). Yet these services may not fully cover all appliances, accessories, or STC items; therefore, a process must be devised to track all required reference materials. Even with subscription services, someone must ensure that the periodic subscription is received and not lost in the mail or subject to a subscription expiration.

Reliability

Reliability is an important aspect of the corporate aviation mission. Therefore, this department shall provide mission-ready aircraft to meet flight schedules so that every flight is launched within 15 minutes of its scheduled time or upon passenger availability. This is to be accomplished for a minimum of 99 percent of all scheduled aircraft launches.

Each person performing maintenance...shall use the methods, techniques and practices prescribed in the current manufacturer's maintenance manual or Instructions for Continued Airworthiness prepared by the manufacturer.

—FAR PART 43.13

Parts Inventory and Control

The number of spare parts, both consumable and rotable, should be kept to a minimum. Parts are expensive to keep on hand and account for, and they may become obsolete. Most parts, even major or rotable items, can be obtained within 24 hours or less through a number of vendors. Aircraft-on-ground (AOG) parts are usually available even sooner. These "on demand" parts services have allowed flight departments to reduce their inventories to a minimum, freeing up both storage space and parts personnel and reducing inventory costs.

Parts should be ordered only from vendors who have been investigated properly and found to have a good reputation and to charge competitive rates. New and additional vendors should be constantly sought to ensure that the best possible product is available at the best possible price.

Parts ordering and control should be accomplished by an individual who will be responsible for all parts-related functions. The advantage to having a single individual perform these tasks is one of control and quality control. If more that one individual attempts to work with parts, there inevitably will be gaps in communication and miscommunications that inject errors into the system.

A parts usage and inventory system is essential to maintain adequate stocks of parts. Available software programs for ordering, tracking, and billing may simplify the process of parts control and certainly will provide better records of parts transactions. However, small inventories may be maintained using paper records with only a minimal effort.

All parts must be identified properly to ensure that they are approved by the regulatory authority. A receiving inspection and verification system should be instituted to verify the authenticity and proper documentation of all aircraft parts coming into the department. Similarly, an outgoing identification and shipping and inspection function should be performed to ensure that the receiving vendor is properly supplied with authentic documentation (see Table 7.3).

TABLE 7.3 Aircraft Parts Acceptance and Identification (FAA)

- Confirm that the packaging of the part identifies the supplier or distributor and is free from alteration or damage.
- Verify that the actual part and delivery receipt reflect the same information as the purchase order regarding part number, serial number, and historical information (if applicable).
- Verify that the identification on the part has not been tampered with (e.g., serial number stamped over, label or part/serial numbers improper or missing, vibro-etch or serial numbers located at other than the normal location).
- Ensure that the shelf life and/or life limit has not expired, if applicable.
- Conduct a visual inspection of the part and supporting documents to the extent necessary to determine if the part is traceable to an FAA-approved source. For detailed guidelines on the identification of replacement parts, refer to AC 20–62. The following are examples of positive forms of identification:
  - FAA Form 8130-3, Airworthiness Approval Tag
  - Joint Aviation Authorities (JAA) Form One
  - Maintenance records or release document with approval for return to service
  - FAA TSO markings
  - FAA PMA markings
  - Shipping ticket/invoice from the Production Approval Holder.
  - Direct ship authority letter from PAH.
- Evaluate any visible irregularities (e.g., altered or unusual surface, absence of required plating, evidence of prior usage, scratches, new paint over old, attempted exterior repair, pitting or corrosion).
- Conduct random sampling of standard hardware packaged in large quantities in a manner which corresponds to the type and quantity of the parts.

Duty Time

Flight time and duty time are always hot topics for flight crews but rarely heard of when speaking of AMTs. Traditionally, technicians work until the job is complete, be it a critical repair that affects the airworthiness of the aircraft or a single inspection work card. Many late nights are spent in lonely hangars by single technicians working to make the morning launch. However, if a pilot cannot be expected to be productive, alert, and safe after 12 or 14 hours (during which some rest time may have been available), is it possible for a technician to be safe after the same interval?

Technicians work with complex machines that require high levels of understanding; theirs is a world of complicated detail. It is reasonable to assume that their comprehension of the task at hand and the detailed procedures to complete it require great insight and concentration. Fatigue, poor lighting, heat, cold, humidity, noise, and frequent distractions are the enemy of this type of work, all conditions common to a technician's work life. Controlling these factors should make the technician a more productive, safer worker. Fatigue is the perhaps the easiest to control.

> ### Duty Time
>
> AMTs will work not more than 12 continuous hours in any 24-hour period. The minimum acceptable rest period following a duty period is 10 continuous hours. Each AMT should be relieved from all duty for at least one period of 24 continuous hours during any 7 consecutive days.

A number of flight departments have placed duty time limits on their technicians' work in much the same manner as they have for pilots. The most common limit seen is 12 hours, with provision for finite extensions at the discretion of a lead technician or the director of maintenance. If an early launch and late recovery are planned, wherein the technician is required to be present, credit can be given for time off during the day to extend the duty day. However, this should not be done for more than 2 or 3 days in a row. Further, consideration must be given to when work begins and ends. If the technician arrives at 5 A.M. to launch an aircraft, a normal work day should end at 1 to 2 P.M. Similarly, this technician will have difficulty performing/resting if the next day begins at 4 P.M. and goes to midnight.

Quality Control

This is a safety issue that is difficult to resolve in smaller departments. Airlines and repair stations require that certain critical maintenance actions be inspected by a designated inspector prior to the aircraft, powerplant, or appliance being approved for return to service. These required inspection items (RIIs) are listed in the operations specification or general maintenance manual. While there is no requirement to do so in most corporate operations (U.S. FAR Part 91), some departments have instituted their own RIIs that call for a designated inspector, usually a lead technician or director of maintenance, to inspect certain items of work before the aircraft is released; some departments go so far as to double inspect all work performed. This is especially difficult for a single technician working on a weekend or late at night. This situation should be considered when setting work rules for technicians.

Continuing quality requires that the quality be built into each procedure used by the technician. That is, instead of relying on inspection procedures to ensure quality work, the process that created the work must have procedures and checks built into each action to ensure accuracy and safety. While many manufacturers' maintenance instructions strive to accomplish this in each work card and procedure, some fall short and must have procedures devised to preclude error.

Did It Get Done?   This question normally comes to mind when the you are driving home from the hangar at 2 A.M. wondering whether you safety wired the final bolt on the hydraulic pump you just replaced. This is an occupational hazard of those who performance solo maintenance work.

To an even greater degree, this question comes to mind when a high-priority nonscheduled maintenance task has been completed, and it is time to return the aircraft to service. The question refers not just to the many actions required to accomplish the actual maintenance task but also to the paper trail that will prove that the action has occurred.

If you operate small aircraft with no maintenance record tracking system, work exclusively by yourself, or have a maintenance paperwork checklist you use regularly, this section may not apply to you. However, if you are like the great majority of technicians who work with others, perform complex tasks, and have a maintenance recordkeeping system in addition to the actual aircraft, powerplant, and accessory logs, this section is probably for you.

Traditionally, the paperwork is saved until the maintenance task has been accomplished and tested and the aircraft is given to the pilots to fly. (Do not forget, however, that the aircraft may not be approved for return to service until an official logbook entry has been made—paperwork first.) In the heat of battle to get the aircraft fit to fly, certain items may get overlooked. For instance:

- Was the received part logged in correctly and its inspection recorded properly?

- Was the serviceable part tag attached to the work order/work card prior to filing?

- Did the unserviceable part tag get filled out completely and attached to the part prior to return/disposal?

- If consumable or standard parts were used, was an inventory debit made?

- Was the proper maintenance record tracking system work card completed/entered into the system?

- Was the aircraft/powerplant/accessory logbook entry made (strange as it may seem, this important step is sometimes neglected, yet all the ancillary paperwork has been accomplished).

- The airworthiness directive (AD) was accomplished and recorded, but was the AD status record updated?

This is a representative sample of some of the many records that should be kept to ensure a comprehensive view of accomplished maintenance actions—do you have a means for making sure that all necessary recordkeeping is accomplished?

Airlines and repair stations are required to have systems in place to ensure that all their record entries are accomplished. These systems are set forth in their general maintenance/inspection manuals and may provide checklists for technicians to use. In the fully integrated recordkeeping systems, internal edits prevent certain entries from being made if other, more fundamental record actions were not accomplished first.

Some flight departments use recordkeeping checklists temporarily attached to maintenance action packages or simple checklists posted at all normal recordkeeping locations around the shop to ensure all the *i*'s are dotted and *t*'s crossed. Others impose a strict sequence of recordkeeping actions that forces technicians to complete all required actions. Still others either use a single individual to make all record entries or a quality control person to ensure that the recordkeeping actions of others are complete and correct.

Maintenance Inspection Accuracy.   The airworthiness of aircraft depends heavily on the scheduled maintenance that they are required to undergo. The items to be inspected and the frequency with which they must be inspected are specified in the manufacturer's continuing airworthiness instructions and the applicable regulations. However, a critical part of the inspection process is the ability of the inspector to reliably and correctly perform the required inspection task.

If the aviation maintenance technician is inadequately trained in inspection techniques, does not know the possible fault conditions specified in the task, is not psychologically or physically prepared, or is performing the inspection in less than favorable environmental conditions, the outcome of the procedure may be in doubt. Inherent in inspection task design is the notion that human beings are fallible and that some are better prepared to detect fault conditions than others; defining the specific abilities and inabilities to perform is the subject of ongoing maintenance human factors systems design studies.

A recent study[3] examined the ability of a number of technicians to detect surface fatigue in aircraft fuselage skins using high-frequency eddy current inspections. The experiment was taken to nine maintenance facilities, where inspectors examined a large number of rivet sites for skin cracks known to the test conductor. Various controlled factors were incorporated into the experiment, including painted versus bare surfaces, accessibility to the inspection site, and type of specimen. Other, uncontrolled areas of environmental and personnel factors also were considered for their impact on the task. Environmental factors included noise level, instrument calibration, temperature, lighting, procedures used, and scanning techniques. Personnel factors included both physical and psychological factors, including age, amount of sleep, time on duty, work patterns, type of training, attitude, education level, and recency of inspection experience.

Results were predictable in some cases and surprising in others. For example, the length of the crack to be detected determined the probability of detection (small cracks were more difficult to detect), and painted surfaces made reliable crack detection significantly more difficult. In this latter case, the number of false detections increased dramatically when painted surfaces were inspected.

The most interesting results came from the uncontrolled personnel and environmental factors. A number of these included the following:

- Inspectors overcame poor lighting in the inspection area by using flashlights, but when portable lighting was used, the process speeded up significantly. Quality and amount of lighting did not, however, appear to affect the accuracy of the inspection tasks.

- A wide range of eddy current calibration techniques and inspection procedures were observed. Some nonstandard and substandard calibration techniques measurably affected the outcome of the tests.

- Fatigue caused performance to suffer, especially for those who had already worked a full shift prior to engaging in the test. However, a direct correlation between amount of recent sleep and inspection performance was not possible.

- Younger inspectors tended to perform better than older inspectors. While not fully verified, the training received by the younger inspectors may have caused the difference.

- A less desirable behavioral climate in an individual facility or the perceived poor attitudes of management did not appreciably affect inspector performance because of the apparent personal and professional pride they exhibited in their work.

- Even formalized on-the-job training did not seem to produce the quality of inspectors that formal classroom training produced.

- Inspectors who took more work breaks tended to be more accurate than those who worked straight through.

- The quality of inspection teams (two-persons) was dragged down by the poorest member of the team rather than being pulled up by an excellent team member. Preliminary findings indicate that single inspectors were better and more effective.

Be aware of these factors when assigning and engaging in inspection activities. There is more to it than meets the eye.

Maintenance Error. Maintenance errors occur through lapses in attention, distractions, racing to finish a job, and just plain carelessness. Traditionally, quality lapses, unsafe acts, and less than adequate maintenance performance are sorted according to their adverse impact on the aircraft. These error types fall into two general classes:

- The introduction of an aircraft discrepancy that was not there before the maintenance activity began.
- The failure to detect damage or incorrect components during maintenance inspections.

Such errors may be further broken down into specific categories, as was done, for example, in a Pratt and Whitney study of the causes of 120 inflight engine shutdowns (IFSDs) on Boeing 747s in 1991 (see sidebar, ranked according to frequency). This study provides examples of typical maintenance errors.

Analysis of 122 quality lapses detected by a major airline over a period of 3 years revealed very similar discrepancy types:

- Omissions (56 percent)
- Incorrect installations (30 percent)
- Wrong parts (8 percent)
- Other (6 percent)

When omissions, the largest single category, were examined further, the following categories of error were identified.

- Fastenings left undone or incomplete (22 percent)
- Items left locked or pins not removed (13 percent)
- Filter/breather caps loose or missing (11 percent)
- Items left loose or disconnected (10 percent)
- Spaces, washers, etc. missing (10 percent)
- Tools, spare fastening, etc. not removed (10 percent)
- Lack of lubrication (7 percent)
- Panels left off (3 percent)
- Miscellaneous (11 percent)

Another study conducted by the British Civil Aviation Authority in 1992

Pratt and Whitney In-Flight Shutdown Causes

- Missing parts
- Incorrect parts
- Incorrect installation of parts
- Use of worn or deteriorated parts
- Careless installation of O-rings
- B-nuts not safety wired
- Nuts tightened but not torqued
- B-nuts overtorqued
- Seals overtorqued
- Not loosening both ends of connecting tube during replacement
- Replacing tube assembly without first breaking connections between matching parts
- Loose or missing oil-tank caps
- Dirty or loose cannon plugs
- Water in fuel
- Foreign objects dropped into engines
- Hydraulic fluid in oil system

found that the most frequently occurring maintenance problems, in order of occurrence, were

- Incorrect installation of components
- Installation of incorrect parts
- Electrical wiring discrepancies (including cross-connection)
- Loose objects (tools, etc.) left in aircraft
- Inadequate lubrication
- Cowlings, access panels, and fairings not secured
- Fuel/oil caps and refuel panels not secured
- Landing gear ground lock pins not removed before departure

Although these studies tell us little about why individuals made these particular errors, they tell a great deal about the relative error proneness of the different phases of the aircraft maintenance task.

The cure? Perhaps the best overall cure is a well-developed safety culture that places high value on quality work. Other measures include required inspection items, attention to maintenance instructions and procedures, and a supportive management structure.

While business aviation suffers very few accidents due to maintenance error, less serious incidents cause unnecessary aircraft reliability problems and wasted time and money. Quality control and maintenance error should never be far from the mind of each technician and manager.

Maintenance Manual

- Organization/job descriptions
- Safety
- Technician qualifications
- Training
- Inspection programs
- Quality control
- Work procedures and performance criteria
- Discrepancy management
- Maintenance scheduling
- Unscheduled maintenance away from home base
- Recordkeeping
- Vendor selection
- Spare parts control
- Support equipment
- Facility maintenance

Maintenance Manual

An operations manual was discussed in Chap. 6, and the chapter contains a brief recommendation that a section of it be devoted to maintenance procedures. This brief treatment may be adequate for departments that are small or have most of their maintenance performed by vendors, but large departments possessing capabilities to perform a variety of tasks should consider developing a separate maintenance manual.

The manual is primarily a communications tool to control expectations and provide guidance for all people within the department. Making sure technicians perform actions the same way every time and to a set of standards goes a long way toward ensuring excellence within the maintenance function.

Ideally, this manual should be developed in-house and by the department technicians themselves. If a generic manual is adopted by the department, it probably will not be used as a reference because it does not reflect actual practices used by the department. Developing a manual in-house also serves to clarify and reinforce existing policies and procedures and to indicate the need for additional ones.

Aircraft Handling

The high value of corporate aircraft demands great care during moving and parking. Therefore, the following procedures should be considered for all aircraft movements:

- Training should be provided for all personnel.
- Only qualified personnel will move the aircraft.
- Tugs and towbars should be rated adequately for the gross weight of the aircraft to be handled.
- The aircraft will be chocked whenever parked.
- At least one wing walker, in addition to the tug driver, will be employed to determine adequacy of clearance between an aircraft and surrounding objects during aircraft movement. Additional wing walkers should be employed when warranted.
- Aircraft spotting marks shall be used.
- Hangar doors will be fully opened during operations in which an aircraft is moved into or out of the hangar.

Security

Security is covered more completely in Chap. 6, but some note of security for maintenance needs to be made. Facility security may be of greater importance for maintenance personnel than for others because maintenance controls so many and such large entrances the hangar. Open hangar doors during warm weather are an invitation to thieves, vandals, and the like; a favorite time for leaving everything unattended and open is lunch time. And maintenance personnel are often the last to leave a facility at night. The duty of locking up and setting the intrusion alarms should be spelled out and briefed to all maintenance personnel.

Another problem area arises when leaving aircraft on the ramp unattended with the airstair, equipment bays, and baggage doors open. Even though the aircraft is in front of the hangar or nearby, it does not take long to get in and out.

Maintenance personnel are quite knowledgeable regarding aircraft movements and, possibly, the passengers being moved. This is not only security-related but confidential information, too. This information must be kept close-hold and passed only to those needing to know aircraft movements.

Evaluating Maintenance Performance

Chapter 4 covered evaluation of the flight department's overall performance, looking at measures such as aircraft cost per mile, load factor, and denied trips. Maintenance activity also can be measured and should be to determine its level of performance. Here are some of the measures that can be used:

- *Aircraft availability.* Answers the question, "How many days was the aircraft available for flight during the month?" The complement of this number is normally the number of days the aircraft was not available due to maintenance, either in-house or contract.

- *Dispatch reliability.* If an aircraft departs within 15 (or 30) minutes of its scheduled departure time or passenger arrival, a successful flight has commenced. If it does not depart within that time frame, something went wrong—weather, ATC, or a mechanical problem. Therefore, a subdefinition of dispatch reliability is required to adequately define the failure. The value is expressed as a percentage arrived at by dividing the number of the number of successful launches by scheduled flights.

- *Quality.* How many errors were made in maintenance monitoring/tracking, actual maintenance functions, recordkeeping, and parts ordering/handling? Most departments do not measure these items, but doing so provides useful feedback to all concerned, especially if the data are not used for disciplinary actions.

- *Maintenance hours per flight hour.* Knowing how much maintenance time, especially nonscheduled time, is spent on a specific aircraft tells a lot about its reliability and general condition. Recording the type of system worked on will help further define issues.

Tracking these values provides information about the effectiveness and efficiency of a maintenance operation, although some issues causing poor numbers may be beyond the control of the maintenance organization. Therefore, each of these measures requires either a footnote or further explanation to describe the cause for either low numbers in the first two measures or a high number in the third.

RECORDKEEPING

The ICAO and all national regulatory systems require that certain records be kept for each aircraft, powerplant, and appliance to determine whether it has been maintained in an airworthy condition in accordance with approved procedures. This is a critical function because it is usually the only means available for an operator to prove compliance with airworthiness requirements. However, there is an even more important reason to maintain complete and correct maintenance records, that of proving to a prospective buyer of the aircraft that not only has it received the required maintenance but also that it has been done properly and in a high-quality manner. The resale value of a turbine-powered aircraft may be decreased by 20 to 30 percent if its maintenance records are poorly maintained or incomplete.

Inspection status and maintenance performed are important components of recordkeeping but are considered perishable records. This means that they must be maintained for only 1 year after the work has been performed or until the work is superseded or repeated. Perhaps the more important records are those that record the status of life-limited and time-controlled items, airworthiness directives (AD), and records of major alterations or repairs. These are permanent records that stay with the aircraft throughout its life. It is these last records that are most important in proving the status and quality of care of the aircraft. If the accomplishment of an AD or important service bulletin or approval for a major alteration cannot be proved, its reaccomplishment can be very costly.

> . . . *Each person who maintains, performs preventive maintenance, rebuilds, or alters an aircraft, airframe, aircraft engine, propeller, appliance, or component part shall make an entry in the maintenance record of that equipment containing the following information:*
>
> *(1) A description (or reference to data acceptable to the Administrator) of work performed.*
>
> *(2) The date of completion of the work performed.*

(3) The name of the person performing the work if other than the person specified in paragraph (a)(4) of this section.

(4) If the work performed on the aircraft, airframe, aircraft engine, propeller, appliance, or component part has been performed satisfactorily, the signature, certificate number, and kind of certificate held by the person approving the work. The signature constitutes the approval for return to service only for the work performed.

—U.S. FAR Part 43.9(a)

Regulations to Comply With

There are many regulations that must be complied with to ensure that every flight is legal in the eyes of the national regulatory authority. The list shown in Table 7.4 includes just those regulations that form the basis for corporate flight department maintenance issues in the United States and that require some form for proof of compliance. Non-U.S. operators will find similar regulations promulgated by their national regulatory authority, usually based on applicable ICAO annexes.

An individual should be tasked with ensuring that all aircraft records are maintained properly. In larger departments, this may become a supervisory function due to the number of people involved in the recordkeeping process. Regardless of the situation, a single individual should be given the task of ensuring that the recordkeeping job is done correctly. It may be desirable to have all recordkeeping work be subject to an additional supervisory or quality control function to make sure that record entries are complete and correct.

TABLE 7.4   Regulations for U.S. Flight Department Maintenance Operations

---

Airworthiness Directives
39.3 General

Maintenance, preventive maintenance, rebuilding, and alteration
43.5 Approval for return to service after maintenance . . .
 .7 Persons authorized to perform maintenance . . .
 .9 Content, form and disposition of maintenance . . .records
 .11 Content, form, and disposition of records for inspections . . .

Certification: Airmen other than flight crew members
65.81 General privileges and limitations
 .83 Recent experience requirements

General operating and flight rules
91.7 Civil aircraft airworthiness
 .9 Civil aircraft flight manual, marking and placard requirements
 .203 Civil aircraft: certifications required
 .213 Inoperative instruments and equipment
 .403 General (maintenance)
 .405 Maintenance required
 .409 Inspections
 .411 Altimeter system and altitude reporting equipment tests and inspections
 .413 ATC transponder tests and inspections
 .415 Changes to aircraft inspection programs
 .417 Maintenance records
 .419 Transfer of maintenance records

Computerized Record Tracking Systems

The complexities of modern turbine-powered aircraft and their required maintenance actions are such that maintaining a clear picture of aircraft airworthiness status is difficult without some form of computerized tracking system. These systems are commonly offered as services to flight departments, providing a required inspection and time-controlled item action and status structure for the department to use. The service provider reviews inputs from the subscriber prior to applying those actions to the database and creates status reports to be used for maintenance planning and scheduling. Some services produce maintenance-due lists and work cards to provide the subscriber with inspection and time-controlled item action checklists.

While these services provide a very useful function, they do not take the place of the official recordkeeping function of the department. For instance, actual signatures are required for inspection, maintenance, and AD actions, and AD methods of compliance are required to determine AD status. This function is not normally available on computerized tracking systems. Paper records and actual signatures may no longer be required in the future, but both regulators and prospective buyers want to see them today.

Selecting a computerized recordkeeping system can be a confusing experience because the available systems contain so many features, some useful and some not so useful. The data input mechanism, application of the data to portions of the record, and creation of status and due lists are all fairly standard. The real variables of the systems are the method of portraying airworthiness status and quality control of the data and reports. Some status reports are easier to read and use than others, but the feature that separates the good from the not so good is the vendor's ability to ensure that the data provided by a client make sense (it is up to the operator to ensure their correctness) and are applied properly to the database. Many a frustrating hour has been spent in trying to correct a data-entry mistake or missing entry.

The only way to determine the vendor's ability to perform well in these areas is to ask those who use the systems. A lot is riding on the ability of a computerized recordkeeping system to provide you with accurate, reliable, timely data regarding the airworthiness status of your aircraft; take time and care in selecting a vendor. Most important is to use a system that fits the department's method of operations and that does not require the department to accommodate a feature of the vendor's system that cannot be modified.

Maintenance Records: Fine Points.   Most operators of aircraft, regardless of size, fail to realize and appreciate the fact that the responsibility for maintaining records that accurately reflect the state of airworthiness of an aircraft rests with the owner/operator, not the technician who maintains it. Yes, the technician is responsible for recording the maintenance and inspection work he or she performs on the aircraft, but the final responsibility for an aircraft's records rests with whoever owns up to operating it.

This is important for several reasons. First, the principal method of determining airworthiness, particularly for complex and/or transport-category aircraft, is through an aircraft's status with regard to inspection, required maintenance, compliance with mandatory manufacturer's service bulletins and ADs, and status of life-limited components. Granted, a detailed preflight or postflight inspection will determine obvious airworthiness discrepancies, but the FAA and other national regulators are concerned with whether the aircraft conforms to its original type design and is in a safe condition for flight; the best means of accomplishing this is to comply with the manufacturer's instructions for continued airworthiness (maintenance program), required as a consequence of the certification process.

While many operators (pilots) rely of the integrity of their technicians and maintenance contractors to ensure that all this paperwork is complete, few understand or appreciate the implications of not being in compliance with whatever maintenance and inspection program they use. Other than being in violation of the regulations, the aircraft may not be in a safe condition for flight. Moreover, when it comes time to sell the aircraft, gaps and inconsistencies in the maintenance records may raise questions regarding its true state of airworthiness and value.

Computerized maintenance recordkeeping systems have enabled the corporate operator to plan for upcoming inspections and required maintenance and life-limited items and to track the status of all these requirements. If the combination of source documents (work cards, parts transaction reports, discrepancy actions, etc.) and tracking lists meets regulatory requirements, these systems may constitute the actual aircraft maintenance records. But a word of caution: Computerized maintenance record tracking systems do not automatically provide the operator with a set of records that meet all regulatory requirements for maintenance records.

For instance, if a discrepancy is corrected (the aircraft is repaired), where is this action recorded? Few record tracking systems record repair-only information, merely the fact that a part may have been replaced. Suppose that no part was replaced. Where is this maintenance action recorded?

Regulations require that a current status of ADs be maintained, imposing specific items to be recorded. Most tracking systems do not note the method used to comply with the AD; this is required to be in compliance with the regulations. And merely noting the manufacturer's service bulletin used for compliance may not be adequate either. Some service bulletins offer alternative means of compliance, and these alternatives are seldom noted in computerized systems.

On a procedural note, most tracking systems provide operators with a monthly transaction report, noting the entries made in the previous month. However, many operators fail to check this list against their submissions over the same time period. This is particularly true if a maintenance contractor performs the action, and a transaction report is not submitted to the tracking system service provider. As a consequence, tracking systems may not reflect the actual status of an aircraft due to entry errors and omissions—garbage in, garbage out.

Most flight departments operating turbine-powered aircraft maintain both the required aircraft records and also participate fully in a records tracking system service. The two systems complement one another and act as a system of checks and balances to ensure that all required maintenance is accomplished. This system is particularly impressive when it comes time to sell the aircraft.

Finally, consider the dilemma of losing an aircraft's official maintenance records due to fire, flood, theft, or carelessness. Attempting to reconstruct those records is a time-consuming and imperfect process that may or may not satisfy the regulatory authority or, more important,

Company Private Airline

A telecommunications company bought a competitor whose headquarters were 300 miles away. Company managers foresaw a lengthy transition period in which employees would travel regularly between the two headquarters. Since airline service was spotty and road conditions between the locations were poor, the purchasing company, which already had used corporate aircraft for years, bought a 12-seat turboprop aircraft to provide twice-a-day shuttle service between the two centers.

Over time, the two locations retained their importance, and a third company was acquired, bringing the same requirements for travel as the initial acquisition. As a consequence, a triangle route was established for the turboprop. Now, years after the merger, the small turboprop has given way to a 30-seat jet, providing daily round trips to the same three locations.

a prospective buyer. Since a great deal of the value of the aircraft depends on its official records, it makes good sense to back up those records either by photocopying or electronic imaging. The latter is particularly attractive because companies providing this service often certify the authenticity of the images they produce.

TRAINING

Technician training does not end with AMT school, an inspection authorization refresher, or even aircraft initial training. The world of aviation continues to change with increasing rapidity, particularly manufacturing and maintenance technology. Nondestructive testing, composite repair, data bus technology, and built-in test equipment have created a new world of wonders for the technician within the past decade. A technician who graduated from school more than a decade ago must struggle to stay abreast of the newest hardware and, yes, software.

Like it or not, our aircraft are constantly changing; service bulletins, ADs, alert bulletins, customer bulletins, and new manufacturing methods are literally making our aircraft obsolete, one piece of paper at a time. Manufacturers release a wealth of information concerning aircraft, powerplants, and appliances, but there is often so much information that not much of it gets read and/or absorbed. Whether this flurry of information is absorbed adequately or not does not guarantee that technicians remain knowledgeable of the aircraft in their charge or their craft in general.

Aircraft-specific recurrent training is a must due to these changes and to hear the latest airworthiness problems and cures. How often? Once every 3 years if there is more than one technician working on an aircraft and every 2 years if there is only one. Some of this recurrent training can be obtained at manufacturer's maintenance and operations (M&O) seminars; departments send their technicians to recurrent training one year and to the manufacturer's seminar the next.

Most maintenance training centers around aircraft-specific recurrent courses, but there is much more of value available. Troubleshooting, avionics, and electrical systems basics are quite popular and are credited with extending the basic knowledge of the technician. Some consider these tools that help the productivity of the maintenance department and provide skills that save maintenance hours and lost flights.

State and local environmental and safety agencies may require toxic chemical handling, waste disposal, and special vehicle and industrial safety qualifications for hangar personnel. First aid, CPR, fire fighting, blood-borne pathogens, refueling, and airport security courses may be required too.

How about training for advancement and promotion? Management, personnel relations, finances, and leadership courses probably will make your technicians more productive, part of the team, and promotable. It is unfair to expect an expert technician to perform as a supervisor without proper training. Perhaps the best reason for training technicians is to show them that you value their contribution to the

Maintenance Training

- Aircraft initial
- Aircraft recurrent
- Selected systems
- Manufacturer M&O
- Troubleshooting
- Electronics/avionics
- Support equipment
- Trade shows
- Maintenance resource management
- Environmental/health/safety
- Personal development/advancement (NBAA PDP)

department's efforts sufficiently to invest in them, to show them that you consider them to be professionals and want them to be the best qualified and most productive employees. Investing in their future sends them a message that says, "We value your services; you're here for the long haul." Returns on such messages cannot be measured.

Flight departments regularly spend $15,000 to $30,000 per year on pilots to keep them current in the aircraft they are assigned to fly. But how much is spent on those responsible for the maintenance and inspection of the machines they fly? No such numbers exist, but casual observation would place the number at between $2000 and $4000 per year. Does this make sense? Should less be invested in the people who maintain the aircraft than in those who fly them?

As increasing numbers of "electronic" aircraft enter the fleet, training will become not just nice to have, but essential. However, the technology of the 1960s and 1970s continues to change as well and demands constant upgrading of skills and knowledge for the technician force.

The most persuasive reason for training is to ensure that the abilities of the technician are equal to efficiently troubleshooting an aircraft problem to save money and time and perhaps even a flight itself. As with pilots, a training plan for the flight department should include planned technician courses for each individual for the following year. And once the technician has been to school, record the fact in an individual training/qualifications folder.

Maintenance Resource Management[4]

Maintenance resource management (MRM) is a general process for improving communication, effectiveness, and safety in aircraft maintenance operations. Attention should be given specifically to the implementation and evaluation of MRM training. Much as crew resource management (CRM) was created to address safety and teamwork issues in the cockpit, the FAA and other national regulatory bodies, in conjunction with industry partners, developed MRM to address teamwork deficiencies within the aviation maintenance environment.

MRM is a team-based safety behavior. It teaches managers and maintenance personnel skills that enable them to work safely in a complex system. MRM teaches more than just team skills; it teaches and reinforces an organizational philosophy in which all members of the organization are oriented toward error-free performance. This is accomplished by teaching

- How the effects of individual actions ripple throughout organizations
- How to use available resources safely and effectively
- How to propagate a positive culture of safety in the organizations through specific individual actions

The overall goal of MRM is to integrate the technical skills of maintenance personnel with interpersonal skills and basic human factors knowledge in order to improve communication effectiveness and safety in aircraft maintenance operations.

PASSENGER HANDLING

The passengers carried in the company aircraft are, first, fellow associates and, second, guests or clients of the company. As such, they deserve courtesy and consideration while they are in and around company aircraft. More important, they often are not familiar with aircraft operations, and their safety and wellbeing should be given special attention any time they are in an aircraft operating area.

Maintenance section personnel are often the first contact that passengers have with corporate aviation. Therefore, maintenance personnel carry a special burden because they must ensure that the passengers are cared for properly. Although passenger service representatives and the flight crew normally are responsible for passenger handling, maintenance personnel are an integral part of their care.

All passengers should be greeted warmly, directed to the aircraft or passenger assembly area, assisted with their luggage, and given answers to their questions. A maintenance segment employee will be available to passengers for every launch and recovery.

Passengers should be escorted at all times on the ramp by a line service technician, mechanic, or flight crew member to ensure their safety and to prevent inadvertent damage to the aircraft. If a qualified person is not available to escort passengers, they may be instructed to remain in a safe location until an escort can be arranged.

The aircraft handler or mechanic should remain available at all times before departure to assist the flight crew with baggage or other passenger concerns.

SAFETY

Safety is as important for the maintenance department as it is for the flying side of the house. Perhaps it is more important because more personal injury accidents occur in maintenance operations and in hangars than they do in flight operations. Management commitment to a safety policy and to its enforcement is an essential part of any flight department. Expediency and just plain sloppiness are the principal enemies; constantly keep these unwanted "visitors" in check.

Chapter 8 is devoted entirely to safety, but much of what is presented relates specifically to operational safety. Maintenance safety is equally important; in an effort to ensure that maintenance personnel do not overlook the safety subject, this special maintenance safety section is inserted into the maintenance chapter. However, make sure that at least the first

Safety Policy

Safety is the most important operating rule. It is an essential ingredient in all measurements of success. It is the *direct* responsibility of all personnel connected with the aviation department.

To accomplish the above safety mandate, the company shall operate under the following safety policy:

- Safety shall be considered by all personnel to be an integral and vital part of the successful performance of any job.
- Safety is a paramount part of good operating practice and, therefore, a management function that will always be given priority.
- Direct responsibility for the safety of an operation will rest with the person performing that operation.
- Each employee is responsible for the performance of his or her duties, giving primary concern to his or her own safety and that of fellow employees. The company's guests, property, and equipment are entrusted to their care.
- Management at all levels shall initiate procedures for prompt corrective action to eliminate unsafe acts, conditions, equipment, or mechanical hazards.

and last sections of the next chapter are also reviewed because a healthy overview of safety and the accident/incident response section applies to all.

Safe Hangars for All

Consider the following:

- A passenger has to duck under a wing to get to her airplane on the ramp. She doesn't duck far enough and gets a nasty gash in her forehead.
- The aviation department manager, in a rush to get to his aircraft, turns from a conversation and moves forward in a darkened hangar, impaling himself on a trailing edge static discharge wick.
- A flight department secretary, looking for a technician, falls from an airstair and breaks her wrist.
- A manufacturer's customer service representative slips and falls on a wet hangar floor, injuring his back.

What do these accidents have in common? They all occurred in hangars. What do they not have in common? None of these accidents involved an aviation maintenance technician. Why is this important?

Most people in corporate aviation think of the hangar floor, its shops, and its equipment to be the sole domain of the technician and not the concern of others in the department or outsiders. The mishaps just mentioned tend to debunk that myth, underscoring the need to provide a safe operating environment for all who may venture into the hangar area.

The aircraft hangar is principally the domain of the technician, aircraft cleaner, and hangar attendant—it is these employees who must be protected first. Most corporate flight departments are aware, at least to some degree, of the requirements of the Occupational Safety and Health Administration (OSHA), mandated by federal and state law. These codes specify equipment standards, personal protection devices, operating procedures, and information elements for all workplaces that involve industrial activity. Companies engaged in this type of work are subject to inspections to ensure compliance with the regulations and sanctions if the codes are not met. However, just being in compliance with OSHA and company safety standards does not guarantee that safe operations will occur.

Rather than just compliance with a set of rules that sometimes seem to be of little value except to hinder the worker and his or her company, it is the concept of *protection* that must be considered to ensure workplace safety. Consider the following:

- Aircraft check stand safety rails are provided but not used by technicians.
- Material Safety Data Sheets (MSDS) are prominently displayed, but no employee has ever read them or understands their value.
- Eye protection devices are provided, but maintenance supervisors do not enforce their use.
- An eye wash station is available on the hangar floor, but it has never been tested or flushed.
- No technician has ever viewed available hangar safety videos.

While this fictitious company seemingly is in compliance with most OSHA standards, it is probably unsafe. Why? The attitude of management and employees seems to be that safety is a paperwork exercise and not a necessity. Like people sitting on their seat belts, these are accidents waiting to happen.

Perhaps one of the reasons companies are seemingly in compliance with regulations but are not in practice is that they do not consider safety to be a part of their standard operating procedures (SOPs). That is, even though they have safety rails for check stands, the requirement to use the safety equipment is not written into their normal procedures. However, the real reason may be that supervisors do not take the time to enforce the few simple rules that go along with safe operations around aircraft.

Safety pays! Try replacing a disabled employee if you don't believe this.

• Provide a safe working environment—walking surfaces, noise, light, temperature.

• Use personal protective equipment.

• Provide proper tools and equipment.

• Report unsafe conditions and practices—correct them as soon as possible.

• Educate for safety.

• Regularly inspect work areas for unsafe operating conditions.

The final item on the list needs some explanation. Work areas and practices are subject to a slow deterioration if they are not constantly looked after. The "we've been doing things this way for a long time and they work OK" syndrome creeps into daily operations, and the downward slide begins. If there are safe working standards in place and they are upheld and enforced on a continuing basis, the battle for safety is more than half won. Take time to inspect the hangar area using a checklist (see the following sidebar) at least quarterly. Better yet, have a company or other safety expert look at your facility annually in addition to your inspection efforts.

Basic Hangar Inspection Checklist[5]

• Fire detection and extinguishing equipment

• Personal protective devices—use, maintain

• Work surfaces—floors, stands, ladders, fall hazards

• Housekeeping—spills, trash, clutter, obstacles

• Storage of flammables

• Compressed gasses—storage/use

• Motorized machines—guarding/anchoring

• Environment—ventilation, noise, light, temperature

• Toxic substances—labeling, storage, use, protection

• Electrical, compressed air, water—safety, integrity, availability

• Work procedures

There must be buy-in to these tenets from all levels of management. Without management educating, coaching, demonstrating, and enforcing safe practices, the troops will not do what's needed. Management "must walk the talk" if a safe operating environment is to be created.

Technicians and other hangar workers must be guided and supported in the extra effort it takes to properly position the right check stand or prepare a safety harness for a fall hazard. Without a cooperative effort between management and the workers, safety will not occur in the hanger.

And remember, hangar safety is for everyone, not just the technicians. Safe operating practices must be taught to and lived by all personnel who have access to the hangar. Any person with access to the hangar should either be educated in its hazards or continuously escorted. This is why your automobile service center prominently displays signs forbidding entry to shop areas—the workers know that hazards exist in those areas for the uninitiated and realize that they incur a liability by admitting nonemployees to their work areas. Everyone must be involved in safe hangar operations.

Steps to take:

- Assign hangar safety as a collateral duty to an individual.
- Create a hangar safety plan.
- Conduct regular inspections (see the sidebar on page 7.30).
- Enforce safety regulations.
- Strive for continuous safety improvement.

Thousands of people will be injured in an aviation ground environment this year. Keep your people out of those statistics.

Solo Technicians

Many flight departments have just one AMT. This is the norm for single-aircraft operators and appears to work well in terms of reliability and safety. However, there are significant challenges associated with this work process.

Regardless of the number of technicians assigned, every department is subject to the single-technician phenomenon. Even in large departments, technicians often work alone or with little supervision. And there may not be enough time to allow a second person to review the work of the individual prior to approval for return to service.

Airworthiness.   The name of the game for any AMT is to maintain assigned aircraft in an airworthy condition. In corporate aviation, the pride and personal integrity shown by most technicians make airworthiness a given rather than the ultimate goal. However, having just one brain, one set of eyes, and two hands presents significant barriers to the solo technician.

Regardless of the experience level of the technician, a second opinion from another is always welcome. And a second set of eyes and hands increases the confidence level and speeds completion of the task.

Perhaps the greatest challenge faced by the solo technician is having to be right all the time—a tall order for mere human beings. Using the specified torque value, getting the sequence of wire clips in the correct order, and servicing the hydraulic system to the proper level are all critical items—were they done correctly? Unfortunately, this thought may occur at 2 A.M. when the technician is on the way home from the hangar. Inspection of critical components during an inspection or verifying one's own work on these systems may be the most difficult part of the AMT's job; on some systems, you only get one chance to get it right. Airlines and repair stations have mandatory inspections imposed on their critical systems/component work via required inspection items (RII). This system is a luxury the single technician can seldom afford.

However, the individual may ask a fellow solo practitioner, a pilot experienced in maintenance issues, or an A&P from a maintenance vendor to perform a quality check on their work. Yes, even pilots can be trained to look for errors if they know what to look for.

Personal Safety.   The AMT works in an industrial setting that contains many hazards. The technician often works in an isolated area, surrounded by hazards, where a serious injury may go undetected for a significant period of time. Some companies do not allow technicians to work alone, instead assigning another individual who may not be a technician to work with them. Alternatively, the solo technician may be required to check in with company security at regular intervals or to wear a wireless alerting device to ensure safety.

Administration.   Some estimates claim that 40 percent of an AMT's time is spent on paperwork. While not seemingly productive time, this function is an essential part of the technician's job. This paperwork includes maintenance recordkeeping; keeping manufacturer's directives current; ordering, receiving, and shipping parts; and vendor management. The company probably adds its own administrative requirements to the aviation-related ones, further compounding the problem. The volume of paperwork requiring the technician's attention and the accuracy of the completed work are both problems for a one-person maintenance operation. Any clerical assistance is appreciated.

Help for Singles. Both the single technician and every member of the flight department must realize the difficulties and hazards that confront these individuals—the concept of looking out for one another is especially important when the maintenance department only has one name associated with it. Judicious amounts of assistance, professional and otherwise, will help to ensure quality work and safe technicians.

UPSTAIRS, DOWNSTAIRS

Keeping all members of the flight department informed and up to speed on current and future operations becomes a challenge when the department consists of more than one person. Communications and coordination tasks of the manager's job begin to multiply rapidly as the number and type of personnel grow. Keeping two pilots in the loop is hard enough in small departments, but when AMTs, schedulers, administrators, and purchasing agents are brought into the picture, more of the manager's time becomes devoted to keeping these diverse elements of the team moving in the same direction.
    One of the greatest communications gaps observed in flight departments occurs

Maintenance and Ops on the Same Team

- Encourage frequent visits between the two camps.
- Hold joint pilot and AMT meetings to discuss areas of mutual interest.
- Locate the pilots and AMTs in the same area of the hangar.
- Create quality action teams that consist of people drawn from all departments to solve specific problems.
- Designate an AMT to be present at the launch and recovery of all flights to discuss the airworthiness of the aircraft with the pilots.
- Take AMTs along on flights as observers.
- Designate pilots to assist/observe with scheduled inspections of the aircraft they normally fly.
- Create pilot/AMT teams to manage each aircraft.
- Use AMTs and pilots to conduct in-house aircraft systems and operations training for their counterparts.
- Provide lunch for all hands on a regular basis to encourage interaction between the groups.

between operations personnel (pilots) and maintenance personnel (AMTs). These two groups are highly specialized and usually work well within their respective departments but may not work well at the interface between their specialities. The "they fix 'em, we fly 'em" and "they break 'em, we fix 'em" mind sets describe the gap that may exist between the pilot and AMT. And because pilots traditionally have offices on the second floor of the hangar and AMTs on the first, this rift has been described as the "upstairs, downstairs" phenomenon, a title borrowed from the PBS Masterpiece Theater series that described the interaction of a nineteenth-century British noble family and their servants.

This communications gap that may exist between the two groups can affect the efficient operation of the department in a variety of ways. Misunderstood aircraft discrepancies, poorly scheduled maintenance planning, handling repeat discrepancies, and just being unaware of either the operations or maintenance schedules can cause increased expenses, lowered efficiency, and flights that do not go. If permitted to exist for long, these conditions may grow into feelings of mistrust and hostility between the two departments.

Just think how the two groups might better operate as a team if there were no "stairs" separating them.

KNOW THE REGULATORS

Horror stories abound regarding interaction with the local aviation regulatory representatives, especially with FAA Flight Standards District Offices (FSDO). Red-tagging aircraft for minor airworthiness items, unreasonable ramp checks, unannounced visits that result in fines and airman certificate actions, and general unreasonableness about interactions with the dreaded airworthiness or operations inspector are common aviation lore. Are they true? Some undoubtedly are. How pervasive are these unjustified federal actions? Probably not very.

Personal and business turbojet operations enjoy one of the best accident records and operational reputations in civil aviation. The insurance industry knows this, so it places few restriction on those operations. Airport operators know this and essentially leave corporate operators alone. And most airworthiness and avionics inspectors know this and do the same.

Most airworthiness inspectors have a massive workload placed on them every year through their national work plan. FSDOs are tasked with visiting and surveilling all air agency certificate holders within their geographic area not once but several times during the fiscal year. Scheduled air carriers, air taxi operators, repair stations, instrument shops, and FBOs are all targets of their scrutiny on a continuing basis. Inspectors will tell you that working with some of these operators can be a complex and challenging task. Keeping these companies in compliance with the myriad of FARs and FAA orders is more than a full-time job.

So how much time do they have to monitor and inspect general aviation? Not much. And for the corporate operator who enjoys such a sterling reputation, not much indeed.

Does this mean that you are home free, that you never have to deal with the feds? Probably. Is this a good thing for you and your operation? Probably not.

While you may consider it dancing with the devil, getting to know at least one contact at your local FSDO will benefit you and your operation someday. An aircraft ferry permit, a field sign-off for a 337, and an interpretation of a regulation or AD are all reasons to know a local FAA inspector. And being able to associate a name with a voice or face makes the transaction more friendly.

If you are really feeling brave, why not invite your local airworthiness inspector to visit your facility? While there is an actual Part 91 maintenance inspection procedure listed in the inspector's handbook, chances are that the inspector will be delighted at your hospitality and limit his or her surveillance activities to a detached admiration of your facilities.

Speaking of "the handbook," FAA Order 8300.10, *Airworthiness Inspectors Handbook,*[6] is an invaluable compendium of the way the FAA expects its inspectors to carry out their activities. This tome (two large loose-leaf binders) is a treasure trove of information about acceptable means of compliance, standards, and regulatory processes. And when an inspector hears you referring to "the handbook," the conversation is automatically elevated to a higher plane.

While it is difficult to have a perfect relationship with those who are paid to ensure compliance with the welter of regulations and orders that govern our activities, these people joined the FAA for the same reason we started in our jobs, a love of aviation. They are kindred spirits in many ways. Get to know your fed.

SELLING MAINTENANCE

Every day you tackle the monthly due list, work off discrepancies, and maintain the hangar. Keeping your aircraft airworthy and in good condition is the reason for your existence, so you do it cheerfully and with satisfaction.

Long hours, knotty problems, bad parts, obscure manuals, and sometimes unappreciative pilots do not make the job any easier, but it is your chosen profession, so you enjoy doing it most of the time. It is what is expected of you, so you do your job with little expectation of recognition other than an occasional "Good job" or "Well done" from those who count.

However, did you ever think of the significant contribution the maintenance section provides to the corporate aviation effort? The name of the game is airworthiness—without it, nothing happens. The complexities and number of items that go into the concept of airworthiness are not well understood outside the AMT fraternity. Pilots and schedulers wonder what takes so long to approve an aircraft return to service, managers wonder why you need another set of hands, and the accountants always ask why windshields cost so much. The truth is that most people, even aviation people, do not understand what it takes to maintain a modern turbine-powered aircraft to the standards required by the FAA, the manufacturer, and most important, you. Aviation maintenance technicians have been doing their job quietly and efficiently for so long that everyone has come to expect miracles from their technicians. And like Rodney Dangerfield, they may not be getting the respect they deserve.

Why not tell them more about what is involved in the maintenance process? Why not let the rest of the department and the folks downtown in on what it takes to keep the aircraft in excellent condition?

The immediate effect probably will be greater respect from all concerned; the long-term effects may be more significant. If the department manager understands how many individual actions and work cards it takes to perform a phase inspection, including those requiring two sets of hands, he or she may be more willing to provide temporary or permanent help or to send the aircraft out to a maintenance contractor to complete the work. If the accounting department understands how hard you try to get the best deal for rotables and replacement parts, there may be fewer questions about the invoices. And if senior company management understands some of your money-saving successes or notable airworthiness safety finds you make in the course of your work, the entire flight department's image will benefit.

By nature, most technicians are not predisposed to blowing their own horn or selling their virtues to anyone. However, a little low-level selling may bring big benefits.

The suggestions shown in the sidebar may help get more recognition for the maintenance function and its personnel. The most important lesson: Don't hide your light under a basket.

Good maintenance is not an option; my airplanes don't fly without it.

—AIRLINE CEO

Techniques for Promoting Maintenance

* Keep records of your searches for major parts and services, recording the quotes for each. When significant differences exist, share these with your manager and those within accounting. A formal memo may be appropriate for major finds.

* When an inspection turns up a significant fault or defect, make a photographic record of it and share it with the pilots and company management. If you can save the part or component, use it as a dramatic visual aid.

* Take the time to show schedulers, dispatchers, and pilots what is involved in a major inspection. Invite them to the hangar deck to observe notable procedures and inspection techniques, e.g., landing gear swings, nondestructive testing, electronic BITE procedures, etc.

* Become involved in a company nonaviation activity such as an employee research team, sports team, or charitable activity. Most people in the company do not know the aviation maintenance section exists. Let them know it does.

REFERENCES

1. *NBAA Management Guide.* Washington: NBAA, 2001.

2. *www.opspecs.com/AFSDATA/MMELs.*

3. Spencer, F. W., and Schurman, D. L., *Reliability Assessment at Airline Inspection Facilities,* Vol. III: *Results of an Eddy Current Inspection Reliability Experiment.* DOT/FAA/CT-92-12. National Technical Information Service, 1992.

4. From FAA Advisory Circular 120-72, *Maintenance Resource Management Training.*

5. See *OSHA Handbook for Small Businesses.* OSHA 2209. Washington: U.S. Government Printing Office, 1992. Also see NFPA 409, *Standard for Aircraft Hangars.* Quincy, MA: National Fire Protection Association, 1995, and NFPA 410, *Standard on Aircraft Maintenance.*

6. *www.faa.gov/avr/afs/faa/8300/8300.html.*

CHAPTER 8
SAFETY

SAFETY PROGRAMS

Corporate aviation enjoys an enviable safety record, maintaining an accident rate equivalent to that of the major scheduled airlines. In fact, corporate aviation has proved safer than the airlines in a number of recent years (see Table 8.1). How does this happen?

Dedicated professional pilots and mechanics, good management, excellent equipment, setting and sticking to standards, and perhaps most important, a corporate and departmental culture of conservatism are the causal factors in a safe operation. This last item is most important because safety as a concept and safe operations specifically are largely intangible; safety is an *attitude,* a mind set established at the highest levels of the organization and projected downward through the ranks. While it is possible to run a safe flight department without a high-level commitment to safety in the organization, this is a rarity and a credit to the professionalism of the individuals within the department.

However, since safety is essentially an attitude and way of life, it must be constantly demonstrated and reinforced within the organization. Merely telling professionals to be safe will not work either. Senior pilots and mechanics who go by the book, take the conservative approach, and comment on unsafe and potentially unsafe practices they observe are the backbone of a safe operation. Other practices reinforce the safety message as well:

- Recurring references to standards
- Constant training
- Required reading of safety materials
- Review of standardization, regulatory, and procedural materials
- Spontaneous discussions of aircraft systems, procedures, and regulations
- Spot inspections of facilities and records

Recognition of safe practices helps, too. Company and departmental recognition serves as local reinforcement, whereas the National Business Aviation Association (NBAA) Corporate Flying Safety Awards Program serves as a national incentive.

Safety as a concept does not sell well, but daily practice of an ingrained safety culture does sell.

Crafting the Safety Function

The notion to start a safety function in the flight department normally comes from the outside. The company safety or audit department discovers that the corporate flight department does not have such a function, is suitably shocked, and decrees that there will be one. Or an insurance safety auditor or outside safety and compliance evaluation consultant similarly clucks his or her tongue and strongly suggests that the department have such a worthy function.

TABLE 8.1 U.S. Aviation Accident Rates (NBAA)

Year	General Aviation, Total/Fatal	Air Taxi, Total/Fatal	Airlines, Total/Fatal	Corporate/Executive,[*] Total/Fatal	Business,[†] Total/Fatal
1992	8.36/1.80	3.86/1.22	0.146/0.032	0.210/0.080	2.17/0.86
1993	8.94/1.74	4.16/1.15	0.181/0.008	0.230/0.070	2.02/0.52
1994	8.96/1.81	4.58/1.40	0.168/0.030	0.180/0.070	1.81/0.51
1995	7.72/1.55	4.39/1.41	0.267/0.022	0.250/0.110	2.04/0.67
1996	7.09/1.34	4.44/1.43	0.276/0.036	0.140/0.060	1.71/0.34
1997	7.26/1.39	2.65/0.48	0.309/0.025	0.230/0.060	1.41/0.39
1998	7.47/1.41	2.08/0.45	0.297/0.006	0.091/0.000	1.14/0.30
1999	6.42/1.15	2.36/0.36	0.296/0.011	0.230/0.130	1.40/0.40
2000	6.32/1.18	2.25/0.62	0.311/0.016	0.125/0.060	1.28/0.37
2001	6.56/1.22	2.12/0.53	0.239/0.036	0.108/0.031	1.06/0.23
2002	6.53/1.31	1.93/0.56	0.217/0.000	0.116/0.029	1.08/0.36

[*]Aircraft owned or leased and operated by a corporation or business firm for the transportation of personnel or cargo in furtherance of the corporation's or firm's business and which are flown by professional pilots receiving a direct salary or compensation for piloting.
[†]The use of aircraft by pilots (those not receiving direct salary of compensation for piloting) in conjunction with their occupation or in the furtherance of a business.

Rarely, if ever, does the realization occur to the flight department manager or an individual within the department that a safety function is needed. And if it does, much of what occurs is done with a strong "cookbook" or fill-in-the-blanks approach:

- Designate a safety person.
- Conduct a safety survey.
- Convene the safety committee(s).
- Devise an action plan.
- Track the program.

And watch the entire concept slowly fade into inactivity.

Yes, most safety programs are started for the wrong reasons, run by the wrong people, and supported by virtually no one. Safety is viewed as being a commodity rather than part of the culture. Unfortunately, safety is often seen as a block to fill in the organizational chart or a function to satisfy someone else's requirement. Many people would like to compartmentalize safety into a commodity or well-defined function. However, it cannot be purchased by the bushel or six-pack.

Reasons. Why do we want a safety program in the first place? Because a consultant said you needed one? Because it looks good to the insurance company? I hope not. I hope that the reason goes something like the rationale in the following sidebar.

Far-fetched? Overstated? Suitable for framing only? I hope not. However, like so many other things in life, the person who issued these words must be willing not only to talk the talk but also to walk the talk.

Unfortunately, safety, accident prevention, and risk management are not all things that can be initiated and sustained by using some organizational, administrative, or dictatorial formula. The old cliché that safety is an attitude, a mind set rather than a function, is never more true than when attempting to set up and maintain the function within an organization. So how should safety and accident prevention be approached?

Rather than using an organizational or functional approach to safety, try a principles approach. This method recognizes the fact that if a set of simple tenets or guidelines is put forth and revisited from time to time, both the principles and dedication to them eventually will become a part of the department's culture.

What should be the principles? Check the Safety Tenets sidebar: These items could be merely items suitable for framing and not for action. Somebody has to get behind these values and ensure that they are lived by members of the department. This means a dedication by the leadership of the organization to promote and defend the concept of safety. The leadership must be willing to draw a distinct line between safe and unsafe—to not equivocate when operational standards are about to be compromised.

While this means that the aviation department manager, chief pilot, and director of maintenance all have to be stalwart and constant supporters of the principles, they may not be enough leadership to make it a reality. The company chairperson, president, chief financial officer (CFO), and flight department reporting senior all have to internalize and live the principles as well.

Standards. Having operational standards that are realistic, written, and supported is certainly more than half the battle on the way to safe operations. However, be careful how you treat your standards. If the runway is 3800 feet long and the minimum length for your type of aircraft is 4000 feet, then look for another airport. Once you start placing conditions on standards—"Harry is the best pilot we have," "The wind is right down the runway," "The brakes are new"—they lose their classification as a standard. They become guidelines, values to be tampered with. While guidelines are needed, too, make sure that guidelines are not used where standards should be.

Safety Rationale

Operating complex, high-speed aircraft involves a certain element of risk. While we provide our pilots and technicians with the best training, exceed Federal Aviation Administration (FAA) and manufacturer maintenance requirements, and set high operating goals for ourselves, an awareness of the potential hazards associated with this type of operation will provide a healthy mind set for all hands. To this end, all department members will be active members of the department's safety team, conditioned to communicate and act on potentially unsafe items when discovered. We prize curious and inquiring minds dedicated to safety and hazard reduction.

Safety Tenets

- Our job involves risk.
- Training is important.
- Exceed FAA and manufacturers' maintenance requirements.
- Set high levels of operating standards.
- Hazard awareness is important.
- Safety belongs to everyone.
- Communicate safety ideas.
- Act on safety issues.
- Curiosity and inquiry about safety are important.

For instance, if you have a guideline stating that flight crews will attempt to touch down with a minimum of 1 hour of fuel on board, this provides some wiggle room when an air traffic control (ATC) delay or weather diversion reduces this margin to 50 minutes. However, if you have a standard that says, "Thou shalt not take off when the prevailing visibility or equivalent RVR is less than one-quarter mile," this means that 10 feet less than that value is not acceptable.

A word about safety being everybody's business: This may mean that the function is so diffuse, so indistinct that it becomes nobody's business. Specific issues and assignments must be made to ensure that all are constantly reminded of the principles. Hangar, passenger, ATC, fueling, industrial, fire, operational, maintenance, and hazardous materials safety are all subsets of the safety equation and should be focused on regularly to ensure that adequate attention is given to them. Individuals can be assigned the task of monitoring and reporting on these individual aspects of safety. How you do that in your operation is best left to individual leadership styles and corporate cultures. However, everyone within the department must be involved.

Communications. Communicating about safety is an important part of maintaining sufficiently high levels of awareness and interest within a group. Safety posters, reading files, and internal training sessions are all means of keeping the subject of safety fresh in the minds of those who need it. However, the most effective means of doing this is personal communications between individuals about specific safety issues. An aware and concerned staff will perpetuate safety concerns if they view it as something that is valued by management.

I think I learned more about flying in general, the aircraft I flew, and handling unusual situations through informal conversations with my fellow pilots and technicians. It is the exchange of ideas among concerned individuals that not only answers immediate questions but also stimulates an abiding curiosity within the participants, providing for a lifetime of seeking and finding. This joint search and discovery technique works well because it is a social activity as well as a learning activity. It works well for learning as well critical assessment of established processes and procedures.

For example, if the standard operating procedure (SOP) regarding checklist usage is unrealistic or undoable on quick-turnaround flights, the person who first realizes this should initiate action to change it. This requires communicating the perceived fault to peers and supervisors alike. Moreover, it means devising a new procedure, testing it, and *selling* it to the rest of the department. Sound like safety? Probably not, but it is this level of curiosity and concern about day-to-day operations that are the embodiment of the safety principle process. However, it will not happen if this type of behavior does not come from the top. This means that the leadership must show the way, prime the pump, and sustain a level of interest and concern about safety.

A footnote has to do with the small flight department, usually defined as comprising a single aircraft and one or two individuals. While it may not be obvious initially, this type of operation may need a safety program more than a larger department. Why? Because there are fewer brains to be curious and creative about safety. And small departments rarely have well-developed standard policies and procedures from which to work. Further, these individuals have many more administrative and operational issues to occupy their time than do individuals within larger organizations. Since there is little formality involved in small operations, well-established principles seem to work better than do hard procedures.

Every accident, no matter how minor, is a failure of the organization.

—JEROME LEDERER

Leadership. Leadership may be the single most important element in ensuring safe operations and continuing awareness of the elements comprising safety. Without an enlightened and credible leadership, safety principles and values will have a hard time penetrating the day-to-day operational tempo or competing for time between the press of making the flight schedule and completing next year's budget.

In addition, decreeing safety or bludgeoning people with safety prescriptions will only drive them further from the safety goal. Constant example, quiet pressure, abiding curiosity, a bias toward action, and upholding established standards will provide the type of leadership necessary to make safe principles a reality throughout the department. The rest of the department is watching: The minute the leaders back away from the principles, the program starts to crumble. Leadership is important. Dedication to standards is important.

In my consulting practice I am often asked about establishing the safety function and making it work. I used to provide a list of organizational, functional, and action elements that seemed to work in other departments. But these measures rarely were effective just because these procedures worked for *other departments*. Trying to graft them onto another organization is difficult and often counterproductive. Thus I started a dialog with those who asked about crafting the safety function, a dialog that went to the heart of their values and principles regarding their company, aviation operations, and safety in general. This dialog usually resulted in the manager arriving at a set of principles that would enable a flight department to view and act on safety in a productive manner.

Learning from Others. Does all this mean that we cannot learn from others, that we cannot borrow ideas that have worked for others? Not at all. Indeed, the very fact that you *talk to others about their safety organization* is part of the process that will help you start successful initiatives within your own organization. However, merely copying another's program by rote without carefully weighing how the elements of that program will fit your organization and culture is a recipe for failure. What works for one organization may not work well for another. However, collecting ideas from others and carefully using them to craft your own safety function should provide you with a better program.

Further, while there does not have to be a standardized organizational or administrative approach to the safety function, some program structure does help. Specifically, a plan stating program goals, someone to shepherd it along, and a means to measure its effectiveness are the minimum elements of a safety program. These are also the basic elements of any management process: Plan, execute, control. Exhaustive plans, program documents, safety committees, routine reports, weekly training, or monthly inspections may prove counterproductive to safety program goals, however. *Simple is better* should be the watchword for a safety program. Perhaps even a minimalist approach is the best guidance for an effective program. Structure, yes; superstructure, no.

There are no prefabricated structures or formulas that lead to successful safety programs. *Each must be crafted individually* to accommodate the leadership styles, operational requirements, and corporate cultures. However, having a set of principles that lead to safety, leading people to believe in them, and stimulating participation by all will build a very adequate safety function.

Model Safety Program

"OK people, let's settle down. Today's topic is thunderstorms; anybody ever get caught in one?" Pete's question brought knowing smiles from the other three pilots as they settled down to 30 minutes of honest discussion about convective weather. At the end of the half hour, the four pilots had reviewed the weather phenomenon, how it was reported, the consequences of getting too close, and how to avoid it.

Did this mini-training session occur at Flight Safety? Simuflite? An airline? None of the above. This was the regular bimonthly pilots meeting at the Acme Corporation Flight Department. While this is not the company's real name, nor is Pete's, the tale you are about to read is real and, hopefully useful. It is the story of a really good safety program, a complete, well-crafted group of exercises, policies, procedures, and reports. More important, it a very workable program for a small flight department.

Small departments traditionally have found it difficult to mount an identifiable safety program. Not enough—pick one—people, time, resources, or money is the usual reason for not having a safety program. In reality, the reason may be lack of appreciation of the need for a *continuing safety consciousness* in aviation (Pete's words).

Pete is Acme's flight department safety manager. He reports directly to the director of aviation and is also a line captain piloting the department's Gulfstream IV. The department's reporting senior, Acme's chairman, occasionally chats with Pete, seeking his opinion about the state of safety within the department. This chain-of-command leaping process is OK with the director of aviation because everybody in the organization is kept in the safety loop—there are no secrets.

Company Program. Not surprisingly, the chairman strongly supports an active and aggressive safety program throughout the company. Each aspect of corporate operations follows both corporate and departmental safety policies and goals. Every employee receives regular safety training, an active safety hazard reporting program exists, and hazard and risk containment is measured. Every employee, especially managers, is graded on his or her safety performance. With this background, the safety manager's job is made easier, but with all the emphasis on safety, his performance is closely noted.

Both company and flight department safety programs start with an identical statement of health and safety policy. From this policy, annual goals are developed within the company and its departments (see following sidebars). Each departmental goal is made a part of both the aviation manager's and Pete's annual reviews. And the goals are substantive, serious goals that drive every part of the department's safety program. This is a serious, substantive program, not just fluff to keep the boss happy.

Sample Flight Department Health and Safety Policy

In all aspects of our operations we will provide a healthy and safe working environment for our employees, contractors, customers, and the public. To accomplish this, we will

- Comply with applicable health and safety laws and regulations.
- Take the initiative to provide appropriate guidance where controlling laws or regulations do not exist, including using the resources of the corporate Environmental, Health, and Safety Department.
- Recognize that health and safety are essential elements of our work and that no task is so important that it will be preformed at the risk of health and safety.
- Use internal and external audits and inspections to eliminate unacceptable hazards that are likely to cause injury or illness.
- Emphasize awareness of safety programs and policies through corporate support and training.
- Set quantifiable safety objectives and targets that result in continuous improvement.
- Set safety performance objectives in employee and contractor evaluations, rewards, and recognition.
- Strive to achieve a healthier and safer workplace.

All employees are responsible for their own safety and the safety of others.

Each company department receives an annual safety, health, and fire audit. Audit findings are discussed, and remedial measures are instituted. These measures and their effectiveness are tracked at the departmental level and reviewed by safety, health, and environment personnel quarterly. Specialized segments of Acme, such as the flight department, are audited every 3 years by an outside organization qualified in the specialty field. The results of these specialty audits are integrated into the department's overall safety goals.

Sounds like a lot of paperwork and bureaucracy, doesn't it? In reality, the safety program is so well integrated and ingrained into the corporate culture that it has become part of the daily routine. Efforts have been made to streamline and simplify the recordkeeping and tracking aspects of the program. This is proved by the fact that risk-factor analysis and good safety practices are a part of every decision and daily operation; employees are safety conscious in every action taken.

Everybody Participates.   Back to the bimonthly pilots' meeting. Safety is just one part of the meeting, although an important part of it. The department manager uses the meeting to disseminate and discuss important departmental issues. An agenda is published prior to the meeting, extraneous discussion is minimized, and a 90-minute time limit is set for the entire meeting.

While we have just talked about the pilots' participation in the safety program, everybody within the flight department participates. The department's three aviation maintenance technicians (AMTs) have their own goals, meetings, and training. Since they also fly as flight technicians, they are often made a part of the pilots' meetings and are consulted on aircraft operational safety issues.

Acme maintains a large hangar that is home for tenant flight departments. Several line technicians and facility maintenance personnel provide necessary aircraft movement, fueling, and cleaning services to the tenants. Because of the variety of tasks they provide, their safety program is extensive, incorporating many fire and facility safety items.

The department flight coordinator gets involved through monitoring all aspects of the program, tracking and ensuring that reports are submitted in a timely manner. She also is responsible for ensuring that flights are not scheduled that exceed flight department standards and limits and that passengers are aware of and understand them.

Standards.   Acme considers written standards and procedures to be the foundation for its safety activities. The reasoning behind this is that doing things the same way every time leaves little room for error. When an activity does not fit exactly into the company SOP mold, existing policies and related procedures form the basis for the new action. If an employee is still unsure, the advice is, "Stop and ask."

Therefore, every aspect of Acme's flight operations is covered by comprehensive, mature, and up-to-date standards, limits, and procedures. All standards are reviewed annually for relevance and for fit with other SOPs. And if a procedure is found to be unsafe or a new procedure is needed, a company "green sheet" is issued to act as an interim change to existing procedures.

Sample Flight Department Safety Program Goals

- Provide safe and efficient air transportation for our customers.

- Maintain an active aviation safety program in which all personnel participate and take an active role in the identification, reduction, and elimination of hazards.

- Incorporate safety planning into all activities.

- Review the safety of all new equipment, facilities, operations, and procedures.

- Reduce insurance costs.

Sample Safety Goals for 2003

- Review crew rest procedures/policies for single-aircraft operations.
- Continue to study department approach and landing procedures.
- Study and suggest runway incursion avoidance countermeasures.
- Investigate extended-range operational procedures for the (soon to be received) G-V aircraft.
- Study the safety, human factors, and procedural aspects of G-V cockpit automation.
- Maintain communication between crew members.

Training. Acme flight department employees probably receive more training than most because of the company's focus on safety. In addition to normal aircraft-related training, they receive a number of safety-related courses on a recurring basis:

- Company/industry safety trends/performance
- Hazardous/toxic materials handling
- First aid/CPR/blood-borne pathogens
- Hangar fire equipment, including fire extinguisher operation
- Hangar/aircraft evacuation
- Environmental issues
- Company/Occupational Safety and Health Administration (OSHA) safety standards

Training is conducted by company safety and health specialists, department personnel, and outside agencies. Completion of training is not optional; it must be conducted within designated intervals, or it is considered a performance issue. It is the responsibility of the individual to ensure that he or she completes the training in a timely manner.

Inspection. Every month Pete and the maintenance and line service safety representatives inspect their areas of responsibility for hazards. Each uses a checklist and takes particular note of changes to the environment since the last inspection. Every other month they select a member of their work group (pilots, technicians, and line service personnel) at random and ask him or her to conduct the inspection; this provides a fresh look at the areas of interest and gets all members of the department involved in the process. Apparently, some of the best observations/comments come from the rank-and-file members of the department. Every few months the aviation manager will accompany one of these inspectors on his or her rounds to remain familiar with the domain.

Discrepancies uncovered during the inspections are recorded and tracked for corrective action. A side benefit of tracking these items is that trends can be spotted easily and long-term remedial action taken.

Reporting. Hazard reporting has been a feature of Acme's corporate life for decades. "See a hazard; report a hazard" has long been a watchword of the company. While employees are not graded on the number of hazard reports they turn in, their submission is encouraged.

Reporting forms are readily available, but because of the natural aversion most people have to paperwork, employees are encouraged to communicate their safety concerns verbally to their safety representatives. The representatives then fill out the form, enter it into their tracking system, and submit it to Pete for coordination, funding, etc. Reports may be submitted anonymously using a serial number to identify the report.

Approximately once every 2 months Pete and the safety coordinators meet to discuss the hazard reports, inspection findings, and progress on ongoing corrective measures. The frequency of this meeting is linked to the number of reports, findings, and actions pending. Once a decision is made, a formal reply is drafted to the submitter to close the loop. Replies to anonymous submissions are made via a sealed envelope placed in the department's report form bin.

Bits and Pieces

- *Safety stand down.* One day a year the entire company stops work to reflect on what each department does, how safely they do it, and how to make their actions safer.

- *Awards celebration.* Safety awards are treated seriously and as a cause for celebration. Each department and individual employees receive their annual awards at a formal dinner held at a classy hotel or restaurant. Spouses and significant others are invited.

- Pete does not lead all safety training discussions; he calls on fellow employees to research a timely topic and act as a group facilitator for the discussion.

- Required reading is accomplished by e-mail. Only high-priority, essential information is e-mailed to employees, emphasizing its importance. Lengthy directives and articles are either summarized or truncated to ease the load on employee mail boxes.

- Brief notes of departmental safety meetings are published to provide absentees with their essential messages.

- The numbers of hazard reports, inspection discrepancies, and other incidents are counted to keep track of them and to establish a measure of safety within the flight department. The numbers are not tied to any absolute measure but are used to measure trends.

Day-to-Day. The safety program has been in place for almost 2 years and has taken root in the flight department culture. Pilots suggest topics for discussion sessions, flight technicians regularly submit anomaly reports, and hangar inspections are done well before they are due. More important, safety issues are discussed regularly at all levels within the department, and recommendations are made informally to management.

Can all this be linked to Pete's energy and enthusiasm? Sorry Pete, the chairman beat you to the punch. While Pete runs an excellent safety program, the boss paved the way for it all to happen.

The Team. Notice that safety is not a one-person operation either at Acme or in its flight department. Everyone gets involved. Everybody has a piece of the action; no one escapes the safety issue. However, since safety is an activity that is held in high regard within the company, no one feels put out by it, and all willingly cooperate in something that is considered *just another part of the job.*

More important, safety literally starts at the top of the organization. The chairman lets his subordinates know that safe operations are a valued goal within the company; the word rapidly filters down to the bottom of the organization. The seriousness with which safety is regarded is proved regularly via hirings, firings, promotions, demotions, bonuses, and lack of bonuses.

Thus Pete's job is made easier by his boss, his boss's boss, and so on. However, because of the emphasis on safety, Pete also has to deliver an active, credible program.

Building In Safety

The old issue of "How safe are we?" keeps coming up. The simplistic answer of "We really must be safe because we've never had an accident" does not really hold water. The flight department could be an accident waiting to happen, just waiting for the right set of circumstances to occur. No, the real answer to the question may be yet another question: "How safe do we want to be?"

Safety comes in degrees. If we kept the aircraft perpetually at rest in the hangar, we would be 100 percent safe because there would be no risk involved. However, the moment that the aircraft is moved, even within the hangar, risk is incurred. If we remain within the design operating envelope, keep the aircraft completely airworthy, and never choose an unfavorable environment, our chances of having an accident are minimized. Yet the variables involved in operating turbojet aircraft around the world are virtually infinite; with this infinitude comes a bottomless pit of *risk*.

Limiting Risk. If we limit exposure to risk, we can make our operation safer. However, limiting our risk also limits our available utility for a given aircraft. If we only put our Citation Bravo into airports with precision approaches, full approach lights, visual approach slope indicators, and sea-level runways at least 300 feet wide and 7000 feet long, we greatly reduce our risk. However, we limit ourselves to a very few airports and thereby reduce our ability to make full use of this wonderful business transportation tool.

At the other end of the risk-avoidance spectrum, if we place no limits on where the aircraft can go except to remain within the specified type design limits of the aircraft, we may be exposing ourselves to significant risk. For example, if our runway calculations show that the Part 91 landing field length is 2980 feet, nicely fitting an available 3000 foot runway, we may not be providing a sufficient margin for error. Wind variability, pilot technique, obstacles, runway surface, and brake condition all bear on our ability to get the beast stopped, regardless what the "certified" runway performance numbers show. However, how much of a safety factor do you build into this process?

Somewhere between "more than enough" and "that's a little tight" lies the right amount. Since Goldilocks is not available to tell us when it is "just right," we have to figure it out for ourselves.

The landing field length example is just one of many risk assessments we make every day. Others include

- Do I have enough fuel?
- Is the balanced field length adequate for a damp runway?
- How much baggage will the chairman's wife bring?
- Will the destination weather stay above minimums?
- Can the newly designated captain handle it?

Every day we make these evaluations and attempt to err on the safe side of these and many other operational decisions. Why not help the process by precalculating the risk and assigning safety factors to the most common elements of our operations?

Increasing the Margins. If you have ever been an airline or charter operator, you are familiar with a few of the other additional regulations that provide an additional measure of safety. Airport weather reporting, takeoff and landing runway requirements, minimum pilot time to act as pilot in command (PIC), takeoff alternates, additional maintenance quality control measures, and the sterile cockpit are but a few. Therefore, why does the traveling public need an additional measure of safety that the business/personal operator does not?

When the U.S. Congress created Title 49 of the *U.S. Code* in the dim recesses of time, it made it clear that "When prescribing a regulation or standard, . . . the Administrator shall (1) consider—(A) the duty of an air carrier to provide service with the highest possible degree of safety in the public interest; and (B) differences between air transportation and other air commerce. . . ." This means that the paying passenger deserves a higher degree of safety and, by implication, that a greater amount of risk aversion is applied to the standards prescribed by the FAA.

Yet the corporate flight department provides its parent company with an *alternative* to the airlines and charter operators. In doing so, there is an implied promise that in providing the alternative, not only will the level of service be equal to or greater than that delivered by the airlines/charter operators but also the level of safety will be equal to or greater than that delivered by the ticket takers. Think about it: The alternative form of air transportation that we offer has to be *at least as safe* or our bosses would likely balk at the deal. Whatever the risk assessment or level of safety you provide, corporate aviation must be doing something right because we are safer than the airlines and charter operators year after year. But, why? Luck? Talent? Good looks? Probably not. Most crews undergo regular recurrent training and adhere to a set of standards and procedures set forth in their flight operations manual (you do have one, don't you?). The point is that someone had the foresight to provide a script for everyone in the department that dictates how each operational evolution within the department is accomplished. From flight planning through conferring with the aviation maintenance technician after the trip, we all abide by a well-defined set of procedures. It is this regularity, this *discipline* of everyone doing it the same way every time, that provides us with a level of *risk reduction,* an additional *safety cushion* that brings predictability and solace to your department.

Well, truth be told, not all flight departments have a good set of standards and limits that will provide this additional safety. Unfortunately, many operations manuals tell more about completing expense reports than safely taking off or landing. There are certain critical areas that require attention regardless of the type of operation.

Critical Areas. Over the past decade the Flight Safety Foundation (FSF) has produced some landmark studies identifying critical areas of both airline and corporate operations that lead to a high incidence of accidents. The Controlled Flight into Terrain (CFIT) and Approach and Landing Accident Reduction (ALAR) studies have unearthed a number of problem areas that require our attention (see sidebar).

A casual glance at the list may elicit such comments as, "We know that" or "We practice that in the simulator." However, does everyone in your flight department have the same understanding of the hazard and consider similar limitations and procedures to reduce the potential risk? If not, you are literally winging it, leaving the decision-making process up to individuals, without the benefit of guidance that will permit everyone to approach these hazards with a common understanding. While your captains are well paid to recognize and evaluate potential hazards and to take appropriate action, the variability in each individual's approach to these hazards is

CFIT/ALAR Problem Areas

- Nonprecision instrument approaches
- Lack of altitude call-outs
- Lack/nonuse of SOPs
- Failure to execute a missed approach
- Unstabilized/rushed approaches
- Approaches in low light/darkness
- Approaches in poor visibility
- Wet/contaminated runway operations
- Optical illusions associated with above
- Disregard of radio altimeter

CFIT/ALAR Antidotes

- SOPs
- Approach briefings
- Altitude call-outs
- Stabilized approach parameters
- Sterile cockpit
- Automation awareness
- Runway safety factor
- Contaminated runway factors
- Nonprecision approach procedures
- Night approach visual vertical guidance lighting
- Crew resource management policy

Courtesy of the Flight Safety Foundation (see *www.flightsafety.org/cfit1.html*).

often quite great. Why not provide them with the guidance they need to reduce risk to a minimum?

Safer Operations.   As you begin to build additional safety into your operations manual, consider the best approach to take before ruling out possible procedures or limits. For instance, instead of issuing a "no nonprecision approaches" decree, take a look at the FSF ALAR recommendations: Construct constant-angle approaches, use visual descent points, employ VNAV, and explore possible pitfalls. Thus, while nonprecision approaches have been identified as a significant hazard, intelligent *risk-reduction techniques* can reduce the potential hazard and still allow the use of this common instrument approach procedure.

Similarly, short, slippery runways can be handled if some forethought is applied. Many flight departments arbitrarily set minimum runway lengths for their various aircraft: "The Citation will never be operated out of runways less than 4000 feet long." While this may be a good guide for the scheduler to use when dealing with passengers wishing to go to inappropriate destinations, this provides very little substantive guidance to flight crews regarding "how much is enough runway?"

Airline and charter crews have lived with the fact that they can only count on 60 percent of the runway when planning a destination. While the addition of a runway safety factor makes good sense, does the arbitrary reduction of 40 percent of the runway make sense? Apparently not, since the FAA is actively considering a change to Part 135 that would impose a reduction of just 15 percent of the available runway. Whatever the reduction, the concept of providing for a bit more runway to accommodate the previously mentioned variables that affect every takeoff and landing makes good sense.

However, how much is enough safety factor? Since the FAA's original 60 percent was apparently an arbitrary figure, the factor remains up to the individual flight department. Is 10 percent enough? How about the proposed 15 percent? How comfortable do you want to be when your pilots are going about their daily business? The concept is valid: Choose your factor, and make sure everybody in the department uses it. A final thought: Why not add the safety factor to the computed runway requirement? This makes the computation easier— it's just like figuring how much of a tip to add to the dinner check.

While I am on the subject, how much runway do you add for a wet or snowy runway? If you are operating a newly certificated aircraft, the decision is made for you within a special section of the runway performance tables; these numbers are a part of the certification criteria and not subject to negotiation. Most aircraft certified more than a few years ago provide supplementary data for contaminated runway operations; these data are not mandatory, merely available to use as the operator sees fit. The point is that adding an arbitrary 15 percent, as required for charter operations, or 50 percent, because the guy you flew with in the simulator last time said so, may not be an adequate amount to get the machine stopped. Use the supplementary data, even though they may recommend a 200 percent addition in icy conditions. No supplementary data for your aircraft? Do some research into what other manufacturers recommend, and adopt what you feel is reasonable. But do adopt something.

Back to a question raised earlier: How much fuel? While the FAA and the International Commercial Aviation Organization (ICAO) require enough to get to the destination and alternate plus 45 minutes, this may not be enough because of a variety of delays encountered along the route. A number of flight departments designate a minimum landing fuel quantity for each aircraft type, normally equating to at least 30 minutes of flight time based on low-altitude holding airspeed fuel consumption. This number provides the pilot with an in-flight target value to shoot for that lies somewhere between the FAA requirements and low-level fuel light illumination. Whatever the amount, it provides an additional safety factor that flight crews can use in-flight.

Perspective.   Obviously, the addition of limitations, standards, and procedures can be overdone. The reason the boss bought the aircraft in the first place was to have some additional flexibility that the airlines do not have. Taking away all or most of that flexibility robs the company of a valuable business tool. However, operating just to Part 91 standards does not meet the implied contract between the flight department and the company to provide on-demand air transportation that is *at least as safe as the airlines.* The answer lies somewhere in between Cessna 152 and Boeing 757 operations—you choose the point along that continuum you wish to be.

Do not overlook limitations imposed by your insurance policy. Flight crew qualifications, supplementary maintenance procedures, and minimum airport requirements may be specified for your operation. Additional guidance may be found in the *NBAA Business Aviation Safety Program Manual* (*www.nbaa.org/member/safety/manual*).

And SOPs should be designed to provide flight crews with guidance regarding a desired outcome, not to tell the pilot what technique to use for a given situation. Again, impinging on pilot technique prerogatives may alienate pilots and accomplish little. Good SOPs reduce surprises in the cockpit and provide a means to achieve a desired outcome in the same manner, regardless of the personalities involved. Predictability is the goal.

The concept of building safety into every process and procedure the flight department engages in includes actions that occur long before the flight begins, too; runway safety factor is a good example of this. However, specifying minimum qualifications for pilots and technicians, detailed training requirements, and a list of required maintenance inspection items contributes significantly to risk reduction and safety within the department. Want to be safe? Build some safety in to your operation.

Passenger Safety

What do our very important passengers (VIPs) want from corporate on-demand air transportation? While no definitive polls are available on this issue, most would bring it down to a very few wishes: safety, reliability, and good service—in that order of importance: Get me there in one piece, do it on time every time, and make it a pleasant experience. This is not surprising or unreasonable.

Most flight departments go to great lengths to ensure that the pilots and technicians are well qualified and trained, that the aircraft are airworthy, and that appropriate policies and procedures are in place to ensure the safety, effectiveness, and efficiency of the entire operation. Understandably, these measures are principally oriented toward operational considerations for pilots, technicians, and aircraft. However, what about keeping the precious cargo, the passengers, safe? What policies and procedures are in place to ensure their health and well-being? In most flight departments, the answer is not many.

This omission is not intentional but stems from the belief that passengers will be safe if the rest of the operation is. If

Ways to Injure

- A passenger runs back across a crowded ramp to retrieve a forgotten article of baggage and is blown to the ground by a large jet at breakaway thrust.

- Passengers refuse to wear their seat belts or ignore the seat belt sign when illuminated.

- Individuals use galley facilities without being properly instructed and are burned.

- A passenger's child darts dangerously close to a running turboprop.

- An unescorted passenger disembarks a helicopter with engaged rotors and walks aft.

- Individuals under the influence of alcohol or drugs become unruly or refuse to take directions from the flight crew.

- A passenger attempts to carry a toxic chemical or loaded weapon on board.

airworthy aircraft are provided, aircrews are properly qualified and trained, and the SOPs are appropriate, then passenger safety can be assumed, right? Maybe not, since there are many nonaircraft, non-SOP items that can reach out and grab an unsuspecting passenger.

The preceding sidebar contains just a few of the many different ways passengers inadvertently expose themselves to the potential hazards associated with flight. The point is that unless the subject of passenger safety is focused on, too much will be left to chance. And given the importance of keeping passengers safe and pleased, leaving this subject to chance is an unacceptable risk for the health and well-being of the flight department.

Sadly, every year a number of unfortunate and avoidable passenger-related accidents occur in on-demand air transportation. Death from being struck by a moving tail rotor, broken limbs and sprains from airstair falls, slip-and-fall accidents in hangars and on ramps, burns from galleys, head gashes from baggage doors, and eye injuries from blowing ramp debris are a few examples of these personal injuries. Are they avoidable? Certainly, but passengers are quite ingenious in their ability to harm themselves, so precautions must be equally thorough and ingenious.

Create Expectations.   Therefore, flight departments should give this subject significant attention if a relatively hazard-free environment is to be achieved for its prized customers. A reasonable means of accomplishing this is to select several flight department members and at least one relatively inexperienced passenger to explore the potential hazards associated with passenger-carrying operations. The passenger's participation is essential to provide department personnel with a nonaviation perspective.

This group should step their way through the entire air transportation process, looking at common (and uncommon) hazards and using the passenger perspective to formulate policies and procedures designed to protect passengers and prevent accidents. Then publish the committee's work and ensure that passengers know what to expect when they fly.

Many potentially hazardous situations may be avoided if the passengers know what to expect in the aviation environment and are apprised of policies and procedures designed to protect them from harm. Therefore, creating expectations regarding preflight through postflight activities will set the scene for a safe and enjoyable flight.

Preflight.   On arrival at the departure facility, be it the hangar at home base or a lean-to at a small airport, passengers should know the scheduled departure time and have a clear idea of where to meet the flight crew and what to do with their baggage. Additionally, they should understand that they will *never* be allowed to move about the ramp area unless they are escorted by competent personnel, be it corporate staff or qualified fixed-base operations (FBO) employee.

Boarding.   Again, no unescorted passengers are allowed on the ramp. When approaching the aircraft, the route should be one that does not require walking under wings, engines, or baggage doors. A crew member should stand by the door/airstair to ensure that passengers are not injured while boarding. Once aboard, each passenger should be shown to a seat and have his or her carry-on items stowed by a crew member.

Briefing.   In addition to the required safety briefing, passengers should be made familiar with *all* cabin safety features, not just how to operate the airstair and use the seatbelt. Primary and secondary emergency exit operation, fire extinguisher locations, and emergency oxygen use should be covered thoroughly (comply with FAR Part 91.519 as a starting point). This is also a good time to brief passengers regarding anticipated enroute weather conditions, point out the fasten seat belt sign, and advise them about the desirability of keeping their seat belt fastened at all times.

Comprehensive knowledge of galley, refreshment center, and lavatory features and operation will go a long way toward preventing injuries associated with these items. Additionally, this briefing will allow the passengers to fend for themselves during flight, allowing the cockpit crew to remain at their stations, as required by law.

Enroute.   Perhaps the greatest hazard during the cruise phase of flight is unexpected turbulence. A policy should be developed to ensure the seat belt sign is turned on at appropriate times with accompanying cabin public address (PA) announcements alerting passengers to the possibility/presence of turbulence.

Descent/Landing.   Again, perhaps the most hazardous condition associated with this phase of flight is the possibility of a passenger not being seated with his or her seat belt fastened. Visual inspection of the cabin by flight crew members and cabin PA announcements should preclude this possibility.

Postflight.   If passengers are properly briefed and controlled, they will remain in their seats until a crew member has opened the entrance door and announced the possibility of deplaning.

Prima Donnas.   By their very nature, corporate aircraft passengers are independent thinkers and used to being treated with deference and respect. Occasionally, these people believe that policies and procedures designed to protect them are meant for others. Examples of passengers wishing to stand between pilots during takeoff or landing, opening the airstair door themselves, and bounding across the ramp unescorted abound. What is to be done with these headstrong free spirits?

Normally, a discreet appeal to the chairperson or chief executive officer (CEO) will put a stop to this activity. However, if the offending party is one of those individuals or close to them (wife, child, etc.), the situation becomes problematic. If the flight crew's repeated requests for compliance with established policies go unheeded, the offender must take personal responsibility for his or her actions and be prepared to accept the consequences. A possible exception may be the ramp escort requirement; ramps are potentially hazardous places at all times. Accompanying a passenger at all times on the ramp is a highly desirable procedure, whether the gesture is appreciated or not.

Emergencies.   While emergencies directly involving passenger participation are rare in corporate air transportation, procedures for cabin fires, passenger medical emergencies, cabin decompression, and emergency evacuation should be developed. These procedures do not necessarily have to be briefed to the passengers prior to flight, but flight crew members should be very familiar with them. Practicing them, as indicated below, will prepare the crew for these events that are hopefully as rare as commonly simulated (and practiced) emergencies such as engine fires or emergency descents.

Practice Makes Perfect.   While the passenger-participation emergencies just mentioned are quite rare, informal surveys indicate that many passengers would like to take part in training sessions in which these events are practiced. Some flight departments do so using their own resources, allowing passengers to remove emergency exits, exit the aircraft through those openings, discover the contents of the first aid kit, practice CPR, and extinguish a fire under controlled conditions. Others contract for this service to be done on a regular basis. Either way, both passengers and crew will learn from the experience. Moreover, the passengers will appreciate the additional level of care and attention provided them.

Passenger Safety Checklist

- Passenger policy/procedures documents
- Ramp access/control
- Activities in the hangar and around the aircraft
- Baggage (including carry-on) control
- Cabin briefing—safety, cabin features, flight activities
- Seat belt policy—takeoff, enroute, landing, taxiing
- Handling unruly passengers
- Cabin emergency procedures
- Passenger safety training
- Reporting safety hazards

The Name of the Game. Pleasing passengers is a highly desirable goal in corporate aviation. However, keeping them safe is essential. Months or years may pass in peace and harmony, with little of note occurring regarding passenger safety. However, when least expected, passengers will unwittingly attempt to do harm to themselves.

Remember, safety, reliability, and good service are what passengers want. Make sure these goals are prioritized in the order shown.

ACCIDENT/INCIDENT PLANNING*

Business aviation is safe, perhaps the safest form of transportation available on the face of the earth. But accidents happen. While no one ever anticipates an aircraft accident or incident, each flight department should have a plan for such an eventuality. The two key factors in preaccident planning are education and communication. Educating all flight department personnel *and* key company personnel about what to expect in case of an emergency will ease the confusion and uncertainty of the event. Connecting the proper people with adequate information after an accident or incident will allow established procedures to be set in motion with a minimum of confusion. Experience has shown that gathering and disseminating information concerning the accident in the few hours after its occurrence are critical to controlling the situation and minimizing the trauma associated with the event. If the company has an overall crisis or disaster plan, the aircraft accident/incident plan should conform to and be integrated with it.

Accident/Incident Flow

- Receive information.
- Verify information.
- Notify crisis management team.
- Log all telephone calls.
- Initiate crisis management plan.
- Communicate frequently with team members.
- Limit and *control* contact with media.
- Each team member must maintain a chronological record of events.

The Plan

A section in the operations manual should be devoted to the subject, providing references, procedures, and lists of people to contact. Key elements of this section are procedures to obtain essential information and then to disseminate it to the proper individuals within the company.

Having a plan is the key to coping with an aircraft accident or incident. A flood of human emotions comes into play in the aftermath of such a traumatic event—disbelief, denial, shock, fear. Couple these with the confusion, conflicting reports, inability to communicate with key persons, rumor, and lack of verifiable information that accompany such events, and the flight department's tasks become more than difficult.

As with any other emergency event, having developed a plan, practiced it, and communicated the contents of the plan are the keys to getting through the first days following an accident. Pilots have extensive emergency and abnormal procedures checklists, regularly practice them during recurrent training, and work with other crew members to successfully handle the emergencies. Why not such a system for accident/incident planning (see Fig. 8.1)?

---

*Portions of this section appeared in "Preparing for the Worst," *Professional Pilot,* October 1997.

- **RECEIVE INFORMATION** – Use Aviation Accident/Incident Reporting Form

- **VERIFY INFORMATION** – Obtain an independent second report

- **NOTIFY CRISIS MANAGEMENT TEAM** – Always notify *the Manager of Corporate Aviation* first -- Use emergency response telephone numbers

- **LOG ALL TELEPHONE CALLS** – Use a permanent log

- **INITIATE CRISIS MANAGEMENT PROCEDURE** – See plan

- **COMMUNICATE FREQUENTLY WITH TEAM MEMBERS**

- **LIMIT AND *CONTROL* CONTACT WITH MEDIA** – Work with Corporate Communications

- **EACH TEAM MEMBER MAINTAIN A CHRONOLOGICAL RECORD OF EVENTS**

FIGURE 8.1 Aircraft accident plan action items.

If there is single goal for those who may be involved directly in postaccident matters, it would be: Control chaos. The minutes and hours following an accident are fraught with disorder and competing demands on one's time; controlling these events and demands will have long-term implications.

The best way to start the process of planning for the worst is to engage in a role-playing exercise with your peers. Pilots, flight attendants, technicians, schedulers, and receptionists all have unique perspectives that will prove useful as you develop the plan. Also seek the advice of members of your aviation network; they will provide still other perspectives and experiences relative to your search. The object of the role-playing is to explore all probable scenarios of how notification could take place, what support may be needed, who should be notified, how information should be disseminated, and who can properly represent the company to members of the media, government investigators, and employees.

If the company has a disaster or crisis response plan, the aviation plan should follow its guidelines as closely as possible. In fact, the aviation plan should be integrated into the company plan.

Elements of the Plan

Here are some elements of an aviation crisis response plan that should be considered:

- *Initial notification.* Word of an accident could come from a variety of sources: media, law enforcement, airport, FAA, or the National Transportation Safety Board (NTSB).

Each will have a different level of information and expertise. How will you handle them? What information elements do you need to get from them?

- *Anybody can get the word.* Company security guards, public relations personnel, and receptionists may receive word of the event prior to an aviation-literate person. How should those people be prepared to receive the information?

- *Verification:*

  - Never accept a single report from an unknown source regarding an accident/incident, no matter how authoritative it sounds. Get the basic facts before the word is spread: what, where, when, who and damage/injury assessment (see Fig. 8.2).*
  - Ensure that the crew and passenger manifest is accurate. Once verified, release the manifests only to corporate human resources or corporate counsel for further dissemination.

- *Communications:*

  - After informing necessary flight department personnel, notify essential corporate managers (see the sidebar on page 8.19). Key personnel should have up-to-date telephone lists for these people to facilitate the communications process. Company receptionists, security guards, and all flight department personnel should have these lists available and be trained in collecting and transmitting the information to the proper people. This process should be tested periodically to ensure its validity.
  - The NTSB must be notified immediately of a reportable accident/incident. While someone else may have done this, verify by calling a NTSB field office.
  - Notification/release of crew and passenger names should be done only by corporate human resources or other designated and experienced persons.
  - No, *absolutely no* communications regarding the event should be attempted with media, press, insurance companies, attorneys, and curiosity seekers. Any outside communications must be accomplished by corporate communications or legal counsel; aviation personnel are too close to the problem to provide objective answers about accidents/incidents, particularly in the first hours following the event.
  - Log all telephone contacts and significant events for postevent reconstruction purposes.

- *Preservation:*

  - Provide assistance to injured.
  - Protect the aircraft from further damage or vandalism.
  - Protect crew members from providing possibly self-incriminating answers to NTSB/FAA officials. Those involved in an accident/incident always may be represented by counsel.
  - Obtain photographs of the event scene.

- *Participation.* Owner/operators are normally afforded official status as parties to the accident investigation by the NTSB/FAA. An operator may wish to participate to protect his or her interests and to provide necessary background information for the event. However, participants should be familiar with aircraft accident investigations and the NTSB rules and rights regarding investigations

- *Data collection.* As an investigation unfolds, large amounts of data will be required. It should be collected expeditiously, impounded, and released only on advice of counsel. Such information may include

  - Flight crew employment, operational, and training records
  - Flight schedule and passenger manifests

---

*See also NTSB Part 830, *Notification and Reporting of Aircraft Accidents or Incidents.* Washington: National Transportation Safety Board; ICAO Annex 13, *Aircraft Accident Investigation.* Montreal: International Civil Aviation Organization.

Date _____   Time _____
Name of person taking the report _____
Person providing the report: Name _____
                                Location/Phone _____
Aircraft involved: Type _____ Registration _____
Crew: Pilot in Command _____ Condition _____
      Second in Command _____ Condition _____
Location of occurrence _____
Time of occurrence _____
Details of the occurrence _____
_____

Injuries _____

Damage to aircraft _____

Damage to property _____

Passenger names/condition_____
_____

Names/phone of available witnesses _____
_____

Other pertinent information _____
                                            (continue on back)

Reminders at the scene: **Reminders at home base:**
• Care for injured   • Notify corporate officers
• Protect wreckage   • Notify NTSB
• **No contact with media**   • **No contact with media**
• Only minimum facts to FAA/NTSB   • Collect/impound crew,
• Photograph the scene   flight and maintenance
• Physical examinations for crew/passengers   records

FIGURE 8.2   Incident/accident reporting form.

• Maintenance discrepancy, inspection, and airframe/powerplant/accessory maintenance records
• Flight plan and weather briefing information
• Fueling records

• *Control.* A single individual within the flight department should be designated as the central control point for all communications and actions relating to the event. This is normally the flight department manager or director of operations. While this individual may, and should, delegate certain tasks, the responsibility for overall control of the communications and investigation must lie with this individual for purposes of continuity.

People to Notify within the Company

Companies vary, but here is a basic list:

• Flight department manager or chief pilot

• Chairperson and/or president

• Legal counsel

• Risk manager

• Public affairs/corporate communications

• Human resources

- *Format.* While nicely crafted prose and attractive formatting are expected for most corporate communications, these may not be useful for the accident plan. Events will unfold rapidly after initial notification. There will be little time to pour through detailed directives and instructions. Therefore, checklist and brief outline formats will be useful for all concerned.

More information regarding plans and their structure is available at the NBAA Web site (*nbaa.org/safety*) and the United States Aircraft Insurance Group Web site (*www.usau.com/ USAU.nsf/Doc/CorporateAccidentResponsePlan*).

Implement It

Once a draft plan has been devised, it should be tested by conducting at least a notification exercise to ensure that essential individuals or their surrogates can be contacted at any time. Note how long it takes to complete the notification process and how accurately the individuals involved received the notification information. Then revise the plan to accommodate its shortcomings.

Prior to publishing the plan, obtain the blessing of applicable company personnel, especially human resources, communications, risk management and legal. Once the plan is published, your job is not finished. Training company personnel to use it properly and react to its contents is essential. If the security guard or receptionist who receives the initial call does not know how to complete the initial notification form or who should be called, then the plan will be only marginally effective. And all flight department personnel must be thoroughly familiar with all aspects of the plan because any one of them may be the person who has to "hold down the fort" until designated department managers arrive.

Anyone who may become involved in an aircraft accident/incident should receive applicable portions of the plan. Each aircraft, all flight department personnel, human resources, risk management, communications, and corporate counsel should be provided with the complete plan. Security guards, receptionists, and others who may be involved in the initial notification process only need those portions of the plan that apply to their level of involvement.

Just to make sure the plan works, conduct at least one communications drill annually to ensure that it still works. People, places, and missions change; so should the plan.

Once a basic plan is in effect, you may want to consider enhancing it to include such items as passenger/crew incapacitation, passenger/crew ground injury, vandalism, terrorism, or hijacking.

However, the principal purpose of the plan is to control the confusion that inevitably follows an aircraft-related mishap, to provide organization and structure to a highly disturbing and unstructured event; simple is better. The plan should serve as a guide to those who will become involved in the notification, communication, and investigation processes. Without a plan, chaos may occur.

No job is so important and no task so urgent that we cannot take time to perform our work safely. The safety of people must come first.

—ENDURING SAFETY SLOGAN

CHAPTER 9
PUTTING IT ALL TOGETHER

INSTITUTIONAL FLIGHT DEPARTMENTS

Taken by themselves, the rules, suggestions, and guidelines presented in this book will create pockets of excellence within flight departments. However, there must be a more cohesive, centering force that will enable an on-demand flight department to succeed. This largely undefined force comes from both the experience and insight of those managing the operation.

Most flight departments seek to and succeed at operating safely, keeping up with the flight schedule, and keeping the budget under control. In short, they do the technical stuff fairly well. But many fail at being truly superior service providers.

Call it the big picture, the ability to accurately read the need of the parent organization, or merely organizational talent, but the best flight department and all successful organizations seem to have it. They are constantly seeking to make themselves better, to exceed the needs of their customers, and to achieve excellence for the sake of being excellent. All this takes good management and leadership skills, but it also requires the realization within the flight department and company/principal that on-demand air transportation is an essential part of the larger organization. In such an organization, aircraft are not just limousines with wings, and the people at the airport are not just taxi service order-takers. The flight department is an integral part of the organization.

Few business organizations could do without their accounting, human resources, or information technology departments; these are essential support functions of the company. Although these groups do not produce, market, or sell the company's goods and services, they nonetheless perform critical functions within the organization. It is this revered status that flight department's should be striving for.

MOST ADMIRED

The list is in: General Electric, Procter & Gamble, Wal-Mart, and Southwest Airlines—all traditionally are in the upper strata of *Fortune*'s annual "Most Admired Companies" list. Each year *Fortune* surveys 4000 businesspeople in all industries to see which companies they admire the most—all very subjective, yet with structure.

"Tireless innovation. Robust financials. The ability to lure and keep the smartest people." These are but a few of the features of the much admired. The following equally weighted criteria are used to arrive at which companies enjoy the finest reputations:

- Innovativeness
- Quality of management
- Employee talent
- Financial soundness

- Use of corporate assets
- Long-term investment value
- Social responsibility
- Quality of products/services

Great. But why is it important to be admired? Isn't a profit enough? Well, profitability isn't specifically mentioned, but "financial soundness" is close enough for government work. No, if you cannot attract and retain talent, stay ahead of the pack in developing new products and services, and convince investment bankers and fund managers that your stock has merit, your financials will not be sound for long. The same is true for flight departments: Sheer numbers of passengers flown does not a success make.

While we have a difficult time showing financial soundness in a profit-and-loss sense, the ability to show that we are good stewards of the company's funds through a healthy budget variance report and financial goals met should mean a lot to your company. Real profit for the flight department is measured in broad-based company support, passengers who are raving fans, and people clamoring to use the aircraft.

The other issues mentioned earlier are applicable to any business venture, be it selling lemonade on the sidewalk or producing world-class on-demand air transportation services. For instance:

- *Innovation* means providing transportation solutions for the movers and shakers within your company. Finding these solutions requires cleverness, forward thinking, creativity, and sensitivity to corporate needs. Innovation is a natural product of smart people working to please customers.

- *Quality of management* means people having the best interests of the company at heart and working to fit people to tasks with the goal of winning situations for both the company and individuals. *Quality* means adherence to standards, consistency, and good leadership traits.

- *Talent* means the best people being used for jobs in which they can excel. Knowing raw talent when first seen and then developing it is an artform. The real key to the talent issue is working every day to help your employees realize their personal and corporate goals.

- *Exemplary use of corporate assets* means using the aircraft effectively and efficiently to accomplish stated goals. This means that you have to measure results, compare them with benchmarks or self-trends, and evaluate the result.

- *Long-term investment value* is important to the flight department because it addresses the issue of whether the capital or lease payments invested in the aircraft result in reasonable returns on investment. This is measured in terms of *value created* for the company through use of its aircraft. (*Hint:* Use Travel$ense.)

- *Social responsibility* relates to participation in larger corporate programs that demonstrate that the company cares about the people within its community more than just self-centered profitability. Your company does not have such a program? Start your own—it may become a trend.

- The name of the game—*quality products and services*—if you do not make this the "holy grail" of your operation, the flight department may soon be found only as a chapter in the corporate history book. It is *not* about flying; it is *not* about producing handsome reports; it is *not* about making the budget numbers to the penny—*it is about the customers.* How we serve their needs and treat them while we are serving those needs is the fulcrum around which we leverage our department. Ask them if you are meeting (exceeding?) their expectations on a regular, structured basis. This should be the department's true measure of success.

Staying ahead of these issues not only will make your flight department admired but it also should ensure your place as a significant contributor to the success of the company. In reality, *admired* really means "successful."

PROFIT AND LOSS

Companies thrive on profit and avoid loss. The concept of keeping one's corporate head above a sea of red ink drives everything the company does. One quarter of decreased profits or (shudder) losses is OK; two consecutive poor quarters is grounds for drastic action. It is a basic fact of the business world: No profit, no business; contain and minimize the losses.

Since we all realize that the flight department is a business unit unto itself (we do, don't we?), we should explore the profit-and-loss (P&L) concept as a means of determining our relative level of success. Unfortunately, we do not have the convenient performance measure our parent company does—dollars—but it is possible to assign some value to our performance.

First, understand what business you are in: the transportation solutions business, not the airplane business. The flight department is there to help individuals within the company achieve success by moving them to their desired destinations in a timely manner. Realize that this may not always involve company aircraft; alternate transportation resources outside the company occasionally may be necessary in achieving this goal.

The market for this mission is literally everyone within the company *and* all of its existing and potential customers. While corporate aircraft traditionally have been reserved for a select group of employees, new utilization strategies have opened the door to a wide variety of uses and groups within the company [see the excellent National Business Aviation Association (NBAA) publication, *Business Aircraft Utilization Strategies*].

This market must be researched and cultivated constantly to gain maximum effect from existing and potential customers. The movers and shakers in the company are constantly on the move, exploring new markets and revisiting old ones. How can you help them with their quest? This process requires some marketing of your own—ask your marketing department how it does it.

At the end of every month, sit down and assess that month's performance. Conventional measures of dispatch reliability, number of denied trip requests, and cost per hour all provide *quantitative* measures, but the *qualitative* measures may be more important. Check the sidebar to see how well you did last month.

Is it possible to assign absolute values to these qualities? No, but it is possible to assess the department's relative and ongoing position within a spectrum of these items. Start with a baseline at the beginning of the year, and chart your performance throughout the year using anecdotes,

Profit

- Excellent *relationship* with passengers
- Repeat business
- Respect from all
- Increasing demand
- Broad-based support from the company

Loss

- Unexplained decreasing demand
- Budget under fire
- Increasing micromanagement from above
- Constant review of department activities
- Poor reliability record
- Apprehensive passengers

random comments, and actual numbers (such as demand). Ask other members of the department to help with the process, and do not forget to include the boss in your calculations; he or she will be glad to know that you are concerned and attempting to *qualify* your performance.

The flight department is a service organization, one that supports the company mission. All service organizations within the company—human resources, information services, planning, legal, etc.—must measure their value to the company. If that value sinks below a predetermined level, the service organization's utility to the company is brought into question, and its viability may be jeopardized; personnel changes, reorganization, and outsourcing are all options for the ailing service organization.

How does your service organization measure up? Remember, it is *the little things that count.*

THE EXCELLENT FLIGHT DEPARTMENT

Most corporate flight operations regularly deliver the boss to his or her destination and make it back to home base safely—and do it on time. However, some operations do it better than others, and the ones that do it really well gain the admiration and respect of the boss *and* ensure the longevity of the flight operation. These are important considerations in these lean times, well deserving of the attention of the entire flight department, from the manager to the hangar sweeper. What makes some better departments than others? Consider the following scenarios.

The boss shows up at Frantic Industries' hangar for a scheduled flight only to find that the assigned aircraft is not ready because the ordered fuel load had not been added. While the top man cools his heels for 20 irritating minutes, the flight department rushes to fix the problem. Much shouting and running about ensues, capped off by the chief of maintenance being chewed out by the department manager, unfortunately within earshot of the boss. Eventually, the flight departs, yet no follow-up action is taken by either supervisor concerning the incident.

Coincidentally, a very similar incident occurs at the Frantic flight department's neighbor, Squared Away, Inc., on the same day. However, during the delay, the flight department uses the moment to discuss the proposed acquisition of a new aircraft with the boss. The maintenance manager quietly tells the lineman to bring the fuel load up to the proper amount and actually assists the fueler with the task.

Immediately after seeing the boss off, the department manager launches a quiet but thorough investigation into why the fuel load was incorrect. In so doing, a procedural glitch in the way fuel orders are filled is discovered. The department manager asks the maintenance manager to find a better way to accomplish the procedure, who involved all his people in the process of finding a simple yet effective solution.

Obviously, Squared Away had a better day than did Frantic. Frantic's boss is left wondering whether his department manager is rehearsing for a TV sitcom or running a multimillion-dollar flight department, to say nothing about the departure delay. Further, all the flight department personnel involved in this episode are left in a unhappy mood.

Squared Away fared somewhat better. The boss got to discuss a topic of interest with a trusted manager, while the head of maintenance showed that he is a team member. A hidden problem was uncovered and presented to the people who were most involved in the procedure. The solution to the problem involved everyone; they were all given ownership of the new procedure.

Here's another set of contrasting scenarios: The Stackum and Packum (S&P) Company flight department knew it had to put some procedures and standards on paper because it had just taken delivery of its second aircraft and was in the process of negotiating for a third.

New people were rapidly being hired and had to be indoctrinated and trained into the S&P way of running the "airline." The department manager gave the responsibility to the chief pilot.

Being a hands-on person, the chief pilot worked long hours and weekends and her scheduled vacation period to complete a master training plan and an operations manual. As she tried to implement these directives, major flaws and oversights were discovered, to the point where training courses were considered meaningless and most of the department ignored the new operations manual.

Meanwhile, in a flight department several hangars down, Paradigm Enterprises, an equally fast-growing company was faced with a similar situation. At Paradigm, however, the department manager sat down with his chief pilot and maintenance manager and told them he wanted a comprehensive training plan and operations manual, stating that he wanted every manager and supervisor to have a part in their development.

Because the department manager selected effective project leaders, all the members of the department were soon energized. Within a week, everybody in the hangar was working on some aspect of the projects. The best news was that because all members of the organization had worked on the projects, both directives were embraced and followed by all concerned.

Ways and Means

Attitude, attention to detail, leadership, good communications, customer orientation, personnel empowerment, and a willingness to go the "extra mile" made the difference in these little morality plays. It is these few management and behavioral traits that spell the difference between "merely adequate" and "excellent" in any organization, corporate flight department's included.

Sounds easy, doesn't it? Just put those magic words to work, and excellence will soon follow. Not! Throughout many flight department evaluations and consultations, the preceding characteristics stand out as common threads of excellence. But just talking about them in the abstract will not make them so. Lots of hard work and constant attention to making them all work together just may yield the desired superior performance. Let's take them one at a time.

Attitude.   Does the department manager think that he or she has reached the pinnacle of his or her profession? Does he or she believe that the department personnel are the best available? Is providing on-time, smooth, and safe air transportation that exceeds airline standards his or her top priority? Does all this flow to every subordinate? If not, then excellence for the department is doubtful.

Conversely, if the manager views his or her job as a stepping stone to an airline cockpit or a larger flight department, he or she may not be putting his or her best into the job. If he or she thinks that some of his or her people are not good at their jobs and chooses to accept this, how can he or she expect superior performance? And if better than airline standards are not set and compliance demanded, then mediocre or uneven performance is the inevitable consequence.

Details.   This is why we delegate, right? Yes, but if attention to detail is not demanded on a continuing basis and followed up on, delegation is a shallow exercise of avoiding responsibility. But micromanagement is a danger if supervisors go overboard in their attention to detail. This is a trait best passed onto the troops by example rather than by oversight and second-guessing.

Leadership.   Unfortunately, we spend too much time concentrating on building managers and not enough time on growing leaders. *Growing* is the operative term here; all the training and authority in the world will not create a leader. It is often said that the leader gains his or her authority from his or her subordinates and not his or her supervisor. This is certainly true of the flight department, since most of its occupants are highly trained professionals who expect to be treated as such and look to their supervisor for intelligent direction and mutual respect.

However, John Wayne types cannot run the flight department by sheer force of will and charisma. Good management and planning are essential adjuncts to the total view of running the operation. The good leader must provide firm and consistent direction while giving his or her people the opportunity to make self-realized decisions of their own.

Communications. Perhaps the most important failing of flight departments is their failure to adequately communicate within their organizational boundaries. This is especially true of the often not-so-thin line that separates the operations types from the maintenance types. Up, down, and crossways are all essential interpersonal communications models that must be emphasized and fostered, whether it be intradepartmental or interdepartmental.

If there is a simple way to foster the communications habit, it is to ask lots of questions. Research has shown that only when we are actively listening do we understand problems and form solutions to be transmitted eventually to the sender. Too many of us try to transmit simultaneously; all we get is a squeal as a result.

Customer orientation. Too often flight departments get the mistaken notion that they are in the flying business and not the customer satisfaction business. True, flight departments do a lot of flying in the pursuit of pleasing the customer, but this is only a part of it. Is the transportation service done pleasantly and on time? Moreover, does the service meet the expectations of the customers? When was the last time you asked your customers what they thought of or expected of the service you provide?

Customer orientation means selling the product, too. Even if you are flying all your aircraft more than 700 hours per month with a 50 percent load factor, you must be constantly marketing the flight department to the entire company. Divisions come and go, plant locations come and go, and chief executive officers (CEOs) come and go; constant marketing to all parts of the company will ensure that the flight department will not fall victim to the impermanence of the business world.

Personnel empowerment. A new touchy-feelie buzzword? Not really, if used properly. This is the concept that people, especially subordinates, often have good, creative, and useful ideas that will benefit the organization if those people are presented with the proper environment in which to implement those ideas. The subsets of empowerment are delegation, trust, and support for subordinates. Inherent in the concept is that people can be more productive if they work in an environment that recognizes their value to the organization. It does not mean that the inmates are in control of the asylum, however. See "Leadership."

The Extra Mile. Adequate service is the goal of the mediocre provider. Excellent service is the goal of the organization that wants to be held in high esteem and to be considered invaluable. Don't you want your department to be considered at least invaluable or, preferably, indispensable? If you don't, your company may not be able to justify just an adequate operation for very long.

Attainment

So how does one attain this high level of management purity and excellence? Unfortunately, there is no right or single answer. There are just too many variables involved. Good people, a clear sense of mission, and a good product to sell make the job easier, but the basic tenants remain: Attitude, leadership, good communications, customer orientation, and extra effort make it happen every time.

However, since most of us have not attended the Peter Drucker or Tom Peters schools of management, how does one get the ball rolling on the road to a excellent flight department? Fancy techniques and programs with impressive-sounding acronyms do not make it happen. The attributes I have mentioned involve commitment, dedication, and hard work by all managers associated with the enterprise. Here are some starter ideas:

• Establish/reestablish contact with key company personnel in planning, accounting, human resources, production, etc. Know what the company needs.

- Start a "Market the Flight Department" campaign within the department. Ensure that all department members realize the value of the flight operation to the company and "sell" the concept whenever possible.

- Get the pilots talking to the maintenance crew. Form a safety committee, a training committee, a service-upgrade committee, anything to get all the players talking.

- Have an independent party perform a management and safety evaluation of the department and make specific recommendations to improve all aspects of the operation.

- Hold a planning retreat for the department to find out where you want to be in the next 3 to 5 years.

- Hold brief in-house training sessions each month. While department personnel can act as instructors in some cases, draw on company, airport, service representative, and FAA personnel for these functions.

- Ensure that your routine reports and budgeting documents are adequately supporting your needs. Are you reporting information that is no longer relevant? Does corporate headquarters have a full appreciation for your efforts and problems?

These are just a few ideas on how to get started on the road to a better running department. Want more ideas? Ask your people.

SAFETY, SERVICE, VALUE

We all pride ourselves on providing good service to our passengers. Show up on time with a shiny airplane, be nice to the people in back, get them to the destination with minimum hassle, say "Please" and "Thank you," and smile as they deplane. What more do they want? Well, maybe a bit more.

While most chairpersons or CEOs will not articulate the reasons they have a corporate aircraft, experience has shown that they are looking for an alternative to airline travel. This alternative must be as safe as, or safer than, the airlines, provide high-quality service to the passengers, and ensure that good value is received for the company in the process. With this in mind, the corporate flight department can structure its organization and operations to incorporate features that will focus on *safety, service,* and *value.*

Safety First, Last, and Always

I have never met a flight department manager or chief pilot who said that the boss ever grabbed him or her by the lapels, pulled him or her close, and said, "You'd better be safe!" Hardly ever is the subject of safety raised with regard to corporate aircraft operations. Why? It is taken for granted that all aspects of the flight department will be conducted as safely as possible. This is the most important tenet that underlies corporate aviation: We are as safe (hopefully safer) as the airlines. Without this essential foundation, we might as well pack up and go home.

Fortunately, turbine-powered corporate aviation regularly betters the airlines accident rate. This segment of corporate aviation has beat the airlines accident rate for the past 7 years and should continue to do so, given the current culture within the community. And culture is the key.

You cannot go to the corner store and buy a six-pack or half-gallon of safety; it is not something that can be readily defined or obtained. It is a *culture* or state of being that provides us with the safety we seek. However, culture is one of those Psych 101 terms that normally eludes definition. The best definition of a safe aviation operation I ever heard was one in which every decision started with the subject of safety, i.e., an assessment of the risks involved with any and every decision made. Doing so is not all that difficult; assessing relative risk sometimes can be tricky. Yet practice should make the act second nature.

Make sure *everybody* in the company knows about this decision process, too, especially the boss and all flight department members. If everybody understands that safety is not only first but also last and always, decisions will be accepted more readily and less subject to challenge.

Service with a Smile

Most flight department members will tell you that good service for their passengers goes without saying; they always give good service. And therein lies the problem; it usually goes without saying.

Few, if any, flight departments abide by written passenger service standards, yet they maintain volumes of administrative, financial, and operational standards. The problem is that every flight crew member thinks that he or she knows what constitutes good service. However, this is exactly the reason that standard operating procedures are published in such great detail—everybody has a different opinion about how things, everything, should be done.

Flight crews take great pride exhibiting their professionalism in how they train and plan for and fly their flights. This professionalism involves both ongoing training and adherence to standards. Why not for the customer, too?

Every time you walk up to the check-in counter of a major hotel chain or call the help line of a major company, you should witness the results of a carefully crafted customer standards and training program. These people are trained to help, to be pleasant, and to provide *results*. Why not your flight department, too?

How and by whom are passengers greeted prior to a flight at home and on the road? Which crew member provides both the required safety brief and the "soft" trip brief prior to flight? What are the contents of the soft briefing? How is catering handled before and during flight? These may seem to be small items, but the passengers *always* notice how well they are done.

Good service provides your flight department with its reputation. That reputation should be impeccable. It should generate raving fans. It should make the flight department an indispensable part of the corporate culture. Work at it.

Good Value Creates Job Security

A common expression within the community says that a sustained high level of demand for the flight department's services creates job security. This may or may not be true. If you fly the aircraft 800 hours per year, you may just be creating wear and tear on the aircraft if the company does not perceive that it is receiving good value for its transportation dollar.

Companies often confuse the concept of *cost versus value*. Just about everything costs something, but many things may not provide a value that makes the cost worthwhile. For example, your aircraft may cost $1000 per hour to operate, but can you prove that the company gets at least $1000 in value per hour out of that expenditure? Well, it depends on how you define value.

In this case, *value* refers to the usefulness or importance of a product or service. In the case of corporate aviation, just the availability of rapid and reliable on-demand air transportation creates usefulness for the company. That is, the ability to visit a customer, plant in trouble, or supplier at will should *create value* for the company. Then individual trips themselves create value, depending on the mission and desired outcome of the trip.

Creating one's own schedule, security, confidentiality, and lack of the hassles associated with airline travel complete the value equation.

Much of this is measurable via the NBAA Travel$ense software program. Being able to measure the *value* of a single flight, series of flights, or an entire year's worth creates a powerful impression on the corporate aviation detractors within the company.

Hierarchies

Safety, service, and value always should be prioritized in the order stated. That is, safety first (naturally), service next, and finally, value. If taken out of order (i.e., if value is sought before either safety or service), the equation breaks down. If safe, service-oriented operations are not desired before calculating the value, the company and, likely, the passenger will be disappointed in the long run. Similarly, if a disproportionate amount of emphasis is placed on value or service over safety, warning flags should be raised.

All this revolves around the reason the company got an airplane in the first place. This reason, hopefully, was to provide safe, reliable on-demand air transportation to serve company interests in achieving its basic mission. *Safety, service,* and *value* always should support this basic thought.

When in Doubt

Flight department personnel are faced with decisions, great and small, every day. If they are taught to always consider *safety, service,* and *value* in the decision-making process, they probably will choose wisely most of the time. Finally, they must see this process being used by both flight department and company management on a daily basis. Management by example is a powerful tool.

Use your own best judgment at all times.

—Entire contents of Nordstrom Corporation Policy Manual

APPENDIX A
BUSINESS AVIATION BACKGROUND

ORGANIZATIONS

Aircraft Owners and Pilots Association (AOPA)

421 Aviation Way

Frederick, MD 21701

Tel: + 1 301 695 2000

www.aopa.org

Represents the interests of aircraft owners and pilots in the United States. For foreign affiliates, see IAOPA.

Airports Council International–North America (ACI-NA)

1755 K Street, NW Suite 500

Washington, D.C. 20006

Tel: +1 202 293-8500

www.aci-na.org

Represents major airports.

American Association of Airport Executives (AAAE)

601 Madison St., Suite 400

Alexandria, VA 22314

Tel: +1 703 824 0504

www.airportnet.org

Represents airport managers/executives.

Flight Safety Foundation (FSF)

601 Madison St, Suite 300

Alexandria, VA 22314

Tel: +1 703 739 6700

www.flightsafety.org

Promotes civil aviation safety worldwide.

International Council of Aircraft Owner and Pilot Associations (IAOPA)

421 Aviation Way

Frederick, MD 21701

Tel: +1 301 695 2220

www.iaopa.org

Represents interests of small aircraft pilots and owners in 57 countries (see Web site for a list of countries represented).

International Business Aircraft Council (IBAC)

999 rue University, Room 16.35

Montreal, Quebec H3C 5J9

Canada

Tel: +1 514 954 8054

www.ibac.org

Represents a number of national business aviation organizations, including NBAA.

IBAC Member Organizations

Associaçao Brasileira de Aviçáo Geral (ABAG)

Rua Simões Magro, 155

Sao Paulo 04342-100

Brasil

Tel: +55-11-5583-3032

Fax: +55-11-5583-2405

E-mail: *mail@abag.org.br*

Web: *www.abag.org.br*

Australian Business Aircraft Association (ABAA)

c/o Southern Commander Pty. Ltd.

Hangar 6, Wirraway Street

Essendon Airport, VIC 3041

Tel: +61-3-9374-2044

Fax: +61-3-9379-8460

E-mail: *jasouth@ozemail.com.au*

Business Aircraft Users Association (BAUA)

Crossmount House, Kinloch Rannoch

Perthshire PH16 5QF

Scotland

Tel: +44-1882-632-252

Fax: +44-1882-632-454

E-mail: *dcl@uku.co.uk*

Business Aviation Association of Southern Africa (a CAASA Division) (BAASA)

P. O. Box 807

1620 Kempton Park

Republic of South Africa

Tel: +27-11-394-5316

Fax: +27-11-975-5147

E-mail: *caasa@iafrica.com*

Canadian Business Aviation Association (CBAA)

Suite 304, 99 Metcalfe Street

Ottawa, ON, KIP 6L7

Canada

Tel: +613-236-5611

Fax: +613-236-2361

E-mail: *info@cbaa.ca*

Web: *www.cbaa.ca*

European Business Aviation Association (EBAA)

Bldg. 27

Brussels National Airport

B-1930 Zaventem

Belgium

Tel: +32-2-766-0070

Fax: +32-2-768-1325

E-mail: *ebaa@compuserve.com*

Web: *www.ebaa.org*

European Business Aviation Council–France (EBAA France)

BP. 10 Aéroport du Bourget

93352 Le Bourget Cedex, France

Tel: 33 1 49 34 22 31

Fax: 33 1 49 34 31 28

E-mail: *EBAAFRANCE@aol.com*

German Business Aviation Association (GBAA)
c/o BDI. Federation of German Industries
Breite Str. 29
10178 Berlin, Germany
Tel: +49-30 2028-1424
Fax: +49-30-2028-2424
E-mail: *k.probst@bdi-online.de*
Web: *www.bdi-online.de*

Italian Business Aviation Association (IBAA)
349 G.se Vittoria Emmanuele II
00165 Rome,
Italy
Tel: +39-6-687-2097
Fax: +39-6-687-3830
E-mail: *bizjet-italia@uni.net*

Japan Business Aviation Association (JBAA)
Toranomon MK Bldg. 4F
5-11-11 Toranomon Minato-ku
Tokyo 105-10001, Japan
Tel: +81-3-5405-2136
Fax: +81-3-5405-2239
E-mail: *webmaster@jbaa.org*
Web: *www.jbaa.org*

National Business Aviation Association (NBAA)
1200 Eighteenth Street, N.W.
Washington, DC 20036-2598 USA
Tel: +202-783-9000
Fax: +202-331-8364
E-mail: *info@nbaa.org*
Web: *www.nbaa.org*

International Civil Aviation Organization (ICAO)
999 rue University
Montreal, Quebec H3C 5H7
Canada
Tel: +1 514 954 8219

www.icao.int

Maintains international civil aviation standards and recommended practices.

Joint Aviation Authorities (JAA)

Saturnusstraat 8-10, PO Box 3000

2130 KA Hoofddorp

The Netherlands

Tel: +31 23 5679 741

Fax +31 23 5621 714

www.jaa.nl

Develops regulatory standards for European nations.

National Air Transportation Association (NATA)

4226 King St.

Alexandria, VA 22302

Tel: +1 703 845 9000

www.nata-online.org

Represents U.S. charter operators, flight schools, and FBOs.

National Aircraft Resellers Associations (NARA)

4226 King St.

Alexandria, VA 22302

Tel: +1 703 671 8273

www.nara-dealers.com

Represents business aircraft brokers and aircraft sales organizations.

PERIODICALS

AOPA Pilot

421 Aviation Way

Frederick, MD 22153

USA

Tel: +1 301 695 2000; fax: 2375

www.aopa.org/pilot

Aviation International News

214 Franklin Ave.

Midland Park, NJ 07432

USA

Tel: +1 201 444 5075; fax: 4647

www.ainonline.com

Aviation Week and Space Technology

2 Penn Plaza

New York, NY 10121

USA

Tel: +1 212 904 2000; fax 6068

www.aviationnow.com

Business and Commercial Aviation

4 International Drive

Rye Brook, NY 10573

USA

Tel: +1 914 939 0300; fax: 1184

www.aviationow.com

BART International (Business Aviation Real Tool)

20 rue de l'Industrie

B1400 Nivelles

Belgium

Tel: +326 784 3299; fax: 3599

www.bartintl.com

Flight International

Quadrant House

Sutton, Surrey

SM2 5AS

United Kingdom

Tel: +44 (0)1444 475 603; fax: 445 447

www.flightinternational.com

Flying

500 West Putnam Ave.

Greenwich, CT 06830

USA

Tel: +1 203-622-2700; fax: 2725

www.flyingmag.com

Professional Pilot

3014 Colvin St

Alexandria, VA 22314

USA

Tel: +1 703 370 0606; fax: 7082

www.propilotmag.com

Weekly of Business Aviation

1200 G Street N.W., Suite 200

Washington, D.C. 20005

USA

Tel: +1 202-383-2350; fax: 2438

www.AviationNow.com/bis

World Aviation Directory

1200 G Street N.W.

Washington, D.C. 20005

USA

Tel: +1 800-551-2015

Fax: +1 202-383-2478

www.wadaviation.com

AIR TRANSPORTATION REQUIREMENTS

AIR TRANSPORTATION NEEDS ANALYSIS CHECKLIST

The ability of the aviation department to successfully support the air transportation needs of the company depends heavily on its ability to provide support *when* and *where necessary.* A clear understanding of company strategy and *anticipated* air transportation requirements is essential in being able to provide transportation services when and where needed.

Historical Research

Airline Activity.   Obtain the following data for the previous 12 months for key executives/personnel from corporate travel department:

- City-pair analysis (note multiple-leg trips)
- Most popular destination frequency
- Total and average fares
- Average trip length in days
- Include or factor out international trips, as applicable

On-Demand Air Transportation.   Develop data similar to airline activity (above) for corporate, charter, and fractional operations. Record positioning (deadhead) trip frequency, if applicable.

- Executive use—individual/average
- Popular destinations
- Costs versus *value*
- *Evidence of value created* (reasons for trips)

Company Strategy.   Obtain access to company strategic plans and/or interview key employees to gain knowledge of company plans (see below).

- Overall change goals/mission
- Mergers/acquisitions
- New products/territories
- Customer targets
- Unique transportation requirements

Analyze Data

Develop tables showing

- Top 10 airline destinations, with frequency
- Top 10 corporate/charter destinations, with frequency
- Average time away from home base per trip
- Costs per trip/leg or other relevant measure

Create maps portraying frequent trips/destinations for both airline and on-demand air transportation operations.

Develop Interview Information

Schedule 30-minute private interviews with key employees/air transportation users. These should be done in the subject's office to put him or her at ease and to imprint you into his or her territory.

Create Baseline Information

- Understand the interviewee's area of responsibility.
- Individual estimates of
  - Airline travel frequency.
  - On-demand travel usage (breakout by type).
  - Load factors.
- Why these trips are critical to accomplishing individual/company goals.
- Opinions regarding quality/efficiency of current/previous service
  - Airline travel.
  - On-demand travel.

Develop Projected Usage (use 18-month time horizon)

- Ask interviewee to explain planned new products/markets for his or her organization.
- List estimates for interviewees and their direct reports of anticipated
  - New destinations.
  - Airline travel.
  - On-demand travel by type.
  - Special needs.
  - Load factors.
- Why new trips are required and/or their effect on individual/company goals.

Create Projection

Alternatives

- Tabular data by individual or organizational subdivision
- Overall narrative estimates of change
- Graphic presentation of old/new destinations/frequencies
- Maps showing current and projected destinations

Analyze Data.   Create an aggregate of

- Current uses, destinations, frequencies
- Projected uses, destination, frequencies
- Special needs
- Innovative uses
- Impact of anticipated travel on company goals/objectives

Analysis

Aircraft.   Requirements:

- Average and longest trip lengths
- Load factors
- Cabin comfort requirements and amenities
- Airport/range-payload performance requirements
- Special equipment (international)
- Trip frequency, RONs, simultaneous trip requirements (how many aircraft?)

People.   Requirements:

- Type
- Skills
- Number

Facilities/Infrastructure.   Requirements:

- Hangar
- Office
- Equipment
- Services

Financial.   Resources:

- Capital expenses
  - Current
  - Projected
- Operational expenses (present as direct and indirect)
  - Current
  - Projected

Alternatives

- Corporate aviation
- Joint ownership/interchange/time share
- Charter
- Fractional ownership

- Airlines
- Combinations of the above

Impact

- Competitive advantage. Beat the competition.
- Time saved. Time away from office, nights away from home.
- Value provided. *Competitive advantage,* productivity, force multiplier, schedule prioritization, customer orientation.
- Intangibles. Safety, security, confidentiality, lifestyle, image, hassle factor.

Presentation

Use maps, graphics, table, narrative.

- Current situation
- Future needs
- *Transportation solutions*
- Options/alternatives

Specifics

- Methods
- Aircraft
- People
- Facilities
- Finances
  - Capital
  - Operating expenses

Recommended alternative

CHOOSING AN AIRCRAFT CHECKLIST

Background

- Who uses the aircraft?
- How much did they use it last year?
- How much did they use the airlines?
- Where did they go?
- How long did they stay?
- What are the shortcomings, if any?

Analysis

- Number of trips

- Popular destinations
- Load factor
- Leg length
- Trip length (days)
- Charter used
- Costs involved – capital + operational

Future (18-Month Time Horizon)

- Determine strategic direction of the company.
- Who could/should use the aircraft?
- Interview movers and shakers:
  - How do they travel now?
  - What will their part of the company be doing next year?
  - How will this affect their and their direct reports' travel needs?
  - What unique travel needs will they have?

Analysis

- Summarize company strategic direction.
- Compile travel requirements.
- Note changes from past.
- Consider preferences of senior staff.
- Build travel resource alternatives—value, suitability, utility, flexibility, cost.
- Choose one alternative.

Presentation

- Build a story.
- Use charts and graphs rather than tables and data.
- Present strategic direction for company departments.
- Provide resource alternatives.
- Use anecdotes to describe value of on-demand air transportation to company.
- Recommend one alternative.
- Provide cost impacts as long-term (life cycle) values.

Reference *http://www.nbaa.org/resourcing, NBAA Management Guide,* Appendix B.

AIRCRAFT PURCHASE CHECKLIST

Background

- Perform air transportation analysis (see checklist).
- Choose likely aircraft types.

- Query personal network regarding likely types and sources.
- Research aircraft choices in detail.
- Research market.
- Determine company acquisition format and financing preferences.
- Decide on broker/dealer, if appropriate:
  - Reputation
  - Years in business
  - Expertise/experience in your area of the market

Purchase Considerations

- New/used:
  - Resale value
  - Warranty provisions
  - Maintenance costs, special maintenance items
  - Customer support
  - Insurance restrictions
- Installed equipment
- Parts availability
- Repair station/service center availability
- Cabin appointments
- Pilot/maintenance training available
- Demonstration flight for principal passengers

Purchase Specifics

- Insurance coverage desired and operating restrictions imposed (see checklist)
- Inspection:
  - Qualifications of inspector
  - Statistics on airframe, powerplants, accessories—time in service, cycles
  - General condition—paint, interior, hidden areas
  - Major repair/damage history
  - Modification/alteration status/documentation (Form 337)
  - Equipment list and parts authenticity validation (Form 8130/yellow tags)
  - Discrepancy list/deferred items review
  - Logbooks/records—status of inspections, life-limited items, AD/SB, required overhauls, and accessory/appliance items
- Specific inspections/tests:
  - Engine borescope, hot section, APU, accessories, oil analysis
  - Test flight/functional checks—all systems, cabin features, avionics, flight envelope
- Legal review of sale/lease documents

Documentation

- Purchase contract/lease

- Bill of sale
- Aircraft registration certificate/application
- Certificate of airworthiness
- Title/title search (release of lien, if necessary)
- Certificate of insurance
- Aircraft records/logbooks (FAR Part 91.417)

Reference: Manufacturers, brokers, dealers: *www.nbaa.org/emarkets* and *www.nbaa.org/prodsvcs.*

ON-DEMAND AIR TRANSPORTATION POLICY AND PROCEDURES (EXAMPLE)

Purpose

The Ace Widget Corporation operates its own aircraft and contracts for charter air transportation for use as a management tool in improving its efficiency and effectiveness in the marketplace. The rationale for use of on-demand air transportation must be consistent with the overall management policies and practices of the corporation.

Use of on-demand air transportation should be considered when significant advantages or savings over airline travel may be realized in terms of time, money, security, or productivity.

Methods

Ace Widget maintains a Cessna Citation aircraft in Anytown to provide air transportation services for its employees and customers. This aircraft is capable of carrying up to seven passengers for distances of up to 1200 statute miles. Certain other restrictions such as minimum runway length and maximum weight apply to the aircraft.

Additional on-demand air transportation is available via aircraft charter. A wide range of aircraft types are available, priced at an equally wide variety of hourly rates. In using these services, the type of aircraft chartered must fit the proposed travel mission and not unduly exceed the desired level of capability.

Only the company Citation and authorized charter aircraft will be used for on-demand air transportation. The standards set for these aircraft operations will ensure that the highest levels of safety and efficiency are received by corporate travelers. *All flights, regardless of supplier, will be scheduled through the Corporate Aircraft Coordinator.*

Authorization

Individuals occupying the following positions within Ace Widget may authorize the use of on-demand air transportation:

Chairman	Strategic Planning
Chief Executive Officer	Corporate Counsel
Chief Financial Officer	Administration
Group Presidents	Treasurer
Government Affairs	

These individuals may authorize on-demand air transportation for use of their direct reports and other activities directly related to essential business purposes, when required.

Scheduling Procedure

Priority for the use of the Citation aircraft will be determined by the Office of the Chairman and will be chosen on the basis of the business purpose containing the greatest benefit for the company.

Those authorized to use on-demand air transportation will supply the following information via e-mail/fax to the Corporate Aircraft Coordinator as far as possible in advance of the requested use date:

Dates desired

Business purpose(s)

Type of aircraft desired

Detailed itinerary, including specific times and locations

Passenger manifest, including applicable cost centers

Special requirements

Ground transportation required

Catering requests

Travelers will make their own lodging arrangements.

The Aircraft Coordinator will make appropriate arrangements and provide an e-mail/fax copy of the proposed trip sheet to the traveler, requesting confirmation of the travel details shown. Once confirmed, a final trip sheet will be transmitted to the requester. Any desired changes to this document must be communicated the Aircraft Coordinator as soon as possible; direct communications between a requester and the charter broker or charter provider are discouraged because this procedure will deny the Aircraft Coordinator needed information.

Charges

At the completion of each trip, the flight department/charter company will supply the Aircraft Coordinator with a final manifest and flight times/charges accruing to the trip. The Aircraft Coordinator will verify the data received and provide the accounting department with appropriate charges by cost center number of the travelers.

Charges for the Citation will be computed at the direct operating cost for the aircraft, currently $650 per flight hour. Charter charges will be actual costs billed by the charter company.

Restrictions

The knowledge and expertise of senior corporate executives are such that the loss of more than one of them may jeopardize the continuity and smooth operation of the company. Therefore, in an effort to manage the risk associated with such losses, the following travel restrictions apply:

1. No two persons in the Office of the Chairman may travel together.

2. Not more than five corporate officers may travel together.

3. Not more that one direct report may travel with a Group President.

[This list needs a detailed review prior to implementation; keep it simple.]
It shall be the responsibility of the executive authorizing the flight to ensure the restrictions above are not violated.

Security

A principal reason for using on-demand air transportation is to protect the well-being of individual travelers and to ensure privileged information regarding corporate activities is not compromised. Therefore, information regarding travel plans, potential or actual, will be treated as corporate confidential information. Specific details of trips will be made know only to those requiring that information.

International Travel

International travel requires an additional level of planning and detail due to the customs, immigration, and aircraft operating facilities requirements; adequate time to plan and make arrangements for these items is essential for a trouble-free trip. Therefore, each executive authorizing an international trip will appoint a contact person to work with the Aircraft Coordinator to gather the information and documentation required for the requested trip.

Special Uses

The Federal Aviation Administration (FAA), Federal Election Commission, and Internal Revenue Service (IRS) regulate the operational and business use of on-demand air transportation. Compliance with applicable regulations is essential for Ace Widget aircraft operations. Since each of the uses listed below may be subject to several regulations and interpretations, further guidance from the Corporate Aircraft Coordinator and Corporate Counsel should be sought when seeking definitive answers for specific usage situations.

Elected Officials

In general, carriage of candidates for elected office or their agents must be paid for by the candidate *prior to the flight.* Carriage of office holders is generally prohibited except in cases where fact-finding trips or activities in which substantial participation by the official is involved. Obtain clearance from Corporate Counsel prior to carrying any candidate or office holder.

Empty Seat Provisions

Each employee traveling on Ace Widget aircraft or aircraft charters must do so for a stated business purpose. However, if more than 50 percent of the aircraft seats are filled on a single flight by those with a valid business purpose, any remaining seats may be used by employees, spouses, and children traveling for nonbusiness reasons without assigning a value to that transportation.

Personal Use

Personal and family use of Ace Widget on-demand air transportation may be available to employees and their guests only with the express permission of the Office of the Chairman.

Such use is subject to IRS rules that impose imputed income for the value of the flight to the employee(s) using the service, normally at a standard industry fare level (a per-mile rate issued periodically by the Department of Transportation) and multiplier factor based on aircraft size and employee position. Note that some spousal services may qualify as business purposes.

Aircraft Operating Standards

Although both corporate and charter aircraft activity are regulated by the FAA, those regulations provide only minimum operating standards. It is the desire and policy of the Ace Widget Corporation to provide the safest possible air transportation offering the highest service standards to its employees and customers.

Therefore, corporate aircraft operations will be conducted in accordance with the Ace Widget Flight Department Flight Operations Manual. All aircraft charter operations provided by the charter broker will incorporate the provisions of the Standards for Qualifying Outside Charter Companies attached to this directive.

In all cases, the pilot in command of the aircraft has full authority over the conduct of that flight and shall not be interfered with.

APPENDIX C
OWNER FLOWN PROCEDURES

OWNER/EMPLOYEE-PILOT OPERATING LIMITATIONS

Aircraft

- No operations in crosswinds that are in excess of 75 percent of the maximum demonstrated crosswind component should be attempted.
- All aircraft will be maintained in accordance with the manufacturer's inspection program or 100-hour inspection cycle, as applicable.
- Each aircraft will be equipped with appropriate emergency and survival equipment.

Pilots

- No pilot will be allowed to fly the aircraft unless he or she has received a formal checkout from a certificated flight instructor and is listed on the insurance policy.
- No pilot having less than 25 hours in type will be allowed to act as PIC.
- An instrument competency check is required of each pilot annually.
- Annual recurrent training from a training vendor employing classroom instruction and a simulator/flight training device is required of all pilots.
- Flights operating with a single-pilot crew shall plan to arrive at the final daily destination not later than 10 P.M.
- All instrument approach weather minimums will be increased by 200 feet and ½ mile and takeoff minimums increased by $1/4$ mile until the PIC has logged 100 hours in type.
- Single-pilot IFR flights must have a functioning autopilot available that provides at least a heading-hold function.

Operations

- Only airports having at least 50 percent more landing and takeoff runway available than required by the airplane flight manual performance charts will be used.
- An approved checklist will be used for *all* aircraft operations.
- Takeoff minimums for all flights require a minimum prevailing visibility of ¼ mile or 1200 RVR, or as published. Takeoffs when ceiling and visibility are less than specified for an available instrument approach at the airport of departure require a takeoff alternate less that 30 minutes flying time from the departure point. This takeoff alternate must be forecast

to have at least alternate weather minimums for the instrument approach providing the lowest approach minimums at the proposed time of arrival.

- Only one instrument approach should be attempted when weather for the approach is reported to be less than published minimum values.
- No night circling instrument approaches are allowed, unless at home base.
- No aircraft will land with less than one hour of fuel on board, computed at normal cruising speed consumption.
- Weather: Takeoff is not permitted when a thunderstorm is located within 5 nautical miles of the airport and within 60 degrees of the departure course.
- Takeoff is not permitted when wind shear warnings of 15 knots airspeed or wind speed are reported.
- Flights will not be operated into areas of known or forecast thunderstorms without an operational weather radar or other thunderstorm detection device.
- No flight will be flown into areas of known or forecast moderate icing or greater or severe turbulence.
- Takeoff or landing is not permitted when winds or wind gusts exceed 40 knots.
- Aircraft are not allowed to take off when weather conditions are such that frost, ice, or snow may be expected to adhere to the aircraft unless it is deiced and operated in accordance with AC 135-17, Appendix A.
- The PIC will always observe the fueling of the aircraft.

OWNER/EMPLOYEE-PILOT STANDARD OPERATING PROCEDURES

Note: The SOPs listed here are only suggested and should not be adopted without a thorough evaluation of their usefulness and effect on other operations. They have been compiled from a variety of sources, including air carriers, corporate flight departments, training vendors, and other good operating practices.

Preflight Preparation

Preflight planning should commence not less than 30 minutes prior to desired departure time. Preflight preparation duties shall consist of

- Ensuring that the appropriate flight information publications are available for the flight.
- Preparing a full flight log, listing all locations that will define the route of flight, times enroute, and total fuel required.
- Obtaining a full weather and NOTAM briefing, either from a computerized briefing service or from a flight service station.
- Filing a flight plan for all flights, except local flights.
- Computing aircraft weight and balance for the load to be carried.
- Reviewing the airworthiness status of the aircraft.
- Ensuring that the proper amount of fuel is on board the aircraft.
- Completing a walk-around inspection of the aircraft as described in the pilot's operating handbook or airplane flight manual.

- Ensuring that passengers are properly briefed concerning the flight including normal and emergency procedures. The briefing will cover the following items:

  - The duration of and flight conditions expected on the flight
  - Smoking
  - Use of safety belts and shoulder harnesses
  - Location and operation of normal and emergency exits
  - Location and use of safety and survival equipment
  - Use of normal and emergency oxygen equipment

Engine Start and Taxi

- All crew members and passengers must be on board, briefed, and seated with seat belts fastened prior to engine start.
- Airport Traffic Information Service (ATIS), ATC clearance, and taxi clearance will be received prior to commencing taxi.
- Taxi at a reasonable and safe speed.
- Check gyro instruments, including horizontal situation indicator (HSI), alignment with magnetic compass during taxi.

Takeoff

- Have departure, initial segment, and departure airport approach charts readily available.
- Compute takeoff safety data (use Takeoff and Landing Data Card).
- Ensure the chosen/assigned runway is suitable regarding length, width, and surface. Note any climb-out limitations regarding required climb gradient or controlling obstructions prior to departure.
- Conduct a takeoff briefing or self-briefing to include

  - Speeds, power settings, aircraft limitations, and special conditions
  - Communications and navigational frequencies for normal departure and emergency return
  - Departure procedures
  - Initial assigned/chosen altitude
  - Emergency/contingency procedures

- Use an appropriate aircraft lighting configuration to ensure conspicuity.
- Select go-around mode on flight director (if installed) for initial pitch attitude guidance.
- Cross-check pitch and roll indications with all available instrumentation.

Climb-out

- Engage autopilot only after reaching 500 feet AGL or twice the altitude loss associated with autopilot failure as specified in the AFM/POH, whichever is higher.
- Maintain a constant lookout for other aircraft.
- Note/callout assigned altitudes 1000 feet prior to reaching each altitude change; use an altitude alerter if installed.
- Cross-check instruments for pitch and roll information.

Cruise

- Recompute fuel required to reach destination at least hourly.
- Obtain an updated destination weather forecast hourly.
- Cross-check navigational accuracy by all available means.
- Cross-check instruments for pitch and roll information.
- Cross-check and note engine instruments at least every quarter hour.

Descent/Approach

- Plan/conduct descents to maintain a cabin rate of descent not greater than 1000 feet per minute.
- Note/callout assigned altitudes 1000 feet prior to reaching for each altitude change; use an altitude alterter, if installed.
- Conduct an approach briefing to include
  - Destination airport features, including approach and runway to be used and lighting to be anticipated
  - Destination weather
  - Navaids setup
  - Field elevation
  - Initial approach altitude
  - Final approach course
  - MAP/timing required
  - DH/MDA
  - Missed-approach procedure
- Note/callout the following during approach:
  - Localized/final approach course capture
  - 500 and 100 feet above DH/MDA
  - DH/MDA
  - Runway in sight/no contact
  - Landing/go-around decision
- Stabilize approach at least 1000 feet above DH/MDA (aircraft in landing configuration and rate of descent stabilized)
- Maintain approach deviation from course/glideslope within 2 dots deflection and $V_{ref} \pm 10$ knots during an instrument approach.
- Place aircraft in landing configuration no later than the final approach fix during an instrument approach.
- Complete landing checklist prior to reaching 500 feet above the runway.
- Execute missed approach at the DH/MAP if visual reference requirements of FAR Part 91.175(c) are not met.
- Configure aircraft lights to provide maximum conspicuity.
- Maintain continuous lookout for other aircraft.
- Cross-check instruments for attitude and position.

Landing

- Maintain V_{ref} (adjusted for condition correction factors) to -5 and $+10$ knots limitations until over the runway threshold.

- Leave configuration of aircraft unaltered until after clearing the runway, unless required by the POH/AFM.

Postflight

- Complete aircraft log and flight record prior to deplaning.
- Conduct brief postflight inspection to determine aircraft's airworthiness.
- These standard practices should be reviewed regularly to ensure their validity and conformance with other procedures and limitations used for a specific aircraft operation. At a minimum, they should be reviewed annually.

APPENDIX D
BUDGET JUSTIFICATION

BUDGET JUSTIFICATION

Replacement Aircraft Tug (Example)

Background. The aviation department uses a special motorized vehicle known as an aircraft tug to move aircraft in and out of the aircraft hangar at the Orville Wright Airport. The weight and size of the department's two aircraft make their movement impossible to accomplish by hand and dangerous to do so except with a specially designed vehicle.

The current tug used by the department, a Fleetway Model 102, has been in service for 12 years. The commonly expected service life for this type of vehicle is 8 years. While the tug has been well maintained, it has reached a point beyond which economic repair is not possible. This conclusion was reached by director of aviation maintenance in consultation with the Fleetway service representative.

Prior Expenses. The current tug was purchased from the Fleetway Corporation in 1984 for $23,000. The following major expenses have been incurred in the recent past:

1993: Transmission overhaul	$1100
1991: Engine overhaul	$1600
1989: Steering mechanism repair	$900
1989: Electrical repairs (3)	$650

Current Situation. The tug has become unreliable for its use of moving company aircraft around the hangar and airport ramp areas. It requires large amounts of aviation department maintenance technician and outside mechanic assistance to keep it in running order.

Engine starting in cold weather is very difficult even when the tug is fresh out of preventative maintenance. Four times during the past winter aircraft launches have been delayed due to an inability to start our tug, necessitating the use a commercial aircraft handler's tug. Additionally, the tug's transmission and braking systems have chronic difficulties that have caused a potential safety problem during aircraft movements.

Since the initial purchase of the tug, the company has upgraded its aircraft fleet, moving to the larger Gulfstream III aircraft. The weight of this aircraft exceeds the Fleetway maximum aircraft weight recommendations, making handling of the Gulfstream aircraft difficult and potentially unsafe during wet weather and on the sloped portions of the airport ramp.

Assumptions

1. The current aircraft tug has exceeded its service life.
2. The current tug is incapable of moving some company aircraft safely and effectively.

3. A replacement tug will have a service life of 8 years (manufacturer's data).
4. The most suitable replacement for the current tug is a Tractionmaster 204. Purchase price: $34,000.
5. Value of the current tug (Fleetway 102) is $600.

Proposal. Purchase a new Tractionmaster Model 204 aircraft tug to replace the existing tug. [This should be accomplished prior to the wet spring weather (May).]

Justification. The current aircraft tug moves the two company aircraft approximately four times each per day in preparation for flight operations, for maintenance purposes, and to store them after completion of flight operations. Additionally, the tug is used for trips to local parts suppliers and other corporate aviation departments located on the airport ramp area. Occasionally, the tug is used to move heavy equipment within the hangar.

When the tug is unserviceable, either flight or maintenance operations must be halted for as long as it takes to repair the tug. Given the on-demand nature of the company flight operations, such delays affect critical operations. Reliable, safe aircraft movements are essential to the aviation department's operations.

The current state of repair of the existing aircraft tug is such that its reliability is never assured. Excessive amounts of maintenance technician and management time are spent on this support device. Repeated visits by the factory service representative and other automotive mechanics have not improved its reliability appreciably.

The current tug is barely adequate to move the Gulfstream aircraft under ideal circumstances. During wet weather and for operations on sloped portions of the ramp, it is sometimes impossible to safely control the movement of the tug-aircraft combination. During these times, a rental tug from a nearby aircraft service company is engaged to ensure the safe movement of the aircraft. Renting a tug is often difficult due to its high demand and limited hours of availability.

Used tugs of the proper size and state of repair are not in ready supply within the aviation community. A number of types of tugs have been investigate, both new and used; a new Tractionmaster 204 is the best replacement choice.

Benefits

- Reliable and safe aircraft ground movements
- High-quality, new-technology, low-maintenance vehicle
- Eight-year service life is high, considering the type and amount of usage

APPENDIX E
EMPLOYEE JOBS AND PERFORMANCE

FLIGHT DEPARTMENT COLLATERAL DUTY
JOB DESCRIPTIONS

Safety. Responsible for ensuring that the flight department maintains a high level of safety consciousness and active safety program promotion. Advises management on safety issues.

* Helps formulate/reviews all operational procedures and policies to ensure safety is included in the process.
* Conducts a semiannual safety review of the entire department.
* Maintains the flight department hazard reporting system.
* Works with flight department management to ensure that safety-related training is accomplished.
* Provides or arranges for monthly safety training for pilots and technicians.
* Maintains a pilot and technician safety reading file.
* Conducts quarterly safety inspections of the hangar.

Training. Responsible for ensuring flight department personnel receive appropriate training.

* Devises and maintains a long-range training plan for the department.
* Arranges for and schedules pilot training and oversees technician training.
* Devises/reviews pilot training curriculum and syllabuses.
* Maintains pilot training records.
* Regularly reports to management on the state of department training.

Standardization. Responsible for maintaining a high level of flight procedure standardization among department pilots.

* Devises and maintains standard operating procedures for all aircraft types.
* Coordinates SOP training with training vendors.
* Conducts and/or supervises regular standardization checks for flight personnel.
* Maintains standardization evaluation records for flight department personnel.
* Works closely with the aircraft manufacturer, training vendors, and the FAA to ensure that SOPs are correct and current.
* Regularly advises department management regarding the state of department flight standardization.

Flight Information Publications/Planning. Responsible for ensuring that current flight information publications and flight planning devices (FLIPPs) are available to department personnel.

- Devises and maintains a FLIPP plan for the department.
- Orders and ensures timely delivery of required FLIPPs.

Automation Support. Responsible for ensuring that appropriate automation support is available to the department.

- Devises and maintains an automation support plan for the department.
- Evaluates additional automation support/upgrade needs for the department.
- Arranges for computer/software training for department personnel.
- Ensures automation devices are properly maintained.

Catering. Responsible for providing consumable products for use by passengers.

- Maintains a standard inventory of consumable materials/food for the aircraft.
- Evaluates and contracts with catering services to provide food service for passengers at home base and at normally used enroute stops.
- Regularly evaluates the quality and adequacy of aircraft consumable products and food service and takes action to ensure a high quality of service to the passengers.

Records/Reports. Responsible for maintaining adequate flight operations and financial records and producing relevant management reports from these sources.

- Devises and maintains appropriate data recording and storage systems for flight department operations.
- Devises and produces operational and management-level reports that adequately describe department operations to the levels needed.

EMPLOYEE PERFORMANCE MEASURES

Writing skills:

- Writes clearly and informatively.
- Edits work for spelling and grammar.
- Varies style to meet the needs of the audience.

Team participation:

- Balances team and individual responsibilities.
- Exhibits objectivity and openness to other views.
- Gives and welcomes feedback.
- Contributes to building a positive team spirit.

Quantity:

- Completes work in a timely manner.
- Achieves established goals.

Quality:

- Demonstrates accuracy and thoroughness.
- Displays a commitment to excellence.
- Looks for ways to improve and promote quality.
- Applies feedback to improve performance.
- Monitors own work to ensure quality.

Problem solving:

- Identifies problems in a timely manner.
- Gathers and analyzes information skillfully.
- Develops alternative solutions.
- Resolves problems in early stages.
- Works well in group problem-solving situations.

Planning and organization:

- Prioritizes and plans work activities.
- Uses time efficiently.
- Plans for additional resources.
- Integrates changes smoothly.
- Sets goals and objectives.

Organization support:

- Follows policies and procedures.
- Completes administrative tasks correctly and on time.
- Supports the organization goals and values.
- Benefits the organization through outside activities.

Oral communication:

- Speaks clearly and persuasively.
- Listens and obtains clarification.
- Responds well to questions.
- Demonstrates group presentation skills.
- Participates in meetings.

Judgment:

- Displays a willingness to make decisions.
- Exhibits sound and accurate judgment.
- Includes the appropriate people in the decision-making process.

Job knowledge:

- Competent in the required job skills and knowledge.
- Exhibits ability to learn and apply new skills.
- Keeps abreast of current industry developments.

- Requires minimal supervision.
- Displays an understanding of how the individual's job relates to others' jobs.

Initiative:

- Volunteers readily.
- Undertakes self-development activities.

Dependability:

- Responds to requests for service and assistance.
- Follows instructions and responds to management direction.
- Takes responsibility for own actions.
- Commits to doing the best job possible.
- Meets attendance and punctuality guidelines.

Customer service:

- Displays courtesy and sensitivity.
- Meets commitments.
- Responds to customer needs.
- Manages difficult or emotional customer situations.

Cooperation:

- Establishes and maintains effective relations.
- Displays positive outlook and pleasant manner.
- Offers assistance and support to coworkers.
- Works actively to resolve conflicts.
- Works cooperatively in group situations.

Communications:

- Expresses ideas and thoughts verbally.
- Expresses ideas and thoughts in written form.
- Exhibits good listening and comprehension.
- Selects and uses the appropriate communication methods.

Analytical skills:

- Synthesizes complex and diverse information.
- Collects and uses data.
- Uses intuition and experience to compliment data.
- Identifies data relationships and dependencies.

GLOSSARY

Abort   To terminate a preplanned aircraft maneuver; e.g., an aborted takeoff.

ACAS   Airborne Collision and Avoidance System (See *TCAS*).

ADF   Automatic Direction Finder—Aircraft radio receiver that will point to a ground based radio transmitter (See *NDB*).

Aerial work   An aircraft operation in which an aircraft is used for specialized services such as agriculture, construction, photography, surveying, observation and patrol, search and rescue, aerial advertisement, etc.

Aeronautical Information Publication (AIP)   A publication issued by or with the authority of a state and containing aeronautical information of a lasting character essential to air navigation.

Air taxi operator   Company providing on-demand (non-scheduled) commercial air transportation. Also known as an aircraft charter operator.

Air transportation   An aircraft operation involving the transport of passengers, cargo, or mail.

Airworthy (aircraft)   Conforms to the type design specifications and is in a safe condition to fly.

ALAR   Approach and Landing Accident Reduction. An extensive study resulting in a series of recommendations to reduce accidents in the stated regime. The Flight Safety Foundation has promoted the work.

Annex (ICAO)   Method of promulgating ICAO standards and recommended practices (SARPS).

AOG   Aircraft on ground. Parts needed to repair an aircraft, without which the aircraft remains unflyable.

ASOS/AWOS   Automated Surface/Weather Observation System. Remote sensors that record and broadcast weather conditions at an airport.

ATC   Air traffic control. A service operated by an appropriate authority to promote the safe, orderly, and expeditious flow of air traffic.

ATIS   Automated Terminal Information Service. Recorded message broadcast by air traffic control towers providing weather and operational conditions at an airport.

Block time   See *Flight Time.*

Business aviation   On-demand air transportation used in support of a business.

CAA   Civil Aviation Authority (United Kingdom and other countries).

Category I/II/III operations   Precision instrument approach operations providing landing minimums as follows:
- Cat. I. Decision height (DH) 200 feet and runway visual range (RVR) 2600 ft (these are the normal precision approach minimums)
- Cat. II. DH 100, RVR 1200
- Cat. IIIa. DH (N/R), RVR 700
- Cat. IIIb. DH (N/R), RVR 150
- Cat. IIIc. DH (N/R), RVR (N/R)

Note: Special ground and aircraft equipment, aircraft maintenance, and pilot training required for operations below Cat. I.

CFIT Controlled flight into terrain. Causal factor in a significant number of aircraft accidents. CFIT awareness and education programs have been developed by the Flight Safety Foundation.

Chargeback An internal charge levied on the user of a business/corporate aircraft.

Commercial air transportation An aircraft operation involving the transport of passengers, cargo, or mail for remuneration or hire.

Contaminated runway A runway is considered contaminated whenever standing water, ice, snow, slush, frost in any form, heavy rubber, or other substances are present.

Corporate aviation Noncommercial on-demand air transportation used in support of a business, employing professional pilots (normally two) compensated specifically for their piloting duties.

CVR Cockpit voice recorder. Device installed in most turbojet aircraft that records the most recent 30 minutes of intracockpit conversation and radio transmissions/reception.

CRM Cockpit resource management. A series of recommended practices designed to promote harmony, safety, and efficiency among flight crew members.

DH Decision height. Height above the terrain during a precision instrument approach at which a decision must be made to either continue the approach or execute a missed approach (go-around).

Direct operating costs Operating costs applicable only when an aircraft flies. Also known as *variable costs.*

Dispatch rate Percent of time flights depart within a specified time frame (normally 15 minutes) relative to the scheduled time or time passengers are available for flight. Failure to meet this criterion may be due to weather, air traffic control, or aircraft malfunction.

EFIS Electronic flight instrument system. CRT/LED-based flight and engine instrument.

EGPWS Enhanced ground proximity warning system. Electronic system installed in an aircraft to warn of approaching terrain that may endanger the aircraft.

ELT Emergency locator transmitter. An aircraft radio transmitter designed to activate automatically on impact; it aids in locating downed aircraft by transmitting signals to a locating satellite after an accident.

Employee (owner)–flown business aviation Aircraft operated in support of a business and using a pilot or pilots not specifically employed or compensated to fly the aircraft.

ETA Estimated time of arrival.

ETE Estimated time enroute.

ETOPS Extended-range operations. Flight operations in which a suitable emergency airport is more than 90 minutes distant during some portion of the flight.

FAA Federal Aviation Administration. U.S. aviation regulatory body.

FAR Federal Aviation Regulations. U.S. federal rules controlling aviation operations.

FBO Fixed-base operator. Aircraft service company providing fuel, transient parking, passenger waiting areas, and often aircraft hangars and maintenance services.

FDR Flight data recorder. Electronic device installed in some larger turbojets that records a number of aircraft flight and systems operating parameters.

Fixed costs Operating costs applicable whether an aircraft flies or not. Also known as *indirect costs.*

FOQA Flight operational quality assurance. Program for the routine collection and analysis of digital flight data gathered during aircraft operations; intended to amass data to be used in assessing operational quality and safety.

Flight plan Routing, aircraft, passenger, and pilot information relating to a specific flight, usually filed with government agency; used for air traffic control and search and rescue purposes.

Flight time (airplane) The total time from the moment an airplane first moves for the purpose of taking off until the moment it finally comes to rest at the end of the flight. Also known as *block time.*

Flight time (helicopter) The total time from the moment a helicopter's rotor blades start turning until the moment the helicopter finally comes to rest and the blades are stopped.

FMS   Flight management system. A computer system that uses a large database to allow routes to be preprogrammed and fed into the system by means of a data loader. The system is constantly updated with respect to position accuracy by reference to a variety of navigation aids.

Fractional ownership   An arrangement whereby an individual or company purchases a share of an airplane (normally not less than one-sixteenth) that is placed in a pool of similar aircraft to be shared with other similar owners. The pooled aircraft are operated and managed by a company that provides all necessary personnel and services.

FSF   Flight Safety Foundation. Organization promoting safe flight operations worldwide.

GA   General aviation.

General Aviation (ICAO)   An aircraft operation other than a commercial air transport operation or an aerial work operation.

GMT   Greenwich Mean Time. Now correctly called *Coordinated Universal Time (UTC)*. Time at the prime meridian. Also known as *Zulu time*.

GNSS   Global navigation satellite system. Generic term for any satellite-based navigation system.

GPS   Global Positioning System. A space-based radio positioning, navigation, and time-reference system. The system provides highly accurate position and velocity information and precise time, on a continuous global basis, to an unlimited number of properly equipped users.

GPWS   Ground proximity warning system. Aircraft electronic system that warns of inadequate separation from ground and excessive sink rate close to ground.

IBAC   International Business Aviation Council. An association representing business aviation associations around the world.

ICAO   International Civil Aviation Organization. A specialized agency of the United Nations whose objective is to develop the principles and techniques of international air navigation and to foster planning and development of international civil air transport.

IFR   Instrument flight rules. Regulations designed to provide safe operating procedures for aircraft operating in weather conditions less that the minimums required for flight under visual flight rules (VFR). IFR flights usually receive a route clearance and flight monitoring by air traffic control agencies.

ILS   Instrument landing system. Short-range navigation system that uses precision localizer and glide-slope radio transmitters near a runway to provide landing approach guidance. See *Cat. I, II*, etc.

IMC   Instrument meteorological conditions. Meteorological conditions expressed in terms of visibility, distance from cloud, and ceiling less than the minimums specified for visual meteorologic conditions.

Instrument approach procedure   A series of predetermined maneuvers for the orderly transfer of an aircraft under instrument flight conditions from the beginning of the initial approach to a landing or to a point from which a landing may be made visually.

Interchange agreement   Method of mutual leasing of aircraft between parties in exchange for equal time in the other's aircraft. No charge or fee may be made except for the difference in aircraft operating costs.

JAA   Joint Aviation Authorities. European-based regulatory body that generates aviation standards.

JAR   Joint Aviation Requirements. Standards produced by the JAA.

Joint ownership   Operating agreement under which two or more entities own an aircraft, one party provides the flight crew, and each party pays a share of charges specified in a legal agreement.

Kts   Knots. Nautical miles per hour. Speed measurement; 15 percent greater than miles per hour.

Life-limited items   Aircraft parts that must be overhauled or discarded after a certain number of hours or calendar interval.

LOA   Letter of agreement/authority. Letter from a state regulatory authority permitting a specific type of operation, e.g., MNPS, RVSM, etc.

LORAN   Long Range Navigation. An electronic navigational system by which hyperbolic lines of position are determined by measuring the difference in the time of reception of synchronized pulse signals from two fixed transmitters.

Maintenance   Aircraft inspection, overhaul, repair, preservation, and replacement of parts; excludes preventative maintenance.

Manifest   A document that lists the number/names of passengers and weight of baggage and/or freight carried on an aircraft.

MDA   Minimum descent altitude. The lowest altitude, expressed in feet above mean sea level, to which descent is authorized on final approach or during circle-to-land maneuvering in execution of a standard instrument approach procedure where no electronic glideslope is provided.

MEA   Minimum enroute altitude. The lowest published altitude between radio fixes that ensures acceptable navigational signal coverage and meets obstacle clearance requirements between those fixes.

MEL   Minimum equipment list. A document issued by the country of registry's regulatory authority that permits operation of a specific aircraft with certain installed systems inoperative or removed.

MLS   Microwave landing system. Precision instrument approach system used primarily in Europe.

MMO   Maximum operating Mach number.

MNPS   Minimum Navigation Performance Specification. Standards that require aircraft to have a minimum navigation performance capability in order to operate in MNPS-designated airspace; regulatory authority certification required.

MOA   Memorandum of agreement (also military operating area).

MOCA   Minimum obstruction clearance altitude. The lowest published altitude in effect between radio fixes on VOR airways, off-airway routes, or route segments that meets obstacle clearance requirements for the entire route segment

Missed approach   A maneuver conducted by a pilot to pull up and go around when an instrument approach cannot be completed either due to weather being less than published minimums or the aircraft not being in a position that will permit a safe landing.

Mode S   Type of secondary surveillance radar (SSR) equipment that provides Mode A and Mode C interrogations, discrete address (Mode S) interrogations from the ground or air, and a data link capability.

Nav   Navigation.

Navaid   Navigational aid.

NBAA   National Business Aviation Association.

NDB   Nondirectional beacon. Ground-based radio transmitter designed to be located by an aircraft ADF.

NM   Nautical mile. 1 NM = 1.15 SM (statute miles).

NMC   National Meteorological Center.

NOAA   National Oceanic and Atmospheric Administration.

Nonprecision approach procedure   A standard instrument approach procedure in which no electronic glide slope is provided.

NOTAM   Notice for airman. Advisories to pilots regarding inoperative features of airports, navigation aids, or air traffic control facilities.

NTSB   National Transportation Safety Board. Independent federal agency responsible for investigating transportation accidents and incidents.

NWS   National Weather Service.

On-demand air transportation   The transportation of passengers and cargo by aircraft from one point to another in a manner and at a time designated by the person exercising operational control.

Operational control   The exercise of authority over initiating, conducting, or terminating a flight.

PAR   Precision approach radar. Ground-based radar providing precision approach capability to aircraft, normally associated with military installations.

Personal aviation   On-demand air transportation used in support of personal needs and desires.

PF   Pilot flying. The pilot actually controlling the aircraft at a given time during flight.

PIC   Pilot in command. The person who (1) has final authority and responsibility for the operation and safety of the flight, (2) has been designated as pilot in command before or during the flight, and (3) holds the appropriate aircraft category, class, and type rating, if appropriate, for the conduct of the flight.

Pilot in command time   Flight time logged while the pilot is (1) the sole manipulator of the controls of an aircraft for which the pilot is rated or (2) the sole occupant of the aircraft or (3) acting as pilot in command of an aircraft on which more than one pilot is required under the type certification of the aircraft or the regulations under which the flight is conducted.

PIREPS   Pilot reports. Enroute weather conditions reported by pilots.

PNF   Pilot not flying. Sometimes referred to as the *monitoring pilot.*

Positioning flight   Relocating an aircraft to another airport, normally without passengers on board, to meet a specific mission or need. Also known as *deadheading* or *ferrying.*

Precision approach procedure   A standard instrument approach procedure in which an electronic glide slope is provided, such as ILS and MLS.

Preventive maintenance   Simple or minor preservation operations and the replacement of small standard parts not involving complex assembly operations.

RNAV   Area navigation. Generic acronym for any device capable of aircraft guidance between pilot-defined waypoints.

Rotable parts   Aircraft parts subject to reuse after overhaul or repair and recertification have taken place.

RNP   Required navigation performance. Enroute and terminal navigation performance standards imposed on aircraft operating in specified areas.

RTCA   RTCA, Inc., formerly Radio Technical Committee on Aeronautics. U.S. federal advisory committee that develops aircraft electronic equipment standards.

RVR   Runway visual range. Runway visibility measured in feet by precision instruments located on a runway.

RVSM   Reduced vertical separation minimums. Areas of the upper airspace in which aircraft vertical separation requirements have been reduced. Requires special aircraft modification and certification.

SATCOM   Satellite communications. Normally associated with commercially available nonaviation communications.

SATNAV   Satellite navigation. Usually associated with a global navigation satellite system (GNSS).

SIC   Second in command. Pilot who is designated to assist the pilot in command during flight.

SOP   Standard operating procedure.

Stabilized approach   Defined safe aircraft operating condition, not to be exceeded during approach and landing.

Standard industry fare level (SIFL)   U.S. Internal Revenue Service's aircraft valuation formula used to compute the value of nonbusiness transportation aboard employer-provided aircraft.

Standards and recommended practices (SARPS)   ICAO guidance promulgated to member states via 18 separate annexes.

Stage 2 or 3 aircraft   Noise emission classifications for aircraft defined by ICAO and state regulatory standards. Stage 2 aircraft are several times more noisy than stage 3 aircraft, creating a number of airport restrictions on those aircraft.

Sterile cockpit   An SOP designed to minimize flight crew distractions in which unnecessary conversation and paperwork are restricted when operating on the ground and at low altitudes (usually up to 10,000 feet AGL).

TAWS   Terrain awareness warning system. See *GPWS/EGPWS.*

TCAS   Traffic alert and collision avoidance system. Electronic system installed in aircraft designed to detect nearby aircraft that may create a collision hazard. Some systems provide escape maneuver directions known as *resolution advisories*. Also known as *ACAS*.

Time in service   Time from the moment an aircraft leaves the surface of the earth until it touches it at the next point of landing. Principally used in determining maintenance time intervals.

Time sharing   A method of leasing an aircraft for discrete periods to a second party and recouping only a portion of the total operating costs of the aircraft.

Transponder   The airborne radar beacon receiver/transmitter portion of the Air Traffic Control Radar Beacon System (ATCRBS) that automatically receives radio signals from interrogators on the ground and selectively replies with a specific reply pulse or pulse group only to those interrogations being received on the mode to which it is set to respond.

Type rating   A special pilot rating required to act as pilot in command of specific types of large, turbo-jet, or special aircraft.

V_1 Takeoff decision speed. The computed speed beyond which an aircraft can no longer stop within the available runway but can sustain flight in the event of an engine failure.

V_2 Takeoff safety speed/takeoff climb velocity.

VFR   Visual flight rules. Rules that govern the procedures for conducting flight under visual meteoro-logical conditions (VMC). The term *VFR* is also used in the United States to indicate weather conditions that are equal to or greater than minimum VFR requirements. In addition, it is used by pilots and con-trollers to indicate type of flight plan.

VMC   Visual meteorological conditions. Defined ceiling, visibility, and cloud clearance values that permit VFR flight.

VOR   Very high frequency omnidirectional range. Ground-based radio navigational aid.

V_R Takeoff rotation velocity. Speed during the takeoff roll at which the airplane's pitch attitude is positioned for liftoff.

V_{REF} Reference velocity. Computed speed used during landing approach.

Windshear   A change in wind speed and/or direction in a short distance resulting in a tearing or shearing effect. Constitutes a hazard for aircraft when windshear is severe. ·

Zulu   Designator for Coordinated Universal Time (UTC). Time at the prime meridian.

INDEX

ABOUT THE AUTHOR

John J. Sheehan has extensive experience in aviation, beginning his career as a Navy carrier pilot. After a 21-year Navy career he flew corporate and charter aircraft and worked as an aviation association executive and consultant, assisting airlines, government agencies and corporate aviation with management and operational issues. In 1995 he established Professional Aviation Inc., which specializes in aircraft selection, management and safety issues for corporate flight departments. He presents management and operational workshops for the National Business Aviation Association and writes extensively for industry publications.

Mr. Sheehan holds an FAA Airline Transport Pilot certificate and a Master of Business Administration degree. He resides in Wilmington, NC.